THOMAS JEFFERSON

The Apostle of Americanism

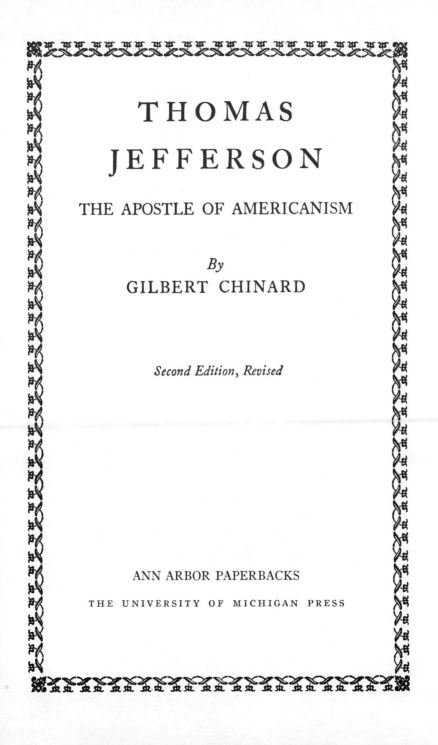

THOMAS JEFFERSON

THE APOSTLE OF AMERICANISM

By
GILBERT CHINARD

Second Edition, Revised

ANN ARBOR PAPERBACKS
THE UNIVERSITY OF MICHIGAN PRESS

Seventh printing 1975
First edition as an Ann Arbor Paperback 1957
Copyright © 1929, 1939 by Little, Brown and Company
Reprinted by special arrangement
All rights reserved
ISBN 0-472-06013-9 (paperbound)
ISBN 0-472-09013-5 (clothbound)
Published in the United States of America by
The University of Michigan Press and simultaneously
in Don Mills, Canada, by Longman Canada Limited
Manufactured in the United States of America

CONTENTS

BOOK FIVE: *The Presidency*

BOOK SIX: *The Sage of Monticello*

BOOK ONE

The Virginian

CHAPTER I

A VIRGINIA BOYHOOD

THE peoples of the Old World worship at the birthplaces of their national heroes and bury their mortal remains in splendid mausoleums, pantheons or Westminster Abbeys. By a significant and symbolic contrast, the memories of Washington and Jefferson are enshrined in no ancestral homes, but in the mansions planned with loving care, in which they so expressed themselves that their very spirit seems to haunt the deserted rooms of Mount Vernon and Monticello. They are buried according to their wishes on their own land, at the very center of the acres they had themselves surveyed and reclaimed from the wilderness, close to nature and Mother Earth. However great may be their debt to the past and their remote ancestors, they stand by themselves at the threshold of America's national history, — master builders who wrestled with gigantic tasks and first thought of their country as the future home of unborn millions.

The boy who was born on April 2, 1743, in the recently erected farmhouse at Shadwell, on the bank of the Rivanna, never gave much thought to his lineage in his later life. Yet Virginians of good stock were always proud of their ancestry, and more than once he was told by his mother that the Randolphs could "trace their pedigree far back in England and Scotland." Jefferson's mother and John Marshall's grandmother were descended from William Randolph and Mary Isham, both of the English gentry, and Jane Randolph, issued from the best blood in the Old Dominion, had married when she was nineteen a man without means, whose education had been neglected, but sturdy and industrious and belonging to one of the proudest and most aristocratic lines of old Virginians.

Of his mother, Jefferson has told us very little either in his letters or in his "Autobiography." We may surmise she had the refined, modest, unobtrusive and yet efficient qualities so marked in the Virginia girls of the Colonial days and so often noticed by travelers. Sons are apt to mold their feminine ideal on the memory of their mother, and Jefferson may have been thinking both of her and of his wife when, many years later, he contrasted French frivolity with Virginian virtues:

In America, the society of your husband, the fond cares for the children, the arrangements of the house, the improvements of the grounds, fill every moment with a useful and healthy activity. . . . The intervals of leisure are filled by the society of real friends, whose affections are not thinned to cobweb, by being spread over a thousand objects. This is the picture, in the light it is presented to my mind.[1]

The fond cares for her children would have been ample to fill all the minutes of Jefferson's mother. Large families were the rule in Virginia; fifteen children were born to Thomas Marshall and Mary Keith, and Jefferson's family was no exception to the rule. Between 1740 and 1755, Jane Randolph gave ten children to Peter Jefferson; Thomas was the third child and the first son.

What information he gave about his father has to be completed from other sources. The tradition in the family was that "the first paternal ancestor came from Wales, and from near the mountain of Snowdon, the highest in Great Britain." Peter Jefferson, landowner, practical surveyor, of gigantic stature and strength, had the sturdy qualities and ambition of the pioneer. He received a colonelcy in the militia, became a member of the House of Burgesses in 1755, and in 1749 had

[1] To Mrs. Bingham, Paris, February 7, 1787, Memorial Edition, VI, 81.

been chosen with Joshua Fry, professor of mathematics in William and Mary College, to continue the boundary line between Virginia and North Carolina. "He was afterwards employed with the same Mr. Fry to make the first map of Virginia which was ever made." Besides his association with Fry, from whom he drew the theoretical knowledge of mathematics in which he was lacking, Peter Jefferson improved himself by much reading, not novels, but the serious and sound books which constituted the ordinary family library in colonial Virginia, — historians, essayists, and most of all Shakespeare. For in Virginia as well as in New England, Shakespeare and the Bible were the two books found in every household, the two richest springs of the modern English language. Religion took up as much of their life as in New England. Prayers were said three and sometimes four times a day, and from his earliest infancy, Jefferson became familiar with the liturgy of the Church of England, and had stamped in his memory the strong old words, vigorous phrases and noble speech of King James' version.

He was only five years old when his father, already planning to give him the education of which he himself had been deprived, decided to send the boy to the best school in the neighborhood. He stayed two years at the English school; then, when nine, he went to the school of Mr. Douglas, a Scotch clergyman, who taught him French and the rudiments of Latin and Greek. Most of his childhood was spent away from home, as a boarding student, and the silence maintained by Jefferson with reference to his parents is thus easily explained. It explains also the lack of spontaneity and the awkwardness which always prevented him from expressing freely his emotions and sentiments. What may seem in him a national characteristic was largely a matter of training and early discipline.

He was fourteen when his father died, with a last recommendation that his son be given a classical education. Still a mere boy, Thomas Jefferson had become the oldest living male of the family and to a certain extent its head. Whether he was at first fully aware of his new responsibility is very doubtful. He could not remember without a retrospective fear in his later years how close he had come to wasting his whole life:

> When I recollect that at fourteen years of age, the whole care and direction of myself was thrown on myself entirely, without a relation or friend, qualified to advise or guide me, and recollect the various sorts of bad company with which I associated from time to time, I am astonished I did not turn off with some of them, and become as worthless to society as they were.[1]

The next two years were spent as a boarding student with Reverend Mr. Maury, "a correct classical scholar" — probably not a very inspiring one, if we interpret rightly the adjective used by Jefferson. We may well imagine him at sixteen, a tall, slim boy, with auburn hair and clear eyes, fond of fowling, horse-riding and outdoors, fond of reading also, but disposing of very few books; for his father's library was not large and, if the Reverend Mr. Maury followed the tradition of many old school-masters, he seldom opened his library to his students. Still, he knew his Bible, had read a few English classics, was well grounded in Greek and Latin, and had perfected his knowledge of French; but it is doubtful whether he was acquainted with any French writer except the old standard authors — "Télémaque", Berquin, perhaps "Gil Blas" and Pascal's "Pensées." But, even at that age, Jefferson necessarily knew something of the many duties of a landowner; for the slaves he was the young master, and during the summer he had to become somewhat acquainted with the management of a large estate. The education he had received was not exactly a frontier education with the usual connotations of that word. He had not been brought up in a log cabin, he had never engaged in back-

[1] To Jefferson Randolph, November 24, 1808, Memorial Edition, XII, 197.

breaking tasks of felling trees or of splitting rails; he probably had never put his hand to the plow except as an experiment. He had heard his father tell of long journeys in the wilderness and of treacherous Indians, but no Red Men roamed the forests near Shadwell. The only Indians he knew were peaceful, almost romantic characters who stopped at the house of Colonel Jefferson on their way to Williamsburg.

I knew much — he said — of the great Ontasseré, the warrior and orator of the Cherokees; he was always the guest of my father on his journeys to and from Williamsburg. I was in his camp when he made his great farewell oration to his people, the evening before his departure for England. The moon was in full splendor, and to her he seemed to address himself in his prayers for his own safety on the voyage, and that of his people during his absence; his sounding voice, distinct articulation, animated action, and the solemn silence of his people at their several fires, filled me with awe and admiration.[1]

This youthful impression left an indelible mark on his mind and was not without some influence on the "Notes on Virginia" as well as on the letters he wrote to Indian chiefs when he was President.

Nor was Shadwell exactly in the "howling wilderness", even if there was no large city near it. It was located on the road to Williamsburg, and many travelers stopped at the house on their way to the capital. Hospitality to friends and strangers was a sacred rite and most scrupulously observed. Much visiting was done in Virginia, and men particularly spent considerable time traveling from house to house; slaves were put up, horses were sent to the stable, while the best was spread on the table for the master. During the summer months, when roads were not made impassable by deep mudholes, one visitor had hardly left when another came. They had to be entertained, sometimes at a considerable expense, always at a considerable

---

[1] To John Adams, June 11, 1812. Memorial Edition, XIII, 160.

loss of time. Young Jefferson soon realized, after returning to Shadwell, that he would never amount to much and would probably become an idler, if he stayed on the estate like so many of his young friends. The wasting of precious moments irritated and disturbed him when he wanted to do some reading or some study, and he felt that the condition of the estate hardly warranted such a generous hospitality. He therefore decided to leave, and the letter he wrote on this occasion to his guardian, Mr. John Hervey of Bellemont, shows him fully aware of his responsibilities and perfectly definite in his plans.[1]

In the spring of 1760, the young man, then exactly seventeen, went to Williamsburg and enrolled in the College of William and Mary. Quite possibly it was his first visit to the capital of Virginia, his first contact with urban life. It was, for the time, a place of very respectable size and considerable activity. Old Professor Hugh Jones, a man much traveled and much read, described it enthusiastically in his "Present State of Virginia", published in London in 1724:

Williamsburg is a market town, and is governed by a mayor and aldermen. It is a town well stocked with rich stores, all sorts of goods, and well furnished with the best provisions and liquors. Here dwell several good families, and more reside here in their own houses at publick times. They live in the same neat manner, dress after the same modes, and behave themselves exactly as the Gentry in London; most families of note having a coach, chariot, Berlin, or chaize. . . . Thus they dwell comfortably, genteely, pleasantly, and plentifully in this delightful, healthful, and (I hope) pleasant city of Virginia.

Great occasions were receptions given by the Governor, meetings of the Assembly, occasional performances by regular companies from New York, semi-professional players and later, by the Virginian Company of Comedians. Horse races

[1] "Domestic Life of Thomas Jefferson", by S. N. Randolph. New York, 1857, p. 27.

attracted every year a large concourse of people, for every true Virginian is a lover of horseflesh. Betting was active and large sums of money changed hands, particularly for the four-mile heat race given each year on the course adjoining the town.

Ladies in all the glory of their imported dresses, gentlemen in brilliantly colored knee breeches and coats, with elegantly chased swords at their sides and the best beaver hats made in London under their arms, attended the receptions, the dances, the theater, and more than once adjourned to the famous Apollo room in the Raleigh Tavern, where they indulged in much drinking of "punch, beer, Nantes rum, brandy, Madeira and French claret." The first time young Jefferson went to the Raleigh he was probably shown the largest punch bowl in the house, which had played a part in the purchase of Shadwell, for had not Colonel Jefferson bought the site from William Randolph of Tuckahoe, for "Henry Weatherbourne's biggest bowl of arrack punch"?

The college itself was no less an attraction than the town. Built originally on the plans of Christopher Wren, it had un-fortunately been remodeled after a fire, "a rude, misshapen pile, which but it had a roof would be taken for a brick-kiln", wrote Jefferson in his "Notes on Virginia." Such as it was, however, with the Capitol, of much better style, it was the first large building and monument the young man had ever seen and he probably admired it at the time as much as most Virginians did.

It was by no means a university, not even a real college. Like most institutions of learning in the colonies, it had been established "to the end that the church of Virginia may be furnished with a seminary for ministers of the gospel, and that the youth may be piously educated in good letters and man-ners, and that the Christian faith may be propagated amongst the Western Indians, to the glory of the Almighty."

The lack of preparation of the students, the fact that the sons of the wealthiest were sent to England to finish their education, perhaps also an aristocratic scorn for specialized and intensive learning among the gentry of Virginia, all had contributed to keep down the standards of the institution. Much to his disgust, Jefferson found

. . . that the admission of the learners of Latin and Greek had filled the college with children. This rendering it disagreeable and degrading to young gentlemen, already prepared for entering on the sciences, they were discouraged from resorting to it, and thus the schools for mathematics and moral philosophy, which might have been of some service, became of very little. The revenues, too, were exhausted in accommodating those who came only to acquire the rudiments of the sciences.[1]

Thus the problem of caring for the many, the danger of keeping together in college the prepared and the unprepared students, which is still with us, existed already in America one hundred and fifty years ago. Evidently Jefferson considered himself as one of those young gentlemen who were prepared for entering upon the study of the sciences; he was certainly more mature for his years than most of his fellow students and looked down upon them as well, we may surmise, as upon the teachers themselves. On the other hand, the town offered many temptations and he probably yielded to some of them. He was often thrown into the society of horse-racers, card-players, fox-hunters, and at the end of his first year in college it appeared to him that he had spent more than his share of the income of the estate. He therefore wrote to his guardian to charge his expenses to his share of the property : "No," Colonel Walker is reported to have said, — "if you have sowed your wild oats thus, the estate may well afford to pay the bill."

We possess no precise information upon the amount spent by Jefferson nor any account book for that year, but we may

[1] "Notes on Virginia." Query XV.

surmise that Colonel Walker would not have been so lenient if the total sum had been spent in reprehensible dissipations. Williamsburg boasted of a large bookstore, and in 1775 Dixon and Hunter published a list of more than three hundred titles in their stock. Book lovers are born and not made. Jefferson had never been able to satisfy fully his passion for books, and as the college library offered him only very meager resources, he must have plunged with delight in the bookshop of Williamsburg and bought extravagantly, an expense the estate "could well afford to pay." But the fact remained that what he had learned he had learned by himself, and that college life had not furnished him the guidance and direction he was looking for.

It was at this juncture that Doctor Small, professor of mathematics, was appointed *ad interim* professor of philosophy and soon developed an interest in the young Virginian. Jefferson himself paid a grateful tribute to the man who just in time rescued him from his frivolous companions and brought back to his mind the serious purpose he had entertained when he entered William and Mary.

It was my good fortune and that probably fixed the destinies of my life, that Doctor William Small of Scotland was then Professor of Mathematics, a man profound in most of the useful branches of science, with a happy talent of communication, correct and gentlemanly manners, and an enlarged and liberal mind. He, most happily for me, became soon attached to me, and made me his daily companion when not engaged in the school; and from his conversation I got my first views of the expansion of science, and of the system of things in which we are placed. Fortunately, the philosophical chair became vacant soon after my arrival at college, and he was appointed to fill it *per interim:* and he was the first who ever gave, in that college, regular lectures in Ethics, Rhetoric and Belles-Lettres.[1]

[1] "Autobiography." Memorial Edition, I, 3.

For Jefferson Doctor Small was the prime awakener and inspirer. Through him the young man was introduced to George Wythe who soon accepted him as a student of law, and through him again he was received by Governor Fauquier. Such were the first really cultured men with whom Jefferson ever came in contact: William Small, the mathematician and philosopher, would not have been a true Scot if he had not had that passionate love for discussion and logic which seems the innate gift of so many sons of the Highlands. Francis Fauquier, "the ornament and delight of Virginia", generous, liberal, elegant in his manners and requirements, was the son of Doctor Fauquier of Floirac, near Bordeaux, who had worked under Newton in the mint and become a director of the Bank of England. His early biographer Burke, the Virginia historian, has chiefly emphasized his propensity to gaming. But Fauquier was an economist of no mean distinction and had written an important tract on the basis of taxation. He was interested in physics or natural philosophy and had become a Fellow of the Royal Society. He was a student of natural phenomena and sent to the Society the description of a hail-storm in Virginia. Finally, there was George Wythe, whose virtue was of the purest tint, his integrity inflexible, and his justice exact. Last and most important of all his qualities, perhaps, was the characteristic peculiarity mentioned by Jefferson in the sketch he wrote after the death of his old master: "he was firm in his philosophy, and neither troubling, nor perhaps trusting any one with his religion."

Such were the true masters of Thomas Jefferson, and from their conversations around the table, after bottles of port had been brought, he learned more than any student at William and Mary ever acquired in college. It was a rare privilege for a young man of Jefferson's age to be admitted to the " *parties carrées* ", and he must have already given singular promise to have been invited at all into the society of these three luminaries of Virginia. What topics were discussed among them can easily be imagined. Fauquier would speak of old England, the theaters of London, the monuments and works of art, of his colleagues of the Royal Society, or discuss a problem of taxation or a recent meteorological phenomenon. A man of the world, a friend of Admiral Anson whom he had met after his circumnavigation of the globe, a director of the South Sea Company, he would speak of ships, strange lands, and reveal to the young man the existence of a world extending far beyond his native Virginia. Thus was born in Jefferson that ardent desire to travel and most of all to see England which appears in some letters written in the early sixties.

Philosophical and religious subjects perhaps were introduced, although that is rather doubtful, in my opinion. The passage on George Wythe, already quoted, mentions his reticence on religion. Whatever may have been the propensity of Fauquier to gaming, he was never accused by his contemporaries of being a religious libertine. It is also very doubtful whether any of the group would naturally have discussed such subjects, particularly in the presence of a young student whose education had been deeply religious. Finally it must be remembered that in Virginia, as well as in New England, there always existed some "reserved questions", that it was not good form to criticize established institutions and current beliefs. It is quite possible that Fauquier may have lent to Jefferson certain volumes of Shaftesbury and Bolingbroke, but in spite of the contrary opinion expressed by some biographers of Jefferson, it seems very unlikely that any of the three older men should have undertaken to shake the foundations of his faith. The "parties carrées" could not have lasted very long, since William Small went back to Scotland in 1762. But Jefferson's acquaintance with Fauquier and Wythe was continued for many years after the departure of the philosopher and, in both cases, until the death of the older men.

The master of Shadwell had sown his wild oats; he had had his brief flight of dissipation and had reformed; but he had by no means become a hermit. He had not entirely given up attending horse races and fox hunts.

Many a time — he wrote in 1808 — have I asked myself, in the enthusiastic moment of the death of a fox, the victory of a favorite horse, the issue of a question eloquently argued at the bar, or in the great councils of the nation. Well, which of these kinds of reputation would I prefer? That of a horse jockey? a fox hunter? an orator? or the finest advocate of my country's rights?[1]

What young man has not thus dreamed of serving his country and devoting himself to some noble cause, what student preparing for the bar has not pictured himself winning a difficult case, forcing the judge's attention and swaying a reluctant jury? The ambition to become an orator may have been awakened in his mind by the acquaintance he had made of the "uncultured Demosthenes" of the Old Dominion. In the winter of 1759–1760, he had met at the house of Mr. Dandrige, in Hanover, a tall, ascetic-looking fellow, rather disdainful of finery and careless in his wearing apparel, but "with such strains of native eloquence as Homer wrote in" — "I never heard anything that deserved to be called by the same name with what flowed from him," wrote Jefferson later, "and where he got that torrent of language is unconceivable. I have frequently shut my eyes while he spoke, and, when he was done, asked myself what he had said, without being able to recollect a word of it. He was no logician. He was truly a great man, however — one of enlarged views."

His name was Patrick Henry. Far less uncultured than Jefferson's portrait would lead us to believe, related to very good families, although poor and a complete failure as a merchant, Patrick Henry had suddenly decided to enter the legal profession, and after borrowing a "Coke upon Littleton" and a

[1] November 24, 1808. Memorial Edition, XII, 197.

"Digest of the Virginia Acts", he had appeared after six weeks' preparation before the board of examiners. He won his diploma through logic, clear presentation and common sense rather than through his knowledge of the law, and commenced practicing in the fall of the same year. Whenever a case appeared before the General Court sitting at Williamsburg and consisting of the Governor and his council, "he used to put up" with Jefferson, borrowing books which he seldom read, always ready with stories of the backwoods. Fame came to him soon after, when his fiery eloquence in the "parson's case" drew down upon him clerical hostility and public admiration. "Instead of feeding the hungry and clothing the naked," he cried out in the courtroom, "these religious harpies would, were their powers equal to their will, snatch from the hearth of their honest parishioner his last hoe-cake, from the widow and her orphan children their last milch cow, the last bed, nay, the last blanket, from the lying-in woman." [1] Not even in the days of the Convention did the halls of Paris echo with more vehement vituperations and more indignant denunciations. A magnetic power, an emotional appeal to elementary passion, to a sense of justice in the mass rather than to the letter of the law fitted him for political life. He was soon to have his opportunity; in the meantime he awoke in Jefferson a revolt against clerical usurpations that was to bear its fruit in time. Usually passed over by Jefferson's biographers, the plea made by Patrick Henry in the "parson's case" seems to have been the incident that called the young man's attention to the position occupied by the established Church in its relations to the civil power. It started in him the train of thought that culminated in the "Bill for religious freedom."

It has been sometimes said that Jefferson used to spend fourteen hours a day in study when he was at Williamsburg; his correspondence with John Page shows him in a very different

---

[1] William Wirt Henry: "Life of Patrick Henry." New York, 1891, vol. I, p. 41.

light. He was not in any sense a bookworm, even though he read enormously, but he played as strenuously as he studied. A good horseman, a good violin player, a good dancer, he was a much-sought-after young man. He had a keen eye for the ladies, and very early in 1762 he had fallen in love with Miss Rebecca Burwell, the *Bell-in-day, Belinda, campana in die, Adnileb* of his letters to Page. The young lady had given him her profile cut in black paper which he carried in his watch case. Far from her, life lost all interest : "all things appear to me to trudge in one and the same round : we rise in the morning that we may eat breakfast, dinner and supper, and to go to bed again, that we may get up the next morning and do the same, so that you never saw two peas more alike than our yesterday and to-day." He had in mind to go back to Williamsburg, to propose, receive his sentence and be no longer in suspense : "but reason says, if you go, and your attempts prove unsuccessful, you will be ten times more wretched than ever." [1] Spring, then summer came, and he could not muster up enough courage to declare himself. Madly in love as he was, he was not intending to marry at once. He had formed great plans for traveling. He was dreaming of hoisting his sail and visiting England, Holland, France, Spain, Italy (where I would buy me a good fiddle), and Egypt, and return home through the British provinces to the northward. This would take him two or three years. Was it fair to ask Belinda to wait so long for him? And yet he could not leave without speaking and remain in suspense and cruel uncertainty during the whole trip. "If I am to meet with a disappointment, the sooner I know it, the more of life I shall have to wear if off . . . If Belinda will not accept of my service, it will never be offered to another. That she may I pray most sincerely : but that she will, she never gave me reason to hope." [2]

[1] January 20, 1763. Memorial Edition, IV, 6.
[2] July 15, 1763. *Ibid.*, IV, 8.

When college opened again at the beginning of October, he had made up his mind to make his position clear. A dance was to be given in the Apollo room of the Raleigh Tavern. He dressed up in all his finery, he rehearsed in his head such thoughts as occurred to him and made a complete fiasco. "A few broken sentences, uttered in great disorder, and interrupted with pauses of uncommon length were the too visible marks of my strange confusion" (October 7, 1763). Belinda did not say a word to relieve him in his embarrassment, did not manifest in any way that she understood his purpose, and several months were to elapse before Jefferson had another opportunity to express himself. This time he had learnt his piece perfectly, and from what we know of him already it is probable that he made a very clear presentation of his case, too clear and too logical even, for he concluded by saying that the decision rested with her and that a new interview would not serve any purpose. A strange lover indeed, apparently as madly in love as a young man could be, and yet too respectful of the free will of his beloved to attempt to sweep her off her feet by too frequent interviews and too passionate pleas! Belinda listened attentively but did not give any indication that Jefferson's speech had convinced her and won her heart. A few weeks later the bashful suitor heard indirectly of her answer when she announced her marriage to Mr. B . . . Whether it was "for money, beauty, or principle will be so nice a dispute, that no one will venture to pronounce", wrote Jefferson at the time. To crown the joke, his happy rival, who evidently had been kept in blissful ignorance of Jefferson's sentiments, asked him to act as a best man at the wedding. A more ironical trick of fate could scarcely be imagined; but, all considered, Belinda was not altogether to blame.

Thomas Jefferson did not think of committing suicide, he did not swear revenge, nor did he curse the ungrateful one in any of his letters. We have some reason to believe, however, that his affair with Belinda marked a decisive turn in his life. It killed whatever romantic strains may have existed in his heart; it matured him, and it was probably at that time that the long-belated metaphysical crisis took place, the disappointed lover evolving a certain philosophy of life which he was to retain to the end of his days.

CHAPTER II

AN AMERICAN DISCIPLE OF GREECE AND OLD ENGLAND

UNTIL very recently the material for a study of the formative years of Thomas Jefferson was very scanty. Many of his earliest letters have disappeared and he always felt a strong disinclination to analyze himself in writing. It was also contrary to his training and to the customs of his milieu to discuss personal matters too frankly and too openly. An American Jean-Jacques Rousseau baring his heart to posterity would have been as out of place as a man from the moon in New England or Virginia. But what he did not express as his personal feelings, he copied from the philosophers and poets he read during his studious nights or when resting under a tree on one of the hills surrounding Shadwell. The two commonplace books I have recently published, written by Jefferson during his student days and consulted by him throughout his life, could rightly be called "Jefferson self-revealed." [1] They enable us at any rate to determine with a fair degree of certainty the sentimental and intellectual preoccupations that filled his mind when examining the problems of society and the universe.

It does not seem that, until 1764, that is to say until the unfortunate ending of his love affair with Belinda, Jefferson had ever been touched by any religious doubt. When, in July, 1763, he foresaw the possibility of being rejected, he wrote to Page a long letter in which he appears still strongly marked

---

[1] "The Commonplace Book of Thomas Jefferson." Paris, Baltimore, 1927. "The Literary Bible of Thomas Jefferson." Paris, Baltimore, 1928.

by the Christian training he had received in his family and at the hand of Mr. Douglas and the Reverend Mr. Maury:

> Perfect happiness, I believe, was never intended by the Deity to be the lot of one of his creatures in this world; but that he has very much put in our power the nearness of our approaches to it, is what I have steadfastly believed.
>
> The most fortunate of us, in our journey through life, frequently meet with calamities and misfortunes which may greatly afflict us; and, to fortify our minds against the attacks of these calamities and misfortunes, should be one of the principal studies and endeavors of our lives. The only method of doing this is to assume a perfect resignation to the Divine will, to consider that whatever does happen, must happen; and that, by our uneasiness, we cannot prevent the blow before it does fall, but we may add to its force after it has fallen. These considerations, and such others as these, may enable us in some measure to surmount the difficulties thrown in our way; to bear up with a tolerable degree of patience under this burden of life; and to proceed with a pious and unshaken resignation, till we arrive at our journey's end, when we may deliver up our trust into the hands of him who gave it, and receive such reward as to him shall seem proportioned to our merit. Such, dear Page, will be the language of the man who considers his situation in life, and such should be the language of every man who would wish to render that situation as easy as the nature of it will admit. Few things will disturb him at all: nothing will disturb him much.[1]

This note of Christian stoicism is exactly what might be expected from a young Protestant whose mind was not particularly perturbed by metaphysical problems. At that time Jefferson did not even conceive that there might exist a code of ethics resting on a different basis. If Doctor Small had helped him to find his exact relation to "the system of things in which we are placed", he was satisfied that complete resignation to Divine Will was the only wisdom. It may be safely assumed

[1] To John Page, Shadwell, July 15, 1763. Memorial Edition, IV, 10.

that three years after meeting Governor Fauquier, Thomas Jefferson had retained intact the faith of his youth.

What brought a change in his attitude and disturbed his equilibrium is certainly not the influence of the "infidel French philosophers." The volume of extracts which I published under the title of "The Literary Bible of Thomas Jefferson" does not contain a single quotation from Voltaire, Diderot, or Rousseau, and French literature is represented only by a few insignificant lines from Racine. It is more likely that the first doubts were injected into his mind by the reading of Bolingbroke. He did not even need the assistance of Fauquier to lead him to the English philosopher. The catalogues of the old libraries of Virginia frequently mention Shaftesbury's "Characteristics" and Bolingbroke's "Works." [1]

Whether it was from the town bookstore or from Fauquier's own library, the fact remains that sometime, when still a student, but certainly after 1764, Jefferson obtained a copy of Bolingbroke and came to question the authenticity of the Bible as a historical document. It may have been due to the sentimental shock he had suffered, or simply to the critical attitude developed in him by his study of legal texts and decisions, but there is little doubt that he put into practice at that time the advice he gave later to Peter Carr, when he told him to "question with boldness the existence of a God; because, if there be one, he must more approve of the homage of reason, than that of blindfold fear. You will naturally examine first, the religion of your own country. Read the Bible, then, as you would read Livy or Tacitus." [2] He therefore went systematically through Bolingbroke, learned from him methods of historical criticism and scientific doubt, weighed the evidence with a legal mind and came to very definite conclusions. At this decisive turn in his life, Jeffer-

[1] Mary Newton Stanard: "Colonial Virginia." Philadelphia, 1917, p. 306.
[2] To Peter Carr. Memorial Edition, VI, 258.

son might easily have become a sceptic and a cynic, like so many men of the eighteenth century. As a matter of fact, a careful study of his "Literary Bible" indicates that at least for a time he was extremely cynical in his attitude towards women. This may have been due to the cruelty of Belinda, but it was more than a passing mood, for as late as 1770, two years before his marriage, he scribbled on the margin of his account book a Latin doggerel clearly indicating his distrust of the female kind:

> *Crede ratem ventis, animum ne crede puellis*
> *Namque est foeminea tutior unda fide.*
> *Foemina nulla bona est, sed si bona contigit ulla*
> *Nescio quo fato mala facta bona est.*

From Euripides particularly he collected with a sort of waggish pleasure the strongest denunciations of women in the old poet and repeated with him "Mortals should beget children from some other sources, and there should be no woman-kind: thus there would be no ill for man" — and again, "O Zeus, why hast thou established women, a curse deceiving men, in the light of the sun?"

In Milton he found an echo of Euripides' misogynism and from "Paradise Lost" and "Samson Agonistes", he compiled a pretty set of accusations against female usurpations. His conclusion at that time was probably that of the old English poet, and he affirmed his superiority over the treacherous sex by repeating after him:

> Therefore God's universal law
> Gave to man despotic power
> Over his female in due awe.[1]

His outlook on life must have been very gloomy, if we are to trust certain quotations from Greek and Latin authors. To matters of mythology, descriptions of battles, and grandiose

---

[1] "Samson Agonistes", v, 1025.

comparisons in Homer, Jefferson apparently paid no attention. He saw in the old poet a repository of ancient wisdom and the ancient philosophy of life. From him he collected verses in which he found expressed views on human destiny, — a courageous, stoic, yet disenchanted philosophy, summed up in two lines from Pope's translation :

> To labour is the lot of man below
> And when Jove gave us life, he gave us woe.

When he read from Cicero's "Tusculanae" he selected passages with a view to confirm the deistic and materialistic principles towards which he was leaning at the time : "All must die ; if only there should be an end to misery in death. What is there agreeable in life, when we must reflect that, at some time or other we must die." This particular piece of reasoning seems to have struck Jefferson quite forcibly, for he repeated it again and again fifty years later in his letters to John Adams : "For if either the heart, or the blood, or the brains, is the soul, then certainly the soul, being corporeal, must perish with the rest of the body ; if it is air, it will perhaps be dissolved ; if it is fire, it will be extinguished." [1]

It was then that he copied and evidently accepted the statement of Bolingbroke that "it is not true that Christ revealed an entire body of ethics, proved to be the law of nature."

The "law of nature" — what was meant by the word? Was it the Epicurean maxim of Horace, — "enjoy to-day and put as little trust as possible in the morrow?" If such had been the conclusion reached by Jefferson he could have followed the line of least resistance and enjoyed the good things of life, the good wines of the Raleigh Tavern, the pretty girls and all the social dissipations of many of his contemporaries. Such would have been Jefferson's destiny, had he been born in the Old World.

---

[1] See also "Commonplace Book", p. 330, and "Writings." Memorial Edition, XV, 239, March 14, 1820.

Had he been made of weaker stuff he would have become one of the fox-hunters, horse-racers and card-players of the Virginian gentry. But he was saved by his aristocratic pride and the stern teaching of the old Stoics.

He was conscious that he was of good stock, and he had read in Euripides that "to be of the noble born gives a peculiar distinction clearly marked among men, and the noble name increases in lustre in those who are worthy." [1]

To be ever upright and to be worthy of one's good blood, this was the simplest, most obvious and most imperious duty. It would have been very difficult for Jefferson to believe any longer that "at the end of the journey we shall deliver up our trust into the hands of him who gave it and receive such reward as to him shall seem proportionate to our merit", which was his belief in 1763. There was not even much to obtain in our life as a reward, for most societies are so organized that "whenever a man is noble and zealous, he wins no higher prize than baser men." [2] Still the fact remained that, after the collapse of all the religious superstructure, the foundations of morality were left unshaken, so Jefferson undertook to rebuild his own philosophy of life according to Bolingbroke's advice, with the material at hand. For it was evident that "a system thus collected from the writings of ancient heathen moralists, of Tully and Seneca, of Epictetus, and others, would be more full, more entire, more coherent, and more clearly deduced from unquestionable principles of knowledge." [3]

But he would take nobody's word for it, he would accept the teachings of no professor of moral philosophy; every man had to think for himself and to formulate once for all his own philosophy. When writing to his nephew, who he thought might go through the same crisis, Jefferson declared some forty years later that:

---

[1] "Hecuba", 592, in "Literary Bible of Thomas Jefferson."
[2] "Hecuba", 306.   [3] Bolingbroke, in "Literary Bible."

Man was destined for society. His morality, therefore, was to be formed to this object. He was endowed with a sense of right and wrong, merely relative to this. This sense is as much part of his nature, as the sense of hearing, seeing, feeling; it is the true foundation of morality and not the TO KALON, truth, etc. as fanciful writers have imagined. The moral sense, or conscience is as much a part of man, as his leg or arm.

But this is the Jefferson of 1808, the mature man, almost the aged sage of Monticello. How far he was from having reached that poise and that clear vision of the moral world, appears in the confusion and contradictions of the abstracts collected in the "Literary Bible." Yet when he read Homer, Euripides, Cicero, Shakespeare, and even Buchanan, Jefferson had a clear and single purpose. He was reading more for profit than for pleasure, to gather material with which to build anew, by himself and for himself, a moral shelter in which he could find refuge for the rest of his days. He was not thinking then of devoting his life to his country; if he had any patriotism, it was dormant, and if he had any sense of abstract justice it is nowhere manifest. And yet, quite in contrast with the general run of quotations in the "Literary Bible" are some maxims scribbled in one of his unpublished Memorandum books under the year 1770. He had already levelled the top of the hill on which he was to build Monticello and was digging the cellar. But one day, after noting carefully that " 4 good fellows, a lad and two girls, of about 16 each, have dug in my cellar a place in 8 hrs. $\frac{1}{2}$, 3 feet deep, 8 feet wide and $16\frac{1}{2}$ feet long," he stopped to recapitulate the most striking maxims by which he intended to regulate his life :

. . . no liberty no life — endure and abstain — *bonum est quod honestum, macte virtute esto, nil desperandum, faber suae quisque fortunae, fari quae sentiat,* what is, is right — *ex recto decus — ne cede malis sed contra audientior ito* — long life, long health, long pleasure and a friend — *non votum nobis sed patriae — fiat justitia ruat cœlum.*

Clearly between the time he compiled his "Literary Bible" and this entry in the Memorandum book, a considerable change had taken place in Jefferson's mental world. What was dormant had been awakened, what was non-existent had been created. Let those who are looking for influences hunt for pale reflections of these maxims in the writings of the French philosophers. I cannot perceive any. I would even say that there is no distinct influence of Bolingbroke, for Jefferson borrowed from Bolingbroke methods of approaching certain problems rather than definite ideas. The young Virginian made use, for a short time only, of the critical reasoning employed by the English philosopher, but when it came to building anew, he gathered all the material, stone by stone and maxim by maxim, from the old Greek Stoics. It was a pessimistic yet courageous philosophy of life, far different from eighteenth-century optimism. By a strange anomaly, the son of the pioneer, the young man supposedly brought up under frontier influence, felt more kinship with Greece and republican Rome than with the philosophers of London, Paris or Geneva. During this early period of his life and when he had rejected the Christian system of ethics, the young Virginian found the moral props he needed in Homer's simple code of honor and friendship; in echoes from the Greek Stoics discovered in Cicero; and through them also was revealed to him a conception of patriotism and devotion to public duty which was to mold the rest of his life.

In the transformation that took place in Jefferson's attitude towards life, it would be unjust to leave out the influence exerted by Patrick Henry. The young student was present when Henry delivered his famous speech in the House of Burgesses in 1765 and ended the speech with the defiant declaration, "If this be treason make the most of it." "He appeared to me," wrote Jefferson, "to speak as Homer wrote; his talents were great indeed, such as I never heard from any man." From

Henry he did not receive any particular political philosophy, but from him he learned the value of those striking formulas which remain in the memory of men, become mottoes and battle cries of political campaigns. He liked the vehemence and completeness of Henry's affirmation and when, in 1770, he wrote in his memorandum that maxim of all revolutionists and radicals of every age — *fiat justitia ruat cælum*, let there be justice, even if the heavens should crumble down — he was thinking as much of the Virginia orator as of the Romans of old.

A last item in the same memorandum book of 1770 may justify the supposition that still another influence had entered Jefferson's life. By that time he had forgotten the fickle Belinda who had played with his heart, but he was no longer a woman-hater. When he quoted from Pope "the sleepy eye that speaks to the melting soul", he was already thinking of the young and attractive widow he was to marry two years later.

In the meantime he had been pursuing assiduously his law studies and his readings of political philosophers. Very early after entering college, he had decided that he would not be satisfied with the study of belles-lettres, or the life of a gentleman managing a large country estate. The clergy and the law were the only two professions open to a young man of distinctly aristocratic tendencies. He chose the law and began his training under the direction of Mr. Wythe. This training was markedly different from the instruction he would have received in Europe. There was no regularly organized law school at Williamsburg; candidates for the Bar had to prepare themselves under the direction of an old practitioner; they attended the sessions of the court and prepared briefs for their master; they studied by themselves and consequently were much more familiar with the practice than with the theory of jurisprudence. No examination was given by a regular faculty; but a license to practice law and to hang out his shingle was obtained by the candidate after appearing before a special board of examiners. In the case of Patrick Henry, the examiners had been John Randolph, afterward Attorney-general for the Colony, Peyton Randolph, Mr. Wythe and perhaps Robert C. Nicholas. If Henry "got by" after six months' study, thanks to his phenomenal fluency and "aplomb", it took Jefferson six years before he considered himself sufficiently prepared to appear before the examiners. A large part of his time however was spent at Shadwell in agricultural pursuits and independent study; but he came regularly to Williamsburg to consult Mr. Wythe, to attend the sessions of the Court, to buy books, and also to attend during the winter the many functions given by the brilliant society of the capital of Virginia. These years, the most important of all in the formation of Jefferson's political theories, can now be studied in the "Commonplace Book", long thought destroyed, which even Randall had not been able to find, but which is now safely deposited in the Library of Congress. It is a most revealing compilation and throws an unexpected light on the origin of Jefferson's political doctrines.

It contains first of all no less than five hundred fifty-six articles analyzing special cases from the Reports of Cases in the King's Bench, George Andrews, Robert Raymond, William Salkeld and Coke's "Institutes", for in a colony where no attempt had been made to codify the body of existing laws, and where the common law was the supreme law of the land, the first prerequisite to becoming a good lawyer was to assimilate an enormous number of cases and precedents. Jefferson proceeded, like all the law students of his time, to dig in "Coke upon Littleton" and others, putting down in his "Commonplace Book" decisions, discussions, definitions, matters of importance to a country lawyer, such as wills, devises, commercial contracts, cases on larceny, trespassing, debts, damages, bankruptcy, leases, libels; and he did it with his customary thoroughness and clarity. A detailed study of the "Commonplace Book" would be most illuminating for those who, in spite of all evidence to the contrary, still maintain that Jefferson was an impractical philosopher, interested only in abstract principles and in theory. On the other hand, he was not simply a country lawyer, either. If he had not seemed to manifest any interest in the abstract study of the principles of law, in what he used to call "metaphysical disquisitions", he was keenly interested in the historical development of the legal structure on which rested modern society and particularly the colonial society of Virginia.

He carefully went through Lord Kames' "Historical Law Tracts" and studied from him the history of criminal law, promises and covenant, property, securities upon land, courts, briefs. It is in Kames that he found a definition of society which he could have written himself and which expresses his political individualism and subordination to law:

Mutual defence against a more powerful neighbor being in early times the chief, or sole motive for joining society, individuals never thought of surrendering any of their natural rights which could be retained consistently with their great aim of mutual defence.

This is elaborated upon in the passage quoted from the "History of Property":

Man, by his nature, is fitted for society, and society by its conveniences is fitted for man. The perfection of human society consists in that just degree of union among the individuals, which to each reserves freedom and independency, as far as is consistent with peace and good order. The bonds of society where every man shall be bound to dedicate the whole of his industry to the common interest would be of the strictest kind, but it would be unnatural and uncomfortable, because destructive of liberty and independence; so would be the enjoyment of the goods of fortune in common.

I am perfectly aware of the undeniable influence of Locke upon the theory of Kames; and it would be very unlikely that Jefferson had not read at that date Locke's "Treatise on Civil Government." The fact remains, however, that neither Locke, nor so far as I know any political thinker of the period, had yet so clearly defined that particular combination of individualism and respect for peace and order so characteristic of American democracy. We shall see in one of the following chapters how Jefferson, elaborating on this statement of Kames, derived from it all his conception of natural rights. The Scottish Lord was for him a master and a guide.

In Sir John Dalrymple, author of an "Essay Towards a General History of Feudal Property", in Francis Stoughton Sullivan's "An Historical Treatise of the Feudal Laws and the Constitution of the Laws of England", Jefferson studied the history of primogeniture and of entails and came to the conclusion that both of them had foundation neither in nature nor in law, and certainly did not appear in England before the Norman Conquest. He reached to the same finding in his long dissertation on the original common law, and thus we can trace directly through the "Commonplace Book" the sources of the Bill on Primogeniture, of the Bill for Religious Freedom, and of the Law to Abolish Entails, which Jefferson considered as forming a system "which would eradicate every fibre of ancient or future aristocracy and lay a foundation for a government truly republican."

Some of the entries in the "Commonplace Book" were evidently made after the period with which we are dealing in this chapter, although most of them can be dated before 1776. We have no means of determining whether Jefferson had undertaken a systematic study of federative governments when he was still a student, or at what time he copied the many extracts and quotations from Montesquieu. Nor can we enter here into a detailed discussion of all the articles. One or two facts, however, stand out even after a superficial glimpse of this repertory of ideas on government and society. The first is that Jefferson at that date, and indeed during most of his life, was not interested in abstract principles or in theoretical discussions. His was eminently the mind of a lawyer, and it is not for a lawyer to arrive at a definition of justice but to determine what the law says on a particular point. Yet in a country where law is not codified and the common law is the basis of the legal structure, it is impossible to find out what the law is without undertaking a historical study of the cases at hand in the different repertories. Men are either fallible or dishonest, false interpretations creep in, texts are distorted from their original meaning, and thus it becomes necessary to apply to legal decisions the rules of historical evidence formulated by Bolingbroke.

After undertaking such a study, Jefferson arrived at a very curious conclusion; that at a time which was not buried in a mythological past, the Anglo-Saxons had lived under customs and unwritten laws based upon the natural rights of man and permitting the individual to develop freely, normally and happily. In the course of time, these free institutions deteriorated through the nefarious influences of several agencies. Unwritten law became written law and jurists succeeded in concealing under their sophistry and verbiage the primitive intent of natural legislation. Priests, striving to extend their domination over a realm which primitively was foreign to them, introduced religious prescriptions into civil laws and thus diminished the rights of the individual. Conquerors and a long lineage of hereditary kings further modified primitive institutions in order to provide an apparently legal foundation for their usurpations, until the people, no longer able to withstand patiently the evils of tyranny, arose and recovered at least some of their rights.

Such a conspectus of the history of England was neither new nor original; it was one of the favorite contentions of English jurists during the eighteenth century, and nowhere perhaps is it more forcibly developed than in the last chapter of Blackstone's "Commentaries", "Of the rise, progress and gradual improvements of the laws of England." It is fundamentally also the doctrine of Jefferson, who went much farther than any of the English political thinkers in his revindication of the Saxon liberties.

One may see already how such a conception differs from the theories of Rousseau and the French philosophers, and indeed from those of the English philosophers. And this is easily explained, even if too seldom realized. Born in the eighteenth century, Jefferson is in some respects a man of the eighteenth century, but no greater mistake could be made than to apply to him the same standards that apply to European political thinkers. The very fact that he was born and grew up in a remote colony prevented him from joining any particular school of political philosophy. He had comparatively few books at his disposal, certainly fewer gazettes, and only faint echoes of the philosophical battles raging in Europe reached the capital of Virginia. During the long winter evenings at Shadwell, he had ample time to think, to sift from the books he was reading, not matter of passing interest, but matter of practical value and principles susceptible of being applied to the society which he knew and in which he lived. He could not have the cosmopolitan and universal outlook of thinkers who had traveled and met with representatives of many nationalities. His "Literary Bible", as well as his "Commonplace Book", contains many examples which might be used to illustrate his provincialism or, if one prefers, his regionalism.

No man can become genuinely interested in things he has never seen and cannot imagine. He had never seen the English countryside and so, when he copied from Thomson's description of spring, he selected only passages that could apply as well to the landscape of Virginia as to the scenery of old England. Even when he read Horace he eliminated verses with too much local color, unknown plants, unfamiliar dishes and beverages, until the descriptions of a Roman farm by the old poet would fit a typical Virginia plantation with the slaves singing in the great courtyard after the day's work is done. He knew Latin and Greek, French and Italian, and perhaps even German; for the time and place his library was rich and varied. He had read Milton, Shakespeare, Dryden, Buchanan, Thomson, Thomas Moss; he had studied Kames, Pelloutier, Stanyan, Eden, Baccaria, Montesquieu and possibly Voltaire's "Essai sur les Moeurs", but from each of these he had culled facts and definitions rather than principles and theories. He had read some books of travel and listened with enjoyment to Fauquier's accounts of his long voyages. He was dreaming of visiting England, the continent and the Mediterranean, but the only form of society he knew was the colonial society of Virginia. No cosmopolitan tendencies would develop in such surroundings. Superior as he was in intelligence and culture to his fellow students and to the young gentry of Williamsburg, Jefferson, at the age of twenty-five, was not yet an American; he was distinctly a Virginian.

CHAPTER III

A VIRGINIA LAWYER

IN 1767, Thomas Jefferson, then twenty-four years of age, was "led into the practice of the law at the bar of the General Court" by his friend and mentor, Mr. Wythe. He was the owner of a substantial estate inherited from his father, and he managed the family property of Shadwell, but he had already formed plans for an establishment of his own and begun preparations to build Monticello on the other side of the Rivanna. The only future open to him seemed to be that of any young Virginian of his social class. He occasionally joined them in fox-hunting and attended the races, enjoyed a dance, a concert, and a good play at the theater. The following year was particularly brilliant at Williamsburg. The governor held stately receptions and the Virginian Company of Comedians presented a rich program: "The Constant Couple or a Trip to Jubilee", a farce called "The Miller of Mansfield", "The Beggar's Opera", "The Anatomist or Sham Doctor", besides the ordinary plays of the repertory, were given during the spring and summer of that year.[1]

Jefferson had his share of all these social pleasures, together with others, but there were also simpler and more austere occupations. First of all he had to look after his plantation. Agriculture, so long a haphazard and empirical affair, was making great strides in Europe, particularly in England. Treatises on the subject and special magazines were read eagerly in Virginia; the choice of cultures, the improvement of seeds, the introduction of new crops greatly concerned the minds of pro-

[1] Stanard, p. 240.

gressive planters like Colonel Washington and the young master of Shadwell.

The "Garden Books" kept by Jefferson and now published only in part, reveal him as a forerunner of modern efficiency engineers. Fences, walls, roads and bridges had to be built on the 1900-acre estate left him by his father; trees had to be planted and vegetables raised for the large family at Shadwell, for the slaves and for the many travelers and visitors who continued to drop in. If all the seeds planted in Jefferson's vegetable garden and orchards did well, he must have had an extraordinary variety of produce, considerably larger than is to be found on the best appointed farms of to-day. For he was not satisfied with the staple vegetables which appear on the American table with clocklike regularity; he sowed "salsifia, peppergrass, sorrel, salmon radishes, nasturtium, asparagus, all sorts of lettuce, cresses, celery, strawberries, snap-beans, purple beans, white beans, sugar beans, cucumbers, watermelons, cherries, olive stones, raspberries, turnips", and — horrors! — garlic. He was led into many such experiments by his neighbor and friend Philip Mazzei, formerly of Tuscany and now of Albemarle County, for many of the entries in the Garden Book are in Italian and "*aglio de Terracina* (*vulgo* garlic), *radiocchio di Pistoia* (succory or wild endive), *cavolo broccolo Francese di Pisa, fragole Maggese* (May strawberries)" and dozens of other imported varieties appear in his garden lists. Then there were the horses, for, true to the Virginia tradition, Jefferson kept no less than half a dozen blood mares of good pedigree. Above all, the regular crops of wheat, corn and especially tobacco had to be looked after; for tobacco was the only crop that could be marketed for solid cash or sent to London to be exchanged for books, furniture, fine clothes, musical instruments, and the choice wines of Europe. As a practical farmer Jefferson was rather successful, since during these early years his land brought him an average return of two thousand dollars.

This was ample for his needs. But his main resources were procured from the practice of law.

He kept a complete memorandum of all the cases in which he appeared before the courts of Virginia and opposite each case entered the fee received for his professional services.[1] These fees would seem very moderate to the least ambitious practitioner of our days. In many cases no fee is mentioned at all, and we are at liberty to suppose that Jefferson took some charity cases, or that the defendants were not always scrupulous in paying their bills. Yet, altogether, the total averaged close to three thousand dollars a year, a nice fat addition to the income from Shadwell and Monticello. Starting with one hundred and fifteen cases in 1768, Jefferson was retained as attorney or counsel in no less than four hundred thirty cases in 1771, and it is no exaggeration to state that no day passed during the twelve years he remained engaged in the practice of law without his giving considerable time to his profession. The moderate amount of these fees and the large number of cases indicate the kind of practice in which Jefferson was employed. Trespassing of cattle on a neighbor's field, destruction of fences, robbery committed by a clerk, wills, administration of estates, interest, quarrels between two goodwives, with a lively exchange of actionable words, assault and battery, all the seamy, sordid, petty side of life, constituted for these twelve years the daily practice of Thomas Jefferson, an apprenticeship of life and a training in the knowledge of human nature enjoyed by very few abstract philosophers.

In the old days of the bar, one of the earmarks of most lawyers was a fluency of speech, unsurpassed except perhaps by the ministers. But words never came easily to Jefferson, or in great abundance. His voice, pleasant and modulated in ordinary conversation, "sank in his throat", if raised higher, and became

---

[1] These memoranda are in the Jefferson Coolidge Collection of the Massachusetts Historical Society.

husky. He was clearly a business lawyer, an office lawyer, whose clear, precise, meticulous presentation of facts fitted him particularly for appearing before a court of appeals like the General Court, rather than for moving and emotionally convincing a jury of twelve men good and true.

His scorn for oratory, long sentences, images, apostrophes may have been a case of sour grapes, for in his youth he admired tremendously Patrick Henry. As we have seen, he was wise enough not to aim higher than he could reach. Not only did he never crave the fame of the popular orator, but, conscious of his limitations, he always showed a real repugnance to addressing a large assembly. Particularly brilliant in conversation, he was destined to be a committee man, to win his ends by the pen rather than by the silver tongue of the politician. Yet if he had been fond of rhetoric, rhetoric would have found its way into his writings, but no man of the period wrote less figuratively, employed fewer artifices of style; metaphors, comparisons were unknown to him. Ideas remained ideas and were never clad in the flowing garments of mythology; facts remained facts and never became allegories. Liberty never appeared before his eyes and was never represented by him as a goddess, and neither America nor Britannia were majestic figures of heroic size that passed in his dreams. He was neither emotional nor imaginative, yet his eyes were keen and quick to note and establish distinctions between different varieties of plants or animals. His mind was alert and always on the lookout for new facts to add to his store of knowledge, after proper cataloguing. Surely he was not the man to make startling discoveries in the realm of natural history, or to propose a new system of the universe, nor was he one to conceive, in a moment of inspiration, a new political gospel and a new system of society; when he took up the practice of law in Williamsburg, the greatest future that destiny had in store for him, promising as he was, seemed to become as upright and sound a lawyer as Mr. Wythe, and a legal authority as good and learned as Mr. Pendleton.

He was admitted to the Bar in 1767, and two years later was chosen as a member of the House of Burgesses and placed on the committee appointed to draw up an answer to the Governor's speech. His draft was rejected, however, and Colonel Nicholas' address substituted.[1] A few days later Governor Botetourt, unable to endorse the spirited remonstrance to the King on the subject of taxation, dissolved the Assembly.

The next day — wrote Jefferson — we met in the Apollo of the Raleigh Tavern, formed ourselves into a voluntary convention, drew up articles of association against the use of any merchandise imported from Great Britain, signed and recommended them to the people, repaired to our several counties, and were re-elected without any other exception than of the very few who had declined to follow our proceedings.[2]

A spirit of discontent was abroad and had spread throughout the colonies, but it was neither disloyalty nor rebellion. Easily satisfied with this gesture, which for many remained a mere gesture, the Virginians paid little attention to public affairs during the next two years. In the words of Jefferson "nothing of particular excitement occurring for a considerable time, our countrymen seemed to fall into a state of insensibility and inaction." His private life was more eventful. The first of February, 1770, the house at Shadwell in which he lived with his mother, his brother and his unmarried sisters, was burnt to the ground, and with it every paper he had and almost every book.

On reasonable estimate — he wrote to Page — I calculate the *cost* of the books burned to have been £200 sterling. Would to God it had been the money, then it had never cost me a sigh. To make the loss more sensible, it fell principally on my books of Common

---

[1] To Wirt, August 5, 1815. Memorial Edition, XIV, 335.
[2] "Autobiography." *Ibid.*, I, 6.

law, of which I have but one left, at that time lent out. Of papers too of every kind I am utterly destitute. All of these whether public or private, of business or of amusement, have perished in the flames.

The disaster had not been quite so complete as Jefferson indicates. His "Commonplace Book" was saved, his account books, garden books and many memoranda and family papers escaped the flames and were discovered again in 1851 at the bottom of an old trunk.[1] Even as far as books were concerned, the loss was not altogether irretrievable. Jefferson wrote at once to Skipwith for a catalogue of books, sent orders to London, and two years later he could proudly enter in a diary not yet published that his library consisted on August 1, 1773, of twelve hundred and fifty books, not including volumes of music or "his books in Williamsburg." A very substantial store of printed matter for the time.

Another event of quite a different order took place in his life. Jefferson had lost a home, but he was building another, soon to be ready for occupancy, on the hill of Monticello, and he already knew that the house would not be left long without a mistress. On the third day of December, 1771, he filled out a formal application for a marriage license in the court of Charles City County and on the first of January he was married to Martha Skelton, widow of Bathurst Skelton, and daughter of John Wayles, then twenty-three years old. John Wayles of "The Forest" was a lawyer with a large practice, a man of worth if not of eminence, a boon companion welcomed in every society, who had amassed quite a large fortune. His daughter Martha, a true type of Virginia girl, of medium height and well-formed figure, had been well educated and possessed all the social accomplishments of the time. She danced gracefully, played the harpsichord and the spinet, was well read and, above all, was a very efficient housekeeper, for she knew how to man-

[1] Randall, "Life of Jefferson", I, 16, *n*.

age the slaves and care for them in their illnesses, knew how to keep accounts and to arrange for a reception. If the family tradition is true, she was receptive to music, for Jefferson had won out over two rivals because of his talent on the violin and his ability to sing duets. It was a *mariage de raison*, to be sure, and two years later Jefferson noted with undisguised satisfaction that, following the death of his father-in-law, the portion that came to Martha was equal to his own patrimony and consequently "doubled the ease of our circumstances." But it was also a marriage of love, not without romantic color, with a wedding trip from Charles City to Monticello through a snowstorm, and a late arrival at night in the cold new house. Jefferson did not take any of his friends into his confidence and did not celebrate his connubial bliss ; but at the very end of the pages given to Milton in his "Literary Bible", as an afterthought and a recantation from his misogynism, are found the following lines copied, we may surmise, during his honeymoon :

> Nor gentle purpose, nor endearing smiles
> Wanted, nor youthful dalliance, as beseems
> Fair couple, linkt in happy league
> Alone as they . . . [1]

Belinda had been forgotten, and the young woman-hater had found his fair conqueror.

But death again took its toll and cast its cloud over Monticello. With Page, Dabney Carr, Jefferson's fellow student at William and Mary, had been his closest friend. Carr, a frequent visitor at Shadwell, had married in 1764 Jefferson's sister Martha. Not a wealthy man, he was described by his brother-in-law as living in a very small house, with a table, half a dozen chairs, and one or two servants, but the happiest man in the universe.[2] He died when hardly thirty and Jefferson had him buried beneath the shade of their favorite tree at

---

[1] "Paradise Lost", l. 4, v., 337.
[2] To John Page, February 21, 1770. Memorial Edition, IV, 17.

Monticello under which they had so often read, dreamed and discussed; and such was the origin of the little cemetery in which Jefferson was to bury so many of his dear ones before he joined them himself in his last sleep. For Carr he went to his "Literary Bible", as he himself felt unable to write a fitting tribute, and copied from Mallet's "Excursion" an inscription to nail on the tree, by the grave of the friend "who of all men living loved him most."

Honored by the Royal Government and made by Botetourt "Lieutenant of the County of Albemarle, and Chief Commander of all His Majesty's Militia, Horse and Foot in the said county of Albemarle"; honored also by his Alma Mater and appointed by the President of William and Mary "Surveyor of Albemarle County",[1] a member of the Assembly, one of the richest landowners of his county, one of the most successful lawyers of Virginia, happily married, busy with his estate, his books, his violin, his law practice, Jefferson could look forward to a long, quiet and moderate life, the ideal life of a farmer, a gentleman and a scholar. For a man who took his duties seriously it was by no means an existence of idleness, in nowise to be compared with the life of an English gentleman farmer. Every planter was to some extent a captain, and every plantation was to a large extent self-sufficient and self-supporting. In the case of Jefferson, who had recently increased his domain, difficulties and new problems requiring inventiveness, resourcefulness and ingenuity arose every day. Slaves had to be taught new trades and trained, the wilderness had to be reclaimed. Thus were developed qualities of leadership and qualities of class pride. A young planter related to the best families of the colony felt that he belonged to a ruling class, above which could only exist the remote power of the British Parliament and the majesty of the king represented by a governor who

[1] June 9, 1770, and June 6, 1773. The diplomas are preserved in the Jefferson papers of the Library of Congress.

never really belonged, and who in spite of his exalted position, always remained a stranger.

An English tourist, Burnaby, traveling in Virginia in 1760, had already noted signs of impatience and restlessness among the colonists of Virginia. "They are haughty," he wrote, "and jealous of their liberties; impatient of restraint and can scarcely bear the thought of being controlled by superior power. Many of them consider the Colonies as independent states, not connected with Great Britain otherwise than by having the same common King." [1]

When the delegates from Virginia were sent to the first Continental Congress, Silas Deane noted that "the Virginia, and indeed all the Southern delegates appear like men of importance ... they are sociable, sensible, and spirited men. Not a milksop among them." [2]

They were aristocrats wont to give orders and resentful of any interference; they were lords and almost supreme rulers on their plantations; they were owners of many slaves and they had been accustomed to call no man master; and Jefferson was one of them.

The change in the situation had come very abruptly. It is not the purpose of this book to present an elaborate discussion of the causes of the American Revolution, whether they were economic or political or philosophical, or whether they were of mixed motives, varying with each colony and in each colony with every man, did not impel the colonies to revolt against the mother country. I am aware of the present tendency to attribute most of the agitation preceding the revolution to purely economic causes; it must be remembered however, that, if the ulterior motives of the promoters of the American Revolution were selfish and interested, Jefferson was one of those who were moved by entirely different considerations, as

[1] Quoted by Stanard, p. 163.
[2] Quoted by T. N. Page, p. 147.

were, as a matter of fact, most of the members of the First Continental Congress.

While life was still moving easily and happily in Virginia, where in 1772 the theatrical season had been particularly brilliant, things were coming to a head in New England. News of the Bill closing the Port of Boston on the first of June, 1774, reached the Virginia Assembly during the spring session; how it was received had better be told in the words of Jefferson. As so often happens in history at the decisive turn of events, the leadership was taken by a very small group of men who made up their minds at once, assumed responsibility and changed the course of the ship of state. So far no strong protest had been made by Virginia to the British Government. Dunmore was far from being tyrannical; the order imposing duties on many English products had been largely rescinded, except on tea, but it may not be sacrilegious to state that the Virginia gentry were more partial to French wines, Madeira and Nantes rum than to the English national beverage. If Virginia had not declared at that particular time her solidarity, if Jefferson and his friends had not taken the right steps and found the right words to "arouse the people from the lethargy into which they had fallen", even New England steadfastness and stanchness of heart would have been unequal to the task. It was on this occasion, rather than on the Fourth of July, 1776, that the fate of the British colonies of America was decided.

According to Jefferson's own statement, leadership in these subjects was no longer left to the old members of the Assembly, but Patrick Henry, R. H. Lee, F. L. Lee, three or four other members and he himself met in the library after agreeing that they must take "an unequivocal stand in the line with Massachusetts." They decided that the best means of calling the seriousness of the situation to the attention of the public was to appoint a day of general fasting and prayer, quite an unprecedented measure in Virginia; but they rummaged in old books "for revolutionary precedents and forms of the Puritans", and they finally "cooked up a resolution, somewhat modernizing their phrases, for appointing the 1st day of June on which the port-bill was to commence, for a day of fasting, humiliation, and prayer, to implore Heaven to avert from us the evils of civil war, to inspire us with firmness in support of our rights, and to turn the hearts of the King and Parliament to moderation and justice." [1] Clearly the day of fasting and prayer did not appear to any of the members of the unofficial committee as springing from a profound religious sentiment, but they knew how strong over the people was the power of the Church, and how impossible it was to unite them except by giving a religious appearance to a purely political manifestation. These young Virginia lawyers knew their people and were not totally unacquainted with mass psychology; they knew how to play the game of practical politics, despite their high and disinterested ideal.

The next day Governor Dunmore pronounced the usual English remedy in such circumstances: the dissolution of the Assembly. Once more the members met in the Apollo room, and "they agreed to an association, and instructed the committee of correspondence to propose to the corresponding committees of the other colonies to appoint deputies to meet in Congress at such place *annually* as would be convenient, to direct, from time to time, the measures required by the general interest."

This passage in the "Autobiography" has led historians into a spirited controversy as to whether the proposal to form a Congress originated in Virginia or in Massachusetts, and whether such a plan had not been discussed in Boston as early as 1770. Whatever the case may be, the most important part of the resolution passed in the Raleigh Tavern was not the establishment of a coördinating organism; it was the declara-

[1] "Autobiography", p. 10.

tion recorded by Jefferson, "that an attack on any one colony should be considered as an attack on the whole." This last part was not a simple administrative provision, it was more than a promise of a union; it was the constitution of a new society, since according to Kames as quoted by Jefferson in his "Commonplace Book" "mutual defence against a more powerful neighbor is in early times the chief, or sole motive for joining society."

The deputies went back home and, on the first of June, met the assemblies of the people "to perform ceremonies of the day and to address to them discourses suited to the occasion. The people met generally, with anxiety and alarm in their countenance, and the effect of the day, through the whole colony was like a shock of electricity, arousing every man and placing him erect and solid on his centre." [1]

As a result of the train of thought started by the meeting, the freeholders of Albemarle County adopted on June 26 a series of resolutions evidently written by Jefferson. Here for the first time Jefferson declared that:

The inhabitants of the several States of British America are subject to the laws which they adopted at their first settlement, and to such others as have been since made by their respective Legislatures, duly constituted and appointed with their own consent. That no other Legislature whatever can rightly exercise authority over them; and that these privileges they as the common rights of mankind, confirmed by the political constitutions they have respectively assumed, and also by several charters of compact from the Crown.

The originality of this theory cannot be determined without comparison with the resolutions adopted a few days before by the Assembly of Fairfax County presided over by Colonel George Washington. These came from the pen of George Mason and they stated with equal emphasis the contractual

[1] "Autobiography." Memorial Edition, I, 11.

theory of the government of the British colonies. Whether Jefferson knew them or not, the similarity with the views expressed by the freeholders of Albemarle is most striking.

The first article averred the principle also found in Jefferson's "Commonplace Book" that "this colony and Dominion of Virginia cannot be considered as a conquered country, and as it was, that the present inhabitants are not of the conquered, but of the conquerors." It added that:

Our ancestors, when they left their native land, and settled in America, brought over with them, even if the same is not confirmed by Charters, the civil constitution and form of Government of the country they came from and were by the laws of nature and nations entitled to all its privileges, immunities and advantages, which have descended to us, their posterity, and ought of right to be as fully enjoyed as if we had still continued with the realm of England.

The second article enunciated the most essential and "fundamental principle of government", that the people "could be governed by no laws to which they had not given their consent by Representatives freely chosen by themselves."

The third article declared that the colonies had some duty to fulfill towards the mother country and admitted that the British Parliament might, "directed with wisdom and moderation", take measures to regulate "American commerce", although such action was in some degree repugnant to the principles of the Constitution.[1]

Whether or not Jefferson had received the Fairfax resolutions before writing the Albemarle declaration, this is the capital difference between the two documents and the two doctrines. On the one hand, George Mason accepted the theory that the first settlers had brought over with them the civil

---

[1] This passage has been overlooked by Randall, and naturally by Mr. Hirst, who follows Randall very closely here as elsewhere. Hirst, p. 69. The Fairfax resolutions did not recognize the right of the British Parliament to regulate the commerce of the colony; they admitted the *expediency* but denied the *right* of such a procedure.

constitution and form of government of the mother country, and consequently admitted a permanent connection between the colony and the metropolis. Jefferson, on the contrary, asserted with great strength and clarity the complete independence of the colonists from the British constitution. They were subject to no laws except those they had freely adopted when they had consented to a new compact and formed a new society. He was perfectly justified when he declared in his "Autobiography":

Our other patriots, Randolph, the Lees, Nicholas, Pendleton, stopped at the half-way house of John Dickinson, who admitted that England had a right to regulate our commerce, and to lay duties on it for the purpose of regulation, but not of raising revenue. But for this ground there was no foundation in compact, in any acknowledged principles of colonisation, nor in reason; expatriation being a natural right, and acted on as such by all nations, in all ages.

This was really the core of the question. Jefferson had reached that conclusion, not from following a certain line of abstract reasoning, but after studying the history of the Greek colonies in Stanyan, and the history of the Saxon settlement of Great Britain in many authors, as may be seen in his "Commonplace Book", and he was soon to reaffirm the doctrine of expatriation as the fundamental principle on which rested all the claims of the American colonies.

The Virginia Convention was to meet at Williamsburg on August 1, to select delegates to a General Congress of the colonies. With all his books at hand, all his legal authorities, the precious "Commonplace Book" and all the repertories he had gathered in his library, Jefferson proceeded to draft a project of instructions for the future delegates. He was taken ill on his way to Williamsburg but forwarded the plan to Peyton Randolph and Patrick Henry. Henry never mentioned it; Randolph informed the convention that he had received such a paper from a member, prevented by sickness from offering it, and laid it on the table for perusal. It was read generally by the members, approved by many, though thought too bold for use at that time; but they printed it in pamphlet form, under the title of "A Summary View of the Rights of British America."

In some respects it is a more original and more important document than the Declaration of Independence itself. With the detailed account of the grievances enumerated by Jefferson we cannot deal here. A few points, however, deserve special attention. The difficulties that had arisen between the colonies and the home government had occasioned the publication of many pamphlets dealing with the situation. Most of Jefferson's predecessors, however, had attempted to define *in jure* the rights of the British colonies. Thus George Mason had made his "Extracts" from the Virginia charters, "with some remarks on them" in 1773, and he had come to the conclusion already given in the "Fairfax resolves", that "the ancestors of the colonists when they had left their native land and settled in America had brought with them, although not confirmed by Charters, the civil government and form of government of the country they came from." [1] But he had gone back no farther in history and had not formulated the principles of the "constitution" of England. Not so with Jefferson, who emphatically denied that the colonists had anything to do with the British constitution or with its form of government. He had studied the history of the settlement of England in Molesworth, in Pelloutier, in Sir William Temple, in Dalrymple, and had come to the conclusion enunciated in the "Rights of British America":

That our ancestors, before their emigration to America, were the free inhabitants of the British Dominions in Europe, and possessed a right which nature has given to all men of leaving the country in which chance, not choice, had placed them, and of seeking out new

[1] George Mason, I, 393.

habitations, and there establishing new societies, under such laws and regulations as, to them, shall seem most likely to promote public happiness.

That their Saxon ancestors had, under this universal law, in like manner, left their native wilds and woods in the North of Europe, possessed themselves of the Island of Britain, then less charged with inhabitants, and established there a system of laws which has been so long the glory and protection of that country.

On another and not less important point, Jefferson was indebted to his "Commonplace Book." He had taken great care to determine through historical and judicial authorities the origin of land tenures in the kingdom of England and he had found that in the good old Saxon times, "upon settling in the countries which they subdued, the victorious army divided the conquered lands. That portion which fell to every soldier he seized as a recompense due to his valour, as a settlement acquired by his own sword. He took possession of it as a freeman in full property. He enjoyed it during his own life and could dispose of it at pleasure, or transmit it as an inheritance to his children." It was not until after the fifth century that the king, because as general he was thought fittest to distribute the conquered lands to each according to his merits, assumed to himself and was quietly allowed the entire power of the partition of lands. This abominable system however was not introduced into England before the Norman Conquest, and thus was spread the false notion that all lands belonged to the crown.[1] Against this last claim, which he believed to rest on a false conception of history, Jefferson raises an emphatic protest. Backed by his knowledge of the gradual encroachment of the feudal system on the natural rights of his Anglo-Saxon ancestors, he claimed for the American colonists the same rights as belonged in the good old Anglo-Saxon days to those who had acquired a settlement by their own sword.

[1] See "Commonplace Book", 229–257.

It is time for us to lay this matter before his Majesty, and to declare, that he has no right to grant lands of himself. From the nature and purpose of civil institutions, all the lands within the limits, which any particular party has circumscribed around itself, are assumed by that society, and subject to their allotment; this may be done by themselves assembled collectively, or by their legislature, to whom they may have delegated sovereign authority; and, if they are alloted in neither of these ways, each individual of the society, may appropriate to himself such lands as he finds vacant, and occupancy will give him title.

According to this theory, one of the mainstays of the doctrine of Americanism, of which Jefferson made himself the advocate, is the right of conquest. But here Jefferson would have introduced a distinction borrowed from Lord Kames, for "the northern nations who overran Europe fought not for glory or dominion but for habitation" and invaded only countries which were sparsely populated.[1] Whether such a position was tenable historically is quite another matter. The important point maintained by Jefferson is that when the first settlers left Great Britain for the shores of America, they were not colonists but free agents. By the mere fact of expatriating themselves they had severed all ties with the mother country, they had recovered full possession of all their natural rights and were at liberty to agree on a new social compact; they derived their rights of property not from the king but from their occupancy of a new and unsettled territory. All considered, this curious doctrine was nothing but a sort of sublimation and legal justification of the pioneer spirit.

This historical and legal demonstration, in which Jefferson had gone back to the very beginnings of Anglo-Saxon society, transcended all contemporary discussions on the Rights of the British Parliament. Jefferson was perfectly aware of its originality and not a little proud of it. It was in his opinion

---

[1] "Commonplace Book", p. 135.

the only orthodox or tenable doctrine — that our emigration from England to this country gave her no more rights over us, than the emigration of the Danes and Saxons gave to the present authorities of the mother country, over England. In this doctrine, however, I have never been able to get any one to agree with me but Mr. Wythe. He concurred in it from the first dawn of the question, What was the political relation between us and England?

Once the question was clearly put, Jefferson went at it with the methods used by a lawyer to prove the title to a piece of property. The first point to be settled was to determine who was the legitimate owner of the territory occupied by the American "colonists", the king or the colonists themselves; thus presented, the question became very simple:

For it is thought that no circumstance has occurred to distinguish materially, the British from the Saxon emigration. America was conquered, and her settlements made and firmly established, at the expense of individuals, and not of the British public. Their own blood was spilt in acquiring lands for their settlement, their own fortunes expanded in making this settlement effectual. For themselves they fought, for themselves they conquered, and for themselves alone they have a right to hold.

This was the keystone of Jefferson's social system at that time. It is not unimportant to note that it was a doctrine that could apply only to Anglo-Saxon colonies, more particularly to American colonies, and not a doctrine susceptible of universal application. Whether or not the principle might also be advanced by other peoples or nations, Jefferson did not state and did not care. His was not a mind to generalize and to extend universally any given principle. For the present, at least, he was satisfied to claim for the American settlers not the rights of man, but the rights of their Saxon ancestors. His position was legal and historical, not philosophical.

It was also to some extent an aristocratic position. Since the land was theirs by right of conquest, it almost necessarily ensued that only landowners, or to use the old colonial word, freeholders, were entitled to the rights, privileges, and happiness of self-government. The consequence was not expressed but it was implied. The analogy with the doctrine of the Physiocrats strikes one at first; but this analogy is only superficial. True enough, only freeholders are really worth considering and can raise a legitimate protest; but in a country as new and as extensive as America, it is within the power of every inhabitant to become a freeholder. For it is another iniquity to suppose that the Crown has the right to give grants of land:

It is time for us to lay this matter before his Majesty, and to declare, that he has no right to grant lands of himself. From the nature and purpose of civil institutions, all the lands within the limits, which any particular party has circumscribed around itself, are assumed by that society, and subject to their allotment; this may be done by themselves assembled collectively, or by their legislature, to whom they may have delegated sovereign authority; and, if they are alloted in neither of these ways, each individual of the society may appropriate to himself such lands as he finds vacant, and occupancy gives him title.

Thus spoke the pioneer, a pioneer who had studied law and history and could express in clear and forcible terms what the pioneers had felt only confusedly. Unless I am much mistaken, it is the first enunciation of one of the cardinal principles of Americanism; but, as far as Jefferson is concerned, it did not rest upon any political philosophy, either Hooker's or Locke's. The American settlers resumed and resurrected on a new soil the tradition interrupted by Parliamentary and kingly usurpations. By a sort of curious primitivism they renounced their immediate and degraded British forbears to claim as their true ancestors the Saxon conquerors of the British Isles. Can any one imagine anything farther from the theory of Rousseau in the "Discourse on the Origin of Inequality", or in the

"Social Contract", anything farther from the universal humanitarianism of the French philosophers? In a last analysis, American society as it existed, and as it expressed its will to exist through its young spokesman, rested essentially not on an *a priori* principle but on the right of conquest, or more exactly, of discovery.

The best student of William and Mary, the young artist who wanted to make Monticello a thing of beauty, the lover of the literature of Greece and Rome, proclaimed loudly that "our ancestors who migrated hither were laborers, not lawyers." His was not a political philosophy dealing with "fictitious principles", it was the harsh, hard-headed, practical and fierce determination of the pioneer who stakes out a piece of land in the wilderness, ready to hold it against all claim jumpers.

The Virginia convention dominated by "Randolph, the Lees, Nicholas, Pendleton" was not ready to go so far as the young master of Monticello. The instructions to the delegates finally adopted and printed in an appendix to Jefferson's own "Autobiography" were exceedingly tame, but his declaration was printed, widely circulated among the people, and even reached England. It was just what was needed to set afire the public mind, for no people will rise, fight and die for an economic doctrine or in defense of its commercial interests. They have to be provided with mottoes which appeal to their imagination, they have to be raised above the ordinary trend of things; they must have a banner, a flag and a battle cry, and such was the object of Jefferson's peroration, which no Pendleton and no Lee could have written:

That these are our grievances, which we have just laid before his Majesty, with that freedom of language and sentiment which becomes a free people claiming their rights as derived from the laws of nature, and not as the gift of their Chief Magistrate. Let those flatter, who fear: it is not an American art. To give praise where it is not due might be well from the venal, but it would ill beseem those who are asserting the rights of human nature. They know and will, therefore, say, that Kings are the servants, not the proprietors of the people.

Congress assembled at Philadelphia on September 4, 1774, under the presidency of Peyton Randolph of Virginia and adjourned in October, not without a recommendation "to discountenance every species of extravagance and dissipation, especially all horse racing, all kinds of gaming, cock-fighting, exhibitions of shows, plays and other diversions and entertainments." [1] The colonies were girding their loins for the fight, society life came to a standstill; the brilliant days of the little capital of Virginia were over.

When the counties organized committees of safety, Jefferson was at the top of the list of appointees in his county. He was again sent to the second convention of Virginia as representative from Albemarle. The convention met in Richmond, March 20, 1775, and it was then that Patrick Henry poured out in a fierce outburst the famous speech ending with the war cry of "Give me liberty or give me death." The resolution to arm passed with a decided majority and a plan of defense was adopted. Collisions threatened between the militia and the regulars on several occasions. But when Lord North's "Conciliatory Proposition" was received, Lord Dunmore convened the House of Burgesses on the first of July to take it into consideration. Peyton Randolph was then recalled from Congress and Jefferson appointed to succeed him. He did not leave, however, before an answer to the proposition had been drafted. The Virginians did not close the door to a compromise, but insisted that the final answer did not depend on them, for they considered that they were "bound in honor as well as interest, to share their general fate with their sister Colonies, and should hold themselves base deserters of that Union to

[1] Stanard, p. 250.

which they had acceeded, were they to agree to any measure distinct and apart from them."

A few days later Lord Dunmore left the city and took refuge on board a man-of-war lying at York, declaring he had taken this step for his safety. Jefferson departed from Williamsburg for Philadelphia on the eleventh of June, 1775, and reached the capital of Pennsylvania on the twentieth. The national rôle of the young Virginia lawyer and landowner was about to begin.

BOOK TWO

Jefferson and the American Revolution

CHAPTER I

THE DECLARATION OF INDEPENDENCE

WHEN Thomas Jefferson arrived in Philadelphia and took lodgings with "Ben Randolph" on Chestnut Street, he was only thirty-three years old, "the youngest member of Congress but one." But he was already known as the author of the "Summary View of the Rights of British America", he was bringing with him Virginia's answer to Lord North's "Conciliatory Proposition," and he had been appointed to succeed as delegate the former President of Congress. Most of all he had behind him, not only the first colony in population, but also, to a large extent, all the Southern colonies, which were bound to follow the course of Virginia.

Unassuming and straightforward, he was at once welcomed with open arms by the New England leaders, and years later John Adams still remembered the first impression he made upon him :

Mr. Jefferson came into Congress in June 1775, and brought with him a reputation for literature, science and a happy talent of composition. . . . Though a silent member in Congress, he was so prompt, frank, explicit and decisive upon committees and in conversation — not even Samuel Adams was more so — that he soon seized upon my heart.

Five days later, he was placed on the committee appointed to draw up a "Declaration of the Causes of Taking Up Arms." Through deference for the authority of Dickinson, leader of the conservative party, he withdrew a draft he had prepared and in the final text he claimed as his only the last four paragraphs. But these last paragraphs contained some of the sharply coined sentences that impress themselves on the mind, the final expression of so many ideas ever since repeated in political speeches whenever an attempt is made to define America's ideal policies.

The drafts of Jefferson rejected by the committee have been found by Mr. Worthington Chauncey Ford, and by him published in his edition of the "Journals of the Continental Congress." Much more fiery than the final text, they contain a long and detailed enumeration of the wrongs suffered by the Colonies, and, to a certain extent, may be considered as a preliminary draft of the special part of the Declaration of Independence dealing with the denunciation of George the Third. Once again the young lawyer reiterated the historical theory already presented in the "Rights of British America":

Our forefathers, inhabitants of the island of Great Britain, left their native land to seek on these shores a residence for civil and religious freedom. At the expense of their blood, to the ruin of their fortunes, with the relinquishment of everything quiet and comfortable in life, they effected settlements in the inhospitable wilds of America; and there established civil societies with various forms of constitution. . . . The political institutions of America, its various soils and climates opened a certain resource to the unfortunate and to the enterprising of every country, and ensured to them the acquisition and free possession of property.

If the text finally adopted fails to justify entirely the claim of Jefferson, there is little doubt that Dickinson used many of the ideas expressed by his younger colleague and that the final paragraphs have a Jeffersonian ring.

Our cause is just. Our union is perfect — our internal resources are great. . . . We fight not for glory or for conquest. We exhibit to mankind the remarkable spectacle of a people attacked by provoked enemies, without any imputation or even suspicion of offense. They boast of their privileges and civilization, and yet proffer no milder condition than servitude or death.

Thus was the uniqueness of America's position emphasized and called to the attention of her own people. Nor was it forgotten that the country was particularly favored by God, for it declared that:

We gratefully acknowledge, as signal instance of the Divine towards us, that His providence would not permit us to be called into this severe controversy, until we were grown up to our present strength, had been previously exercised in warlike apparatus, and possessed of the means of defending ourselves.

Finally, once more was reiterated Jefferson's favorite contention, the theory which has become one of the fundamental axioms of the doctrine of Americanism: that America did not owe anything to the older civilization of Europe, and was a self-made country:

In our native land, in defence of the freedom that is our birthright, and which we ever enjoyed until the late violation of it; for the protection of our property, acquired solely by the honest industry of our forefathers and ourselves, against violence actually offered, we have taken up arms. We shall lay them down when hostilities shall cease on the part of the aggressors, and all danger of their being renewed shall be removed, and not before.

Then came a perfunctory appeal to conciliation, and a final religious note strictly nonsectarian; for of his religious faith the young delegate had retained the form and the tone which scarcely concealed his deism:

With an humble confidence in the mercies of the supreme and impartial Judge and Ruler of the Universe, we most devoutly implore his divine goodness to conduct us happily through this great conflict, to dispose our adversaries to reconciliation on reasonable terms, and thereby to relieve the empire from the calamity of civil war.

No wonder this "Declaration" was read amid thundering huzzas in every market place and amid fervent prayers in nearly every pulpit in the colonies. With an extraordinary "felicity of expression", with a unique sense of fitness, Jefferson had struck every chord susceptible of response in every American heart. He had drawn for the people an ideal picture of the nation and themselves, he had portrayed them as they yearned to be looked upon by posterity and the nations of the world : he had formulated the creed of Americanism.

Far more judicial in tone was the neat state paper prepared by Jefferson to answer Lord North's "Conciliatory Proposition." The committee appointed consisted of Benjamin Franklin, Thomas Jefferson, John Adams and Richard H. Lee. The youngest member of the committee was chosen to draw up the document, the answer of the Virginia Assembly he had brought with him having been approved. Not for nothing had Jefferson attended the courts of justice of Albemarle County and Williamsburg for more than ten years and listened to decisions from the bench. The answer strives to be a cold, dispassionate enumeration of facts, with its short paragraphs beginning : "we are of opinion" — recalling the "Whereases" of legal documents. But there is an undertone of indignation, cropping up in every sentence, which belies the studied reserve. The conclusion, one might call it a peroration, is a genuine specimen of revolutionary eloquence :

When it considers the great armaments with which they have invaded us, and the circumstances of cruelty with which these have commenced and prosecuted hostilities ; when these things, we say, are laid together and attentively considered, can the world be deceived into an opinion that we are unreasonable? Or can it hesitate to believe with us, that nothing but our own exertions may defeat the ministerial sentence of death or abject submission?

Truly Jefferson might have become a great orator had he chosen to correct his handicap in speech and train his voice. Historians who attribute much importance to racial traits and inherited characteristics may believe that this was due to the Welshman that reappeared in him at times ; but the Welsh temperament was suppressed and checked by the puritanical restraint of Mr. Small, Mr. Maury, the judicial reserve of Mr. Wythe, the example of Mr. Peyton Randolph; and, carried away as he was by Patrick Henry's oratory, Jefferson saw in him impulsive and emotional qualities to be admired but to be shunned. More than any of his contemporaries, however, he was unconsciously influenced by reminiscences of speeches he had read and memorized in Livy, Cicero and perhaps Demosthenes. These sentences have a classical ring; his true models were the Greek and Latin orators, and if a critical edition of Jefferson's early papers were ever attempted, a careful investigation could not fail to bring to light the classical sources of his inspiration.

The report was adopted on July 31, and Congress adjourned the next day. Jefferson returned at once to Monticello, to stay in Virginia until the opening of Congress. In spite of the fiery tone of the answer to Lord North's proposition, it seems that neither he nor any of his friends seriously entertained nor even considered the possibility of the colonies separating entirely from the mother country. War had already begun, but it was a civil war. There still remained some hope that an "everlasting avulsion from Great Britain would be avoided." Yet it could be avoided only on one condition: that the British Government should accept, without reservation or restriction, the minimum terms of Congress. Jefferson then wrote to his friend, John Randolph, who had decided to remove to England:

I would rather be in dependence on Great Britain, properly limited, than on any nation upon earth, or than on no nation. But I am one of those, too, who, rather than submit to the rights of legislation for us, assumed by the British Parliament, and which late experience has shown they will so cruelly exercise, would lend my hand to sink the whole island in the ocean.[1]

[1] To John Randolph, Attorney-general, August 25, 1775. Memorial Edition, IV, 28.

The manuscript letter in the Library of Congress is not the one that was used in the different editions of Jefferson's "Works." It is a much corrected and written-over draft, containing several passages which have disappeared in the published text.[1] It contained particularly a request to John Randolph who was going to "the hub of literature", to buy him "books of parliamentary learning." It also included a request to Randolph to sell him his fine violin, to which Randolph acceded, averring that "Tho we *may politically* differ in sentiments, yet I see no reason, why *privately* we may not cherish the same esteem for each other which formerly I believe subsisted between us. We both of us seem to be steering opposite courses: the success of either lies in the womb of Time."[2]

Such letters are very significant, for they express better than long dissertations the state of mind of the leading men of the day. The question at issue was still a political question; it was a question of internal politics on which men could differ without necessarily becoming enemies or losing each other's esteem and affection. Less than a year before the Declaration of Independence, independence seemed to Jefferson the worst possible solution, to be delayed and avoided if it were possible.

Chosen again as delegate to Congress, but delayed by the illness and death of his second child, Jefferson reached Philadelphia on September 25, twenty days after the opening of the session. He stayed only until the twenty-eighth of December, and resumed his seat on May 13 of the following year. In the meantime events were moving rapidly. Congress had been advised of the king's refusal even to notice their second petition; and Jefferson, writing a second time to John Randolph, could declare:

Believe me, my dear sir, there is not in the British empire, a man who more cordially loves a union with Great Britain than I do. But

---

[1] Jefferson Papers, Library of Congress.　　[2] August 31, 1775.

by the God that made me, I will cease to exist before I yield to a connection on such terms as the British Parliament propose; and in this I think I speak the sentiment of America. We want neither inducement nor power, to declare and assert a separation. It is will alone which is wanting, and that is growing apace under the fostering hand of our King.[1]

On the sixth of December, a declaration was adopted repudiating allegiance to the king, and the British Constitution was proclaimed "our best inheritance." Four days previously Jefferson had drafted a declaration concerning Ethan Allen, when news arrived of his being arrested and sent to Britain in irons to be punished for pretended treason. For the first time the delegate from Virginia referred to the British as "our enemies" and called upon them to respect "the rights of nations."

At this juncture and shortly after being appointed on an important committee, Jefferson abruptly left Congress and set out for home. The reason for his sudden departure has never been satisfactorily explained. It may have been due to news of the bad health of his mother: she died on March 31, 1776, and this is the only explanation that Randall could offer. It was more probably due to his anxiety about the fate of his family. Communications with Virginia were rare and difficult. He wrote home regularly every week, but on October 31 he had not yet received a word "from any mortal breathing", and on November 7 he repeated:

"I have never received the script of a pen from any mortal in Virginia since I left it, nor been able by any inquiries I could make to hear of my family. I had hoped that when Mrs. Byrd came I could have heard something of them. The suspense under which I am is too terrible to be endured. If anything has happened, for God's sake let me know it!" Two weeks later he urged his wife to keep herself "at a distance from

[1] November 29, 1775. Memorial Edition, IV, 31.

Ld. Dunmore", and he was planning to meet Eppes "as proposed."

There seems to be very little doubt that he yielded to his anxiety and to the entreaties of Eppes who seems to have urged him to come back. He had left at Monticello a sick mother, his sisters, a wife who had recently lost a child and had hardly recovered from the blow, and he was in constant fear that a raid from the British troops, who had already burnt Norfolk, should endanger the lives of his dear ones. Furthermore he believed that his presence in Philadelphia was not indispensable; for he was never one who overrated himself. Finally, a document overlooked by his biographers informs us that on September 26, 1775, he had been appointed by the Committee of Safety for the Colony of Virginia, Lieutenant and Commander in chief of the Militia of the County of Albemarle.[1] In view of Lord Dunmore's impending attacks his presence was evidently required to organize local forces. All these are reasons enough to explain why he left Philadelphia. We do not even know that he hesitated at all or experienced any conflict of duties. National patriotism was still limited by family duty, and local patriotism was stronger in him than obligations to a country which did not yet exist.

So it happened that the man who wrote the Declaration of Independence was to miss many of the preliminary steps and discussions that preceded it. He did not resume his seat in Congress until May 14, 1776. Five days before, a resolution framed by Adams and R. H. Lee had been adopted, instructing the colonies to form governments. It was passed the very day Jefferson arrived in Philadelphia. Not only had he come back rather reluctantly, but he was anxious to return to Virginia in order to participate in the work of the Colonial Convention, as appears from his letter to Thomas Nelson, Junior:

[1] Jefferson Papers. Library of Congress.

Should our Convention propose to establish now a form of government, perhaps it might be agreeable to recall for a short time their delegates. It is a work of the most interesting nature and such as every individual would wish to have his voice in. . . . But this I mention to you in confidence, as in our situation, a hint to any other is too delicate however anxiously interesting the subject is to our feelings.

With all his attention turned towards the Old Dominion and in his anxiety to participate in establishing a model form of government for his "country", he then decided to send to Pendleton, President of the Assembly, the draft of a proposed constitution for Virginia, or rather, as he termed it, "A Bill for new modelling the form of government and for establishing the Fundamental principles of our future constitution." [1] This is a capital document for the history of Jefferson's political thought. For the first time he had the opportunity to develop fully his views on society and government. How clear in his mind were the theories of which he later became the advocate will be easily perceived. The draft started with a recital of the grievances of the colony against "George Guelph King of Great Britain", which Jefferson was to utilize in the Declaration of Independence. It declared that "The Legislative, Executive, and Judiciary shall be forever separate" and continued with a description of the three branches of government. For the Legislative, Jefferson proposed a bicameral system, consisting of a House of Representatives and a Senate. The House was to be elected by "all male persons of full age and sane mind having a freehold estate in (one fourth of an acre) of land in any town or in 25 acres of land in the county and all persons resident in the colony who shall have paid scot and lot to government the last two years." The Senate was to be appointed by the House of Representatives. The death penalty was abolished for all crimes except murder and offences

[1] The full text will be found in the Ford Edition, II, 7.

in the military service; torture was abolished in all cases whatsoever. Some of these provisions were incorporated later in the "Bill for Apportioning Crimes and Punishment." The Administrator was to be appointed by the House of Representatives, as well as the Attorney-general and the Privy Council. Judges were to be appointed by the Administrator and Privy Council; the High Sheriffs and Coroners of counties were to be elected annually by the voters, but all other officers, civil and military, to be appointed by the Administrator. The bill proposed that "descents shall go according to the laws of Gavelkind, save only that females shall have equal rights with males." — "All persons shall have full and free liberty of religious opinion; nor shall any be compelled to support or maintain any religious institution." "Printing presses shall be free except so far as by commission of private injury cause may be given of private action. There shall be no standing army but in time of actual war." The introduction of slaves into the State was forbidden. Finally provisions were made for the revision of the Constitution.

Truly most of the reforms advocated by Jefferson are already contained in this document, not implicitly but explicitly: religious freedom, freedom of the press, abolition of slavery, the laws of descent and the bill to abolish entail, the "Bill for Proportioning Crimes and Punishment" are all here. It was a bold and radical proposal, and no wonder the young delegate from Virginia was anxious to go home in order to defend it before his colleagues of the Assembly. The delegates, after much wrangling, had come to practical agreement on the most important points. It was too late and they were too "tired" of the subject to resume the discussion. From Jefferson's plan they simply borrowed the long recital of grievances which became the preamble to the Virginia Constitution.[1]

[1] See "Life of G. Mason", I, Appendix.

As finally adopted, the Constitution was far less liberal than the plan proposed by Jefferson, and this may explain his severe criticism of it in his "Notes on Virginia" (Query XIII). It embodied, however, some of the same essential principles; it proclaimed the separation of powers and established two Chambers. It retained the name of governor, redolent of the English régime, instead of "administrator"; it made no mention of slavery, entails, descents and freedom of the press, but in some respects it was even more democratic than the Jefferson plan since both houses were directly elected. In the meantime things were coming to a head in Philadelphia, and on June 7 "certain resolutions concerning independence being moved and adopted, it was

Resolved, That these United Colonies are, and of right ought to be, free and independent States, that they are absolved from all allegiance to the British Crown, and that all political connection between them and the State of Great Britain is, and ought to be, totally dissolved.

That it is expedient forthwith to take the most effectual measures for forming foreign Alliances.

That a plan of confederation be prepared and transmitted to the respective Colonies for their consideration and approbation.[1]

On June 10, it was

Resolved, That the consideration of the first resolution be postponed to this day, three weeks (July 1), and in the meanwhile, that no time be lost in case the Congress agree thereto, that a committee be appointed to prepare a declaration to the effect of the said first resolution.

The next day it was resolved, That the committee to prepare the declaration consist of five members: The members chosen, Mr. [Thomas] Jefferson, Mr. J[ohn] Adams, Mr. [Benjamin] Franklin, Mr. [Roger] Sherman, and Mr. R[obert] R. Livingston.[2]

[1] "Journals of Congress", V, 425.   [2] *Ibid.*, V, 431.

Jefferson's biographers have indulged in a great many discussions about the reasons which determined the selection of the committee. Jefferson certainly did not seek the honor, and little did he dream at the time that it would bring him such fame. Without renewing the old controversy on the participation of the other members of the committee in the drawing up of the famous document, a few facts have to be considered. First of all it was not an improvisation. The committee appointed on June 10 reported only on June 28. A written draft was submitted to Adams and Franklin, whose advice could not be neglected, and they suggested several modifications, additions and corrections. Furthermore, Jefferson was too good a harmonizer not to discuss many points with his colleagues of the committee, so as to ascertain their views before writing down the first draft. Even the desirability of having a declaration was a highly controversial question, and Jefferson himself, in the detailed notes he took of the preliminary discussion, indicates that when the committee was appointed "the colonies of New York, New Jersey, Pennsylvania, Delaware and South Carolina were not yet matured for falling from the parent stem."[1]

On June 28, the committee appointed to prepare a declaration brought in a draft which was read and "*Ordered* to lie on the table." On July 2, Congress resumed the consideration of the resolution agreed to by and reported from the committee of the whole; and the same being read, was agreed to as follows.

Resolved, That these United Colonies are, and, of right, ought to be Free and Independent States; that they are absolved from allegiance to the British crown, and that all political connexion between them, and the state of Great Britain, is, and ought to be, totally dissolved.

[1] "Autobiography." Memorial Edition, I, 25.

Properly speaking this is, as Mr. Becker has remarked, the real Declaration of Independence. But the principle once adopted, it remained to proclaim and explain the action taken by Congress not only to the people of the Free and Independent States, but to the world at large. Congress then resolved itself into a committee of the whole, only to decide that it was too late in the day to take up such a momentous question. The discussion continued on the next day but Harrison reported that the committee, not having finished, desired leave to sit again. On July 4, Congress resolved itself into a committee of the whole to take into further consideration the Declaration ; and after some time, the president resumed the chair. "Mr. (Benjamin) Harrison reported, that the committee of the whole Congress have agreed to a Declaration, which he delivered in. The Declaration being again read, was agreed to." Congress then ordered that the Declaration be authenticated and printed, and the committee appointed to prepare the Declaration "to superintend and correct the press."

Such is briefly told from the "Journals of Congress" the story of the momentous document in its external details. It has been too well related by Mr. Becker and Mr. Fitzpatrick to leave any excuse for a new account. Writing many years later, John Adams declared "there is not an idea in it but what had been hackneyed in Congress two years before," and replying to Adams' insinuations, Jefferson admitted that :

Pickering's observations, and Mr. Adams' in addition, that it contained no new ideas, that it is a commonplace compilation, its sentiments hacknied in Congress for two years before . . . may be all true. Of that I am not judge. Richard H. Lee charged it as copied from Locke's treatise on Government . . . I only know that I turned to neither book nor pamphlet while writing it. I did not consider it as any part of my charge to invent new ideas altogether and to offer no sentiment which had never been expressed before.

In another letter to Lee, written in 1825, a year before his death, Jefferson had given, as his last and final statement on the subject:

Not to find out new principles, or new arguments, never before thought of, not merely to say things which had never been said before; but to place before mankind the common sense of the subject, in terms so plain and firm as to command their assent. . . . Neither aiming at originality of principles or sentiments, nor yet copied from any particular and previous writing, it was intended to be an expression of the American mind. . . . All its authority rests on the harmonizing sentiments of the day, whether expressed in conversation, in letters, printed essays, on the elementary books of public right, as Aristotle, Cicero, Locke, Sidney, etc.

Two phrases in this letter deserve particular notice, "an expression of the American mind" and "the harmonizing sentiments of the day." This is truly what Jefferson had attempted to express in his "felicitous language" — the confused yearnings, the inarticulate aspirations, the indefinite ideals of the speechless and awkward masses. He did it in words so simple that no man could fail to understand it, in sentences so well balanced and so rhythmic that no artist in style could improve upon them. The Declaration of Independence is not only a historical document, it is the first and to this day the most outstanding monument in American literature. It does not follow, however, that Jefferson had no model. Mr. Becker in his masterly study has demonstrated that it was the final development of a whole current of thought, the origins of which can be traced back in history even farther than he has done. The Declaration of Independence is essentially of Lockian origin, but it does not ensue that Jefferson had memorized Locke, nor even that he was conscious, when he wrote the document, that he was using a Lockian phraseology. As a matter of fact, even if he remembered Locke, it is more than probable that reminiscences from two other more modern expressions of the same idea haunted his mind. The first was a pamphlet of James Wilson, written in 1770, published in Philadelphia in 1774 and entitled "Considerations on the Nature and Extent of the Legislative Authority of the British Parliament." Mr. Becker has pointed out the similarity between a passage in Wilson and the preamble. Since then I have found that, in his "Commonplace Book", Jefferson copied passages from Wilson's pamphlet, although for reasons which I could not determine he omitted the very passage which presents the most striking resemblance :

All men are, by nature, equal and free : No one has a right to any authority over another without his consent : All lawful government is founded on the consent of those who are subject to it : Such consent was given with a view to ensure and to increase the happiness of the governed above what they could enjoy in an independent and unconnected state of nature. The consequence is, that the happiness of the society is the First law of every government.

A Lockian theory to be sure, but Wilson in the footnote to this paragraph quoted Burlamaqui to the effect that "This right of sovereignty is that of commanding finally but in order to procure real felicity; for if this end is not obtained, sovereignty ceases to be legitimate authority." But this is not all! The Declaration of Rights of 1774 ("Journal of Congress", I, 373) stated in somewhat similar terms the rights of the inhabitants of the English colonies. Finally the "Virginia Bill of Rights" written by George Mason, adopted by the Virginia Assembly on June 12 and necessarily forwarded to the delegates in Congress, contained articles resembling more closely those of the Declaration of Independence :

I. That all men are by nature equally free and independent, and have certain inherent rights, of which, when they enter into a state of society, they cannot, by any compact, deprive their posterity; namely, the enjoyment of life and liberty, with the means of acquiring and possessing property, and pursuing and obtaining happiness and safety.

II. That all power is vested in, and consequently derived from the people; that Magistrates are their trustees and servants, and at all times amenable to them.

III. That government is or ought to be, instituted for the common benefit, protection and security of the people, nation, or community; of all the various modes and forms of government, that is best, which is capable of producing the greatest degree of happiness and safety, and is most effectually secured against the danger of mal-administration; and that when any government shall be found inadequate or contrary to these purposes, a majority of the community has the undubitable, unalienable right, to reform, alter, or abolish it, in such manner as shall be judged most conducive to the public weal.[1]

This time it is no longer a question of analogy, or similarity of thought — the very words are identical, "Unalienable rights" is the expression which finally replaced "undeniable" in the final form — and "pursuing and obtaining happiness" has become the well-known "pursuit of happiness." Does it mean that Jefferson should be accused of plagiarism? Not in the least, since, as the French author said, "*l'arrangement est nouveau*", and, in a work of art, "*l'arrangement*" constitutes true originality, according to the formula of the classical school. Furthermore, it was clearly Jefferson's rôle and duty as a delegate from Virginia to incorporate in the Declaration as much as he could of the "Bill of Rights" recently adopted by his native dominion. The only fault that could be found is that he did not more clearly acknowledge his indebtedness to George Mason. But his contemporaries, and particularly the Virginians, could not fail to recognize in the national document the spirit and expression of the State document. Jefferson had expressed the American mind but he had above all expressed the mind of his fellow Virginians.

[1] "Life and Correspondence of G. Mason", I, 438.

Whether the doctrine enunciated in the Declaration of Independence is founded in fact and is beyond question "undeniable", is a problem which cannot even be touched upon here. We cannot dismiss it, however, without mentioning a feature which seems to have escaped most American students of political philosophy, probably because it has become such an integral part of American life that it is not even noticed. I do not believe that any other State paper in any nation had ever proclaimed so emphatically and with such finality that one of the essential functions of government is to make man happy, or that one of his essential natural rights is "the pursuit of happiness." This was more than a new principle of government, it was a new principle of life which was thus proposed and officially indorsed. The most that could be asked from governments of the Old World was to promote virtue and to maintain justice; honor, "*amor patriae*" and fear were the essential principles on which rested the governments described by Montesquieu. But in spite of the eternal and unquenchable thirst for happiness in the heart of every man, what European, what Frenchman particularly, could openly and officially maintain that the "pursuit of happiness" was a right, and that happiness could be reached and truly enjoyed. This quest of happiness had been the main preoccupation of French philosophers during the eighteenth century, but in spite of their philosophical optimism, they were too thoroughly imbued with pessimism ever to think that it was possible to be happy; the most they could hope for was to become less unhappy. The whole Christian civilization had been built on the idea that happiness is neither desirable nor obtainable in this vale of tears and affliction, but as a compensation Christianity offered eternal life and eternal bliss. The Declaration of Independence, on the contrary, placed human life on a new axis by maintaining that happiness is a natural right of the individual and the whole end of government. To be sure, the idea was not original with Jefferson, it had been mentioned more than once in official or semi-official documents, it was in James Wilson, as in the Bill of Rights, but I cannot quite conceive that such a formula could have originated in New England. I cannot conceive either that it could have been proclaimed at that date anywhere except in a new country where the pioneer spirit dominated, where men felt that they could live without being crowded or hampered by fierce competition, traditions, and iron-bound social laws.

In his plan for a *Déclaration des droits de l'homme et du citoyen*, Lafayette some twelve years later included "*la recherche du bonheur*", in memory of the American Declaration of Independence, but "*la recherche du bonheur*" disappeared in the committee and was never mentioned again in any of the three Declarations of the French Revolution. The nearest approach to it is found in the first article of the Declaration of June 23, 1793; but it simply states that the aim of society is common happiness — and this is quite a different idea. Whether it was right or not, Jefferson, when he reproduced the terms used by George Mason in the Virginia Bill of Rights, gave currency to an expression which was to influence deeply and even to mold American life.

In that sense, it may be said that the Declaration of Independence represents the highest achievement of eighteenth-century philosophy, but of one aspect of that philosophy that could not develop fully in Europe. Trees that are transplanted sometimes thrive better under new skies than in their native habitat and may reach proportions wholly unforeseen.

Thus the Declaration of Independence written to express the sentiments of the day probably shaped the American mind in an unexpected manner. It was essentially a popular document planned to impress the masses, to place before the young nation at its birth a certain ideal and a certain political faith, but it was also a legal and judicial document intended to make more precise the reasons why the united American colonies had finally resolved to separate from the mother country.

For this part of the Declaration Jefferson drew largely from the "Constitution" he had drafted for Virginia and sent to Randolph by Mr. Wythe. He was his own source — the more so as he substantially repeated many of the grievances enumerated two years earlier in the "Rights of British America." But here again he markedly improved the first version, which was a monotonous recital of dry facts, starting with a legal "Whereas" and beginning each article with a clumsy participle. "By denying his Governor permission : . . . By refusing to pass certain other laws . . . By dissolving Legislative Assemblies," became in the Declaration the dramatic presentation of facts by a prosecuting attorney and not the summing-up of a case by a judge. But the final renunciation of the mother country has an unsurpassed dignity, a finality more terrible in its lofty and dispassionate tone than any curse :

"We must, therefore, acquiesce in the necessity, which denounces our Separation, and hold them, as we hold the rest of mankind, Enemies in War, in Peace Friends." There again one is reminded of the well-known French formula : "*beau comme l'antique.*" Twice in its history the supposedly young and uncultured people had the rare fortune to find spokesmen who, without effort and laborious preparation, reached the utmost heights. The Declaration of Independence, with its solemn renunciation of ties of consanguinity, reminds one of the tone of the Greek tragedy; while the only parallel to the Gettysburg address is the oration pronounced by Pericles over the warriors who had laid down their lives during the first war of Peloponnesus.

Such heights can only be reached if the author is moved to his innermost depths. Singularly unimaginative in ordinary circumstances, for once in his life Jefferson was superior to himself : the student of Greece, the refined Virginian, became truly the voice of the people. But great effects often have small causes. We may wonder if he would have spoken with that same suppressed emotion, fiercely burning and yet controlled, if at that very time he had not been laboring under an emotional stress that never recurred in his life.

While he was in Philadelphia, writing the first draft in which he opened to the people of America "the road to glory and happiness", he could well wonder whether his personal happiness was not about to be destroyed. — His mother had recently died, he had just lost a child and had left in Monticello a beloved companion dangerously ill. "Every letter brings me such an account of the state of her health, that it is with great pain I can stay here," he wrote to Page (July 20, 1776), and for those who knew how reserved he was in the expression of personal feelings, the restraint in his expression hardly conceals the anxiety and distress by which he was torn.

There were also other reasons for his desiring to go home. Jefferson had always understood that as a delegate to Congress his duty was not so much to make a record for himself as to voice the *sentiments of the people he represented and to carry out their instructions*.[1] He was much worried about his standing with the Virginia Convention and suspected that some members were trying to knife him in the back. The Convention had just proceeded to elect delegates for the next Congress. Harrison and Braxton had failed to be reappointed, and Jefferson was "next to the lag." — "It is a painful situation," he wrote to William Fleming, on July first, "to be 300 miles from one's county, and thereby opened to secret assassination without a possibility of self-defence." [2]

A week later, he wrote to Edmund Pendleton to decline his new appointment as a delegate to Congress:

[1] To Thomas Nelson, May 16, 1776. Memorial Edition, IV, 253.
[2] "Writings", Ford, II, 41.

I am sorry that the situation of my domestic affairs, renders it indispensably necessary that I should solicit the substitution of some other person here in my room. The delicacy of the House will not require me to enter minutely into the private causes which render this necessary. I trust they will be satisfied. I would not urge it again, were it not unavoidable.[1]

On July 8 he announced to R. H. Lee that he would return to Virginia after the eleventh of August. It was not until September 2 that, his successor having arrived, he considered himself as free to go. His final reason, possibly not the least important, is given by Jefferson himself in his "Autobiography":

Our delegation had been renewed for the ensuing year, commencing August 11; but the new government was now organized, a meeting of the legislature was to be held in October, and I had been elected a member by my county. I knew that our legislation, under the regal government, had many vicious points which urgently required reformation, and I thought I could be of more use in forwarding that work. I therefore retired from my seat in Congress on the 2d of September, resigned it and took my place in the Legislature of my State, on the 7th of October.

"My state," wrote Jefferson in 1818, but in his letters to William Fleming he was speaking of Virginia as his "country", and at that time constantly referred to the colonies and not the United States.

The necessity of some sort of a union or confederacy had been keenly realized for a long time, but the ways and means were far from receiving unanimous support. As a matter of fact, union had been obtained just on the point of secession, or as Jefferson had it "avulsion from Great Britain"; but the consciousness of solidarity, the community of ideals and interests which constitute an essential part of patriotism hardly existed at that date. Thus the man who had just been the voice of America probably felt himself more of a Virginian than of an American,

[1] Ford, II, 61.

for local patriotism was very strong, while national patriotism was still in a larval stage. For a student of government this was the most fascinating situation which could be devised, since he was to witness the formation of a new society and the signing of a social compact. Jefferson attended all the meetings of Congress in which the Articles of Confederation were discussed. He took copious notes and inserted them in his "Autobiography", but he refrained from expressing his own opinion on the matter. It is not unlikely, however, that he had already given considerable attention to the subject, as appears from many entries in his "Commonplace Book." [1]

In the first edition of this study was inserted at this point a document which I erroneously attributed to Jefferson, when, in fact, it came from the pen of Thomas Paine and was probably written ten years later. While expressing my regrets and apologies to the writers who have been misled by this false attribution, I still believe that it sums up so concisely the early philosophy of Thomas Jefferson that it may not be out of place to reproduce it again. [2]

After I got home, being alone and wanting amusement I sat down to explain to myself (for there is such a thing) my Ideas of natural and civil rights and the distinction between them — I send them to you to see how nearly we agree.

Suppose 20 persons, strangers to each other, to meet in a country not before inhabited. Each would be a sovereign in his own natural right. His will would be his Law, — but his power, in many cases, inadequate to his right, and the consequence would be that each might be exposed, not only to each other but to the other nineteen.

[1] See my edition, Baltimore, 1926, particularly Articles 750 and 783 and supra, pp. 46–49.

[2] The initial sentences had already appeared in "Common Sense" and the whole discussion was printed in a more didactic and positive form in the "Rights of Man." The document as published here had already been printed by Conway in his "Life of Thomas Paine", I, 235. I had already called attention to this error in my edition of "The Correspondence of Jefferson and Du Pont de Nemours", Baltimore, 1931, p. lxxiii.

It would then occur to them that their condition would be much improved, if a way could be devised to exchange that quantity of danger into so much protection, so that each individual should possess the strength of the whole number. As all their rights, in the first case are natural rights, and the exercise of those rights supported only by their own natural individual power, they would begin by distinguishing between these rights they could individually exercise fully and perfectly and those they could not.

Of the first kind are the rights of thinking, speaking, forming and giving opinions, and perhaps all those which can be fully exercised by the individual without the aid of exterior assistance — or in other words, rights of personal competency — Of the second kind are those of personal protection of acquiring and possessing property, in the exercise of which the individual natural power is less than the natural right.

Having drawn this line they agree to retain individually the first Class of Rights or those of personal Competency; and to detach from their personal possession the second Class, or those of defective power and to accept in lieu thereof a right to the whole power produced by a condensation of all the parts. These I conceive to be civil rights or rights of Compact, and are distinguishable from Natural rights, because in the one we act wholly in our own person, in the other we agree not to do so, but act under the guarantee of society.

It therefore follows that the more of those imperfect natural rights, or rights of imperfect power we give up and thus exchange the more securely we possess, and as the word liberty is often mistakenly put for security Mr Wilson has confused his Argument by confounding the terms.

But it does not follow that the more natural rights of *every kind* we resign the more securely we possess, — because if we resign those of the first class we may suffer much by the exchange, for where the right and the power are equal with each other in the individual naturally they ought to rest there.

Mr Wilson must have some allusion to this distinction or his position would be subject to the inference you draw from it.

I consider the individual sovereignty of the States retained under the Act of Confederation to be of the second Class of rights. It becomes dangerous because it is defective in the power necessary to support it. It answers the pride and purpose of a few men in each state — but the State collectively is injured by it.

There remains little doubt that these views were entirely shared by Jefferson if indeed they had not been suggested by him in conversations with his friend. He expressed them as his own in a letter written to Colonel Humphreys, in March 1789, and wrote to Monroe after the publication of "The Rights of Man" that he professed the same principles as the author.[1] It remains however to determine whether he professed them earlier in his career. This would probably be unlikely, if these views and this distinction were as original as I represented them ten years ago. As a point of fact, they were nothing more than the elaboration of a distinction with which all law students of the time were familiar and which had necessarily been established during the long controversy about the origin of natural laws. Thomas Paine and Jefferson may have drawn from Burlamaqui who had simply followed Christian Wolff as pointed out by Professor Wiltse and more recently by Professor Harvey.[2]

More immediately, the document sent by Paine to Jefferson, "to see how nearly we agree", reflects the distinction found in Blackstone, who simply sums up many other jurists, between "the law of nature" and "municipal law . . . being thus defined by Justinian *jus civile est quod quisque sibi populus constituit.*" [3] Blackstone did not fail either to distinguish between "absolute" and "relative rights" and to declare significantly that:

[1] "Memorial edition", VII, 323; VIII, 207, and this volume, p. 201.

[2] C. M. Wiltse, "Jeffersonian Tradition in American Democracy", Chapel Hill, 1935, p. 74; R. E. Harvey, "Jean Jacques Burlamaqui", Chapel Hill, 1937, p. 122. See also the remarkable discussion of James Truslow Adams, "The Living Jefferson", New York, 1936, pp. 79–84.

[3] "Commentaries on the Laws of England", Introduction, sect. 2, 44.

The principal aim of society is to protect individuals in the enjoyment of those absolute rights which were vested in them by the immutable laws of nature; but which could not be preserved in peace without that mutual assistance and intercourse which is gained by the institution of friendly and social communities. Hence it follows that the first and primary end of human laws is to maintain and regulate these *absolute* rights of individuals. Such rights as are social and *relative* result from, and are posterior to, the formation of states and societies." [1]

This is the general idea that underlies the second paragraph of the Declaration of Independence in which it is stated that "to secure these rights, governments are instituted among men, deriving their just powers from the consent of the governed." Thus, in forming a social compact, men do not abdicate all their sovereignty; they do not even abdicate a certain portion of all their rights. On the contrary, they obtain from society a security and a fuller enjoyment of their natural rights than they could enjoy in a complete state of nature. The social compact is no longer a *pactum subjectionis;* there is no longer any question of deciding whether in a society the individual or the society are sovereign, since the primary object of society is to increase the security and the rights of its members.[2]

That not only Jefferson, but also the other members of the committee, had such a distinction in mind appears clearly in the enumeration of "certain unalienable rights" with which men have been endowed by their Creator, "that among these are life, liberty and the pursuit of happiness."

It is worth noticing that the "Declaration on Violation of Rights" adopted by the First Continental Congress had

[1] *Ibid.*, Book I, ch. I, 124.
[2] Such an idea reappears in the speeches of James Wilson. In addition to his speech "On the Legislative Authority of The British Parliament", discussed by Professor Becker, see his "Speech delivered in the Convention for the Province of Pennsylvania, in January 1775", and particularly his declaration that "our ancestors were never inconsiderate enough to trust those rights, which God and nature had given them, unreservedly into the hands of their princes."

specified that the inhabitants of the British Colonies were "entitled to life, liberty & property." [1]

The Virginia Bill of Rights had similarly declared that among the inherent natural rights was the means of acquiring and possessing property.

Now, in the preamble to the Declaration of Independence which follows so closely the Bill of Rights, the word "property" does not appear, while the other rights are reasserted. It is similarly omitted in all the preliminary drafts which have been preserved. The omission of such an important term could hardly be accidental, and it must certainly have been noticed by the different members of the committee, and particularly by Adams and Franklin who inserted several corrections in the rough draft. It becomes particularly significant if we remember, in addition, that when Lafayette submitted to Jefferson his "Déclaration des droits de l'homme", Jefferson put in brackets the words "*droit à la propriété*", thus suggesting their elimination from the list of "natural rights."

Yet neither Jefferson nor his fellow members on the committee were in any way "communists", and it would be a serious error to see in that deliberate omission the influence of Rousseau's " Discours sur l'origine de l'inégalité." The fact is that Jefferson and his colleagues had taken the position that the rights of acquiring and possessing property had to be protected by society in order to be enjoyed securely.

Such a philosophy of natural rights, far from being revolutionary or "radical", represented the traditional and almost orthodox view of the majority of the political thinkers. In fact, on this particular point Jefferson and his associates departed not from tradition and what was considered at the time as sound legalistic doctrine, but from Locke, who was the first to include property among the natural rights, and from the French Physiocrats who were more interested in property than in liberty.

[1] "Journals of Congress", October 14, 1774, I, 67.

At any rate, it seems that already at that time Jefferson had formulated in his mind a philosophy of society to which he remained loyal and which he reiterated on several occasions during the rest of his career. The words "unalienable Rights" in the Declaration of Independence meant exactly what they said. While Locke had said that one divests oneself of one's liberty in assuming the bonds of civil society, while Rousseau had declared that man sacrifices all his natural rights on the altar of society, Jefferson believed with Blackstone and with Lord Kames, the Scottish jurist from whom he had copied many passages in his Commonplace Book, that "Mutual defence against a more powerful neighbor being in early times the chief, or sole motive for joining in society, individuals never thought of surrendering any of their natural rights which could be retained consistently with their great aim of mutual defence." Hence the necessity of a Bill of Rights, in which the individual accepts certain limitations in order to obtain a corresponding amount of security, and specifically enumerates those of his natural rights he means to keep integrally and wholly.

This at the same time explains clearly why Jefferson, who is represented as the champion of State rights, not only accepted the abridgment of State sovereignty but declared that the retention by the States of certain rights was dangerous and illogical. Hence his insistence throughout his life on the prerogatives of the Federal Government in all matters referring to foreign policies, and his reiterated declarations in favor of State rights. The social compact is not a metaphysical hypothesis, nebulous and lost in the night of ages; it is a very specific and very precise convention to be entered into or to be denounced by men, or groups, who remain free and yet agree to submit themselves to certain rules in order to obtain more security. And thus was evolved and formulated a combination of liberty and order, individualism and discipline which lies at the basis of American civilization.

CHAPTER II

THE REVISION OF THE LAWS OF VIRGINIA

At the meeting of July 4, 1776, Congress, after adopting the Declaration of Independence,

"*Resolved*, That Dr. Franklin, Mr. J. Adams and Mr. Jefferson, be a committee, to bring in a device for a seal for the United States of America." [1]

Among the several suggestions made in the committee, the one proposed by Jefferson, according to John Adams, deserves particular attention: "Mr. Jefferson proposed, the children of Israel in the wilderness led by a cloud by day, and a pillar by night — and on the other side, Hengist and Horsa, the Saxon chiefs, from whom we claim the honor of being descended, and whose political principles and form of government we have assumed."

None of the suggestions made by the committee, or their final report, was ever adopted, but the device proposed by Jefferson is a significant indication that his thoughts were still running in the same channel. "The children of Israel" would remind one of the favorite contention of the settlers, piously preserved by their descendants to this day, that they were a chosen people; but the other side of the seal reminds one that Jefferson's great ambition at that time was to promote a renaissance of Anglo-Saxon primitive institutions on the new continent. Thus presented, the American Revolution was nothing but the reclamation of the Anglo-Saxon birthright of which the colonists had been deprived by "a long trend of

[1] " Journals of Congress ", V., 517.

abuses." Nor does it appear that there was anything in this theory which surprised or shocked his contemporaries; Adams apparently did not disapprove of it, and it would be easy to bring in many similar expressions of the same idea in documents of the time.

The principle once established, there remained to put it into effect, and to make a beginning in Virginia. This was the thought uppermost in Jefferson's mind when he went back to the Old Dominion. "Are we not the better for what we have hitherto abolished of the feudal system," he wrote to Edmund Pendleton. "Has not every restitution of the antient Saxon laws had happy effects? Is it not better now that we return at once into that happy system of our ancestors, the wisest and most perfect ever yet devised by the wit of man, as it stood before the 8th century?"[1] This is the true foundation of Jefferson's political philosophy. No greater mistake could be made than to look for his sources in Locke, Montesquieu, or Rousseau. The Jeffersonian democracy was born under the sign of Hengist and Horsa, not of the Goddess Reason.

On September 26, 1776, Congress proceeded to the election of commissioners to the Court of France, and the ballots being taken, Mr. Benjamin Franklin, Mr. Silas Deane, and Mr. Thomas Jefferson were chosen. This was a signal recognition of the prestige of the young author of the Declaration of Independence. An express was sent at once to Jefferson to inform him of his appointment. For the first time he was offered an opportunity to visit the Old World. His desire to go was so strong that he remained undecided for three days before he made up his mind to decline the nomination and to send his refusal to Hancock. In the letter he then wrote, he alleged that "circumstances very peculiar in the situation of my family, such as neither permit me to leave nor to carry it compel me to ask leave to decline a service so honorable and at the same

[1] August 13, 1776.   Ford, II, 78.

time so important to the American cause." [1]   His biographer
Randall observes on this occasion that "the private causes"
were the precarious situation of his wife's health.   The family
record contains the following entry: "a son born May 28th,
1777, 10 h. P.M." [2]   The true reason, however, is to be found
in the "Autobiography", as given before.

The very day Jefferson answered Hancock, he was put on
several committees, and the next day he obtained leave to bring
in a bill "To enable tenants in taille to convey their land in fee
simple."   The Bill to Abolish Entails was reported on October
14, and after discussion and amendments passed by the House
on October 23, and approved by the Senate on November
first.

The bill was no improvisation and Jefferson intended by it
"to strike at the very root of feudalism in Virginia."   On
August 13, 1776, he had already written to an anonymous
correspondent, probably Edmund Pendleton:

The opinion that our lands were allodial possessions is one which
I have very long held, and had in my eye during a pretty considerable
part of my law reading which I found always strengthened it. . . .
This opinion I have thought and still think to prove if ever I should
have time to look into books again. . . .   Was not the separation
of the property from the perpetual use of lands a mere fiction?
Is not it's history well known, and the purposes for which it was
introduced, to wit, the establishment of a military system of defense?
Was it not afterwards made an engine of immense oppression? . . .
Has it not been the practice of all other nations to hold their lands
as their personal estate in absolute dominion?   Are we not the better
for what we have hitherto abolished of the feudal system? [3]

It was the first great blow at the landed hereditary aristocracy
of Virginia.   The abolition of patrimonial estates, rendering
them subject to all the obligations of personal property "susceptible to be sold, conveyed, seized, exchanged and willed"

---

[1] Ford, II, 91, October 11, 1776.   [2] Randall, I, 196.   [3] Ford, II, 79.

as ordinary property, meant the rapid abolition of that refined class of Virginia planters which constituted such a distinguished feature of colonial life. It was a bold step to take, since it meant the antagonism of a powerful class, the beginning of hatred that pursued Jefferson during his whole life and long after his death. Yet he had the courage to do it and was no little proud of it.[1] He was opposed by both Mr. Pendleton and Patrick Henry, "but the bill passed finally for entire abolition."

With the Bill to Abolish Entails Jefferson introduced another bill on the naturalization of foreigners, containing an expressed recognition of the right of expatriation already defended in the "Summary View" of 1774, — another remarkable instance of Jefferson's persistency and relentless efforts to win his point by legal means.

Simultaneously a committee on religion had been appointed "to meet and adjourn from day to day, and to take into their consideration all matters and things relating to religion and religious morality." Besides Jefferson, there were seventeen members on the committee, including Fleming, Page, and Nicholas. Being in a minority, Jefferson began the struggle which was to end in the famous Bill for Religious Freedom, — a long hard fight of which more will be said later. For the time being, however, Jefferson had to be satisfied with a partial success:

We prevailed so far only, as to repeal the laws which rendered criminal the maintenance of any religious opinions, the forbearance of repairing to church, or the exercise of any mode of worship; and further, to exempt dissenters from contributing to the support of the established church; and to suspend, only until next session, levies on the members of that church for the salaries of their own incumbents.[2]

[1] Concerning the opposition he encountered, see "Autobiography." Ford, I, 54.
[2] "Autobiography", *Ibid.*, I, 58.

Yet this was a very significant victory since, from the days of Sir Walter Raleigh, there had been an express proviso that the laws of the colony "should not be against the true Christian faith, now professed in the Church of England." Dissenters as well as members of the Established Church were assessed for the support of the Anglican ministers, and although other denominations, particularly Presbyterians, had succeeded in gaining more than a foothold in some parishes, a majority of dissenters were still obliged to pay for the support of the minority.

But important as they were, these constituted only minor points. The whole structure of laws had to be remodelled to fit new conditions; a new legal monument had to be erected. Jefferson's practice of law had convinced him of the obscurities, contradictions, absurdities, and iniquities of the assemblage of English laws on top of which had been superimposed local regulations. The Bill for a General Revision of the Laws passed October 26. The fifth of November five revisors were appointed by ballot in the following order: Thomas Jefferson, Edmund Pendleton, George Wythe, George Mason, Thomas Ludwell Lee. As this is a more important contribution of Jefferson, we may omit here the part he played on many committees of the House, drafting and reporting on "Declaring what shall be treason"; bills "For raising six additional battalions of infantry", "For establishing a Court of Appeals", "For establishing a High Court of Chancery", "For establishing a General Court and Courts of Assize", "For establishing a Court of Admiralty", "For better regulating the proceedings of the County Courts." He plunged into the work of the complete reorganization of the State judicial machinery, with all the enthusiastic zeal of a born jurist, and his capacity for precise, minute work was once more brought into play.

The committee of revisors met at Fredericksburg to determine on a manner of procedure and to distribute the work between the five members. First of all a question of methods had to be settled : "It had to be determined whether we should propose to abolish the whole existing system of laws, and prepare a new and complete Institute, or preserve the general system, and only modify it to the present state of things."

Pendleton and Lee stood for the former methods, Wythe, Mason, and Jefferson for the latter, and this was the procedure finally adopted. Rather than the account given by Jefferson in his "Autobiography" we shall follow the contemporary account drawn up at the time by George Mason.

Plan settled by the committee of Revisors in Fredericksburg, January, 1777.

(1) The common law not to be meddled with, except where alterations are necessary. The statutes to be revised and digested, alterations proper for us to be made ; the diction where obsolete or redundant, to be reformed ; but otherwise to undergo as few changes as possible. The acts of the English Commonwealth to be examined. The statutes to be divided into periods ; the acts of Assembly made on the same subject to be incorporated into them. The laws of other colonies to be examined, and any good ones to be adopted.

In the margin is here written :

General rules in drawing provisions &c., which would do only what the law would do without them, to be omitted. Bills to be short ; not to include matters of different natures ; not to insert an unnecessary word ; nor omit a useful one. Laws to be made on the spur of the present occasion, and all innovating laws to be limited in their duration.[1]

Truly an admirable plan ! Not the scheme of rash reformers, of *a priori*-minded legislators, deriving a code of laws from a certain number of abstract principles. It was not their purpose to make a *tabula rasa* of the old structure which had slowly grown stone by stone, statute by statute and to rebuild entirely on new plans. The old house resting on solid Anglo-

[1] "Life and Correspondence of George Mason", I, 276.

Saxon foundations was still substantial and safe and it could serve its purpose if only a few partitions were torn down, a few useless annexes demolished, and better ventilation provided. Nothing was farther from the mind of the committee than to erect in Virginia a Greek or Roman temple of Themis.

The statutes were divided into five parts. Jefferson was to take "the first period in the division of statutes to end with 25th, H. 8th"; Pendleton the second period "to end at the Revolution"; Wythe the third "to come to the present day"; G. Mason the fourth, "to consist of the residuary part of the Virginia laws to which is added the criminal law and land law." The fifth, attributed to Lee, "to be the regulation of property in slaves, and their condition; and also the examination of the laws of the other colonies." [1] Mason soon retired, "being no lawyer", and Lee having died, the work was redistributed which explains the somewhat different allotment indicated by Jefferson in the "Autobiography." On the other hand, he seems to have claimed for himself in the "Autobiography" an honor and an attitude that really belonged to the committee:

I thought it would be useful, also, in new draughts to reform the style of the later British statutes, and of our own arts of Assembly; which, from their verbosity, their endless tautologies, their involution of case within case, and parenthesis within parenthesis, and their multiplied efforts at certainty, by *saids* and *aforesaids*, by *ors* and by *ands*, to make them more plain, are really rendered more perplexed and incomprehensible, not only to common readers, but to the lawyers themselves.

The notes taken by G. Mason leave no doubt that this was also the attitude of the committee and their definite policy. It was a slow, painstaking, meticulous task, requiring common sense, good judgment, a good sense for words and erudition. To make laws intelligible and clear is no small achievement. But certainly it was not the sort of work that an *a priori* philoso-

[1] "Life and Correspondence of George Mason", I, 277.

pher, fond of generalizations and universal principles, would have relished, or would have been willing to submit himself to for more than two years. If in some political matters Jefferson differed from Mr. Pendleton, he admired him and later paid him a handsome tribute in the "Autobiography." Pendleton — cool, smooth and persuasive, quick, acute and resourceful — was a remarkable debater.

George Mason, a man of the first order of wisdom, of expansive mind, profound judgment, cogent in argument, learned in the lore of our former constitution, and earnest for the republican change on democratic principles . . . his virtue was of the purest tint; his integrity inflexible, and his justice exact; of warm patriotism, and, devoted as he was to liberty, and to the natural and equal rights of man, he might truly be called the Cato of his country without the avarice of the Roman.[1]

When the preliminary work was done, the reviewers met at Williamsburg in February, 1779, and "day by day" they examined critically their several parts, sentence by sentence, scrutinizing and amending, "until they had agreed on the whole." "The Revised Laws", comprehending one hundred and twenty-six bills, were reported to the General Assembly June 18, 1779; bills were taken out occasionally from time to time, and because of Madison's efforts fifty-six out of the one hundred and twenty-six were after amendments made laws at the sessions of 1785, 1786. Among the bills reworded or initiated by Jefferson several stood out conspicuously.

The Bill for Proportioning Crimes and Punishments is a particularly good example of the methods used by Jefferson in rewriting the old legislation. On sending it to George Wythe he wrote:

I wished to exhibit a sample of reformation in the barbarous style into which our modern statutes have degenerated from their ancient

---

[1] Note for the biography of John Saunderson, Esq., August 31, 1820. "Autobiography", Appendix A. Ford, I, 107.

simplicity. In its style, I have aimed at accuracy, brevity, simplicity, preserving however the words of the established law, wherever their meaning had been sanctioned by judicial decision, as rendered technical by usage.[1]

The transformation undergone by the old statutes can more easily be observed because Jefferson was careful to indicate in footnotes his authorities from the old texts, in Latin, and even in French and Anglo-Saxon. But the very title of the bill indicates that Jefferson's purpose went farther than a mere codification of the old law. He could not be entirely satisfied with the scale of punishments determined by the committee; he regretted particularly the maintainance of the *Lex Talionis*, "an eye for an eye and a hand for a hand" (Section XV), and he attempted to restrict the penalty of death to a few limited cases, for it was "the last melancholy resource against those whose existence is become inconsistent with the safety of their fellow citizens." His preamble reflects to a large extent the views of Montesquieu and Beccaria which he copied in the "Commonplace Book." But it could hardly be called humanitarian in the modern and sometimes derogatory sense of the word. The provisions of the code itself are far from showing any weakness or sentimentality: the death penalty is provided for treason against the Commonwealth and for whomsoever committeth murder by way of duel; manslaughter, previously "punishable at law by burning in the hands, and forfeiture of chattels", is punished by hard labor for seven years in the public works, and the murderer " shall forfeit one half of his lands and goods to the next of kin of the person slain, the other half to be sequestered during such times, in the hands, and to the use, of the commonwealth." Rape, polygamy, or sodomy "shall be punished if a man by castration, if a woman by boring through the cartilage of her nose a hole of one half inch in diameter at least." Witchcraft, conjuration, or sorcery "shall

[1] Monticello, November 1, 1778. Memorial Edition, I, 216.

be punished by ducking and whipping, at the discretion of a jury, not exceeding fifteen stripes", and, most extraordinary for modern readers, "Whenever sentences of death shall be pronounced against any person for treason or murder, execution thereof shall be done on the next day but one, after such sentence, unless it be Sunday, and then on Monday following" (Section XIII). Truly enough the law of nature is once mentioned in a footnote to the effect that if a prisoner tries to escape from prison he shall not be considered as a capital offender. "The law of nature impels every one to escape from confinement; he should not therefore be subjected to punishment. Let the legislature restrain his criminal by walls, not by parchment." If there is "philosophy" in this statement it is common sense and certainly not sentimentality.

The Bill for the more General Diffusion of Knowledge is far more philosophical in its terms. There for the first time will be found a picture of democracy as Jefferson pictured it to himself at that date. The general statement at the beginning may be an echo from Montesquieu; but while the French philosopher had not indicated any remedy for such a situation, Jefferson was interested in it only in so far as it could be amended.

Experience has shewn, that even under the best forms, those entrusted with power have, in time, and by slow operations, perverted it into tyranny; and it is believed that the most effectual means of preventing this would be, to illuminate, as far as practicable, the minds of the people at large, and more especially to give them knowledge of those facts, which history exhibiteth, . . . and whereas it is generally true that people will be happiest whose laws are best, and are best administered, and that laws will be wisely formed, and honestly administered, in proportion as those who form and administer them are wise and honest; whence it becomes expedient for promoting the publick happiness that those persons, whom nature hath endowed with genius and virtue, should be rendered by liberal education worthy to receive, and able to guard the sacred deposit of the rights and liberties of their fellow citizens, and that they should be called to that charge without regard to wealth, birth or other accidental condition or circumstance; but the indigence of the greater number disabling them from so educating, at their own expence, those of their children whom nature hath fitly formed and disposed to become useful instruments for the public, it is better that such should be sought for and educated at the common expence of all, than that the happiness of all should be confined to the weak or wicked.

Is this a democratic view in the modern sense of the word? At any rate it is not the democratic phraseology of a modern politician. There is no protest at all in the name of immanent justice against the unequality of conditions, there is no desire to give every boy a fair chance in life, no indication that men being born equal, all children should have equal opportunities. We are perfectly free to believe that Jefferson entertained such sentiments at that date. Historically, however, there is no evidence that he did so. All we have here is a hard-headed proposition with the corrective that, under the new system, a child of genius or great talent was to be given an opportunity to develop his native qualities, for it was both the duty and the interest of society to prevent such a waste of intellectual potentialities. Furthermore, Jefferson was manifestly of the opinion that no man could properly participate in the government of society unless he had been rendered worthy to receive and able to guard the *sacred* deposit of the rights and liberties of his fellow citizens. Neither wealth, birth, nor accidental circumstances should determine who is fit for public office, but education should be the criterion. As he was doing his utmost to abolish the last privileges and prestige of the landed hereditary aristocracy of Virginia, Jefferson was striving to constitute and to get recognition for another aristocracy, an aristocracy of learning and intelligence, a true ruling class, or more exactly a governing and legislative class; for he was persuaded that the business of the legislator cannot be learned in a day, that it requires, besides native qualities of mind, a certain expert knowledge of the subject.

The provisions of the bill are most extraordinary for the time. Jefferson provided for the division of the State into a certain number of districts or hundreds; in each hundred a schoolhouse was to be built and so located that all the children within it might daily attend the school.

In each of the schools shall be taught reading, writing, and common arithmetick, and the books which shall be used therein for instructing the children to read shall be such as will at the same time make them acquainted with Graecian, Roman, English and American history. At these schools all the free children, male and female, resident within the respective hundred, shall be entitled to receive tuition gratis for the term of three years.

In addition, the bill provided that a certain number of grammar schools would be erected, "their situation to be as central as possible for the inhabitants of the said counties, the schools to be furnished with good water, convenient to plentiful supplies of provision and fuel and above all things that it be healthy." In all of these grammar schools, which shall receive boarders

shall be taught the Latin and Greek languages, English Grammar, geography, and the higher part of numerical arithmetick, to wit., vulgar and decimal fractions, and the extrication of the square and cube roots. In order to provide proper facilities for children of particular ability, the overseer of the hundred schools (one for ten schools) shall appoint from among the boys who shall have been two years at the least at some one of the schools under his superintendance and whose parents are too poor to give them farther education some one of the best and most promising genius and dispositions to proceed to the grammar schools.

At the end of the first year one third of the boys shall be discontinued as public foundations after examination; "all shall be discontinued at the end of two years save one only, the best in genius and disposition, who shall be at liberty to continue there four years longer on the public foundation, and shall thence forward be deemed a senior." Finally, "the visitors will select one among the said seniors of the best learning and most hopeful genius and disposition who shall be authorized by them to proceed to William and Mary College; there to be educated, boarded, and clothed three years: the expense of which shall be paid by the Treasurer."

This rigorous selective process looks very familiar to any one acquainted with the modern French system of free elementary schools, boarding *collèges* and *lycées*, and the system of competitive scholarships and fellowships of the French. But it was not fully developed in France before the Third Republic and it was not even dreamed of before the Revolution. Many times the French have been criticized for the undemocratic features of an educational system which reserves secondary education to those who are able to pay and to the small number of children who win scholarships. There is no possibility that this scheme was ever borrowed by Jefferson from any French theorician, and there is, on the contrary, some reason to believe that in France it owes its beginning to the publication of Jefferson's plan in the "Notes on Virginia" printed in Paris and in French in 1787.

The educational structure of the State would not have been complete if Jefferson had not provided for a reorganization of William and Mary College. Such is the purpose of the next bill (Bill LXXX) in the Report of the Committee of Revisors. There he was more ruthless and more radical. After a first section which recounts the foundation of the college and its history, Jefferson concluded that "the said college, thus amply endowed by the public has not answered their expectation, and there is reason to hope, that it would become more useful, if certain articles in its constitution were altered and amended."

By one stroke of the pen, Jefferson abolished the school of theology, took the administration out of the hands of the former trustees to place it in the hands of visitors appointed by the Legislature and "not to be restrained in their legislation by the royal prerogatives, or the laws of the kingdom of England, or the canons of the constitution of the English Church, as enjoined in the Charter." The president and faculty were to be dismissed, and six professorships created; to wit, one of moral law and police; one of history, civil and ecclesiastical; one of anatomy and medicine; one of natural philosophy and natural history; one of the ancient languages Oriental and northern; and one of modern languages. —

A missionary will be appointed to the several tribes of the Indians, whose business will be to investigate their laws, customs, religion, traditions, and more particularly their languages, constructing grammar thereof, as well as may be, and copious vocabularies, and on oath to communicate, from time to time, to the said President and Professors the material he collects.

Thus the college was to become the training school in which "those who are to be the future guardians of the rights and liberties of their country may be endowed with science and virtue, to watch and preserve the sacred deposit." It was not a democratic institution, but the finishing school of the future legislators and experts in the science of government.

As to disinterested "researches of the learned and curious", they were to be encouraged by the establishment at Richmond of a Free Public Library with yearly appropriation of two thousand pounds for the purchase of books and maps.

One may state here without any fear of contradiction that no system so complete, so logically constructed and so well articulated had ever been proposed in any country in the world. It already embodied the ideas for which Jefferson stood during all his life, it preceded by more than fifteen years the plans of the French Convention. As the first charter of American public education it is an astonishing document and deserves more attention than it has hitherto received.

The Bill for Establishing Religious Freedom in Jefferson's opinion ranked in importance with the Declaration of Independence. It was not intended to be a revolutionary document, but simply a common-sense adjustment of the situation brought about by the repeal of several provisions of the old Virginia laws. Jefferson took care to explain the true purpose of the bill in the "Notes on Virginia" (Query XVII). The Virginia Bill of Rights had proclaimed "it to be a truth, and a natural right that the exercise of religion should be free." On the other hand, no mention of it had been made in the Convention and no measure had been adopted to protect religious freedom. The Assembly, however, had repealed, in 1776, "all *acts* of Parliament which had rendered criminal the maintaining any opinion in matters of religion", and suspended the laws giving salaries to the clergy. This suspension was made perpetual in October, 1779. But religious matters still remained subject to common law and to acts passed by the Assembly. At Common Law, heresy was a capital offence, punishable by burning, according to the writ *de haeretico comburando*. Furthermore, by an act of the Assembly of 1705, "if a person brought up in the Christian religion denies the being of a God, or the Trinity, or asserts there are more gods than one, or denies the Christian religion to be true, or the Scriptures to be of divine authority, he is punishable on the first offence by incapacity to hold any office or employment ecclesiastical, civil, or military: on the second by disability to sue, to take any gift or legacy, to be guardian, executor, or administrator, and by three years' imprisonment without bail." [1]

This being the situation, the article of the Bill of Rights con-

[1] "Notes on Virginia", Query XVII.

cerning religious freedom remained a dead letter until provisions could be made to take religious matters out of the jurisdiction of the Common Law.

Historians seem to have been somewhat misled both by the lofty and philosophical tone of the Bill for Religious Freedom and the comments made by Jefferson in the "Notes on Virginia", specially written by him, as we always must remember, for a group of French philosophers and the French public. A philosopher he was, but before all he was a purist and a historian of law. For him the main question was first to determine whether the jurisdiction of the Common Law in matters of religion was founded in law. He had already studied minutely the history of Common Law and made copious extracts in his "Commonplace Book"; he had noticed in Houard's "Coutumes Anglo-Normandes" that some pious copyist had prefixed to the laws of Alfred four chapters of Jewish law. "This awkward Monkish fabrication makes the preface to Alfred's genuine laws stand in the body of the Work; and the very words of Alfred himself form the frauds, for he declares in that preface that he has collected these laws from those of Ina, of Offa, Ethelbert, and his ancestors, saying nothing of any of them being taken from the scripture." Consequently the pretended laws of Alfred were a forgery.

Yet, palpable as it must be to a lawyer, our judges have piously avoided lifting the veil under which it was shrouded. In truth, the alliance between Church and State in England, has ever made their judges accomplices in the frauds of the clergy; and even bolder than they are: for, instead of being contented with these four surreptitious chapters of *Exodus*, they have taken the whole leap, and declared at once, that the whole Bible and Testament, in a lump, make part, of the Common law. . . . Finally in answer to Fortescue Aland's question why the Ten Commandments should not now be a part of the Common law of England? We may say that they are not, because they never were made so by legislative authority; the document which imposed that doubt on him being a manifest forgery." [1]

Bolstered up with his texts, references, and authorities, Jefferson could now, if need be, confute the redoubtable Mr. Pendleton in the Committee of Revisors, but such a legal technical presentation of the facts would evidently not appeal either to the Assembly at large or to the public. These had to be approached in an entirely different way; for to speak of frauds, forgeries, and monkish fabrication would not do at all in a public document and, on the contrary, might create a revulsion of feeling. It became necessary to present the reform in an entirely different light and Jefferson did so in the first section of the bill.

The phrasing of these lofty principles is well known; still it may not be out of place to reproduce them once more:

Well aware that the opinions of belief of men depend not on their own will, but follow involuntarily the evidence proposed to their minds; that Almighty God hath created the mind free, and manifested his supreme will that free it shall remain by making it altogether susceptible of restraint; that all attempts to influence it by temporal punishments, or burthens, or by civil incapacitations, tend only to beget habits of hypocrisy and meanness . . . to compel a man to furnish contributions of money for the propagation of opinions which he disbelieves and abhors, is sinful and tyrannical; . . . that our civil rights have no dependance on our religious opinions, any more than our opinions in physics or geometry; . . . that the opinions of men are not the object of civil government.

In Section II, after that preamble, the religious independence of the individual was proclaimed:

We the General Assembly of Virginia do enact that no man shall be compelled to frequent or support any religious worship, place, or ministry whatsoever, nor shall be enforced, restrained, molested, or burthened in his body or goods, or shall otherwise suffer, on

---

[1] "Commonplace Book", p. 362.

account of his religious opinions or beliefs; but that all men shall be free to profess and by argument to maintain, their opinions in matters of religion, and that the same shall in no wise diminish, enlarge, or affect their civil capacities.

Furthermore, in the first section, Jefferson gave the first and final expression of his understanding of freedom of thought:

That it is time enough for the rightful purposes of civil government for its offices to interfere when principles break out into overt acts against peace and good order; and finally, that truth is great and will prevail if left to herself; that she is the proper and sufficient antagonist to error, and has nothing to fear from the conflict unless by human interposition disarmed of her natural weapons, free argument and debate; errors ceasing to be dangerous when it is permitted freely to contradict them.

It is not surprising that the bill was savagely attacked in the Assembly and did not pass until 1786. It simply shows that the Church of England had more supporters than Jefferson led us to believe, when he wrote in the "Notes on Virginia" that "two-thirds of the people had become dissenters at the commencement of the present revolution." The remaining third, if such was the proportion, were at least well organized and offered a strong resistance. This bill marked the beginning of the accusations of impiety and infidelity so often launched at Jefferson. Whatever his private sentiments on the matter may have been, he was not the man to discriminate against any one because of religious beliefs; and at the very time when he was engaged in preparing his bill, he took the initiative of starting a subscription towards the support of the Reverend Mr. Charles Clay of Williamsburg. The document, never before published, is entirely written in his hand and is of such importance that I may be permitted to reproduce it here:

Whereas, by an act of General assembly, freedom of Religious opinion and worship is restored to all, and it is left to the members of each religious society to employ such Teachers they think fit for their own Spiritual comfort and instruction and to maintain the same by their free and voluntary contributions. We the subscribers (professing the most Catholic affection for other religious sectaries who happen to differ from us in points of conscience,) yet desirous of encouraging and supporting (a church in our opinion so truly Apostolick as) the Protestant Episcopalian Church, and of deriving to ourselves, through the ministry of it's teachers, the benefits of Gospel-knowledge and Religious improvement, and at the same time of supporting those, who, having been at considerable expence in qualifying themselves by regular education for explaining the holy scriptures, have dedicated their time and labor to the service of the said church (and moreover approving highly the conduct of the rev^d Charles Clay, who early rejecting the tyrant and tyranny of Britain, proved his religion genuine by its harmony with the liberties of mankind and conforming his public prayers to the spirit and the injured rights of his country, addressed the god of battles for victory to our arms, while others impiously prayed that our enemies might vainquish and overcome us) do hereby oblige ourselves our heirs executors and administrators on or before the 25th day of December in this present year 1777, and likewise on or before the 25th day of December in every year following until we shall withdraw our subscription in open vestry, or until the legislature shall make other provision for the support of the said clergy, to pay to the (reverend) said Charles Clay of Albemarle his executor or administrators the several sums affixed to our respective names : in Consideration whereof we expect that the said Charles Clay shall perform divine service and preach a sermon in the town of Charlottesville on every fourth Sunday, or oftener, if a regular rotation with the other churches that shall have put themselves under his care will admit a more frequent attendence.

And we further mutually agree with each other that we will meet at Charlottesville on the 1st day of March in the present year, and and on the second Thursday in —— in every year following so long as we continue our subscriptions and there make choice by ballot of three wardens to collect our said subscriptions, to take care of such books and vestments as shall be provided for the use of our church, to call meetings of our Congregation when necessary, and to transact such other business relating to our Congregation as we shall hereafter confide to them.

Th. Jefferson, six pounds; Jno Harvie, four pounds; Randolph Jefferson, two pounds ten schillings; Thos. Garth, fifteen schillings; Philip Mazzei, sixteen schillings eight pence.[1]

Far more important than the local reception of the revised laws, since most of them were adopted only years later, and thanks to the efforts of Madison, during the sessions of 1785 and 1786, is the fact that Jefferson had already formulated at that time for himself and his fellow citizens the most essential principles of his doctrine. He was not unaware of this, and stated it himself in his "Autobiography" when he declared: "I considered four of these bills, passed or reported as forming a system by which every fibre would be eradicated of ancient or future aristocracy; and a foundation laid for a government truly republican." [2]

The ideal government he had in mind at the time could perhaps be described as a democracy, but he did not use the word himself, not even many years later in his "Autobiography" where he simply spoke of "a government truly republican." He was much opposed to the perpetuation of an hereditary landed gentry, but I do not see that he would have approved or even conceived the possibility of a government placed entirely under the control of unenlightened men. The Bill for the more General Diffusion of Knowledge makes clear that only through a liberal education can men be "rendered worthy to receive and able to guard the sacred deposit of the rights and liberties of their fellow citizens", and the Bill for Amending

---

[1] This seems to be the first draft of the document; another copy in the Jefferson Coolidge Collection presents few variants, the most important being found in the second sentence which reads, "Yet desirous of encouraging and supporting the Calvinistical Reformed Church, and of deriving" etc. The list of names appended to that second version is considerably longer and besides the original signers includes fourteen other supporters of the Reverend Charles Clay.

[2] "Autobiography." Memorial Edition, I, 73.

the Charter of William and Mary proclaims even more emphatically that the old college must "become the seminary, in
which those who are to be the future guardians of the rights of
liberty of their country may be endowed with science and virtue,
to watch and preserve the sacred deposit." Jefferson was a
friend of the people, but no admirer and no flatterer of the
"plain people", nor did he entertain any illusion about their
participation in all the forms of government. For the present
it was enough, as he wrote in the "Autobiography", if they
were qualified through elementary education "to exercise with
intelligence *their* parts in self-Government." If he rebelled
against aristocracy of wealth, he would have reacted with equal
vehemence against mob tyranny. Neither was he radical
enough to admit *propagandistes par le fait* and to forbid society
the right to intervene "when principles break out into overt
acts against peace and good order." (Bill for Religious Freedom.) For freedom of speech does not entail freedom of action: and the civil rights or rights of compacts are necessarily subject to civil regulations.

It is easily seen now that Jefferson so far remained perfectly
consistent, and followed in practice the distinction between
natural rights and rights of compact mentioned in the preceding chapter, and which already constituted one of the main
tenets of his political philosophy. If this theory is accepted,
it is evident that society being founded upon a legal compact,
the ideal form of government is one in which both parties, the
individual on the one hand and society on the other, scrupulously live up to its terms. A breach of contract can no more
be condoned in the individual than in society. On the other
hand, natural rights remain always truly "inalienable" and
apart from civil rights. When any individual comes to the
conclusion that the sacrifice he has made of certain rights in
order to enjoy more security is not compensated for by sufficient advantages, he has the right to denounce the compact:

hence the right of expatriation always so energetically maintained by Jefferson. This is the very reason why Jefferson could not and did not blame John Randolph for going to England in August, 1775, since "the situation of the country had rendered it not eligible to him to remain longer in it." Thus the conflict seen by so many political philosophers between man and society disappears entirely. The individual cannot stand against society when he is free to break the social bond at any time — nor can society oppress the individual without endangering its very existence. Such a theory was more than a "philosophical construction." It was largely based upon facts and observation; it expressed the current political philosophy of the colonies. It was eminently the juridistic explanation of the pioneer spirit.

Granting what is undoubtedly true, that Jefferson aroused antagonism and enmities in the Assembly, he certainly had also his admirers and followers. If the prophet had preached in the desert, he would not have gained the prompt recognition that came to him when he was chosen Governor of Virginia, the first of June, 1779, to succeed Patrick Henry. He was then thirty-six years old.

CHAPTER III

GOVERNOR OF VIRGINIA — THE "NOTES ON VIRGINIA"

JEFFERSON served two years as Governor of the Commonwealth and when he wrote his "Autobiography" he gave only a short paragraph to this episode of his eventful career, referring for more details to Girardin's continuation of Burk's "History of Virginia." The student of law, the erudite jurist, and classical scholar was by the choice of the Assembly entrusted with the duties and responsibilities of a war chief, and it cannot be said that Jefferson enjoyed the experience. The duties of governor were not only exacting but almost impossible to fulfill satisfactorily. For more than two years, Virginia, without money, with a poorly equipped militia reënforced with an inadequate number of Federal troops, had been overrun by the enemy and had known all the atrocities of the war. The governor had to honor the continuous requests of the general in chief for more ammunition, more equipment and provision, and at the same time had to keep under arms, and as much as possible in fighting condition, militiamen anxious to go back to their farms for the harvest or the plowing, so as to protect the territory of the State against the raids of the invader and prevent Indian uprisings on the western border. Last, but not least, he had to take into consideration the general attitude of the people of the State and the measures adopted by the legislature. Jefferson's correspondence with Lafayette during the first months of 1781 is most illuminating in this respect. When, after Arnold's treason, Lafayette was sent by Washington to apprehend the traitor and give some assistance to the Old

Dominion, he found that there were neither boats, wagons, nor horses to carry his equipment from Head of Elk to the siege of operations. The treasury was empty, the Assembly most chary in granting impressment warrants, and practically all the governor could offer in the way of help was his unlimited good will. Lafayette had to use oxen for his artillery and to mount cannon on barges; but even after powers of impressment were granted to the Marquis, Jefferson had to remind him of the necessity of not impressing stallions or brood mares, so as not to kill the "goose with the golden eggs." [1]

Jefferson's attitude in these critical circumstances reveal his true character to a degree, and without entering into a detailed account of the campaign, a few illustrations may be included here. It may be remembered that four thousand British troops, taken prisoners at the battle of Saratoga, had been ordered by Congress to Charlottesville. The problem of housing and feeding them soon became acute, and Jefferson was called upon to assist in finding a proper solution. The life imposed upon the captive soldiers was comparatively mild. Barracks were erected, while the officers, well provided with money, rented houses in the vicinity of the camp and bought some of the finest horses in Virginia. For most of them the Charlottesville captivity was a very pleasant *villégiature*. On the other hand, some of the inhabitants did not view without alarm this sudden increase in the population of the county, and application was made to Governor Patrick Henry to have at least part of the prisoners removed to another section of the State. This, according to Jefferson, would have been a breach of faith, since the articles of capitulation provided that the officers should not be separated from their men. On this occasion he wrote a very vehement letter to the governor, March 27, 1779, protesting that such a measure "would suppose a possibility that

[1] See my edition of the Jefferson-Lafayette Correspondence, Paris and Baltimore, 1929.

humanity was kicked out of doors in America, and interest only attended to." Yet the governor could not entirely neglect interested consideration, and Jefferson once more revealed that curious mixture of high principles and hard, practical common sense, to which we already called attention. He was aware that the circulation of money was increased by the presence of these troops "at the rate of $30,000 a week at least." The rich planters, "being more generally sellers than buyers", were greatly benefited by these unexpected customers, although the poor people were much displeased by inroads made by them upon the amount of supplies and provisions available in the county.

Never were prisoners better treated or made more welcome, and if Jefferson reflected the feelings of his neighbors there was no animosity against the soldiers in the field:

The great cause which divides our countries is not to be decided by individual animosities. The harmony of private societies cannot weaken national efforts. To contribute by neighbourly intercourse and attention to make others happy is the shortest and surest way of being happy ourselves. As these sentiments seem to have directed your conduct, we should be as unwise as illiberal, were we not to preserve the same temper of mind.[1]

Truly this was a war of philosophers and gentlemen, and the courtly generals of Louis XV would not have expressed more elegantly their consideration for the enemy. Jefferson's declaration was no mere gesture, for he struck up lasting friendships with several of the prisoners. He was particularly interested in a young German officer, Louis de Unger, who showed a remarkable talent for philosophy, in Baron de Geismer with whom he kept up a correspondence for more than ten years,[2] and in Major General Baron de Riedesel who, with his wife, was a frequent guest at Monticello. To many of them

---

[1] Jefferson to General Philips. Quoted by Randall, I, 235.
[2] See his letter dated from Paris, November 20, 1789.

Jefferson opened his house, his library, and his dining room. He discussed philosophy and agriculture with them, played duets on his violin, and sincerely regretted the loss of that pleasant society when he had to leave after his appointment as governor.[1]

Yet a sterner trait in his character was soon to be revealed. While the British prisoners were described as "having thus found the art of rendering captivity itself comfortable, and carried to execution, at their own great expense and labor, their spirits sustained by the prospect of gratifications rising before their eyes", the American prisoners and noncombatants were receiving harsher treatment at the hands of the British. War had become particularly atrocious after Indian tribes had been encouraged to attack the insurgents, and this was an offense that Jefferson could not condone. When Governor Hamilton of Kaskaskia, with his two lieutenants, Dejean and Lamothe, who had distinguished themselves by their harsh policy, surrendered to Clark and were brought to Virginia, Jefferson ordered them confined in the dungeon of the public jail, put in irons and kept incommunicado. On General Philips' protest Jefferson wrote to Washington to ask him for advice, but added that in his opinion these prisoners were common criminals and that he could "find nothing in Books usually recurred to as testimonials of the Laws and usages of nature and nations which convicts the opinion I have above expressed of error."[2] To Guy Carleton, Governor of Canada, he answered that "we think ourselves justified in Governor Hamilton's strick confinement on the general principle of National retaliation", and no punishment was too severe for a man who had employed "Indian savages whose known rule of warfare is an indiscriminate butchery of men, women and children."[3]

---

[1] To Baron de Riedesel, July 4, 1779. Ford, II, 245.
[2] July 17, 1779. *Ibid.*, II, 247.   [3] July 22, 1779. *Ibid.*, II, 249.

When a few weeks later, upon Washington's request, the irons were taken from the prisoners and a parole offered to them, Jefferson obeyed very reluctantly and informed the general that "they objected to that part of it which restrained them from *saying* anything to the prejudice of the United States" and insisted on "freedom of speech"; they were in consequence remanded to their confinement in the jail, "which must be considered as a voluntary one until they can determine with themselves to be inoffensive in words as well as deeds." [1]

Even when the prisoners were freed, Jefferson wrote again to Washington:

I shall give immediate orders for having in readiness every engine which the Enemy have contrived for the destruction of our unhappy citizens captivated by them. The presentiment of these operations is shocking beyond expression. I pray heaven to avert them: but nothing in this world will do it but a proper conduct in the Enemy. In every event I shall resign myself to the hard necessity under which I shall act. [2]

Writing the same day to Colonel George Mathews, Jefferson defined with more precision what he understood by these "operations" when he declared that "iron will be retaliated by iron, prison ships by prison ships, and like for like in general." [3]

The faults of his own people did not find him any weaker, for he declared: "I would use any powers I have for the punishment of any officer of our own who should be guilty of excesses injustifiable under the usages of civilized nations." He was not slow either in punishing mutineers, in having the ringleaders seized in their beds "singly and without noise" and in recommending cavalry, "as men on horseback have been found the most certain Instrument of public punishment." [4]

---

[1] October 1, 1779.   Ford, II, 258.   [2] October 8, 1779.   *Ibid.*, II, 261.
[3] *Ibid.*, II, 263.
[4] To The Virginia Delegation in Congress, October 27, 1780.   To Colonel Vanmeter, April 27, 1781.   *Ibid.*, III, 24.

This trait of Jefferson's character, hardly ever noticed, was no passing mood. It was little apparent in ordinary circumstances, but it was to reappear with the same stern inflexibility during the prosecution of Aaron Burr twenty-five years later. The dreamer, the theorist, the "philosopher" does not appear in the letters written by Jefferson during his governorship. He was punctual, attentive to details and careful to abide by the measures taken by the legislature. Yet he was subjected to bitter criticism and a sort of legend grew up about his lack of efficiency. He was approaching the end of his second term, which expired on June 2, 1781, and the legislature, feeling that the present danger required desperate action, was thinking of appointing a temporary dictator. Although most decidedly opposed to the creation of such an office, Jefferson believed that the appointment of a military leader was highly desirable (Letter to Washington, May 28), and according to his wishes General Nelson in command of the State troops was elected in his place. But before the Assembly could come to a decision an unexpected incident happened. It has been related at great length, and I am afraid with some embellishments, by Randall, who reconstructed it from Jefferson's papers and from the family traditions. Virginia was literally overrun by the enemy, and the raids of the British cavalry were a common occurrence. During one of these raids Tarleton attempted to capture the legislature and almost succeeded in taking the governor. The account of the incident, as I found it written by Jefferson, is far less picturesque, but probably more reliable than the highly colored narration of the biographer:

This was the state of things when, his office having expired on the 2d June, & his successor not yet in place, Col. Tarlton, with his regiment of horse, was detached by L. Cornwallis, to surprise him (supposed to be still governor) & the legislature now sitting in Charlottesville, the Speakers of the two houses, & some other members of the legislature, were lodging with him at Monticello. Tarleton, early in the morning of June 4. when within 10 miles of that place, detached a company of horse to secure him & his guests, & proceeded himself rapidly with his main body to Charlottesville, where he hoped to find the legislature unapprised of his movement. notice of it however had been brought both to Monticello & Charlottesville about sunrise, by a Mr Jouett from Louisa, who seeing them pass his father's house in the evening of the 3.^{d} and riding through the night along by-ways, brought the notice. The Speakers, with their Colleagues returned to Charlottesville, & with the other members of the legislature, had barely time to get out of the way.[1]

A few days later Jefferson left Amherst and returned to Monticello which he found practically undamaged; it was then that, riding to Poplar Forest, he was thrown from his horse and so seriously hurt that he could not ride horseback for several months. Shortly afterwards he learned that some members of the legislature, probably irked by the humiliation of having fled before the British raiders, not once, but several times, were not unwilling to accuse the governor of having neglected to take proper measures of defense. As I have found nowhere any indication to contradict Jefferson's account of the incident, it had better be given here in his simple words:

I returned to Monticello July 26. & learning some time after that Mr George Nicholas, than a young man, just entered into the legislature proposed to institute some enquiry into my conduct before the legislature, a member from my county vacated his seat, & the county elected me, in his room, that I might vindicate myself on the floor of the house. thro' the intervention of a friend, I obtained from Mr. Nicholas a written note of the charges he proposed to bring forward & I furnished him in return the heads of the answers I should make. on the day appointed for hearing his charges he withdrew from the house; & no other undertaking to bring them forward, I did it myself in my place, from his paper, answering them verbatim to the house. the members had been witnesses themselves to

[1] "A Diary kept by Th: J. from Dec. 31. 1780 to Jan. 11. 1781 and more general Notes of subsequent transactions during the British invasion." Jefferson Papers. Library of Congress.

all the material facts, and passed an unanimous vote of approbation, which may be seen on their journals. Mr. Nicholas was an honest and honorable man, & took a conspicuous occasion, many years after, of his own free will, & when the matter was entirely at rest, to retract publicly the erroneous opinions he had been led into on that occasion, and to make just reparation by a candid acknowledgment of them.[1]

This unfortunate incident revealed another fundamental trait of Jefferson's character, — his total incapacity to accept public criticism with equanimity. It was not until December 19, 1781, that he had the opportunity of presenting his case before the legislature and of receiving the vote of thanks intended "to obviate and remove all unmerited censure." In the meantime, and because he did not wish to leave a free field to his enemies, he had to decline a new appointment from Congress, when on the fifteenth of June he was designated to join the four American plenipotentiaries already in Europe. The letter was transmitted through Lafayette, and to Lafayette alone Jefferson confided his deep mortification at having to

lose an opportunity, the only one I ever had and perhaps ever shall have, of combining public service with public gratification, of seeing countries whose improvements in science, in arts and civilization it has been my fortune to admire at a distance but never to see and at the same time of lending further aid to a cause which has been handed on from it's first organization to its present stage by every effort of which my poor faculties were capable. These however have not been such as to give satisfaction to some of my countrymen & it has become necessary for me to remain in the state till a later period, in the present year than is consistent with an acceptance of what has been offered me.[2]

A letter written to Edmund Randolph hints at other considerations which "that one being removed, might prevent

---

[1] Jefferson Papers. Library of Congress.

[2] Lafayette transmitted the letter on June 26, 1781, but Jefferson did not receive it until the beginning of August. *Ibid.*

my acceptance." The family record shows that Mrs. Jefferson was then expecting a child who was born on November, 1781, and died in April of the following year. Jefferson himself was far from being well and had not yet recovered from his accident; but there is little doubt that he would have gladly seized the opportunity to fulfill one of his earliest dreams and to visit Europe, had he been free to go. However this may be, it was on this occasion that he reiterated once more, but not for the last time, his wish to return entirely and definitively to private life:

Were it possible for me to determine again to enter into public business there is no appointment whatever which would have been so agreeable to me. But I have taken my final leave of everything of that nature. I have retired to my farm, my family and books from which I think nothing will evermore separate me. A desire to leave public office with a reputation not more blotted than it deserved will oblige me to emerge at the next session of our assembly & perhaps to accept of a seat in it, but as I go with a single object, I shall withdraw when that has been accomplished.[1]

I must confess that Jefferson's determination can scarcely be understood or excused. He was not yet forty and, for a man of that age, his achievements were unusual and many, but he had by no means outlived his usefulness or fulfilled the tasks he had mapped out for himself. Even supposing he had done enough for the United States and did not feel any ambition to return to Congress, there was much to be done in Virginia. For one thing the war was not over and the situation of his native State, his "country", as he still called it, was as precarious as ever. Even supposing the war to be of short duration and destined to end in victory, the work of reconstruction loomed considerable upon the horizon. Not only had plantations been burned, houses destroyed, cattle killed off, Negroes decimated in many places, but the financial resources of Virginia

---

[1] To E. Randolph, September 16, 1781. Jefferson Papers. Library of Congress.

were nil, the currency depreciated and valueless. Above all, republican institutions were far from secure, Jefferson was not at all satisfied with the Constitution as adopted, there remained many bills on the Revised Laws to be presented, defended, and approved. The laws adopted so far might have laid the foundations of true republican government, but the task was still enormous. Was Jefferson irritated and despondent at the ingratitude of his fellow citizens who had not rejected at once the charges made by Nicholas? Was he so alarmed by the health of his wife that he did not feel that he could leave her even for a few days? Was he not rather a victim of overwork and overexertion? He had been severely shaken by his accident and seems to have suffered at the time a sort of nervous breakdown, for on October 28, 1781, when writing to Washington to congratulate him on Cornwallis' capitulation at Yorktown he deplores the "state of perpetual decrepitude" to which he is unfortunately reduced and which prevents him from greeting Washington personally.

Several of his best friends were unable to understand or condone his retirement. Madison himself wrote to Edmund Randolph:[1]

Great as my partiality is to Mr. Jefferson, the mode in which he seems determined to revenge the wrong received from his country does not appear to me to be dictated either by philosophy or patriotism. It argues, indeed, a keen sensibility and strong consciousness of rectitude. But his sensibility ought to be as great towards the relenting as the misdoings of the Legislature, not to mention the injustice of visiting the faults of this body on their innocent constituents.

Monroe, ardent friend and admirer of Jefferson's, was even more direct when writing to acquaint his "master" with the criticism aroused by his retirement. To which Jefferson answered with a letter in which he poured out the bitterness of

[1] June 11, 1782. Randall, I, 376.

his heart. He first recited all his different reasons for making his choice; the fact that after scrutinizing his heart he had found that every fiber of political ambition had been eradicated; that he had the right to withdraw after having been engaged thirteen years in public service; that his family required his attention; that he had to attend to his private affairs. But the true reasons came only in the next paragraph:

That however I might have comforted myself under the disapprobation of the well-meaning but uninformed people, yet that of their representatives was a shock on which I had not calculated. . . . I felt that these injuries, for such they have been since acknowledged, had inflicted a wound on my spirit which only will be cured by the all-healing grave.

The man who wrote these lines had an epidermis far too sensitive to permit him to engage in politics and least of all in local politics. Jefferson in these particular circumstances forgot the lesson of his old friends the Greek and Latin philosophers — truly he was no Roman.

Yet we cannot regret very deeply Jefferson's determination to retire from public life at that time, since to his retirement we owe his most extensive literary composition, one of the first masterpieces of American literature. During the spring of 1781 he had received from the secretary of the French legation, Barbé-Marbois, a long questionnaire on the present conditions of Virginia. During his forced inactivity, he drew up a first draft which was sent to Marbois, but extensively corrected and enlarged during the following winter. A few manuscript copies were distributed to close friends, but the "Notes on Virginia" were not given to the public until 1787 and after they had been rather poorly translated into French by Abbé Morellet.[1]

No other document is so valuable for a complete conspectus

---

[1] The story of the publication has been told by P. L. Ford in a most scholarly edition of the "Notes on Virginia" in the "Writings" of Jefferson.

of Jefferson's mind and theories at that time. But two important observations must be made at the very outset. First of all the "Notes" were not intended for publication, and as late as 1785 Jefferson wrote to Chastellux that:

the strictures on slavery and on the constitution of Virginia . . . are the parts I do not wish to have made public, at least till I know whether their publication would do most harm or good. It is possible that in my own country these strictures might produce an irritation which would indispose the people towards the two great objects I have in view, that is the emancipation of their slaves & the settlement of their constitution on a firmer and more permanent basis."[1]

The second point is that the "Notes" were written for the use of a foreigner of distinction, in answer to certain queries proposed by him. Jefferson, therefore, is not responsible either for the plan of the work, or the distribution into chapters, and he necessarily had to go into more details than if he had written solely for his fellow countrymen.

The twenty-three Queries cover such an enormous range of information and contain such a mass of facts that it would have been physically impossible for any one to complete the work in so short a time, if it had been an impromptu investigation. We can accept without hesitation the statement of the "Autobiography" on the methods of composition employed in the "Notes":

I had always made a practice whenever an opportunity occurred of obtaining any information of our country, which might be of use in any station public or private to commit it to writing. These memoranda were on loose papers, bundled up without order, and difficult of recurrence when I had occasion for a particular one. I thought this a good occasion to embody their substance, which I did in the order of Mr. Marbois' queries, so as to answer his wish and to arrange them for my own use.

[1] June 7, 1785. Memorial Edition, V, 3.

The book was printed in France, in England, in Germany, and went through many editions in America. It probably did more than any other publication to propagate the doctrine of Americanism, for, in his retreat of Monticello, Jefferson formulated the creed and gave final expression to the hopes, aspirations, and feelings that were to govern his country for several generations. It also gives a complete picture of the mind of Jefferson at that date, when he thought he had accomplished the task assigned to him and felt he could stop to take stock, not merely of his native "country", but of the whole United States of America.

Unimaginative, unpoetical, unwilling to express personal emotions as he was, he had always been deeply moved by certain natural scenes. His description of the Natural Bridge, the site of which he owned, is well remembered.

You involuntarily fall on your hands and feet, creep to the parapet, and peep over it. Looking down from this height about a minute, gave me a violent head ache. If the view from the top be painful and intolerable, that from below is delightful in an equal extreme. It is impossible for the emotions arising from the sublime to be felt beyond what they are here; so beautiful an arch, so elevated, so light, and springing as it were up to heaven, the rapture of the spectator is really indescribable!

The "passage of the Patowmac through the Blue ridge" is even more famous, and the broad, peaceful, almost infinite scene is painted by the hand of a master:

It is a true contrast to the foreground. It is as placid and delightful as that is wild and tremendous. For the mountain being cloven asunder, she presents to your eye, through the cleft, a small catch of small blue horizon, at an infinite distance in the plain country, inviting you, as it were, from the riot and tumult roaring around, to pass through the breach to the calm below.

Only Bartram a few years later, and Chateaubriand at the beginning of the next century, with much longer and more elaborate descriptions, could equal or surpass these few strokes of description. Jefferson was truly the first to discover and depict to Europeans the beauty of American natural scenery, and to proclaim with genuine American pride that "this scene is worth a voyage across the Atlantic — and is perhaps one of the most stupendous in nature." It matters little that he followed Voltaire in the origin of fossils, to decide timidly in 1787 that we must be contented to acknowledge that "this great phenomenon is as yet unsolved." I shall not even remark on the completeness and exactness of his list of plants, "medicinal, esculent, ornamental or useful for fabrication", of which he gives the popular names as well as the *Linnæan*, "as the latter might not convey precise information to a foreigner", or on his list "of the quadrupeds of North America"; nor shall I mention his long dissertation on "the bones of Mamoths" found on the North American continent and his refutation of Buffon. Far more interesting is his protest against the assertion of the great French naturalist that "the animals common both to the old and new world are smaller in the latter, that those peculiar to the new are in a smaller scale, that those which have been domesticated in both have degenerated in America." He composed with much tabulation a complete refutation of Buffon's error, and demonstrated that plants as well as animals reached a development hitherto unknown under the new conditions and the favorable circumstances of the American climate.

When it came to the aborigines, he had little to say of the South American Indians, but of North American Indians he could speak "somewhat from his own knowledge" as well as from the observations of others better acquainted with them and on whose truth and judgment he could rely.

Not only they are well formed in body and in mind as the *homo sapiens Europaeus*, but from what we know of their eloquence it is of a superior lustre. . . . I may challenge the whole orations of Demosthenes and Cicero, and of many more prominent orators, if Europe has furnished any more eminent, to produce a single passage, superior to the speech of Logan, a Mingo chief, to Lord Dunmore when Governor of this State.

But his temper was thoroughly aroused when he discovered that Abbé Raynal had undertaken to apply the theory of Buffon to the white men who had settled in America.

If this were true and if climateric conditions were such as to prevent mental and physical growth there would be little hope for the newly constituted country to ever become a great nation. Nature itself pronouncing against the Americans what chance could they have to be able to ever come up to the level of the older nations. Sentenced to remain forever an inferior race, this struggle to conquer independence would have proved futile, and sooner or later, they would fall the prey of superior people.

Never before had Jefferson been so deeply stirred and moved, never before had he felt so thoroughly American as in his spirited answer to Raynal, when he claimed for the new-born country not only unlimited potentialities, but actual superiority over the mother country:

"America has not yet produced one good poet." When we shall have existed as a people as long as the Greeks did before they produced a Homer, the Romans a Virgil, the French a Racine and Voltaire, the English a Shakespeare and Milton, should this reproach be still true, we will inquire from what unfriendly causes it has proceeded, that the other countries of Europe and quarters of the earth shall not have inscribed any name in the roll of poet. But neither has America produced "one able mathematician, one man of genius in a single art or science." In war we have produced a Washington, whose memory will be adored while liberty shall have votaries, whose name will triumph over time, and will in future ages assume its just station among the most celebrated worthies of the world, when that wretched philosophy shall be forgotten which would have arranged him among the degeneracies of nature. In Physics we have produced a Franklin, than whom no one of the present age has made more important discoveries, nor has enriched philosophy with more, or more ingenious solutions of the phaenomena of nature. . . . As in philosophy and war, so in government, in oratory, in painting, in the plastic arts, we might show that America, though but a child of yesterday, has already given hopeful proofs of genius, as well as of the nobler kinds, which arouse the best feelings of man, which call him into action, which substantiate his freedom, and conduct him to happiness, as of the subordinate, which serve to amuse him only. We therefore suppose that this reproach is as unjust as it is unkind : and that, of the geniuses which adorn the present age, America contributes her full share. . . . The present war having so long cut off all communications with Great Britain, we are not able to make a fair estimate of the state of science in the country. The spirit in which she wages war, is the only sample before our eyes, and that does not seem the legitimate offspring either of science or civilization. The sun of her glory is fast descending to the horizon. Her Philosophy has crossed her channel, her freedom the Atlantic, and herself seems passing to that awful dissolution whose issue is not given human foresight to scan.

This is the fullest and most complete expression of national consciousness and national pride yet uttered by Jefferson. The American eagle was spreading her wing and preparing to fly by herself. The American transcended the Virginian and looked confidently at the future.

In Query VIII, we come again to a question of national importance. The country being what it is, it would take at least one hundred years for Virginia to reach the present square-mile population of Great Britain. The question then arises whether a larger population being desirable, the State should not encourage foreigners to settle in as large numbers as possible. To unrestricted immigration, Jefferson, fearful for the integrity of the racial stock, fearful also for the maintenance of institutions so hardly won and yet so precariously established, was unequivocally opposed. In a most remarkable passage he stated the very reasons that after him were to be put forth again and again, until a policy of selective and restrictive immigration was finally adopted. I would not say that he was a hundred and fifty years ahead of his time, but a hundred and fifty years ago he formulated with his usual "felicity of expression", feelings and forebodings which existed more or less confusedly in many minds. When he spoke thus he was more of a spokesman than a prophet of America:

Every species of government has its specific principles. Ours perhaps are more peculiar than those of any other in the universe. It is a composition of the freest principles of the English constitution, with others derived from natural right and natural reason. To these nothing can be more opposed than the maxims of absolute monarchies. Yet from such we are to expect the greatest number of immigrants. They will bring with them the principles of the governments they leave, imbibed in their early youth; or, if able to throw them off, it will be in exchange for an unbounded licentiousness, passing, as is usual, from one extreme to another. It would be a miracle were they to stop precisely at the point of temperate liberty. These principles, with their language, they will transmit to their children. In proportion to their numbers, they will share with us the legislation. They will infuse into it their spirit, warp and bias its directions, and render it a heterogeneous, incoherent, distracted mass. . . . Is it not safer to wait with patience 27 years and three months longer for the attainment of any degree of population desired or expected? May not our government be more homogeneous, more peaceable, more durable? Suppose 20 millions of republican Americans [were] thrown all of a sudden into France, what would be the condition of that kingdom? If it would be more turbulent, less happy, less strong, we may believe that the addition of half a million of foreigners to our present numbers would produce a similar effect here. . . . I mean not that these doubts should be extended to the importation of useful artificers. . . . Spare no expence in obtaining them. They will after a time go to the plough and to the hoe; but in the mean time they will teach us something we do not know.

Everything is there!   That America is essentially and should remain an Anglo-Saxon civilization ; the fear that unassimilated immigration may corrupt the institutions of the country and bring into it uneradicable germs of absolutism ; the admission even that America needs a certain class of immigrants, of specialists to develop new arts and new industries.   In 1781, Jefferson was not only an American, but a hundred per cent. American, and the sentiments he expressed then were to reëcho in the halls of Congress through the following generations whenever the question was discussed.

The government as it was presently organized was far from perfect — it even had "very capital defects in it."   First of all, it was not a truly representative government since, owing to the representation by counties, it happened that fourteen thousand men living in one part of the country gave law to upwards of thirty thousand living in another ; in spite of the theoretical separation of powers, all the powers of government, legislature, executive, and judiciary, were vested in the legislative body.   "The concentrating these in the same hands is precisely the definition of despotic government."   Assuming that the present legislators of Virginia were perfectly honest and disinterested, it would not be very long before a change might come, for "mankind soon learn to make interested uses of every right and power which they possess, or may assume."

"With money we will get men," said Caesar, "and with men we will get money." . . .   They should look forward to a time, and that not a distant one, when a corruption in this, as in the country from which we derive our origin, will have seized the heads of the government, and be spread by them through the body of the people ; when they will purchase the voices of the people, and make them pay the price.   Human nature is the same in every side of the Atlantic and will be alike influenced by the same causes.   The time to guard against corruptions and tyranny, is before they shall have gotten hold of us."

Before proceeding any further, it may be well to pause, in order to analyze more carefully these statements of Jefferson's. It will soon appear that they do not form a perfectly logical construction and are not part of an *a priori* system. He had proclaimed his faith in the ultimate recognition of truth, but he did not believe that unaided truth should necessarily prevail, for human nature being very imperfect, very narrow and very selfish, the best institutions have a permanent tendency to degenerate. Jefferson had already clearly in mind the famous maxim "eternal vigilance is the price of liberty." It is this curious combination of unshakable faith in the ultimate triumph of truth and healthy pessimism as to the present possibilities, that distinguishes Jefferson from the "closet politicians" and theoretical philosophers. It is an alliance of the contraries which seems absurd to many Frenchmen, but is often found in English statesmen, and is probably more common in America than in any other nation. In this respect as in many others Jefferson was typically American.

His criticism of the legislature came clearly from two different motives. He attempted first of all to demonstrate to himself that the Assembly that had listened to charges against him was not a truly representative body, not only because the attribution of two delegates to each county, irrespective of the population, was iniquitous, but also because, owing to emergencies, the Assembly had come to decide themselves what number would constitute a quorum. Thus an oligarchy or even a monarchy could finally be substituted for a regular assembly by almost imperceptible transitions. "*Omnia mala exempla a bonis orta sunt; sed ubi imperium ad ignaros aut minus bonos pervenit novum illud exemplum ab dignis et idoneis ad indignos et non idoneos fertur.*"

This is nothing but a re-affirmation of the aristocratic doctrine of the "Literary Bible." Once more, the aristocrat of mind revolts, for "when power is placed in the hands of men who are ignorant or not so good, it may be taken from those who are deserving and truly noble to be transferred to unworthy and ignoble men." This is the constant undercurrent which runs through Jefferson's political theories and unexpectedly reappears at the surface from time to time. A government of the best minds, elected by a populace sufficiently enlightened to select the best minds, — such is at that time Jefferson's ideal of government.

On the other hand his attitude towards dictatorship, as it appears in the "Notes on Virginia", is no less significant for a true estimate of his character. Unless the views expressed there are carefully considered and kept well in mind, we might fall into the common error of attributing to some mysterious influence of the French Revolution and the French philosophers the opinions expressed by Jefferson on presidential tenure, during the debate on the Constitution and his famous quarrel with Hamilton. As a matter of fact, he had expressed the very same views already and even more emphatically on a previous occasion, when George Nicholas had proposed in the Assembly "that a Dictator be appointed in this Commonwealth who should have the power of disposing of the lives and fortunes of the Citizens thereof without being subject to account"; the motion seconded by Patrick Henry "been lost only by a few votes." [1] One may even wonder if the accusation of inefficiency against Jefferson had not been introduced by the same George Nicholas, in order to clear the way for the appointment of a dictator. Hence the impassioned tone of Jefferson's refutation. Deeply stirred and deeply hurt in his *amour-propre*, Jefferson incorporated in the "Notes on Virginia" the speech he would have made on the occasion had he been an orator.

How must we find our efforts and sacrifices abused and baffled, if we may still, by a single vote, be laid prostrate at the feet of one man. In God's name, from whence have they derived this power?

[1] To Arch. Stuart, September 8, 1818. Ford, III, 231, *n.*

Is it from any principle in our new constitution expressed or implied? Every lineament of that expressed or implied, is in full opposition to it. . . . Necessities which dissolve a government, do not convey its authority to an oligarchy or monarchy. They throw back into the hands of the people the powers they had delegated, and leave them as individuals to shift for themselves. A leader may offer, but not impose himself, nor be imposed on them. Much less can their necks be submitted to his sword, their breath be held at his will or caprice. . . . The very thought alone was treason against the people; was treason against mankind in general; as rivetting forever the chains which bow down their necks, by giving to their oppressors a proof which they would have trumpetted through the universe, of the imbecillity of republican government, in times of pressing danger, to shield them from harm. Those who assume the right of giving away the reins of government in any case, must be sure that the herd, whom they hand on to the rods and hatchet of the dictator, will lay their necks on the block when he shall nod to them. But if our assemblies supposed such a resignation in the people, I hope they mistook their character. . . . Searching for the foundations of this proposition, I can find none which may pretend a colour of right or reason, but the defect before developed, that there is no barrier between the legislative, executive, and judiciary departments. . . . Our situation is indeed perilous, and I hope my countrymen will be sensible of it, and will apply, at a proper season, the proper remedy; which is a convention to fix the constitution, to amend its defects, to bind up the several branches of government by certain laws, which, when they transgress, their acts shall become nullities; to render unnecessary an appeal to the people, or in other words a rebellion, on every infraction of their rights, on the peril that their acquiescence shall be construed into an intention to surrender those rights.

This is much more than an occasional outburst written under a strong emotional stress. Jefferson had discovered in his own country the existence of a group of men stanchly opposed to the republican form of government, ready in an emergency to go beyond the powers that had been delegated to them — not necessarily dishonest men, but dangerous because they did not have a correct conception of their rights and duties. All the controversy with the Federalists already exists in germ, in this declaration, and Jefferson from the very first had taken his position. The immediate effect was to sever the last bonds which still tied him to the aristocratic spirit of the social class to which he belonged by birth, and to make him raise a protest against the fact that, "the majority of men in the state, who pay and fight for its support are unrepresented in the legislature, the roll of freeholders entitled to vote, not including generally the half of those on the roll of militia, or of the tax gatherers."

"It has been thought that corruption is restrained by confining the right of suffrage to a few of the wealthier people"; but experience has shown, irrespective of any consideration of justice or right, that a truly republican form of government is not safe in their hands. What will be the conclusion? That suffrage must be extended so as to become universal. The people themselves are the only safe depositories of government. "If every individual which composes this mass participates of the ultimate authority, the government will be safe; because the corruption of the whole mass will exceed any private resources of wealth." But if the people are the ultimate guardians of their liberties, they must also be rendered the safe guardians of it. Hence the necessity of providing for them an education adapted to the years, the capacity, and the conditions of every one, and directed toward their freedom and happiness. On this occasion Jefferson reproduced the view already expressed in the Bill for the More General Diffusion of Knowledge, as well as the tenor of the first section of the Bill for Religious Freedom, but with new considerations which could scarcely be incorporated in a statute.

Then comes a conclusion unexpected and revealing, a sort of pessimism little in accordance with the supposed democratic faith of the writer; there is no inherent superior wisdom in the people, but it happens that under stress they so rise as to be superior to themselves, and it is for those who direct the course of the State to make the best of this fugitive opportunity :

The spirit of the times may alter, will alter. Our rulers will become corrupt, our people careless. A single zealot may commence persecutions, and better men be his victims. It can never be too often repeated, that the time for fixing every essential right on a legal basis is while our rulers are honest, and ourselves united. From the conclusion of this war we shall go down hill. It will not then be necessary to resort every moment to the people for support. They will be forgotten therefore and their rights disregarded. They will forget themselves, but in the sole faculty of making money, and will never think of uniting to effect a due respect for their rights. The shackles, therefore, which shall not be knocked off at the conclusion of this war, will remain on us long, will be made heavier and heavier, till our rights shall revive or expire in a convulsion.

Is this a dreamer, a philosopher, a mere theorician, or a very alert and keen politician with a high ideal and an exact realization of the people's limitations? This pessimistic view of human nature and human society did not make Jefferson entirely cynical, since he kept his faith in his ideal and never questioned the eminent superiority of the republican form of government. But he knew men too well to have faith in their collective intelligence and disinterestedness, the naïve faith of so many French philosophers. If in this passage Jefferson reminds one of any French writers, it is not Rousseau, nor Helvétius, nor even Montesquieu, but of Montaigne, the Mayor of Bordeaux, who after the pestilence retired to his "Library" and composed his famous "Essais." One may well understand why Jefferson took such care to recommend his friends not to let the "Notes" out of their hands, and not to permit it to be published in any circumstances. The French like to say "*toutes les vérités ne sont pas bonnes à dire*" — these were truths that should not be permitted to leak out and to circulate broadcast among the people : at most they were good only to be disclosed to this élite who had at heart the gradual betterment of the "plain people."

Jefferson's opposition to slavery rests on the same calculating motives. The existence of slavery is as degrading for the master as for the slave ; it is destructive of the morals of the people, and of industry.

And can the liberties of a nation be thought secure when we have removed their only firm basis, a conviction in the minds of the people that these liberties are the gift of God ? That they are not to be violated but with his wrath ? . . . It is impossible to be temperate and to pursue this subject through the various considerations of policy, of morals, of history natural and civil.

But it does not ensue that Negroes should ever be placed on a footing of equality with the whites. To pronounce that they are decidedly inferior would require long observation, and we must hesitate

to degrade a whole race of men from the work in the scale of beings which their Creator may *perhaps* have given them. . . . I advance it therefore, as a suspicion only, that the blacks, whether originally a distinct race, or made distinct by time and circumstance, are inferior to the whites in the endowment both of body and mind. It is not against experience to suppose that different species of the same genus, or varieties of the same species, may possess different qualifications. Will not a lover of natural history then, one who views the gradations in all the races of animals with the eye of philosophy, excuse an effort to keep those in the department of man as distinct as nature has formed them.

However the case may be, the blacks cannot be incorporated into the State, and the only solution after they are emancipated and educated is to "colonize them to such places as the circumstances of the time shall render most proper, sending them out with arms, implements of household and of the handicraft arts, seeds, pairs of the useful animals, etc., to declare them a free and independent people, and extend to them our alliance and protection, till they shall have acquired strength." But the freed slave "is to be removed beyond the reach of mixture", and the purity of the white stock must be preserved.

Throughout the book Jefferson untiringly harps on the fact that American civilization is different from any other that has developed in Europe, and that principles of "economy" which apply to European nations should not be transferred "without calculating the difference of circumstance which should often produce a difference of results." The main difference lies in the fact that while in Europe "the lands are already cultivated, or locked up against the cultivator, we have an immensity of land courting the industry of the husbandman." America is essentially agricultural, and agricultural it must remain :

Those who labour in the earth are the chosen people of God, if ever he had a chosen people, whose breasts he has made his peculiar deposit for substantial and genuine virtue. It is the focus in which he keeps alive that sacred fire, which otherwise might escape from the face of the earth. Corruption of morals in the mass of cultivators is a phaenomenon of which no age nor nation has furnished an example. . . . While we have land to labour then, let us never wish to see our citizens occupied at a work-bench, or twirling a distaff. Carpenters, masons, smiths, are wanting in husbandry : but, for the general operations of manufacture, let our work-shops remain in Europe. It is better to carry provisions and materials to work men there, than bring them to the provisions and materials, and with them their manners and principles.

This vision of an American entirely given to agricultural pursuits may look Utopian in the extreme, and would be Utopian if Jefferson had really believed that it was susceptible of becoming an actual fact. But, in practice, this ideal was on the contrary subject to many adjustments and modifications.

Jefferson's relativism is even more clearly marked in the last

chapter, which forms the real conclusion of the book. It outlines the future policy of the United States with regard to
foreign nations; it formulates a peaceful ideal which has
remained on the whole the ideal of America. Once more it
illustrates that curious balancing of two contrary principles so
characteristic of the philosopher of Americanism as well as of
the country itself.

Young as we are, and with such a country before us to fill with
people and with happiness, we should point in that direction the
whole generative force of nature, wasting none of it in efforts of
mutual destruction. It should be our endeavour to cultivate the
peace and friendship of every nation, even of that which has injured
us most, when we shall have carried our point against her. Our
interest will be to open the doors of commerce, and to knock off all
its shackles, giving perfect freedom to all persons for the want of
whatever they may choose to bring into our ports, and asking the
same in theirs. Never was so much false arithmetic employed on
any subject, as that which has been employed to persuade nations
that it is their interest to go to war. Were the money which it has
cost to gain, at the close of a long war, a little town, or a little territory, the right to cut wood here, to catch fish there, expended in
improving what we already possess, in making roads, opening rivers,
building ports, improving the arts and finding employment for their
idle poor, it would render them much stronger, much wealthier and
happier.

"This," adds Jefferson, "I hope will be our wisdom." But
it is only a hope and circumstances which cannot be changed
by pious hopes exist and have to be confronted. In order to
avoid every cause of conflict it would be necessary to abandon
the ocean altogether, and "to leave to others to bring what we
shall want, and to carry what we shall spare." This unfortunately is impossible, since a large portion of the American
people are attached to commerce and insist on following the sea.
What then is the answer? — Preparedness. — "Wars then

must sometimes be our lot; and all the wise can do, will be to avoid that half of them which would be produced by our own follies, and our own acts of injustice; and to make for the other half the best preparations one can."

One would not have to search long in the speeches of Woodrow Wilson to find the same idea expressed in almost identical terms. Even a Republican president such as Mr. Coolidge did not speak differently, when he simultaneously proposed conferences of disarmament and recommended that appropriation for the navy be enormously increased. This combination of will to peace, these reiterations of the pacific policies of the United States have been since the early days combined with the fixed determination to maintain a naval force adequate to cope with any attacking force. For such is the policy advocated by Jefferson. One should not be deceived by his very modest statement, "the sea is the field on which we should meet an European enemy. On that element it is necessary that we should possess some power." What he proposes is simply the building in one year of a fleet of thirty ships, eighteen of which might be ships of the line, and twelve frigates, with eighteen hundred guns. And he significantly adds, "I state this only as one year's possible exertion, without deciding whether more or less than a year should be thus applied." But, so as not to leave any potential aggressor in doubt as to the resources of America, he mentions that this naval force should by no means be "so great as we are able to make it."

After stating categorically his principles, Jefferson did not object to minor modifications when it came to practice. As early as the winter of 1781 he had found and determined the main tenets of his political philosophy. It was essentially American and practical. The idea never entered his mind that in order to establish an American government it was necessary to make a *tabula rasa* of what existed before. As a matter of fact, Americans had certain vested rights through several

charters enumerated by Jefferson in answer to Query XIII;
they had revolted in defense of these rights, but the principles of
their government, "perhaps more peculiar than those of any
other in the universe", were simply "a composition of the freest
principles of the English constitution, with others derived from
natural right and natural reason." Essentially "founded in
common law as well as common right", it was not necessarily
the best possible form of government or the only one imaginable,
"for every species of government has its specific principle."
But despite its imperfections, it was better adapted to American
conditions than any other that could be devised. At that time,
at least, Jefferson did not seem to suspect that it could be taken
as a model by any other nations, or that its main principles
would prove so "contagious." The situation of America was
unique. Unlimited agricultural lands extended to the west,
and one could estimate that it would take at least a century to
reach a density of population comparable to that of the British
Isles. For a long time America would remain mainly agricultural, with a population scattered in farms instead of being
concentrated in large cities, and would keep many of the virtues
inherent in country life. In addition, the country would be
practically free from any attack by land, as she had no powerful
neighbors. She was geographically isolated from the rest of
the world, and even if she were attacked by sea, it would be by a
fleet operating far from its base and therefore at a disadvantage.
No permanent army had to be maintained and a comparatively
small fleet would suffice for protection. Free from the ordinary
"sores" of civilization, not yet wealthy but prosperous, for,
says Jefferson "I never saw a native American begging in the
streets or highways", a country peaceful and with hatred
towards none, not even to "that nation which has injured us
most", — such is the ideal picture of America drawn by Jefferson for himself and his French correspondent during the winter
of 1781–1782.

Whatever faults existed would be corrected in time. If slavery could be abolished and the last vestiges of an hereditary aristocracy eradicated, little would be left to be desired. Yet it would not be a complete Arcadia, for Jefferson did not believe that a state of perfection once reached could be maintained without effort. Several dangers would always threaten America. The influx of foreigners might alter the character of her institutions. In spite of her peaceful ideals, dangers from the outside might threaten her prosperity. But on the whole, the country, even in its "infant state", was in no wise inferior to any European nation. In all the sciences it gave promise of extraordinary achievements. In architecture, to be sure, it seemed that "a genius has shed its malediction over this land", but artists and artisans could be induced to come, and even if America never reached the artistic proficiency of some European nations, it was and would remain more simple, more frugal, more virtuous than nations whose population congregate in large cities.

Such, briefly told, is the conception of Americanism reached by Jefferson when he wrote the "Notes on Virginia." He had not had any direct contact with Europe, but he had read enormously and he had come to the conclusion that, reasonably secure against foreign aggressions, keeping her commerce at a minimum, America could develop along her own lines and, reviving on a new land the old Anglo-Saxon principles thwarted by kingly usurpations and church fabrications, bring about an Anglo-Saxon millennium which no other country might ever dream of reaching. It now remains to see to what extent and under what influences Jefferson came to modify certain of his conclusions, following his prolonged contact with Europe.

CHAPTER IV

A STATESMAN'S APPRENTICESHIP

THE year 1782 was for Jefferson a year of trial and suffering. A child was born to Mrs. Jefferson on May 8; she never recovered fully and soon it appeared that she was irrevocably doomed. This tragic, touching story had better be told in the simple words of his daughter Martha, then nine years of age:

As a nurse no female had ever more tenderness nor anxiety. He nursed my poor mother in turn with aunt Carr and her own sister — sitting up with her and administering her medicines and drink to the last. For four months that she lingered he was never out of calling; when not at her bed-side, he was writing in a small room which opened immediately at the head of her bed. A moment before the closing scene, he was led from the room in a state of insensibility by his sister, Mrs. Carr, who with great difficulty, got him into the library, where he fainted, and remained so long insensible that they feared he never would revive. The scene that followed I did not witness, but the violence of his emotion, when, almost by stealth, I entered his room by night, to this day I dare not describe to myself. He kept his room three weeks, and I was never a moment from his side. He walked almost incessantly night and day, only lying down occasionally, when nature was completely exhausted, on a pallet that had been brought in during his long fainting fit. My aunts remained constantly with him for some weeks — I do not remember how many. When at last he left his room, he rode out, and from that time he was incessantly on horseback, rambling about the mountain, in the least frequented roads, and just as often through the woods. In those melancholy rambles I was his constant companion — a solitary witness to many a burst of grief, the remembrance of which has consecrated particular scenes of that lost home beyond the power to obliterate.

In Jefferson's prayer book is found this simple entry:

"Martha Wayles Jefferson died September 6, 1782, at 11 o'clock 45 minutes A.M."

She was buried in the little enclosure in which rested already three of her children; on a simple slab of white marble her husband had the following inscription engraved:

> To the memory of
> Martha Jefferson,
> Daughter of John Wayles:
> Born October 19th, 1748 O.S.
> Intermarried with
> Thomas Jefferson
> January 1st 1772;
> Torn from him by death
> September 6th 1782
> This monument of his love is inscribed

> Εἰ δὲ θανόντων περ καταλήθοντ' εἰν Ἀΐδαο,
> Αὐτὰρ ἐγὼ κακεῖθι φίλου μεμνήσομ' ἑταίρου.[1]

If in the house of Hades men forget their dead
Yet will I even there remember my dear companion.

Whether, as Tucker thought, Jefferson selected a Greek quotation so as not to make any display of his feelings to the casual passer-by, or whether Greek had so really become his own habit of thought that he could not think of any better way to express his grief, is a matter of conjecture. He was not the man to speak of himself and his sorrows, even to his closest friends. But it was probably at this time that he wrote these lines found after his death in his pocketbook: "There is a time in human suffering when exceeding sorrows are but like snow falling on an iceberg", and in Latin, "*Heu quanto minus est cum reliquis versari quam tui meminisse.*"

[1] Iliad XXII, 389.

At thirty-nine he was left a widower with a house full of children. Martha, born in 1772, Mary born in 1778, Lucy Elizabeth, the baby just born, who was to die two years later, and in addition the children of his friend and brother-in-law Carr, whom he had adopted at the death of their father. As soon as he had recovered from the first shock, Jefferson went with the children to the house of Colonel Archibald Cary, at Ampthill, in Chesterfield County, where he had them inoculated for the smallpox. "While engaged as their chief nurse on the occasion, he received notice of his appointment by Congress as Plenipotentiary to Europe, to be associated with Dr. Franklin and Mr. Adams in negotiating peace (November 13, 1782)." [1]

He was just emerging from the stupor of mind which had rendered him "as dead to the world as she whose loss occasioned it." [2] It appeared to him that "public interest and the state of his mind concurred in recommending the change of scene proposed; and he accepted the appointment." [3]

The next three months were spent in preparing for the journey. He made arrangements for his children and wrote a very touching letter to Washington, evincing once more that reluctance to express affectionate feeling so often found in Americans, a result of early education and training as much as of the national temperament: "Were I to indulge myself in those warm effusions which this subject forever prompts, they would wear an appearance of adulation very foreign to my nature; for such is the prostitution of language, that sincerity has no longer distinct terms in which to express her own truths." [4]

The ship that was to carry him to France was caught in the ice at the entrance of the Chesapeake, with no prospect of sailing before the beginning of March. When news came early

[1] "Domestic Life", p. 67.
[2] To Chastellux, November 26, 1782, in Randall, I, 1782.
[3] "Autobiography", Memorial Edition, I, 76.
[4] January 22, 1783. *Ibid.*, IV, 215.

in February that the negotiations were making satisfactory progress, he felt some doubts about the desirability of a voyage which entailed so much expense, and placed the matter in the hands of Congress.   It was not until April 1, however, that he was informed that the object of his appointment was "so far advanced as to render [it] unnecessary for him to pursue his voyage."   He left for Virginia a few days afterwards.   For the third time his plans for visiting Europe had been thwarted, but he does not seem to have resented it so deeply as previously.

The wounds inflicted to his *amour-propre* by the Virginia Assembly were healing.   He had renewed his contact with public affairs, and when, on June 6, he was chosen as delegate to Congress, with Samuel Hardy, John F. Mercer, Arthur Lee, and James Monroe, he accepted without hesitation.   The two years which were to elapse between June, 1782, and July 5, 1784, the date of his final departure from France on the *Ceres*, are not the most eventful or the most picturesque of Jefferson's career.   In many respects, however, they are the fullest and the most important for a true understanding of his mind and character.   In the absence of Franklin and Adams he stood out in Congress, head and shoulders above his colleagues ; he was placed on most of the important committees, he completed his acquaintance with the internal and foreign policies of the United States, he reported on measures of vital importance and crystallized his opinion on fundamental problems.

Before being chosen as a delegate to Congress, Jefferson had already decided "to lend a hand to the laboring oar" and to participate in the affairs of his State, if not as a legislator at least as an adviser and counsellor.   From the conversation he had held in Richmond with "as many members" of the Assembly "as he could", [1] he had concluded that Virginia was ready to call a convention to revise the Constitution of 1776.   On June 17 he wrote again to Madison, inclosing his ideas on the

[1] To Madison, May 7, 1783.   Ford, III, 329.

"amendments necessary." No convention was called at that time, but Jefferson's memorandum was printed in pamphlet form later in Paris, and he added it to his "Notes on Virginia." First of all he reassured that the Constitution of 1776 had no legal permanent value, being simply the result of the deliberation of a General Assembly, in no way different from the succeeding Assemblies. A power superior to that of the ordinary legislature could alone have authority to decide on a constitution. This could only be done by recommending "the good people of the State" to choose delegates "with powers to form a constitution of government for them, and to declare those fundamentals to which all our laws present and future shall be subordinate." Many of the provisions of the proposed constitution were not original and, as indicated by Jefferson himself in his letter to Madison, had been tried in other States. The document, however, may serve to illustrate the progress accomplished by Jefferson in the science of government since he had written his first State paper, and to show how far he still remained from his reputed views on democracy.

Although still a free State, Virginia was no longer completely independent, since she had entered a society of States, and it was acknowledged that: "The confederation is made a part of this constitution, subject to such future alterations as shall be agreed to by the legislature of this State, and by all the other confederating States."

Almost universal suffrage was granted, the vote being given to "All free male citizens of full age, and sane mind, who for one year before shall have been resident in the country, or shall through the whole of that time have possessed therein real property to the value of —, or shall for the same time have been enrolled in the militia."

This was an immediate consequence of the contractual concept of society and it is not without some interest to remark that this principle stood in direct contradiction to the physiocratic doctrine; for it was the contention of the Physiocrats that, society resting essentially on real property, those who own the land can alone participate in the government of the country. If, on the contrary, society is considered as an association of men who agree to live together in order to secure fuller enjoyment of their fundamental rights, all the signatories to the compact must have the same rights as well as the same obligations in the government of the association thus formed.[1]

Yet it remained understood that the voters were not to be intrusted with all the details of government, and Jefferson thought it desirable to establish certain safeguards against the possible lack of knowledge of the electors. They chose delegates and senators, but the governor was to be appointed by joint ballot of both houses of the Assembly, and the same procedure was to be followed in choosing a Council of State to advise the governor, the judges of the High Court of Chancery, the General Court and Court of Admiralty, while the judges of inferior courts were to be appointed by the governor on recommendation of the Council of State. The powers of the governor were to be strictly limited and it was made clear that although the old English title was preserved, the chief executive of the State had "none of the powers exercised under our former government by the Crown" : "We give him those powers only which are necessary to execute the laws (and administer the government), and which are not in their nature either legislative or judiciary." The governor had a sort of suspensive veto. The military was to be subordinate to the civil power, and the printing press to be subject to no other restraint but liability to legal prosecution for false facts printed and published. The plan provided also for the gradual abolition of slavery after the year 1800.

[1] This point appears even more clearly in Jefferson correspondence with Du Pont de Nemours, to appear shortly.

The most remarkable feature of this scheme was the strict limitation of popular participation in the government. The only power recognized as belonging to the people was that of selecting delegates to both Houses, and of appointing delegates to a constitutional convention whenever "any of the three branches of the government, concurring in opinion each by the voice of two-thirds of their existing number, decided that such a convention is necessary for amending the constitution." We are very far from government by referendum and even by periodic elections, since none of the State officials were directly appointed by the people. Jefferson had not at that time departed from his fundamental idea that government must be placed in the hands of well-qualified experts, carefully selected and appointed. The "Constitution of Virginia" was a "true form of Republican government", but by no means demagogical or even truly democratic. Curiously enough, and through mere coincidence, the essential features of the present constitution of France closely resemble the general outline of the plan proposed by Jefferson. This alone should suffice to demonstrate how far he was at that time from accepting and propounding some of the main tenets of the so-called Jeffersonian democracy. But Virginia was not yet ready for a change; the constitutional convention was not called, and nothing had been done when Jefferson left the State late in November, arriving at Annapolis on the twenty-fourth.

Much to his disgust, he found that, after a fortnight, the delegates from only six States had appeared and that it was impossible to transact any serious business. The Treaty of Commerce had been received and was referred to a committee of which Jefferson was chairman, but a bare quorum was not assembled until December 13, and on the twenty-third, according to the "Autobiography", it was necessary to send to several governors a letter "stating the receipt of the definitive treaty; that seven States only were in attendance, while nine were necessary to its ratification."

In the meantime Washington had come to Annapolis to resign his commission, in circumstances which can scarcely have been as impressive as is generally related, since the whole program carefully laid out by Jefferson took place before a bare majority of Congress. The rest of the month was spent in discussing whether the treaty could be ratified by less than nine states. It soon appeared that "there now remained but scanty sixty-seven days for the ratification, for its passage across the Atlantic and its exchange. There was no hope of our soon having nine States present; in fact that this was the ultimate point of time to which we could venture to wait; that if the ratification was not in Paris by the time stipulated, the treaty would become void . . ." — On January 13, delegates from Connecticut attended, and the next day a delegate from Carolina having arrived, "the treaty was ratified without a dissenting vote."

This was for Jefferson a most profitable experience. As chairman of the committee, he had to familiarize himself with questions of foreign policies and foreign commerce. He had also to put aside whatever remnants of sectionalism and provincialism he unconsciously retained and he realized that "Those United States being by their constitution consolidated into one federal republic, they be considered in all such treaties & in every case arising under them as one nation under the principles of the Federal Constitution." [1]

The same principle is reasserted more strongly in the "Draft for proclamation announcing ratification of definitive treaties", in which all the good citizens of the United States are enjoined to reverence "those stipulations entered into on their behalf under the authority of that federal (moral, political and legal

[1] "Report on letters from the Ministers in Paris." December 20, 1783. Ford, III, 355.

bond) whereby they are called, by which their existence as an independent people is bound up together, and is known and acknowledged by the nations of the world." [1]

On January 16, Jefferson wrote to Governor Harrison enumerating the important objects before Congress:

1. Authorizing our Foreign minister to enter into treaties of alliance and commerce with the several nations who have deserved it; 2. Arranging the domestic administration; 3. Establishing arsenals & ports on our frontiers; 4. Disposing of Western Territory; 5. Treaties of peace and purchase with the Indians; 6. Money.

A full program, requiring for the adoption of any measure the concurrence of nine States, while barely nine were present, seven of which were represented only by two members each; "any of these fourteen gentlemen differing from the rest would stay the proceedings", and it seemed very doubtful whether anything could be achieved during the session.

This brought home to Jefferson the fact that the concentration of the executive functions in Congress was an obstacle to carrying out effectively the business of the Confederation, and he thought it his duty to point out this defect in his "draft of the report on a committee of the States", January 30, 1784. It was a lengthy report, not very accurately summed up in the "Autobiography", authorizing a permanent Committee of the States to act as executive during the recess of Congress, and enumerating very minutely the powers that such a committee might exercise and those from which it would be excluded. The plan as adopted was somewhat different and it was resolved: "That the Committee should possess all the powers which may be exercised by the seven States in Congress assembled", except concerning foreign relations.

Jefferson recalled in the "Autobiography" that during the following recess the committee quarrelled, split into two parties, "abandoned their posts, and left the government without any visible head, until the next meeting of Congress." He significantly added : "We have since seen the same thing take place in the Directory of France; and I believe it will forever take place in any executive consisting of a plurality. Our plan, — best, I believe, — combines wisdom and practicality; by providing a plurality of Counsellors, but a single Arbiter for ultimate decision." This conclusion was already reached in 1784, not following a logical reasoning, or because of an innate need of unity, but as a result of experience. Very early in his life Jefferson became convinced that the country could not be properly administered unless the executive powers were concentrated in one responsible person, with powers strictly defined, but left free to act and to act rapidly within that field. This explains, among other things, not only Jefferson's approval of the powers granted to the Executive under the Constitution, but also his conduct during his two terms as President.

He soon had an opportunity to study the financial problems of the Confederation, when a "grand Committee of Congress" was appointed to take up the Federal expenses for the current year, inclusive of articles of interest on the public debts foreign and domestic." [1] He presented on March 22 a "Report on the Arrears of Interest", in which were carefully tabulated not only the interest on sums due on account of the national debts but an estimate of the expenses for the year 1784, — in other words a budget. An outgrowth of the work assigned to the Committee was the *establishment of a money unit, and of a coinage for the United States.* The report of Jefferson retained some of the essential provisions of the proposal drawn up by the "Financier of the U. S." (Robert Morris, assisted by Governor Morris), and Jefferson himself did not claim so much originality for it as has been given him by some of his biog-

[1] February 1, 1784.   Ford, III, 393.

raphers. The report of the financier proposed that the new coins "should be in decimal proportions to one another", and this was retained. On the other hand, Morris had proposed as a unit "the 1440th part of a dollar", after taking into consideration the old currencies, "all of which this unit measures without leaving a fraction." Jefferson pointed out that, although theoretically perfect, the unit was much too complicated and too small, and he maintained that the unit should be the Spanish dollar "a known coin, and the most familiar of all to the minds of the people." . . . "It is already adopted from South to North," he added, "has identified our currency, and therefore happily offers itself as a Unit already introduced."

In spite of the financier's opposition, the plan as amended by Jefferson was finally adopted and still constitutes the essential foundation of the American monetary system. To the student of psychology this incident affords another illustration of Jefferson's practical-mindedness. Having to choose between two solutions, one mathematically perfect, and another one simply regulating and organizing what already existed, he did not hesitate a minute and practical considerations prevailed at once in his mind.

In the meantime he was working on one of his most important State papers. Randall called attention to it and P. L. Ford maintained that "next to the Declaration of Independence (if indeed standing second to that) this document ranks in historical importance of all those drawn by Jefferson ; and, but for its being superseded by the 'Ordinance of 1787', would rank among all American state papers immediately after the National Constitution." [1] Yet it does not seem that its value is generally recognized and it is but seldom listed as one of the outstanding achievements of Jefferson. For reasons that will shortly appear, Jefferson himself neglected to mention it in his

[1] Ford, III, p. 430.

"Autobiography." It is a capital document by which to understand the growth of the Jeffersonian doctrine.

First of all, it resolved that "so much of the territory ceded or to be ceded by individual States to the United States as is already purchased or shall be purchased of the Indian inhabitants & offered for sale by Congress, shall be divided into distinct states." Which simply meant that the westward growth of the country, instead of being left to the initiative of the individual States, was placed under the ægis of the Confederation and thus became a matter of national importance and significance. It provided for a practically unlimited expansion of the United States by the establishment of States analogous to the already existing Confederacy. It also insisted strongly that all such territory be connected as closely as possible with the already existing Union. Settlers in any of the territories thus organized, had authority to establish a temporary government, adopting with due modification the constitution and laws of any of the original States. A permanent government was to be established in any State as soon as it should have acquired a population of twenty thousand free inhabitants, provided, and here we probably have the most important provisions:

1. That they shall forever remain a part of this confederacy of the United States of America. 2. That in their persons, property and territory they shall be subject to the Government of the United States in Congress assembled & to the articles of confederation. . . . 4. That their respective Governments shall be in republican forms and shall admit no person to be a citizen who holds any hereditary title. 5. That after the year 1800 of the Christian aera, there shall be neither slavery nor involuntary servitude in any of the said states.

Finally, "whenever any of the said States shall have, of free inhabitants, as many as shall then be in any one of the least numerous, of the thirteen original States, such State will be admitted by it's delegates into the Congress of the United States on an equal footing with the said United States."

This report, submitted March 1, recommitted to the committee March 17, was considered again by Congress on April 19, 21, 23, and adopted after amendment by every State except one. But the amendment took the teeth out of the report, since the clause referring to slavery was struck out, as well as that concerning the admission of persons holding hereditary titles. Other provisions concerning the names to be given to the new States were also eliminated. The scholar reappeared in these suggestions. If Jefferson's original motion had been accepted, the present State of Michigan would wear the name of *Chersonesus* and on the map of the United States would appear such designations as *Metropotamia*, *Polypotamia*, and *Pilisipia*.[1]

Finally Jefferson intended to complete the organization and expansion of the United States with "An ordinance establishing a Land Office" for the United States "to give sure title to the settlers and determine the division and subdivision into lots" which was defeated, an entirely new ordinance being adopted April 26, 1785.[2]

The most striking feature of all these bills was the eagerness of Jefferson to consolidate the Union and to strengthen Federal bonds. With a common monetary unit, common interest in a large territory just acquired by cession from Virginia, one more thing remained to be settled: the organization of permanent relations with foreign nations, that is to say, the conclusion of commercial treaties.

It had appeared very soon to Jefferson that if such treaties were to be concluded it was desirable to adopt a working policy outlined in his "Resolves on European Treaties." [3] To have foreign plenipotentiaries come to the United States, discuss with the badly organized body called the Continental Congress, whose members would have to report to their legislatures and

---

[1] See Ford, III, 407 and 429.   [2] *Ibid.*, III, 476.
[3] March, 1784.   *Ibid*, III, p. 428.

after interminable delays accept or reject the proposal, was an impossible procedure. This distrust of Congress was amply justified at the time, and one may wonder whether satisfactory treaties could ever have been concluded under the supervision of Congress; Jefferson therefore proposed that ministers be sent to Europe to negotiate with the old and established nations, who could not be expected to cross the Atlantic.

On May 7, Congress agreed on *Instructions to the Ministers Plenipotentiary appointed to negotiate treaties of Commerce with the European Nations*. Once more it was proclaimed:

"That these United Sates be considered in all such treaties, and in every case arising under them, as one nation, upon the principle of the Federal constitution."

It was also deemed "advantageous that treaties be concluded with Russia, the Court of Vienna, Prussia, Denmark, Saxony, Hamburg, Great Britain, Spain, Portugal, Genoa, Tuscany, Rome, Naples, Venice, Sardinia and the Ottoman Porte. That treaties of amity and commerce be entered into with Morocco, and the Regencies of Algiers, Tunis and Tripoli. To have supplementary treaties with France, the United Netherlands and Sweden in order to incorporate the new policies of the United States."

The plan of treaties contained some remarkable provisions; they were clear departures, not from the theory of international law and *droit des gens*, as Jefferson had found it in the authorities consulted, but from the actual policy of the European nations.

Thus it was proposed that in case of war between the two contracting parties,

The merchants of either country, then residing in the other shall be allowed to remain nine months to collect their debts and settle their affairs, and may depart freely, carrying off all their effects, without molestation or hinderance, and all fishermen, all cultivators of the earth, and all artisans or manufacturers, unarmed and inhabiting unfortified towns, villages or places, who labor for the common subsistence and benefit of mankind, and peaceably follow their respective employments, shall be allowed to continue the same.

That "neither of the contracting powers shall grant or issue any commission to any private armed vessels, empowering them to take or destroy such trading ships, or interrupt such commerce."

In case of war with another nation, "no merchandize heretofore called contraband, such as arms, ammunition and military stores of all kinds, . . . shall, on any account, be deemed contraband, so as to induce confiscation, and a loss of property to individuals." The right to detain vessels carrying such goods a reasonable length of time was granted, as well as the right not to seize, but "to purchase" military stores with a reasonable compensation to the proprietors; in all cases the owners of the ships delayed were to receive a compensation. But all vessels not carrying contraband were to be entirely free, adding that a blockade in order to be recognized had to be effectual, but even in that case "no vessel of the party who is not engaged in the said war, shall be stopped without a material and well-grounded cause."

Besides these general provisions, it was recommended that "each party shall have a right to carry their own produce, manufactures, and merchandise in their own bottoms to the ports of the others, and thence the produce and merchandise of the other, paying, in both cases, such duties only as are paid by the most favored nations."

A paragraph was intended specially for the commerce with the West Indies, "desiring that a direct and similar intercourse be admitted between the United States and possessions of the nations holding territorial possessions in America."

Finally, as Jefferson as well as his contemporaries were already fearful of seeing any influx of foreigners settle in their country and dominate the infant government, it was stipulated that no right be accorded to aliens to hold real property within these States, this being "utterly inadmissible by their several laws and policy."

From the European point of view many things were inadmissible in the plan of treaties. To request the nations of the Old World not only to abandon privateering, but to relinquish their definitions of contraband and their commercial monopolies with their own colonies, was something which must have appeared as the wild dream of a people unexperienced in the handling of foreign relations. As a matter of fact, the treaties were never signed. But if the principles formulated by Jefferson were not accepted by the European powers, they remained nevertheless an essential part of the foreign policy of the United States.

On the very day the "Instructions" were adopted, Jefferson was appointed Minister Plenipotentiary to "negotiate treaties of commerce with foreign nations in conjunction with Mr. John Adams and Dr. Franklin." No man in Congress was better qualified for such a mission. His work for two years on several important committees had acquainted him with the main problems of the Union. He had demonstrated his ability to present clear reports on the most intricate questions. He had completed his apprenticeship of men and things; but it may be wondered whether the delegates who recommended his appointment were not impelled by ulterior motives. The stand taken by Jefferson on slavery had made him decidedly unpopular with the Southern delegates. He had opposed the original statutes of the Order of Cincinnati, in which he saw the beginnings of a new aristocracy. He had made enemies as well as friends and could write to Washington that an experience of twenty years had taught him "that few friendships stand this test, & that public assemblies, where everyone is free to act & to speak, are the most powerful looseners of private friendship." The petty discussions in Congress, the long speeches he had to listen to, the quibbling, lack of initiative and lack of national spirit of the delegates had thoroughly disgusted him.   Before receiving his appointment he had already repented of his return to public life and had signified his intention of going back to his beloved Monticello.

I have determined — he wrote to Washington — to take no active part in this or anything else, which may lead to altercation, or disturb that quiet & tranquillity of mind to which I consign the remaining portion of my life.   I have been thrown back by events on a stage where I had never more thought to appear.   It is but for a time, however, & as a day laborer, free to withdraw, or be withdrawn at will.[1]

He seized with eagerness the opportunity of visiting older civilizations and enjoying a change of scenes.   Having hastily cancelled his order for printing a few copies of the "Notes on Virginia", he at once made preparations for his departure.

The new plenipotentiary decided to take with him his older daughter Martha, then in Philadelphia at Mrs. Hopkinson's, and to leave the two younger ones with their maternal aunt, Mrs. Eppes, in Virginia.   William Short, his "élève" and friend, accompanied him as private secretary and Colonel David Humphreys as secretary of the legation.[2]   From Philadelphia he went to Boston, visiting Connecticut, Rhode Island, and the principal towns on his way, in order to acquire "what knowledge he could of their commerce and other circumstances."   He sailed from Boston on the *Ceres*, Captain Sainte-Barbe, bound to Cowes.

Jefferson was then forty-one years old.   He knew life and men and had no illusions; he had experienced happiness and sorrow; he had had moments of exaltation, of hot patriotic fever; he had occupied the front of the stage in several circumstances never to be forgotten; he had aroused enmities and made devoted and faithful friends, among them Monroe, Madi-

[1] To George Washington, April 16, 1784.   Ford, III, 466 and 470.
[2] To James Madison, February 20, 1784.   *Ibid.*, III, 403.

son, and Short whom he was taking along with him. But neither his disappointments nor his sorrows had made him a misanthrope. Not an orator, he liked to talk, and he could not live without society. The tall spare man in black was no longer able to feel his heart moved by the early emotions of his youth. Next to Washington, who remained in America, and to Doctor Franklin, a debonair patriarch, he was the most famous national figure of America. None was better qualified by his former life and studies to represent America and to speak for his country. Whatever sectionalism he may have had in him had disappeared in these last two years of Congress, when he had striven so strenuously to make the Union an actual fact and to consolidate the loose Federal fabric, for only there could men "See the affairs of the Confederacy from a high ground; they learn the importance of the Union & befriend federal measures when they return. Those who never come here, see our affairs insulated, pursue a system of jealousy and self interest, and distract the Union as much as they can."

Of Europe he knew little, except what he had been able to absorb from books. It was a country of great artistic productivity, of enviable social life. Towards England he was not particularly attracted; towards France he felt much more favorably inclined. He had met many Frenchmen; some of them already had become his close friends, two particularly, the Chevalier de Chastellux and especially the youthful, impulsive, and charming Lafayette, who in a parting note had asked him to consider his house as his and to take the little motherless girl to Madame de Lafayette. He knew he would not be without friends, without society, that he would have an unique chance to meet the best minds of Europe. This practical American, so little given to the "*joie de vivre*" and without *abandon*, wanted primarily to increase his knowledge, to gather facts, to make comparisons. He had retained the taste for society, the good breeding, the polite manners, the artistic tendencies of the Virginian, but in him the American was already fully grown. He felt also that he had a certain mission and intended to fulfill it : it was to convey to the European statesmen whose wiles he distrusted the impression that the United States existed as a country, that they did not form a loose and temporary confederation of States, but a nation to be reckoned with and respected. His country was no longer his native Virginia alone : he was thinking nationally and not sectionally. For the French Jefferson was already a great American figure ; he was going to embody the best there was in the newly constituted Union.

BOOK THREE

An American View of Europe

CHAPTER I

SOCIETY AND TRAVEL

THE *Ceres* reached Portsmouth nineteen days after leaving Boston, a remarkably swift passage, without incident, except for three days spent in fishing on the Banks of Newfoundland, while the ship was becalmed. Jefferson and his companions were delayed a week in Portsmouth by Martha's slight illness, and then went directly to Paris, where he arrived on August 6, 1784. Jefferson was to remain in France till the fall of 1789 — five years crowded with pleasures, social duties, political duties, and hard work. His activities were so varied and his interests so diversified that it is no longer possible to follow any chronological order; we must establish arbitrary divisions, though Jefferson passed at all times from one subject to another and was incessantly busy with undertakings and plans truly encyclopedic.

First of all, he had to find quarters. He had put up at the Hôtel d'Orléans, Rue des Petits Augustins, then he had rented "Hôtel Tête-Bout, cul-de-sac Tête-Bout", and a year later moved to a house belonging to M. le Comte de l'Avongeac "at the corner of the Grande Route des Champs Elysées and Rue Neuve de Berry", where he continued to live as long as he remained in Paris. His secretary Short and Colonel Humphreys, secretary to the legation, lived with him. It was "a very elegant house, even for Paris, with an extensive garden, court and outbuildings, in the handsomest style."

Of Jefferson's first impressions after landing in France we unfortunately know nothing. Not until a full year had elapsed did he express his personal views in writing. Although he deplored the wretched condition of the larger mass of the people, he had already come to the conclusion, probably correct, that life in Paris was more pleasant than anywhere else on earth : "The roughnesses of the human mind are so thoroughly rubbed off with them, that it seems as if one might glide through a whole life without a jostle."[1] It was some time, however, before he felt entirely at home in Parisian society. He was somewhat handicapped and humiliated at first because of lack of means at the disposal of the Minister of the United States for maintaining his rank. In his report on the reduction of the civil list (March 5, 1784), Jefferson, animated with a fine republican zeal, had fixed the compensation of American representatives abroad at ten thousand dollars. Now that he was in Paris he found the allowance very inadequate. A proud Virginian, accustomed to entertain generously, he considered hospitality an imperious duty as well as a pleasure, and his letters to Congress are filled with complaints on the niggardliness of his resources. However, he procured a good French cook in the person of the worthy Petit, who became quite attached to him, and wrote for him recipes for " *poulet en casserole* " and " *café à la française.*" He informed himself concerning the best French wines, some of which he already knew, and made a thorough and scientific study of the different vintages, recording the result of his observations in unpublished notes. Nor was he so selfish as to keep all his knowledge to himself. Adams and Washington used his good offices to keep their cellars well stocked in champagne and sauternes. For them and for Madison he subscribed to "L'Encyclopédie Méthodique", he bought new French books, engravings, plaster casts, and medals, and his willingness to oblige his friends and to go shopping for them was so well known that Mrs. Adams asked him to buy for her daughter "two pairs of corsets", much to his distress, since she had omitted to send him the measure. For Mrs. Bingham he

---

[1] To Mrs. Trist, Paris, August 18, 1785. "Domestic Life", 79.

filled boxes with "caps and bonnets"; for Madison he bought a pocket telescope, a walking stick, a chemical box, for poor little Polly who had remained with her aunt at Eppington "sashes" and Parisian dolls.

Through Franklin, Jefferson was introduced to Madame d'Houdetot, who had unlimited admiration for a man who not only was an American and a philosopher, but who also knew the names of American plants and trees much more thoroughly than her dear Doctor. He obtained for her seeds, bulbs, and trees to be planted in the park of Sannois.[1] Through Franklin also he met Madame Helvétius and her two abbés, who always wrote jointly to Jefferson.[2] At her house, he saw Cabanis, then a very young man, Destutt de Tracy and abbé Morellet. He attended concerts at Madame d'Houdetot's brother's house, but above all he was attracted by Lafayette's family and friends. It was large enough for a man of more leisure and more worldly tendencies. There was the Marquis himself and his charming wife, who befriended Martha and wrote Jefferson several notes filled with that delightful eighteenth-century "*sensibilité*" and amiability of which we have lost the secret. There was also Madame de Tessé, Lafayette's cousin, who was, however, considerably older than the Marquis and whom he called "aunt." Jefferson saw her in Paris and visited her often at Chaville, where Short stayed for weeks at a time, perfecting himself in the French language and the ways of French society. She loved trees, good paintings, fine buildings, statues, and music, and did much to educate Jefferson's taste in these matters. Not mentioned by his biographers, Madame de Corny played a not inconsiderable part in Jefferson's sentimental life. Young, pretty, witty, and married to a husband much older than herself, she enjoyed Jefferson's company, took with him many walks in the Bois de

[1] See G. Chinard, "Les Amitiés américaines de Madame d'Houdetot." Paris, 1923.
[2] May 24, 1785, November 12, 1785, etc. Massachusetts Historical Society.

Boulogne and perhaps, secretly, found him too scrupulously polite and too respectful.[1] There were also several other women, Madame de Tott, a distinguished painter, the vivacious and charming Lucy Paradise, Comtesse Barziza, a real "*enfant terrible*", irresponsible, outspoken, who in her letters to Jefferson listed all the scandals of the days.[2] And one must not forget among Jefferson's feminine acquaintances the old Comtesse de la Rochefoucauld, dignified, sarcastic, a terrible bore at times, whom on many occasions he vainly tried to avoid.

But when all is told, it does not appear that the circle of Jefferson's friends was ever very large. During his first year in Paris he did his best to keep in the background. To Franklin he owed deference, because of his age and the position of the Doctor as the only accredited representative to the Court of Versailles. Adams, the other plenipotentiary, was older than Jefferson, who on every occasion insisted that his colleagues should have precedence over him. A good listener, he was much more reserved than Franklin and always remained somewhat self-conscious when he spoke or wrote French. If the Doctor spoke French as badly as he wrote it, his conversation must have been an extraordinary jargon; but Jefferson was too sensitive and had too much *amour-propre* to venture upon long discussions and conversations with people he did not know intimately. Most of his French letters were written by Short, who became rapidly a master of the language, and we may presume that Jefferson never really felt at home in a purely French circle.

This was true at least of his first year in Paris. He had many fits of despondency and wondered at times whether he was not too old to accustom himself to strange people and to strange manners. He often experienced the usual longing of the trav-

---

[1] Chinard, "Trois Amitiés Françaises de Jefferson." Paris, 1927.
[2] Most of her letters to Jefferson are in the Jefferson Coolidge Collection of the Massachusetts Historical Society.

eler for his native land: "I am now of an age which does not easily accommodate itself to new modes of living and new manners," he wrote to Baron Geismer, the former prisoner of Charlottesville; "and I am savage enough to prefer the woods, the wilds and independence of Monticello, to all the brilliant pleasures of this gay capital. I shall therefore, rejoin myself to my native country with new attachments and exaggerated esteem for its advantages." [1] It was probably on these occasions that he took refuge in the most silent of all places, a Carthusian monastery, a very strange abode for one who has been accused of being a fierce anti-clerical:

He also had rooms in the Carthusian Monastery on Mount Calvary; the boarders, of whom I think there were forty, carried their own servants, and took their breakfasts in their own rooms. They assembled to dinner only. They had the privilege of walking in the gardens, but as it was a hermitage, it was against the rules of the house for any voices to be heard outside of their own rooms, hence the most profound silence. The author of "Anarcharsis" was a boarder at the time, and many others who had reasons for a temporary retirement from the world. Whenever he had a press of business, he was in the habit of taking his papers and going to the hermitage, where he spent sometimes a week or more till he had finished his work. The hermits visited him occasionally in Paris, and the Superior made him a present of an ivory broom that was turned by one of the brothers.[2]

From time to time this same mood recurred:

I am burning the candle of life without present pleasure or future object — he wrote to Mrs. Trist in 1786. — A dozen or twenty years ago this scene would have amused me; but I am past the age for changing habits. I take all the fault on myself, as it is impossible to be among a people who wish more to make one happy — a people of the very best character it is possible for one to have. We have no idea in America of the real French character.[3]

---

[1] April 6, 1785. "Domestic Life", p. 80.
[2] Diary of Martha. *Ibid.*, p. 74.   [3] *Ibid.*, p. 84.

Not foreign to this despondency was the bad news that came from America. His youngest daughter Lucy died in the fall of 1784 and he was not satisfied until he had his remaining daughter near him in Paris, and Mary, familiarly called Polly, had joined her sister in the best convent of the French capital.

Between social duties and pleasures, dinners at the house of Lafayette, meetings of the Committees of Commerce, interviews with Vergennes, preparation of long letters to be sent home to keep his Government informed of the situation in Europe, correction of the proofs of the "Notes on Virginia", interviews with former French volunteers clamoring for their back pay, visits to shops and factories, Jefferson was a very busy man indeed. But exacting as his occupations were, he found time to escape from Paris on three different occasions to see something of France and Europe. In 1786 he journeyed to England, traveled in France and Italy in the spring of the following year, and visited Holland and the Rhine shortly before leaving for home. The diaries he kept during these trips are both revealing and disappointing. They demonstrate how little of European culture had penetrated his American mind, how carefully he preserved himself from the contamination of European manners and ways of thinking. In some respects it must be confessed that Jefferson remained very narrow and provincial, and almost a Philistine in his outlook.

The most damning document is the outline he made for Rutledge and Shippen on June 3, 1788, though in some respects it shows good judgment, as when Jefferson recommends "not to judge of the manners of the people from the people you will naturally see the most of : tavern keepers, *valets de place*, and postillions." — "These are the hackneyed rascals of every country. Of course they must never be considered when we calculate the national character." He manifested the same good sense in recommending always to ask for the *vin du pays* when traveling. But the worst comes in his enumeration of the

"Objects of Attention for an American." It has to be read
to be believed and should be transcribed here almost in full:

1. Agriculture. Everything belonging to this art, and whatever
has a near relation to it. . . . 2. Mechanical arts, so far as they
respect things necessary in America, and inconvenient to be transported thither ready-made, such as forges, stone quarries, boat
bridges, etc. 3. Lighter mechanical arts, and manufactures. Some
of these will be worth a superficial view; but circumstances rendering it impossible that America should become a manufacturing
country during the time of any man now living, it would be a waste
of attention to examine these minutely. 4. Gardens peculiarly
worth the attention of an American, because it is the country of
all others where the noblest gardens may be made without expense. . . . 5. Architecture worth a great attention. As we
double our numbers every twenty years, we must double our
houses. . . . It is, then, among the most important arts; it is
desirable to introduce taste into an art which shows so much.
6. Painting, Statuary. Too expensive for the state of wealth
among us. It would be useless, therefore, and preposterous, for us
to make ourselves connoisseurs in those arts. They are worth
seeing, but not studying. 7. Politics of each country, well worth
studying so far as respects internal affairs. Examine their influence
on the happiness of the people. Take every possible occasion for
entering into the houses of the laborers, and especially at the moment
of their repast; see what they eat, how they are clothed, whether
they are obliged to work too hard. . . . 8. Courts. To be seen
as you would see the tower of London or menagerie of Versailles
with their lions, tigers, hyenas, and other beasts of prey, standing
in the same relation to their fellows. . . . Their manners, could
you ape them, would not make you beloved in your own country,
nor would they improve it could you introduce them there to the
exclusion of that honest simplicity now prevailing in America, and
worthy of being cherished.

The man who wrote these lines was certainly not denationalized; the emancipated Virginian had unconsciously retained a

puritanical distrust of purely æsthetic enjoyments. He seems to have taken a sort of wicked pleasure in denying himself the disinterested joys of the artist and philosopher and his travels in Europe were no "sentimental journey." It cannot even be maintained that the views expressed in the letter to Shippen were a paradox and that he felt free to enjoy the pleasures from which he strove to protect his fellow countrymen. Most revealing in this respect is the following passage from a letter written to Lafayette, when he was traveling along the Riviera:

In the great cities I go to see, what travellers think alone worthy of being seen; but I make a job of it, and generally gulp it all down in a day. On the other hand, I am never satisfied with rambling through the fields and farms, examining the culture and cultivators, with a degree of curiosity which makes some take me to be a fool, and others to be much wiser than I am.[1]

He seems to have been dominated by the same utilitarian preoccupations during his English journey. There he noted carefully all the peculiarities of English gardens, visiting all the show places with Whateley's book on gardening in his pocket: "My inquiries," he himself said, "were directed chiefly to such practical things as might enable me to estimate the expense of making and maintaining a garden in that style." This is why the only thing worth noticing at Kew was an Archimedes screw for raising water, of which he made a sketch. His conclusions were summed up in a letter to John Page after he came back to Paris. England had totally disappointed him. The "pleasure gardens", to be sure, went far beyond his ideas, but the city of London, though handsomer than Paris, was not so handsome as Philadelphia: "Their architecture is in the most wretched style I ever saw, not meaning to except America, where it is bad, not even Virginia, where it is worse than in any other part of America which I have seen." On the other hand,

[1] April 11, 1787. Jefferson Papers. Library of Congress.

the mechanical arts were carried to a wonderful perfection, but he took no joy in visiting manufactures and shops, since the view reminded him that the frivolity of his fellow country-men made them import many articles from London and thus pay tribute to a foreign nation.[1]

When he left Paris for the South of France he was in no more amiable mood. It was his first real contact with the French countryside and he was shocked beyond words at the sight of the first villages he passed through from Sens to Ver-manton. He could not understand why the French peasants insisted on living close together in villages instead of building their houses on the grounds they cultivated. He racked his brains for an explanation and could find no better one than to suppose that they were "collected by that dogma of their religion which makes them believe, that to keep the Creator in good humor with His own works, they must mumble a mass every day." The people were illy clothed; the sight of women and children carrying heavy burdens and laboring with the hoe made the Virginian slave-owner conclude that "in a civilized country, men never expose their wives and children to labor above their force and sex, as long as their own labor can pro-tect them from it." But he nowhere expressed any emotional distress nor heartfelt sympathy for these poor wretches and concluded that if there were no beggars it was probably an effect of the police.[2]

On the other hand, he noted every detail of the fabrication of Burgundy wine, enumerated the different vintages, the cost of casks, bottles, methods of transportation and market-ing, the price of "*vin ordinaire*", of oil, butter, cattle, the culti-vation of olive trees and fig trees and capers. Monuments are described with a mathematical eye, many small points noted, columns described, ornaments studied, but the only personal

---

[1] May 4, 1786. Memorial Edition, V, 303.
[2] *Ibid.*, XVII, 153.

impression elicited by Arles is that "The principal monument here, is an amphitheatre, the external portico of which is tolerably complete."

What is true of France is even more true of Italy. At Milan the cathedral is not even mentioned, but "the salon of the Casa Belgiosa is superior to anything I have ever seen." And he adds immediately, "The mixture called Scaiola, of which they make their walls and floors, is so like the finest marble as to be scarcely distinguishable from it." Pages are given to the fabrication of Parmesan cheese. Once, however, in walking along the shore from Louano to Alberga, he could not resist the enchantment of the landscape. There he noted the remarkable coloration of the Mediterranean and was puzzled by it, but he also added, let it be marked to his credit:

If any person wished to retire from his acquaintances, to live absolutely unknown, and yet in the midst of physical enjoyments, it should be in some of the little villages of this coast, where air, water and earth concur to offer what each has most precious. Here are nightingales, beccaficas, ortolans, pheasants, partridges, quails, a superb climate, and the power of changing it from summer to winter at any moment, by ascending the mountains. The earth furnishes wine, oil, figs, oranges, and every production of the garden, in every season. The sea yields lobsters, crabs, oysters, thunny, sardines, anchovies etc. Ortolans sell at this time at thirty sous, equal to one shilling sterling, the dozen.

A queer mixture of suppressed artistic emotions and avowed culinary preoccupations. Shades of Rousseau and Wordsworth, to mention the nightingale and the ortolans in one breath! But one thing at least we must be thankful for is his lack of pretence and conventional admiration. It is, after all, refreshing to find a traveler who does not copy from his guidebook and does not fall into raptures and worked-up ecstasies. He came back through "Luc, Brignolles, Avignon, Vaucluse", simply noting that "there are fine trout in the stream of Vau-

cluse and the valley abounds particularly with nightingales."
He saw Nîmes, Montpellier, Frontignan, where he discussed
the manufacture and price of wine; he passed through Car-
cassonne and was much interested in the canal and "the carp
caught there", but did not mention the walls; he stayed several
days at Bordeaux, measured the remains of a Roman amphi-
theater and made a thorough study of the wines; "Chateau
Margau, La Tour de Ségur, Hautbrion, Chateau de la Fite,
Pontac, Sauternes, Barsac." He visited Nantes, Rennes,
Angers, Tours, and ascertained the truth of the allegations of
the famous "growth of shells unconnected with animal bodies"
mentioned by Voltaire and discussed in the "Notes on Virginia." He saw Chanteloup and heard a nightingale there,
but was far more interested in "an ingenious contrivance to
hide the projecting steps of a stair-case."

The same utilitarian preoccupation reappears most conspicuously in his "Memorandums on a Tour from Paris to Amsterdam, Strasburg, and back to Paris" (March, 1788). At
Amsterdam he studied the Dutch wheelbarrow, the canal to
raise ships over the Pampus, joists of houses, the aviary of
Mr. Ameshoff near Harlem; he made a sketch of the Hope's
House "of a capricious appearance yet a pleasant one" — an
architectural atrocity if ever there was one. At Düsseldorf
"the gallery of paintings is sublime", but equally interesting
is the hog of this country (Westphalia) "of which the celebrated
ham is made which sells at eight and a half pence sterling the
pound." If he saw the cathedral at Cologne he forbore to
mention it, but at Coblenz he had his first taste of the Moselle
wine. It would be cruel to reproduce his description of the
"clever ruin at Hanau, with the hermitage in which is a good
figure of a hermit in plaster, colored to the life, with a table
and a book before him, in the attitude of contemplation."

And yet, when the worst is told, one may wonder whether
there would not be some unfairness in judging Jefferson merely

from these memoranda. There he noted information for which he foresaw some further use, interesting knowledge which could be utilized at Monticello or for the benefit of his fellow countrymen. How to plant and prune the vines and the olive trees; how to make cheese and oil; how to introduce the "St. Foin", new vegetables, new crops such as rice, new industries such as the silkworm and mulberry tree; how to build a house; all this required exactness and precision and could scarcely be trusted to memory. Pleasant impressions of travel on the contrary, could always be evoked through the imagination and would lose very little of their charm and value with time. Furthermore to put down these impressions in black and white would have required a certain process of analysis entirely foreign to Puritan consciousness, and a Puritan Jefferson had remained in his speech and manners far more than he himself believed. There was in these purely æsthetic pleasures something really too personal to be indulged in, at least in writing. Once, however, he did away with all the restraint imposed upon him by education and the "habits of his country"; it is in the well-known letter written from Nîmes to Madame de Tessé. Parts of it at least, in all fairness to Jefferson, have to be quoted here as a contrast to the dryness and objectiveness of the notes on travel . . .

Here I am, Madam, gazing whole hours at the Maison Quarrée, like a lover at his mistress. . . . This is the second time I have been in love since I left Paris. The first was with a Diana at the Château de Laye-Epinaye in Beaujolais, a delicious morsel of sculpture, by M. A. Slodtz. This, you will say, was in rule, to fall in love with a female beauty; but with a house, it is out of all precedent. No, Madam, it is not without a precedent in my own history. While in Paris, I was violently smitten with the Hôtel de Salm, and used to go to the Tuileries almost daily to look at it. The loueuse des chaises — inattentive to my passion — never had the complaisance to place a chair there, so that sitting on the parapet, and twisting my neck around to see the object of my admiration, I generally left with a torti-colli.

From Lyons to Nismes I have been nourished with the remains of Roman grandeur. They have always brought you to my mind, because I know your affection for whatever is Roman and noble. At Vienna I thought of you. But I am glad you were not here; for you would have seen me more angry than, I hope, you will ever see me. The Praetorian palace, as it is called — comparable, for its fine proportions, to the Maison Quarrée — defaced by the barbarians who have converted it to its present purpose, its beautiful fluted Corinthian columns cut out, in parts, to make space for Gothic windows, and hewed down, in the residue, to the plane of the buildings, was enough, you must admit, to disturb my composure. At Orange too, I thought of you. I was sure you had seen with pleasure the sublime triumphal arch of Marius at the entrance of the city. I went then to the Arenae. Would you believe, Madam, that in this eighteenth century, in France, under the reign of Louis XVI, they are at this moment pulling down the circular wall of this superb remain, to pave a road? And that too, from a hill which is itself en entire mass of stone, just as fit, and more accessible.[1]

This is indeed a charming letter; but why did he not write more often in this vein? Why did he send to Martha moralizing and edifying letters when he was traveling in Southern France and Italy? His latent puritanism, as already shown, may partly account for this reticence, but this came from a deeper feeling. He had already protested in his "Notes on Virginia" against the claim made by Europe to intellectual supremacy. He realized, however, how powerful was the attraction of the great centers of European culture on young America, and was afraid that the introduction of foreign arts, foreign literature, foreign customs, and "mode" might corrupt the very springs of American life. This blind admiration of everything European constituted one of the greatest dangers if America wished to develop on her own soil a civilization

[1] Nismes, March 20, 1787.

of her own.　Friends in Virginia had to be convinced that an American youth, brought up on a strictly American diet, would in nowise be inferior to most Europeans.　If one insisted upon sending a young man to Europe, the chances were that he would learn nothing essential, that on the contrary he would lose many of his native qualities and at any rate his native innocence and purity of mind.　This appears most conspicuously in a letter written to J. B. Bannister, Junior, who had manifested the intention of sending his son to Europe.　There Jefferson proceeded to denounce the features of European civilization as vehemently as any Puritan preacher and with the same frankness of expression.　To enumerate the disadvantages of sending a youth to Europe "would require a volume", so he had to select a few.　England is shortly disposed of: "If he goes to England, he learns drinking, horse racing, and boxing," for those are the peculiarities of English education.　If he goes to the continent he will acquire a fondness for luxury and dissipation, he will contract a partiality for aristocracy and monarchy; he will soon be led to consider "fidelity to the marriage bed as an ungentlemanly practice."　He will become denationalized and recollecting "the voluptuary dress and arts of the European women, will pity and despise the chaste affections and simplicity of those of his own country."　He will return to America "a foreigner", speaking and writing his own tongue "like a foreigner", and therefore unqualified to obtain those distinctions, which eloquence of the pen and tongue ensures in a free country."　There can be only one conclusion after such a fierce denunciation of Europe:

It appears to me, then, that an American, coming to Europe for education, loses in his knowledge, in his morals, in his health, in his habits, and in his happiness.　I had entertained only doubts on this head before I came to Europe: what I see and hear, since I came here proves more than I had expected.　Cast your eye over America: who are the men of most learning, of most eloquence, most beloved

by their countrymen and most trusted and promoted by them?
They are those who have been educated among them, and whose
manners, morals, and habits, are perfectly homogeneous with those
of the country.[1]

Very bold indeed would have been the American father who,
with such a frightful picture before his eyes, would have sent
his son to Europe.

Thus we are led to a very unexpected conclusion. There
is little doubt that Jefferson's democratic theories were confirmed and clarified by his prolonged stay in Europe. But this
was not due to the lessons he received from the French philosophers. He had gone to France under the misapprehension
that he would be considered there as a "savage from the mountains of America"; he had been dazzled at first by the splendor of the old world, but he had soon overcome his admiration
and arrived at the conclusion that the game was not worth the
candle. Life in Paris was very pleasant, but some one had to
foot the bill, and the general fate of humanity was most deplorable in Europe. Such are the general impressions he sent
to his friend Bellini one year after arriving in Paris:

It is a true picture of that country to which they say we shall pass
hereafter; and where we are to see God and his angels in splendor,
and crowds of the damned trampled under their feet. The great
mass of the people suffer under physical and moral oppression; but
the condition of the great if more closely observed cannot compare
with the degree of happiness which is enjoyed in America. Among
them there is no family life, no conjugal love, no domestic happiness;
intrigues of love occupy the young and those of ambition, the elder
part of the great.

Much, very much inferior, this, to the tranquil, permanent
felicity with which domestic society in America blesses most of
its inhabitants; leaving them to follow steadily those pur-

[1] To J. Bannister, Junior, October 15, 1785. Memorial Edition, V, 185.

suits which health and reason approve, and rendering truly delicious the intervals of those pursuits!

If one looks to another field, the situation is very similar. "In science, the mass of the people are two centuries behind ours; their literature half a dozen years before us." But that is no serious inconvenience; books which are really good acquire a reputation in that lapse of time and then pass over to America, while poor books, controversial and uncertain knowledge are naturally weeded out, so that America is not bothered with that "swarm of nonsensical publications which issue daily from a thousand presses, and perishes almost in issuing."

On some points, however, Europeans have a decided superiority over the Americans: they have more amiable manners, they are more polite, more temperate, "they do not terminate the most sociable meals by transforming themselves into brutes. I have never seen a man drunk in France, even among the lowest of the people."

Finally in the arts there is no possible comparison:

Were I to proceed to tell you how much I enjoy their architecture, sculpture, painting, music, I should want words. It is in these arts they shine. The last of them particularly, is an enjoyment the deprivation of which with us, cannot be calculated. I am almost ready to say, it is the only thing which from my heart I envy them, and which, in spite of all the authority of the Decalogue, I do covet.[1]

Nor are we to believe that in Jefferson's opinion this was a small achievement. Had he been more poetically inclined he might have repeated the apostrophe of the old poet: "France mother of all the arts." But when all is told, the fact remained that Europe had more to learn from America than she could possibly give to the new nation, and thereupon Jefferson started to "boost" his own country. Protesting against a pseudo-discovery of an English wheelwright, he de-

[1] To Bellini, September 30, 1785. Memorial Edition, V, 153.

clared that the idea had been stolen from Doctor Franklin who had observed it in Pennsylvania, Delaware and Jersey, and the Jersey farmers might have borrowed it from Homer, "for ours are the only farmers who can read Homer." [1]   Against the architectural feats of the Europeans it is not unfair to claim the superiority of American scenery, particularly of the Virginia marvels, such as the Natural Bridge, for "that kind of pleasure surpasses much in my estimation, whatever I find on this side of the Atlantic." [2]

At the end of his journey in France and Italy he conceded that there are indeed in these countries "things worth our imitation." But he immediately added, "the accounts from our country give me to believe that we are not in a condition to hope of the imitation of anything good." [3]   In the meantime it is better for the Americans to stay at home, for "travelling makes men wiser, but less happy"; and he wrote to Peter Carr, whose education he had undertaken to direct: "There is no place where your pursuit of knowledge will be so little obstructed by foreign objects, as your own country, nor any, wherein the virtues of the heart will be less exposed to be weakened." [4]

[1] To Crevecoeur, January 15, 1787.   Memorial Edition, VI, 53.
[2] To Carmichael, December 26, 1786.
[3] To Skipwith, July 28, 1787.   Memorial Edition, VI, 187.
[4] August 10, 1787.   *Ibid.*, VI, 262.

CHAPTER II

GALLO–AMERICAN COMMERCE AND THE DEBT QUESTION

AFTER Franklin's departure from Paris, Jefferson was left officially in charge of the diplomatic relations of the United States with the French Court. Adams was in London and Carmichael in Madrid, and with them he exchanged extensive communications. But the Paris legation was really the headquarters of American diplomacy, and the problems that came up taxed the ingenuity and all the intellectual resources Jefferson could command.

Summing up his activities in Paris, he declared with too much modesty in his "Autobiography":

My duties, at Paris, were confined to a few objects; the receipts of our whale oils, salted fish, and salt meat, on favorable terms; the admission of our rice on equal terms with that of Piedmont, Egypt and the Levant; a mitigation of the monopolies of our tobacco by the Farmers-general, and a free admission of our productions into their islands, were the principal commercial objects which required attention; and on these occasions, I was powerfully aided by all the influence and the energies of the Marquis de La Fayette, who proved himself equally zealous for the friendship and welfare of both nations."

As a matter of fact, Jefferson's duties extended to many other subjects, of which the most important and at any rate the most perplexing may have been the settlement of the debt question. This problem, as we shall presently see, haunted Jefferson's mind and was never separated by him from the purely commercial questions. In many respects the situation then existing between the United States and France was very similar to the present situation and certainly not easier to solve. An estimate of Jefferson's career that would leave out this particular side of his activities when in France, would necessarily be incomplete, if not misleading. A large part of the minister's time was devoted, not to philosophical conversations with Helvétius' friends but to obstinate, patient, and harassing endeavor to obtain for his country commercial rights and even privileges that would enable her to pay off her debt to Europe. In spite of his affected scorn for figures and statistics, the "philosopher" demonstrated an unusual business ability.

The tobacco trade in which the Southern States and particularly Virginia were vitally interested was at that time entirely in the hands of the Farmers-general, whose monopoly was not administered to the best interests of either the American growers or the French consumers. Being closely allied with some of the prominent economists and entirely in sympathy with their views, Lafayette was naturally against the farming of taxes on tobacco. But as he realized that there was very little hope of doing away entirely with the system, he contented himself at first with employing his best efforts to facilitate the direct importation of tobacco into France. As early as May, 1785, he managed to obtain a copy of a document indicating that some London dealers were offering to the Farmers-general large quantities of Virginia tobacco. He communicated the document at once to Jefferson, and suggested that it was important for both countries to eliminate the London middlemen. Direct commercial relations should be established between France and America, not only as a matter of patriotism, but also as a matter of interest.[1]

This proposed change in the traditional policy of the Farmers-general, who were accustomed to deal with British intermediaries, met with a strong opposition from the Farmers-

[1] Jefferson to the Governor of Maryland. June 16, 1785. Memorial Edition, V, 8.

general. For reasons which they did not state openly, they refused either to deal with independent American growers, or to buy from a new and strictly American company planned by Jefferson.[1]

Unable to overcome the resistance of the Farmers-general, Jefferson decided that the next step would be to fight the monopoly and to persuade the Court to do away with it. It was a logical more than a truly diplomatic procedure, since Jefferson took upon himself to meddle in the internal affairs of the government to which he was accredited. But Jefferson, without being the originator of the famous "shirt-sleeve" diplomacy, was not the man to let diplomatic proprieties stand in the way of the best interests of his country. Furthermore, he was quite sincere in his belief that he was acting to the greatest advantage of both France and America. He therefore wrote to Vergennes a long letter, in which he stated the advantages which would accrue to the royal treasury from the abolition of the tobacco monopoly.[2]

There is no indication that Vergennes resented in any way Jefferson's suggestion; but there is no evidence either that he paid any attention to it. Things remained in the same condition to the end of the year. Up to that date, Lafayette had fought as a free lance the commercial battle of the United States, using his personal influence and family connections to undermine the prestige of the Farmers-general. At the beginning of 1786, Calonne, yielding to his solicitations, formed the Comité du Commerce composed of Farmers-general, inspectors of commerce, and members of the council, in order to study the future of the commercial relations between France and the United States. Lafayette was appointed to the committee on February 9, 1786. He had very little training in economics and had never displayed any particular aptitude for financial

---

[1] To Messrs. French and Nephew. July 13, 1785. Memorial Edition, V, 34.
[2] August 15, 1785. *Ibid.*, V, 68.

problems. But back of him was Jefferson, and on the committee Lafayette was nothing but the spokesman of the American Plenipotentiary. The account of his speeches before the committee, given by Brissot, and reprinted in a note to the "Memoirs of General Lafayette", is simply the résumé of a letter sent by Jefferson to Vergennes six months earlier. Jefferson prompted him, furnished him with figures and statistics, and in a letter written at the eleventh hour urged him to expose the fundamental dishonesty of the Farmers-general. Since, according to their own figures, said Jefferson, they lose annually over four million livres by the farming of tobacco "the king, in favor to them, should discontinue the bail; and they cannot ask its continuance without acknowledging they have given in a false state of quantities and sums." [1]

Standing alone in the committee against a strong combination of skilled financiers, Lafayette was fighting for a lost cause without any profit to himself or any visible hope of success.[2]

Both Lafayette and Jefferson were outmaneuvered by the financiers. They professed that they were willing to denounce their contracts with the London merchants, and thus seemed to accomplish a grand patriotic gesture, but they granted to the American financier, Robert Morris, the exclusive privilege of buying tobacco for them and thus defeated the main purpose of Jefferson. The minister had to confess that he was beaten, although he had spared no pains to strike at the root of the monopoly. "The persons interested in it are too powerful to be opposed, even by the interest of the whole country." [3]

But it was not in his character ever to give up; he soon renewed the attack at another point. First he succeeded in postponing for six months the effect of the new lease to Morris, and thus permitted American importers who had accumulated

---

[1] Jefferson Papers. Library of Congress, Feb. 20, 1786.
[2] Lafayette's letter. March 18, 1786. *Ibid.*
[3] To the Governor of Virginia, January 24, 1786. Memorial Edition, V, 253.

stocks in Lorient to sell them directly to the Farmers-general. Some time later he partially nullified the concession to Morris by obtaining an order from the council "obliging the Farmers-general to purchase from such other merchants as shall offer fifteen thousand hogshead of tobacco", and to grant to the sellers in other respects the same terms as they had granted Robert Morris.

Thus, indirectly but very effectively, Jefferson finally achieved his purpose: to undermine an odious monopoly which caused a great loss to the planters of his country; to enable the American consumers to buy directly from France manufactured products, or at least those "commodities which it is more advantageous to us to buy here than in England, or elsewhere"; finally "to reinforce the motives for a friendship from this country towards ours. — This friendship we ought to cultivate closely, considering the present dispositions of England towards us." [1]

In addition, he flattered himself that he had taught the French some sound economic principles:

I have been for some time occupied in endeavouring to destroy the root of the evils which the tobacco trade encounters in this country, by making the ministers sensible that merchants will not bring a commodity to a market, where but one person is allowed to buy it; and that so long as that single purchaser is obliged to go to foreign markets for it, he must pay for it in coin and not in commodities. These truths have made their way to the mind of the ministry insomuch, as to have delayed the execution of the new lease of the farms, six months. It is renewed, however, for three years, but so as not to render impossible a reformation of the great evil. They are sensible to the evil, but it is so interwoven with their fiscal system, that they find it hazardous to disentangle. The temporary distress, too, of the revenue, they are not prepared to meet. My hopes, therefore, are weak, though not quite desperate. [2]

[1] To James Ross, May 8, 1786. Memorial Edition, V, 321.
[2] To James Ross, May 8, 1786. *Ibid.*, V, 329.

One might well wonder to what extent these "truths" were as new to the French as Jefferson seemed to believe, and to what extent he was operative in strengthening the opposition to the Farmers-general, already very strong in France. However that may be, the American minister learned from the French example as much as he taught the members of the committee. The tobacco monopoly was to him another object lesson on the danger of farming taxes, and he did not forget it.

Even greater obstacles were encountered by Jefferson and Lafayette in their effort to develop commercial transactions with New England. The negotiations extended over three years and would be worth relating in detail.[1]   Jefferson, bent on breaking customs barriers and obtaining free entrance for the products of New England fisheries, brought forward every possible argument to fight the doctrine of commercialism and summed up his case in a letter sent to Lafayette, but evidently intended for the committee.   There for the first time he pointed out the necessary connection existing between the tariff question and the repayment of the French debt.   The problem of "transfers" is not a new one, and Jefferson's reasoning sounds strangely familiar to all those who have paid any attention to our present problems of debt settlement, reparations, and tariff. The following passage seems particularly worth quoting:

On running over the catalogue of American imports, France will naturally mark out those articles which she could supply us to advantage; and she may safely calculate, that, after a little time shall have enabled us to get rid of our present incumbrances, and some remains of attachment to the particular forms of manufacture to which we have been habituated, we shall take those articles which she can furnish, on as good terms as other nations, to whatever extent she will enable us to pay for them.   It is her interest therefore, as well as ours, to multiply the means of payment.   These must be

---

[1] For a brief but satisfactory treatment see W. K. Woolery. "The Relation of Thomas Jefferson to American Foreign Policy, 1783-1793." Baltimore, 1927.

found in the catalogue of our exports, and among these will be seen neither gold nor silver. We have no mines of either of those metals. Produce therefore is all we can offer.[1]

The conclusion was that it was imperative to obtain such abatement of duties and even such exemptions as the importance of the article might justify, in the hope that his country would be enabled to build up a commercial credit of about 275,000 louis, which would provide for the service and amortization of the American debt to France.

Thanks to the unrelenting efforts of Lafayette and also to the sympathetic attitude of the committee, a series of *arrêts du conseil* listed in a letter to Monroe was finally obtained.[2] There was little hope at first that they would be countersigned, but in October of the same year Jefferson, with evident satisfaction, was able to inform Jay of the new regulations granting free ports to America, abolishing export taxes on brandies, and for a year the tax on whale oil and spermaceti, on potash, furs, leather, timber, trees, and shrubbery, brought either in American or French bottoms. Every effort had been made not only to place the United States on the footing of the most favored nation, but to encourage her infant industries and manufactures. The new regulations approved by Calonne did much to free America from her commercial subservience to Great Britain and also reinforce, according to Jefferson's wishes, the motives for a "friendship from France towards America."

This was by no means the end of all difficulties; the abatement on whale oil was only temporary and Jefferson was never able to obtain entire satisfaction in respect to the tobacco trade, but there is no doubt that the situation had greatly improved.

Even during the last months of his stay in France he never overlooked an opportunity to further the commercial interests of the United States. His fear to see his fellow countrymen

---

[1] Letter to Lafayette, July 17, 1786. Library of Congress.
[2] July 9, 1786. Memorial Edition, V, 357.

"over-trade themselves and embark into the ocean of speculation" had not abated. He still believed that "we have no
occasion for more commerce than to take off our superfluous
produce", and tobacco was clearly in that class.[1] But at that
time there arose an opportunity both to develop commercial
relations and to be of distinct service to France. The years
that immediately precede the French Revolution were marked
by a very distressing food shortage in France and particularly
in the capital. This was one of the most disquieting problems
confronting the Committee of Commerce and the city syndics.
Jefferson, because of his connections with Lafayette, Du Pont
de Nemours, and Mr. Ethis de Corny, was particularly well
informed on the situation and he turned his best efforts to
induce the government to remedy it through the importation of
American products. He thought that besides the salt fish
from New England, salt meat and corn beef would constitute
a desirable addition to the French diet and he undertook a
campaign to convert the French to the idea. One of his last
letters to Necker, on September 26, 1789, was to recommend
the importation of salted provisions from the United States,
appraising the quality of American salt meat, for "the experience of a great part of America, which is fed almost entirely on
it, proves it to be as wholesome as fresh meat." [2]

In spite of all the obstacles to the development of the Gallo-
American commerce because of the deep-rooted French horror
of innovations and changes, the efforts of Jefferson and his
friends were not wholly unavailing. According to Mr. Woolery,
in 1789 importations from the United States amounted to
140,959 barrels of flour, 3,664,576 bushels of wheat and
12,340,000 pounds of rice. Vessels coming from the United
States to French ports in this year included thirteen French,
forty-three English and one hundred and sixty-three American ;

[1] To Washington, August 14, 1787. Memorial Edition, VI, 277.
[2] *Ibid.*, VII, 478.

the tonnage of American vessels was 19,173 in 1788 and 24,173 in 1789.   Exports to France in 1788 were valued at $1,384,246; to French possessions in America $3,284,656; and from them, $155,136 and $1,913,212 respectively.   In this trade the American tonnage engaged was approximately ten times that of the French.   The philosopher had proved himself a first-class commercial agent.   He had built up trade relations which would have consolidated the friendship between the two countries if the Revolution had not intervened.   But no real friendship can exist between creditor and debtor; the debt problem was no less important than the commercial problem, and Jefferson displayed on this occasion an ingenuity and a diplomatic skill no less worthy of commendation.

When he took charge of the legation at Paris the finances of the United States were in a deplorable condition.   Loans made by the Farmers-general, by Beaumarchais, by the King of France, and loans contracted in Holland and in Spain, constituted the most important outstanding liabilities of the American Government.   In 1783 the situation as reported to Congress was as follows:

To the Farmers-general of France, livres .	1,000,000
To Beaumarchais	3,000,000
To King of France, to the end of 1782 . .	28,000,000
To same for 1783	6,000,000

To this total was to be added a loan from Holland for $671,200, and $150,000 borrowed from Spain by Jay.   Interest was coming in at the rate of four per cent. on the French loan, making it a total of approximately $7,885,000.   The domestic situation was far worse; the States had plunged into issues of paper money: $241,552,780 had been issued in bills of credit by Congress, and $209,524,776 by the States.

If it is remembered that private investors had bought American paper rather recklessly, that important sums were due to

England, and that the United States could not even meet the interest on the debts without further borrowing, it is small wonder that European creditors began to wonder whether they would ever be repaid. The first task confronting the new Minister Plenipotentiary was to convince them that the United States as then organized had a sufficient stability to allay all fears. Jefferson undertook at once to clarify the situation. In a letter to the Dutch bankers, N. and J. Van Staphorst, he asserted that no man in America had ever entertained any doubt that "our foreign debt is to be paid fully." He significantly added: "Were I the holder of any of them, I should not have the least fear of their full payment." But he had to call the attention of the bankers to the fact that some international notes were issued for paper money debts, and those of course would be subject to a certain depreciation, to be settled by Congress according to carefully worked out tables. The safer thing, therefore, for European investors was to beware of and to avoid any speculation on American bills and "foreigners should be sure that they are well advised, before they meddle with them, or they may suffer." [1] He repeated the same advice on October 25: "It is a science which bids defiance to the powers of reason."

With the particulars of the different loans obtained by Jefferson while he was in France, and with the transactions that took place in Holland, we cannot deal here. It would be a study well worth undertaking separately, and one for which there is abundant material not yet utilized in the Jefferson papers, particularly in his correspondence with Dumas, the agent at the Hague. We shall restrict ourselves, however, to the political aspect of the debt settlement during Jefferson's mission.

The French were at first very polite about it; without insisting in any way on the question of payment, Vergennes simply asked Jefferson whether "the condition of American finances

[1] July 30, 1785. Memorial Edition, V, 45.

was improving." The French minister did not even mention the possibilities of the United States paying the arrears of the interest; but Jefferson suffered and irked, thinking that he was probably expected to mention it first, while he could not do so without instructions and there were "no visible means to pay anything for the present." [1]

Curiously enough, the matter came to a head with England during the trip made by Jefferson in the spring of 1786. He held several conferences with the British merchants and tried to obtain with them a sort of compromise by which American merchants would repay in full the capital of debts contracted before and after the war, but withdrawing payment of the interest for the period of the war. It was then that Jefferson put forth the principle he was to maintain persistently with the French, — namely that the matter of commerce and the question of the debts could not be separated, "were it only as a means of enabling our country to pay its debts." [2]

The chief fault of Jefferson's solution, however, was that there was very little America could sell to England, while the Americans themselves were eagerly buying goods manufactured in England. There was great danger of seeing that economic vassalage perpetuated, for "instead of a proper equilibrium, everything at present lies all in the British scale." [3] Importations being permitted, fashion and folly requiring English products, the country was sinking deeper and deeper into poverty, and all the news on the matter received by Jefferson "filled him with despair."

However, something had to be done at once in the case of the French debt, as Jefferson knew that the French Minister of Finance was "at his wit's end to raise supplies for the ensuing year." [4] It does not appear that the French Court had made

[1] To Jay, August 14, 1785. Memorial Edition, V, 65.
[2] To John Jay, April 23, 1786. *Ibid.*, V, 300.
[3] To T. Pleasants, May 8, 1786. *Ibid.*, V, 324.
[4] To Jay, September 26, 1786. *Ibid.*, V, 426.

any representation on the debt to the American Plenipotentiary, but Jefferson fully realized that he was placed in a position of inferiority as long as the vexing question remained unsettled and payments on the interest were overdue. This was the more deplorable, as France was the only European nation with which the United States could hope to develop really satisfactory relations. It was at this juncture that a very interesting proposition was made through Dumas by the Dutch bankers. The French debt's most objectionable feature was that it placed the American Government under direct obligation to the French; in other words, as we would say now, it was a political debt, but means might be found to change it into a purely commercial debt. If a company of bankers were formed to pay off France at once, the American Government would be able to treat with them on a business basis, the greatest advantage being that in case of delayed payments, no political pressure could be exerted or political advantage claimed.

The only objection to such a combination was that it could not be made without the consent of both the French and American governments, and negotiations to that effect would necessarily take a long time. To provide for the most pressing needs, Jefferson proposed to raise directly in Holland the four and twenty millions due to France as accrued interest. This would make a beginning and create a precedent. In the meantime Adams was urged to go to Holland to acquaint himself with the situation, so as to be able to present a definite solution to Congress on his return to America.[1] The French court remained very considerate and did not make any formal representations; but very harsh criticism of the failure of America to meet her obligations were heard during the Assemblée des Notables. The funds were so low that the American Government could not even pay its debts to the French officers who,

[1] To Jay, September 26, 1786. Memorial Edition, V, 426; to Adams, July 17, 1787. *Ibid.*, VI, 173; to James Madison, August 2, 1787. *Ibid.*, VI, 215.

because of their influence with the Court, should have received special consideration. Yet Congress did not seem to realize how pressing the matter was, and Jefferson could only repeat with real despair and disgust: "Would to heaven they would authorize you to take measures for transferring the debt of this country to Holland before you leave Europe." [1]

On their side, the French Court did their best to reassure the French creditors, and when the written report of the Assemblées des Notables appeared it had been considerably toned down, simply stating that:

. . . the interest of the claims of His Majesty on the United States of America, cannot be drawn out for the present, except as a document. The recovery of these claims, as well as principal as perhaps even interest, although they appear to rest on the most solid security, may, nevertheless, be long delayed, and should not consequently, be taken into account in estimating the annual revenue.

But even that mention seemed to Jefferson a reflection on the national honor of his country. He was harassed by French claimants; Beaumarchais had just placed in his hands a memorial to Congress; French officers were writing to him and calling on him, threatening to sell their claims to a single creditor, or to ask the court to intervene in their favor. But all the unfortunate American minister could answer was that Congress "would do in that business, what justice would require, and their means enable them." [2]

At the end of the same year he learned that Congress had rejected the proposition of the Dutch bankers, and he could not help expressing deep disappointment. One hope was left however: the sale of western lands then going on which would provide Congress with important liquid assets.

[1] To J. Adams, July 17, 1787. Memorial Edition, VI, 173.
[2] To John Jay, August 6, 1787. *Ibid.*, VI, 248.

I turn to this precious resource — he wrote to a friend — as that which will, in every event, liberate us from our domestic debt, and perhaps too, from our foreign one; and this much sooner than I had expected.   I do not think anything could have been done with them in Europe.   Individual speculators and sharpers had duped so many with their unlocated land-warrants, that every offer would be suspected.[1]

In the meantime something had to be done to reassure the creditors of the United States, and Jefferson pressed Dumas to publish a series of articles in the *Gazette of Leyden* to demonstrate the financial stability of his country.   The situation had to be presented as follows: two sales of five million and two million acres respectively had been made, another for four million was in process and Jefferson considered that these sales had absorbed seven million dollars of the domestic Federal debt.   The States had absorbed by taxation and otherwise about ten million dollars, so "that the debt stands now at about ten millions of dollars, and will probably be all absorbed in the course of next year.   There will remain then our foreign debt, between ten and twelve millions, including interest.   The sale of land will then go on for payment of this." [2]   But in spite of this official optimism the Commissioners of the Treasury had informed Willincks and Van Staphorsts that they should "not be able to remit one shilling till the New Government gets into action" and that consequently they were not to pay anything towards the interest of the Dutch loan except out of the proceeds of the last loan.   To which the Dutch bankers had answered that "there was not much prospect to raise as much on that new loan as would cover the next June interest and that the credit of the United States was in danger of being wiped off." [3]   As Adams was about to leave for America, Jefferson, at the request

---

[1] December 21, 1787. Memorial Edition, VI, 394.

[2] To Dumas, February 12, 1788. *Ibid.*, VI, 429.

[3] To Adams, February 6, 1787. *Ibid.*, VI, 419. To The Commissioners of the Treasury, Feb. 7, 1788. *Ibid.*, VI, 421.

of the Dutch bankers, met him at Amsterdam and for several days the two American envoys did their best to convince close-fisted financiers, who had speculated in American bonds and refused to do anything until paid for the interest on the domestic bonds they held. They finally yielded, but to avoid further embarrassment Jefferson and Adams decided to provide at one stroke for the years 1789 and 1790 by signing new bonds for a million florins, subject to approval of Congress.[1]

The real danger, as both Adams and Jefferson saw it, came from unwise speculation in American domestic bonds, since the bankers had tried to use these bonds as a sort of lever; consequently the transfer of domestic bonds to Europe was to be discouraged by every possible means. "If the transfer of these debts to Europe, meet with any encouragement from us, we can no more borrow money here, let our necessities be what they will."[2]

How desperate the situation was at that date appears in two letters written to General Washington May 2, 1788, and to James Madison, May 3, 1788.[3] Jefferson's visit at Amsterdam had convinced him that the credit of the United States was at its lowest ebb and in great danger of being reduced to nil. The nation with the highest credit was Great Britain, because the English never asked for a loan without providing by new taxes for the repayment of it. He indicated that no doubt was entertained by any one in Holland about the ultimate repayment of the capital, but that repeated failures to pay the interest on the old loans had stopped any further borrowing. As to the French debt, the Court had carefully avoided any public mention of it, "the government here, saying nothing about it, the public have supposed they wished to leave us at our ease

---

[1] March 16, 1788. Memorial Edition, VI, 438.
[2] To the Commissioners of the Treasury, March 29, 1788. *Ibid.*, VI, 433.
[3] *Ibid.*, VI, 447 and 445.

as to the payment.   It is now seen that they call for it, and they will publish annually the effect of that call."   The most pressing need was an order from the Treasury to pay the arrears for the last three years to the French officers.   With much difficulty Jefferson had prevented them from holding a meeting to agree on concerted action on the matter, and when he came back he prevented them from taking "desperate measures" till July.   But a solution could not be deferred much longer. The necessary sum was comparatively small: twenty thousand florins a year would have sufficed "to suppress these clamors", and through diplomacy he finally succeeded in staying the address they intended to send to Congress and to the king, asking him to intervene on their behalf.[1]

Fortunately the loan launched in Holland to meet the payment of the June interest had succeeded and had been finally ratified by Congress.[2]   It was a beginning that brought some respite to Jefferson, but he insisted again that the next step to take was the funding of the foreign debt, for the French Government expected "a very satisfactory provision for the payment of their debt, from the first session of the new Congress."[3]   He was enclosing two tables "showing what fund will suffice to discharge the principal and interest, as it shall become due aided by occasional loans, which the same fund will repay." This very detailed and technical proposal now preserved in the Jefferson papers of the Library of Congress would repay careful study.

During the spring of the same year, however, Jefferson made a startling discovery which added to his distress.   The international bankers of Amsterdam were not as politically disinterested as he had thought at first.   He even suspected that,

[1] To the Honorable, The Board of the Treasury, May 16, 1788.   Memorial Edition, VII, 9.

[2] To John Jay, May 23, 1788.   *Ibid.*, VII, 22; To the Commissioners of the Treasury, September 6, 1788.   *Ibid.*, VII, 136.

[3] To James Madison, November 18, 1788.   *Ibid.*, VII, 186.

by careful manipulations, they intended to keep control of the credit of the United States.

I have observed — wrote Jefferson — that as soon as a sum of interest is becoming due, they are able to borrow just that, and no more; or, at least, only so much more as may pay our salaries and keep us quiet . . . I think it possible, they may choose to support our credit to a certain point, and let it go no further, but at their will; to keep it poised, as that it may be at their mercy. By this, they may be sure to keep us in their own hands.[1]

This had to be remedied at once; energetic representations were sent to the bankers and an order of the Treasury was obtained deciding that "money for the captives and foreign affairs was to be furnished before any other payment of interest."[2]

In spite of these tremendous handicaps, due to the apathy of Congress, to the "stagnation" of American affairs, Jefferson succeeded, through sheer persistency and hard work, in gaining at least a few points. The history of his negotiations concerning the debt and the commerce of the United States may not be so dramatic and picturesque as some other episodes of his long career; but it cannot be neglected without doing injustice to his sense of duty, to his industry and above all to his political vision and understanding of international psychology. The application to the present situation is so obvious that it needs not to be elaborated upon. More fortunate than many recent negotiators, Jefferson had been able to obtain a settlement of the debt question satisfactory to both parties, and succeeded in eliminating the political factor from the situation; the debt to France was no longer an obstacle to the maintenance of friendly relations between the two countries. He was not the man to boast of his achievements but the legitimate pride he felt at having done his work to the best of his ability appears in

---

[1] To John Jay, March 12, 1788. Memorial Edition, VII, 296.
[2] To John Jay, May 9, 1788. *Ibid.*, VII, 345.

the letter he wrote to John Jay shortly before his departure from France :

I am well informed that our credit is now the first at that exchange (Amsterdam), (England not borrowing at present). Our five per cent. bonds have risen to ninety-seven and ninety-nine. They have been heretofore at ninety-three. There are, at this time, several companies and individuals here, in England and Holland, negotiating to sell large parcels of our *liquidated debt.* A bargain was concluded by one of these the other day, for six hundred thousand dollars. In the present state of our credit, every dollar of this debt will probably be transferred to Europe within a short time.[1]

[1] To John Jay, September 19, 1789.   Memorial Edition, VII, 471.

CHAPTER III

UNION AND ISOLATION

EVEN an incomplete survey of Jefferson's activities in Paris would convince any one that at all times the preoccupation uppermost in his mind was to defend and further the interests of the United States. He shared practically without any reservation the commonly accepted theory of his time that self-interest is the most powerful motive of human actions, and that enlightened self-interest is the true foundation of morality. Never a sentimentalist, he felt it his duty to put all the questions he had to discuss on a purely practical basis, neglecting every other consideration. He had been welcomed enthusiastically and would have been lionized if he had permitted it. But in the midst of the adulation showered upon him by Madame d'Houdetot, Madame de Tessé and the friends of liberty, he endeavored to keep a cool head; and at the end of his first year in France, he summed up as follows his views of the situation:

The body of the people of this country love us cordially. But ministers and merchants love nobody. The merchants here, are endeavoring to exclude us from their islands, the ministers will be governed in it by their political motives, and will do it or not do it, as these shall appear to dictate, without love or hatred to anybody. It were to be wished that they were able to combine better, the various circumstances which prove, beyond a doubt, that all the advantages of their colonies result in the end, to the mother country.[1]

Representing a country hardly organized, without any diplomatic traditions, and inexperienced in dealing with foreign affairs, Jefferson had no easy task. One of his first duties was

---

[1] To John Langdon, September 11, 1785. Memorial Edition, V, 129.

to convince the diplomats he was dealing with that America was a country to be trusted, in which existed a certain permanency and some sort of responsible organization with which it was possible to deal. This preoccupation influenced to such an extent his views on the American Constitution that they can be considered to a large extent a result of his experiences in Europe.

As chairman of the committee on the ratification of the peace treaties, as plenipotentiary entrusted with the negotiations of the treaties of commerce, Jefferson had more than once felt how insufficient were the Articles of Confederation. He had repeatedly proclaimed that to all intents and purposes the United States were to be regarded as one nation; but as long as treaties with foreign powers had to be ratified not only by Congress but by the different States, as long as delegates had to refer constantly to the particular States they represented, the Federal organization remained a very clumsy, inefficient piece of machinery, and business could not be transacted. He never thought for an instant that it was possible or desirable for the former colonies to remain completely independent; they had at least to form a society of nations in order to insure their very existence and their development. His first months in Europe could only confirm him in these views, and he wrote to Madison at the end of 1786: "To make us one nation as to foreign concerns, and keep us distinct in domestic ones, gives the outlines of the proper division of powers between the general and particular governments. But to enable the federal head to exercise the powers given it to best advantage, it should be organized as the particular ones are, into legislative, executive and judiciary."

At that date, however, he had not admitted the desirability of appointing a single executive and came back to all his proposals of vesting the executive powers in a committee of the States, leaving to Congress the legislative authority.

To Adams, who saw in Congress "not a legislative but a diplomatic assembly", he protested that it was an opinion not entirely correct and not likely to do good. As a matter of fact, in forming a confederation, the individual States yielded some parts of their sovereignty to Congress, and these parts were both legislative and executive. The confederation was part of the law of the land, and "superior in authority to the ordinary laws, because it cannot be altered by the legislature of any one State." It is not without piquancy to remark here that the man who was to become the champion of State rights and decentralization was advocating a strong Federal bond, while the future Federalist was in favor of a very loose association of States, truly a sort of League of Nations. In Jefferson's view, on the contrary, the United States as such were endowed with a sort of super-power, while the independent States retained only those rights which they were able to exercise fully.[1] On the other hand, Congress should have absolutely no authority over acts which do not concern the confederacy. In case of conflict an appeal could be made "from a state judicature to a Federal court", in other words to a Supreme Court, and there again Jefferson takes the position which his enemies were fifteen years later to defend against him, namely that there ought to be some power above Congress to restrain it.

It will be said that this court may encroach over the jurisdiction of the State courts. It may. But there will be a power, to wit, Congress, to watch and restrain them. But place the same authority in Congress itself, and there will be no power above them, to perform the same office. They will restrain within due bounds a jurisdiction exercised by others, much more rigourously than if exercised by themselves.[2]

In a letter to Edward Carrington he summed up his views even more clearly. Reforms are necessary, although with all

---

[1] To John Adams, February 23, 1787. Memorial Edition, VI, 97.
[2] To James Madison, June 20, 1787. *Ibid.*, VI, 132.

its defects the present government of the United States is so far superior to any monarchy that its defects must be viewed with indulgence. If any change is to be made, the general principle ought to be

to make the States one as to everything connected with foreign nations, and several as to everything purely domestic. Then to separate the executive from the legislative in order to avoid the terrible delays which are bound to happen with a large assembly and to have the most important propositions hanging over, from week to week and month to month, till the occasions have passed them, and the things never done.[1]

Even if originally Jefferson had been of another opinion, the situation in Europe would have rapidly brought him to the same conclusion. For the credit of the United States could only be maintained on the condition that the newly formed confederation gave guarantees of permanency and stability. In his letters to foreign correspondents, such as Dumas, financial agent of the United States in Holland, he consequently affected more confidence in the wisdom of the convention than he perhaps felt at heart:

No trouble of any sort is to be anticipated. Happily for us that when we find our constitutions defective and insufficient, to secure the happiness of our people, we can assemble with all the coolness of philosophers, and set it to rights, while every other nation on earth must have recourse to arms to amend or restore their constitutions.[2]

The main principle to observe is a separation of powers into "legislative, executive and judiciary" as complete as possible, and the rest will follow of itself.

Yet as the convention approached, he favored less than ever the possibility of trusting any individual with the executive power for an indefinite length of time. "There are things in

---

[1] August 4, 1787. Memorial Edition, VI, 227.
[2] September 10, 1787. *Ibid.*, VI, 295.

it which stagger all my dispositions to subscribe to what such an Assembly has proposed," he wrote to Adams. His chief objection to the Constitution was the appointment of a President who would be a sort of Polish king. If they wanted a President they could have it, provided they should make him ineligible at the end of four years. He even came to wonder whether too much ado was not made by the convention, for all the good that was in the new Constitution "could have been couched in three or four new articles added to the old articles of confederation." Far from being a radical and one of these reformers who first think of destroying the old order of things in order to build anew, Jefferson proposed to keep as much as possible "the good old and venerable fabric which should have been preserved, even as a religious relic." [1]

At that time Jefferson had not yet received the text of the Constitution and had only vaguely heard of the discussion in the convention. When the newspapers brought him more details, he acquainted Carmichael with his views on the situation. This time his objection to the proposed scheme was more specific. It bore not only on the presidency but on the absence of a Bill of Rights; the thirteen States could not be melted into one government without guarantees to the people, and particularly without the recognition of the freedom of the press. The subordination of the laws of the States to Federal legislation was equally objectionable and he predicted that many States, among them Virginia, would reject several articles, making it necessary to assemble another convention to reach a better agreement.[2]

But it was reserved for Madison finally to become his confident on this question, and Jefferson's letter to him is both a capital document for the history of Jeffersonian democracy

---

[1] To John Adams, November 13, 1787. Memorial Edition, VI, 370. See also letter to Colonel Smith, written the same day. *Ibid.*, VI, 372.

[2] December 11, 1787. *Ibid.*, VI, 380.

and a discussion of the first rank on the science of government. The good things Jefferson saw in the Constitution were many : the division of powers; the election of a greater House by the people directly; the negative given to the executive by a third of either Houses, and many others of less moment. But the absence of a Bill of Rights could not be condoned, for it was a sacred palladium of liberty, nor the abandonment of rotation in office, particularly in the case of the President. He did not despair of the Commonwealth, but he foresaw the necessity of calling another convention to agree on an explicit Bill of Rights and to change the objectionable features of the convention. In a postscript, he made one of those curious proposals which would be disconcerting if it were not remembered that his faith in democracy and representative government was tempered with a great deal of common sense. The people are right most of the time, the people are right in most cases, but the people are not right in all cases : they are apt to be swayed by temporary interests and considerations and they are apt also to pass contradictory laws from day to day. In order to remedy this instability of legislation, Jefferson did not hesitate to recommend that there should always be "a twelvemonth between the engrossing a bill and passing it", adding that if circumstances required a speedier passage, it should take "two thirds of both Houses instead of a bare majority." [1]

Having thus defined his position with regard to the Constitution, he thought it necessary to qualify it. Despite its imperfections, it contained many excellent points; and if it were felt that insistence on a Bill of Rights, or on the principle of rotation for the presidency should cause dissensions between the States, Jefferson declared himself ready "to swallow the two bitter pills" in order to avoid a schism in the Union. For that would be "the incurable evil" because near friends, falling out, never re-united cordially; "whereas, all of us

[1] December 20, 1787. Memorial Edition, VI, 393.

going together, we shall be sure to cure the evils of our new Constitution before they do great harm." [1]

The unlimited confidence he had in the ultimate wisdom of the people convinced him that if they went wrong for a time they would soon admit their mistakes, for there was in America a "good sense and a free spirit" which was the safest guarantee that things will right themselves in time. First ratify and amend afterwards, such was therefore the best procedure to follow, and he prayed heartily that a sufficient number of States would ratify, even Virgina and obstinate little Rhode Island! For after all there was no immediate danger, and the character of Washington was such that nobody could suspect him of coveting a life tenure for himself.[2]

Following anxiously and almost day by day the progress of the ratification, he declared himself perfectly satisfied with the successful result obtained in August, 1788, and was confident that the two main defects would be remedied, the first one, the lack of a Bill of Rights, very soon, the other as soon as General Washington should retire from office. Jefferson had come gradually to this stand, to a large extent under the influence of the *Federalist*, which had "rectified him on several points" and which he considered the "best commentary on the principles of government ever written." [3]

The most complete expression of Jefferson's views at that time is found in a letter to Francis Hopkinson, written at the beginning of 1789. He had been informed that both his friends and his enemies were trying to put a definite label on him and protested on that occasion that he was not a Federalist, because, he said, "I never submitted the whole system of my opinions to the creed of any party whatever, in religion, in

[1] To Donald, February 7, 1787. Memorial Edition, VI, 425.
[2] To Carmichael and to Colonel Carrington, May 27, 1787. *Ibid.*, VII, 27, 29.
[3] To Carmichael, August 12, 1787. *Ibid.*, VII, 124; to James Madison, November 18, 1788, *Ibid.*, VII, 183; to General Washington, December 4, 1788, *Ibid.*, VII, 223.

politics, or in anything else, where I was capable of thinking for myself. If I could not go to heaven but with a party, I would not be there at all." But he added at once, "I am even farther from the anti-federalists." Neither a Federalist, nor an anti-Federalist, nor "a trimmer between parties", he absolutely refused at that date to take sides, for he would have been sure to draw criticism from the other side and to see his name in the papers. This was to be avoided at any cost, for "the pain of a little censure, even when it is unfounded, is more acute than the pleasure of much praise." As a matter of fact, Jefferson was already preparing to become the leader of a new party whose program would combine elements borrowed from the Federalists as well as from their opponents, but which would rest essentially upon principles apparently overlooked by both sides. At that time he formulated in his own words the principles already implied in the Declaration of Independence which he had discussed earlier with Thomas Paine.

In forming a society of States, as well as in forming a society of men, there are rights "which it is useless to surrender to the government, and which governments have yet always been found to invade." These rights which cannot be abridged or alienated are "the rights of thinking and publishing our thoughts by speaking or writing; the right of free commerce; the right of personal freedom." In a similar way, there are some instruments of government which are so trustworthy that they ought to be placed beyond the power of any legislature to alter; the most important of these is probably trial by jury. Scarcely less essential to the permanency of a free government is the absence of a standing army, for such a body of men whether placed at the disposal of the executive or of the legislative power, may always become an instrument of oppression. Hence the necessity of a separate instrument, a Bill of Rights, to secure and protect these fundamental principles of free government. On the whole, Jefferson declared himself well pleased with the Constitution "unquestionably the wisest ever yet presented to men" ; its obvious defects would be remedied in the near future, and in the meantime it had effected its main object, the consolidation of the thirteen States into a Union.[1]

Whether Jefferson would have reached that lofty and disinterested attitude if he had remained in America is quite another question. He was placed in a situation entirely different from that of his countrymen who could not help being influenced by party politics and sectionalism. But it is a fact worth remembering that before the Constitution was adopted, the only men who constantly had to think of the United States as one nation were the American ministers abroad. The very fact that Jefferson was in Paris not only put him above all parties, but brought home to him the fact that the United States could not hope to face successfully external dangers or even survive unless they gave up some of their liberty for more security, while reserving some of their unalienable rights. In his views on the Constitution, Jefferson remained perfectly consistent and followed very closely the principles he had formulated in 1776.

On the other hand, he had found in Europe an opportunity to test his principles by facts and direct observation. He was opposed to monarchy on general grounds, but he had seen in France monarchy and absolutism at their worst. A well-meaning king, not by any means a tyrant, unable to prevent the dissolution of the nation, a corrupt hereditary aristocracy, in the main narrow and selfish, a State religion, monopolies, a standing army, "*lettres de cachet*", no freedom of the press, everywhere ignorance and misery ; such was the picture of France that presented itself to his eyes ; and conditions were such that they could not be remedied effectively except through a bloody revolution, a last and desperate resort, to be dreaded as much as monarchical oppression. In many respects the

[1] To Colonel Humphreys, March 18, 1789. Memorial Edition, VII, 324.

same situation prevailed all over Europe, demonstrating beyond the possibility of a doubt that absolutism does not pay, that it fails to procure the maximum of happiness to the largest number of inhabitants, that it is wasteful, inefficient and leads nations to follies, ruin, and war. America was free from all these evils, but every precaution had to be used lest they should take root there.

This task naturally required constant vigilance, for everywhere men in power have a tendency to continue in power, and to extend the limits of their attributions; some safeguards against these encroachments could be provided, the greatest safeguard being the pressure of public opinion. Public opinion could be misled temporarily; but after a time, in a country where the citizens were reasonably educated, and knowledge more diffused than in any other country, the chances were that in most cases the citizens would see where their true interest lay and correct such evils. This could be achieved only if the citizens were in a position to collect information on the true state of affairs, to discuss freely with their neighbors, and communicate their opinion so as to make that pressure felt. A free press, therefore, was one of the most essential features of a republican government, for one might conceive a modern nation existing without a legislature, but it was impossible even to think of a free government existing without the control of the men who had subscribed to the social compact. Public opinion and a free press were not a fourth estate, they were the true source of all three powers, and superior to all.

Thus, after more than fifteen years of personal reflection aided by direct observation, Jefferson came to formulate very clearly in his own mind a certain number of principles founded on reason and verified by facts. Whether he was at that time under the influence of any particular philosopher cannot be proved satisfactorily. It may even be said that it is very improbable, for he was not a man "to submit the whole system of his opinions to the creed of any party of men whatever." Elements of different origins can be recognized in his political philosophy: the theory of natural rights was perhaps Lockian in its principle, but it had been developed by many philosophers, incorporated in the Virginia Bill of Rights and thus naturalized as American even before the Declaration of Independence. The theory of the social compact, too, may have come from Locke; certainly it did not come from Rousseau; but Jefferson introduced into it a fundamental modification when he distinguished between real natural rights and the civil rights guaranteed by society but limited in order to provide for more safety. At any rate, Jefferson's conception of the social compact was far more rigorous, precise, and specific than any that had been proposed before. A man who had been trained as a lawyer knew exactly what a contract was, and how necessary it is, in such an instrument, to write clauses safeguarding both parties. The Bill of Rights was to serve that very purpose: it was nothing but a document enumerating, defining, and recognizing once for all a certain number of rights that every individual specifically reserved in joining a new society. The constitution on the contrary was purely an instrument of government, susceptible of all sorts of amendments from time to time, and certainly from generation to generation. Public opinion was set up as a court of last resort in all cases; for public opinion, not necessarily right in all cases, is always right ultimately in a nation where people have received a minimum of education and are kept informed by a free press.

Such were the essential lines of Jefferson's political philosophy on the eve of his departure from France. It does not appear that there was in it anything particularly English or particularly French, although the remote source of some ideas may be traced to English and French political thinkers. His principles, as a matter of fact, belonged to the common fund of political thought drawn upon by all the liberal thinkers of the eighteenth century, and Jefferson, calling no man his master, simply reflected the general trend of his time. But whatever may have been the primary origin of some of his ideas, he was fully convinced that they corresponded to conditions existing in America and nowhere else on earth, that in America alone were they susceptible of immediate application and extensive development.

These views on the uniqueness of America's position among the nations of the world contributed to the crystallization of certain principles which Jefferson enunciated when he was sent to Paris and endeavored to apply when Secretary of State and President. They were to exert a tremendous influence upon the destiny of the nation and to a certain extent are still to-day the directing principles of America's foreign policy.

If Jefferson had ever believed that it was possible for the United States to coöperate effectively and satisfactorily with Europe in any common undertaking, after his failure to organize a confederacy of the European States against the Barbary pirates, he soon came to the conclusion that such a hope was chimerical. The question of the navigation of the Mediterranean was not the least complicated of the puzzles that confronted the American minister in Paris. After long hesitations the European powers had finally adopted a *modus vivendi* with the Barbary pirates — a solution far from satisfactory, since it meant the paying of a regular tribute to the Dey of Algiers, the Regency of Tunis, and the Sultan of Morocco. Was the young republic of the United States to follow in their steps and accept such a humiliating compromise? If they refused, their commerce with the Near East was placed on a very precarious foundation. On the other hand, they could hardly maintain a sufficient fleet in the Mediterranean to insure the safety of their merchantmen. To pay tribute, or to give efficient protection to the merchant marine entailing expenditure of sums easily as large as the tribute, or else to give up the Mediterranean trade, were the only solutions to be considered.[1]

The first solution was absolutely repugnant to Jefferson. "When this idea comes across my mind, my faculties are absolutely suspended between indignation and impatience."[2]

He therefore approached Vergennes to sound him on his intention and to determine whether it would not be possible to establish a permanent blockade of Algiers. Although Admiral d'Estaing was in favor of the plan and thought it perfectly feasible, the prudent diplomat did not give Jefferson much encouragement. But in spite of the instructions sent by his government and the pressure exerted by Adams, who thought it cheaper to buy peace, Jefferson's preference for war remained entire. With his characteristic obstinacy, he tried another approach and thought it possible to organize a confederation of all the nations interested in the Mediterranean trade, in order to maintain an international blockade before the ports of the pirates and thus paralyze their operations. He explained his plan in detail to Adams and even drew up the articles of confederation.[3]

At this juncture he took Lafayette into his confidence as he had already done so many times, and discussed the situation with him. The Marquis saw at once another opportunity to be of service to America. He had hardly left Jefferson's house before the idea came to his mind that he could offer his services as chief of the operations against the Barbary pirates, and he wrote at once to Jefferson to that effect.[4] That the project did not come to completion was due to many causes and to a large extent to Adams' opposition, as may be inferred from a letter

[1] Jefferson to Monroe, May 10, 1786. Memorial Edition, V, 327.
[2] To Major General Greene, January 12, 1786. *Ibid.*, V, 246.
[3] "Autobiography", *Ibid.*, I, 97 and July 11, 1786, *Ibid.*, V, 364.
[4] See my edition of the Jefferson Lafayette correspondence, chapter II. Paris, Baltimore, 1929.

written by Lafayette to his "Dear General" during the fall of 1786,[1] but most of all to lack of coöperation between the European powers; and during the rest of his mission Jefferson had to restrict himself to making arrangements in order to obtain the release of the American captives.

On the other hand, if it was evident that Europe was unwilling to coöperate with America in the Mediterranean, it was not so certain that France, England, and Spain had given up their ambitious designs on the New World, and Jefferson considered it his duty to forestall any attempt of theirs to develop or reëstablish colonies on the American continent.

As far as France was concerned, she had given up all claims to her former colonies by the Treaty of Alliance signed on February 6, 1778, but there always remained the possibility that she might attempt to settle on the western coast of the American continent and thus take possession of the back door of the country. The preparations made for "La Peyrouse's voyage to the South Seas" aroused strong suspicions in Jefferson's mind. He could not be persuaded that the French were in a position to spend so much money "merely for the improvement of the geography of that part of the globe." They certainly had some ulterior aims, at least that of establishing fur-trading stations on the western coast, as a first step towards regular colonization; and "if they should desire a colony on the western side of America, I should not be quite satisfied that they would refuse one which should offer itself on the eastern side," wrote Jefferson to Jay. So, to ascertain the true nature of the expedition, he commissioned Paul Jones to go to Brest "to satisfy himself of the nature of the expedition; conducting himself so as to excite no suspicion."[2] This was not a very important incident in itself, but it is not impossible that it attracted Jefferson's attention to the western coast fifteen

[1] "Memoirs", II, 148.
[2] To John Jay, August 14, 1785. Memorial Edition, V, 63.

years before he sent out the Lewis and Clarke Expedition; and his unwillingness to permit France to obtain a footing even in a very remote part of the continent is quite significant.

His fears of the colonizing designs of France were soon allayed, but there remained England to consider, and England still constituted the greatest potential danger for the United States. While in America, Jefferson never manifested any strong animosity against the British as a people, and even expressed the hope that a reconciliation would follow the victory of American arms. Soon after coming to Europe, however, he had to admit that the commercial policy of Great Britain was so obnoxious that the American hatred "against Great Britain having lately received from that nation new cause and new aliment, had taken a new spring."[1] Thus, added Jefferson, "in spite of treaties, England is still our enemy. Her hatred is deep rooted and cordial, and nothing is wanting with her but the power to wipe us, and the land which we live on out of existence." The only hope of avoiding a new war was to make Great Britain realize that her true interest lay in some compromise, and that America had more energy than she suspected. But all told it was "a conflict of dirty passions."[2] Unfortunately the British were absolutely unrelenting in their hostility:

. . . they keep a standing army of newswriters formally engaged in war against America. They dwell very much on American bankruptcies — and thus worked to such good effect that by destroying America's credit they checked her disposition to luxury; and forcing our merchants to buy no more than they have ready money to pay for, they force them to go to those markets where that money will buy most.[3]

---

[1] To Baron Geismer, September 6, 1785. Memorial Edition, V, 128.
[2] To John Langdon, September 11, 1785. *Ibid.*, V, 131.
[3] To Count Hogendorp, October 13, 1785. *Ibid.*, V, 182.

Jefferson's tour in England only confirmed him in his views, for

> that nation hate us, their ministers hate us, and their King more than all other men.   They have the impudence to avow this, though they acknowledge our trade important to them. . . .   They say they will pocket our carrying trade as well as their own.   Our overtures of commercial arrangements have been treated with a derision, which shows their firm persuasion, that we shall never unite to suppress their commerce, or even to impede it.   I think their hostility towards us is much more deeply rooted at present than during the war.[1]

To Dumas, the financial agent at the Hague, he reiterated his views that "the English are still our enemies."   He even predicted war, a war which would renew the scenes of Rome and Carthage : "Peace and friendship with all mankind is our wisest policy; and I wish we may be permitted to pursue it.   But the temper and folly of our enemies may not leave this in our choice." [2]

Finally the Spanish colonies in America constituted another source of danger.   Jefferson was confident that Spain would never be in a position to conduct a war of aggression against the United States; but being a weak country and embroiled in European affairs, her colonies might be used at any time as mere pawns in the unscrupulous game of European politics. In these circumstances the attitude the United States should observe in their relations with the Spanish colonies was to be seriously considered.   A curious illustration of the fears and schemes which passed at that time through Jefferson's mind is found in an episode of his Southern journey during the preceding year.   The gist of his conversation with a Brazilian he met at Montpellier was that an important group of colonists were ready to follow the example of the United States and proclaim

---

[1] To John Page, May 4, 1786. Memorial Edition, V, 306.
[2] To Dumas, May 6, 1786. *Ibid.*, V, 309.

their independence of the mother country. But as **Portugal** was certain to join forces with Spain in repressing such a revolution, the Brazilian patriots had decided not to undertake anything before securing the assistance of some other country. The thinking part of the population had naturally thought of the United States. "They would want cannons, ammunition, ships, sailors, soldiers and officers, for which they are disposed to look to the United States, it being always understood that every service and furniture will be well paid." The answer of Jefferson to that alluring proposition, contains more than one interesting point :

I took care to impress on him, through the whole of our conversation, that I had neither instructions nor authority to say a word to anybody on this subject, and that I could only give him my own ideas, as a single individual; which were, that we were not in a condition at present to meddle nationally in any war; that we wished particularly to cultivate the friendship of Portugal, with whom we have an advantageous commerce. That yet a successful revolution in Brazil could not be uninteresting to us. That prospects of lucre might possibly draw numbers of individuals to their aid, and purer motives our officers, among whom are many excellent. That our citizens being free to leave their own country individually, without the consent of their governments, are equally free to go to any other.[1]

Amusingly enough, Jefferson evidently believed that he had displayed a remarkable caution during the whole conversation. It is doubtful that such would have been the opinion of the Portuguese Government had his letter to Jay been intercepted, and one may wonder what he would have said if he had really intended to encourage a revolution in the Portuguese colonies. With a Mexican who made a similar inquiry he was somewhat more reserved. He had observed that the gentleman was "intimate at the Spanish Ambassador's" and sus-

[1] To John Jay, May 4, 1787. Memorial Edition, VI, 119.

pected that he might be a spy.   He was therefore "still more
cautious with him than with the Brazilian"; mentioning
simply that "a successful revolution was still at a distance with
them": that he feared "they must begin by enlightening
and emancipating the minds of their people."   He finally
recalled that the British papers had mentioned during the late
war an insurrection in Peru "which had cost two hundred thousand lives, on both sides!" — a figure not to be taken too
literally.

During the course of a year, however, Jefferson's views
underwent a remarkable change.   In May, 1788, he mentioned to Carmichael his suspicions that a Spanish squadron
had been sent to South America in order to quell an incipient
revolt started at the instigation of the British.   This placed
the situation in an entirely different light.   The United States
would have very little to gain if a weak neighbor were dis-
placed by a powerful and treacherous nation.   He consequently requested his colleagues to reassure the Spanish Court
that the United States would not favor in any way a revolt of
the Spanish colonies in the New World, for "those who look into
futurity farther than the present moment or age, and who combine well what is, with what is to be, must see that our interests, well understood, and our wishes are, that Spain shall
(not forever, but) very long retain her possessions in that
quarter; and that her views and ours must, in a good degree,
and for a long time concur." [1]

This is the more important as it already defines the position
taken by Jefferson twelve years later during the negotiations
concerning the Louisiana Purchase.   It is also a reiteration
of that desire of isolation which constituted the cardinal principle of American foreign policies and which had been enunciated in the Treaty of Alliance concluded with France in 1778.
Jefferson had not originated the principle, since this article of

[1] To Carmichael, May 27, 1788. Memorial Edition, VII, 27.

the Treaty of Alliance was due to Adams, but his direct and prolonged contact with European affairs had strengthened in him the instinctive conviction that it was the only wise course for America to follow. If he had felt free to indulge in his own theory, he would have gone even further than any of his contemporaries for, as he wrote in 1785, "I should wish the United States to practice neither commerce, nor navigation, but to stand, with respect to Europe, precisely on the footing of China." Unfortunately, this was only a theory and the servants of the country were not at liberty to follow it, since "Americans have a decided taste for navigation and commerce." Being on a mission to protect and further the commerce of his fellow countrymen, Jefferson consequently thought it his duty to forget for the time being his personal preferences. In a similar way, although he strongly believed in free trade and would have seen no objection to "throwing open all the doors of commerce, and knocking its shackles", he realized that such an ideal condition could not be reached unless the European powers granted similar treatment to American goods. He therefore came to the conclusion that, "as this cannot be done for others, unless they will do it for us, and there is no great probability that Europe will do this, we shall be obliged to adopt a system which may shackle them in our ports, as they do in theirs." [1]

We have here another striking instance of the close partitioning established by Jefferson between theory and practice, between his wishes as a political philosopher, and his conception of his duties as a public servant. Far from being a single-track mind, his was decidedly a double-track intellect, with two lines of thought running parallel without any apparent contradiction, for theory never seemed to have interfered with his practice. When a month later he wrote to W. W. Seward about the future of commercial relations between

---

[1] To Count Hagendorf, October 13, 1785. Memorial Edition, V, 181.

Ireland and America, he excellently defined his position by saying that "the system into which the United States wishes to go, was that of freeing commerce from every shackle. A contrary conduct in Great Britain will occasion them to adopt a contrary system, at least as to that island." [1]

There is probably nothing in this to astonish the man in the street, either in Washington or in London, for it seems to be a curious quality of the Anglo-Saxon mind to be able to pursue a very practical and hard-headed policy, while keeping its belief in disinterested and idealistic principles. Yet it may not be out of place to mention that this is the very reason why both England and America have so often been accused of hypocrisy by European public opinion. Without attempting to justify all the foreign policies of the United States on that score, it may be said that in this particular case there was no hypocrisy. Jefferson made no attempt whatever to conceal the difference that existed between his theory and his practice; he even called attention to it. He did not attempt to color unpleasant reality with idealistic camouflage, and gave the European nations a chance to choose between two entirely different courses. He would rather have chosen to follow the more liberal system, but he gave due notice that if it came to playing the game of real politics, America could be just as practical and firm in insisting upon her rights as any nation of the Old World.

The millennium had not yet arrived; and America, in spite of her peaceful attitude, might be caught at any time in European "commotions." While maintaining a policy of strict aloofness, it would have been foolish and ostrich-like for her to ignore that danger, and it became the strict duty of those in power to keep close watch on political developments in the Old World. Such is the conclusion reached by Jefferson as a result of his observations, and in a letter to E. Carrington

[1] November 12, 1785. Memorial Edition, V, 202.

he outlined a policy of watchful waiting to which Woodrow Wilson himself would have subscribed:

I often doubt whether I should trouble Congress or my friends with these details of European politics. I know they do not excite that interest in America, of which it is impossible for one to divest himself here. I know, too, that it is a maxim with us, and I think it is a wise one, not to entangle ourselves with the affairs of Europe. Still I think, we should know them. The Turks have practiced the same maxim of not meddling in the complicated wrangles of this continent. But they have unwisely chosen to be ignorant of them also, and it is this total ignorance of Europe, its combinations and its movements, which exposes them to that annihilation possibly about to take place. While there are powers in Europe which fear our views, or have views on us, we should keep an eye on them, their connections and opposition, that in a moment of need, we may avail ourselves of their weakness with respect to others as well as ourselves, and calculate their designs and movements, on all the circumstances under which they exist. Though I am persuaded, therefore, that these details are read by many with great indifference, yet I think it my duty to enter into them, and to run the risk of giving too much, rather than too little information.[1]

Watchful waiting, no political entanglements, unofficial observers — everything is here and this page could have been written ten years ago or yesterday. It is sometimes said that America, being a young and inexperienced nation, has had no time to develop traditions, but it may be wondered whether any other nation could be found which, after defining so clearly the essentials of a policy, has adhered to them so persistently for a century and a half. There is no doubt, at any rate, that once again Jefferson, although he did not originate the theory, formulated it with his usual felicity of expression, and thus contributed toward giving America what Descartes would have called her "maxims of action."

[1] December 21, 1787, Memorial Edition, VI, 396; see also letter to John Jay, May 4, 1787. *Ibid.*, VI, 122.

CHAPTER IV

JEFFERSON AND THE FRENCH REVOLUTION

JEFFERSON has often been represented, both by his enemies and friends, as the American exponent of the theories of the French Revolution. The possible influence exerted upon the development of his political philosophy by French thought has been the subject of lengthy discussions and probably will never be determined with any degree of exactness. It is very difficult to see how a man of his character could have remained in Paris for more than five years without participating in some manner in the great battle of theories which preceded the French Revolution. He associated with Lafayette and his group of "republicans", exchanged some correspondence with Condorcet, frequently saw Abbé Morellet, was introduced by Benjamin Franklin to Madame Helvétius and her coterie; he worked with Du Pont de Nemours on commercial questions, subscribed to papers and gazettes and to the "Encyclopédie Méthodique", a continuation and systematization of Diderot's "Encyclopédie."

But when all is said, the most careful scrutiny of the letters he wrote during that period fails to reveal any enthusiasm or even any endorsement of the many and somewhat contradictory political doctrines which were preached in France at the time. I do not even see that his prolonged sojourn in France modified to any extent the conclusions he had already reached independently in the "Notes on Virginia." When he arrived in Paris he was over forty and had been in public life for almost fifteen years; he had written not only the Declaration of Independence but many reports on vital questions; he had participated actively and for several years in the deliberations of the Virginia Assembly and of the Congress of the United States and he had been chief executive of his native State. Such a man was not a student coming to Paris to sit at the feet of French masters; he was considered by the French themselves, not only as a master but as the apostle of the religion of liberty.[1] They looked up to him for advice and help, for he had over them the great superiority of having been more than a simple theorizer; he had contributed to a great movement of liberation; he was the promoter of the Bill for Religious Freedom; he had proposed a complete plan of public education and he had proclaimed in a national document the inviolable rights of man. They had much to learn from Jefferson and he was not reluctant to teach them, but he never felt that his French friends could repay him in kind. On the other hand, it cannot be denied that he was very happy to find enunciated in a very clear and logical way some of his favorite ideas; it is equally certain that France was to him a living demonstration and a sort of horrible example of all the evils caused by aristocratic, monarchical, and ecclesiastical oppressions. His sojourn in France had at least the effect of making him more intensely, more proudly American than he was before sailing, and more convinced than ever of the unsurpassed superiority of the civilization which had already developed on the northern continent of the New World.

This sentiment appears even during the first year of his stay in Paris in a letter to Mrs. Trist:

It is difficult to conceive how so good a people, with so good a king, so well-disposed rulers in general, so genial a climate, so fertile a soil, should be rendered so ineffectual for producing human happiness by one single curse — that of a bad form of government. But it is a fact in spite of the mildness of their governors, the people are ground to powder by the vices of the form of government. Of

---

[1] See "Les Amitiés Françaises de Madame d'Houdetot." Paris, 1925.

twenty millions of people supposed to be in France, I am of opinion there are nineteen millions more wretched, more accursed, in every circumstance of human existence, than the most conspicuously wretched individual of the whole United States. . . . Nourish peace with their persons, but war against their manners. Every step we take towards the adoption of their manners is a step to perfect misery.[1]

This was no passing mood : a few weeks earlier he had written much more vehemently to his friend and "*élève*", James Monroe, engaging him to come to France in order to see for himself the extraordinary superiority of America over Europe and particularly France.

It will make you adore your own country, it's soil, it's climate, it's equality, liberty, laws, people & manners. My God! how little do my country men know what precious blessings they are in possession of, and which no other people on earth enjoy. I confess I had no idea of it myself. While we shall see multiplied instances of Europeans going to live in America, I will venture to say no man now living will ever see an instance of an American removing to settle in Europe & continuing there.[2]

But unhappy as they are, the French are lovable, for he loved them with all his heart and thought that, "with a better religion, a better form of government and their present Governors, their condition and country would be most enviable." At any rate they were to be preferred to the "rich, proud, hectoring, swearing, squibbling, carnivorous animals who lived on the other side of the Channel." [3]

At the beginning of his stay, Jefferson paid little attention to the internal affairs of the country ; the only incident worth comment during his first year in Paris was the imprisonment of the chief editor of the *Journal de Paris* who was sent to the Bastille, perhaps to end his days there :

[1] To Mrs. Trist. Paris, August 18, 1785. "Domestic Life", p. 79.
[2] To James Monroe, April 15, 1785. Ford, IV, 59.
[3] To Abigail Adams, June 21, 1785. *Ibid.*, IV, 59.

Thus — wrote he — you see the value of energy in Government for such a measure, which would have been wrapt in the flames of war and desolation in America, ends without creating the slightest disturbance. Every attempt to criticize even mildly the government is followed immediately by stern measures, suppressing the London papers, suppressing the *Leyden Gazette*, imprisoning Beaumarchais, and imprisoning the editor of the *Journal*, the author of the *Mercure*, etc.[1]

It is not until February, 1786, that he gave hints, quite incidentally, that the situation might become critical and that serious disturbances might be feared for the future.

But he did not see anywhere any immediate danger of a political commotion and during that year he continued to repeat in his letters that "Europe was very quiet for the present." As a matter of fact, he had come to the conclusion that the case of the Old World was hopeless; they were past redemption and, "if the Almighty had begotten a thousand sons, instead of one, they would not have sufficed for this task. If all the sovereigns of Europe undertook to emancipate the minds of their subjects, a thousand years would not place them on that high ground on which our common people are now setting out." France has become a horrible example to place constantly before the eyes of America, to remind her that the most important factor for the happiness of the people is the diffusion of common knowledge that will enable them to preserve themselves from kings, nobles, and priests, for it is impossible to imagine a people of more pleasant dispositions, more made for happiness, surrounded by so many blessings of nature, and yet "loaded with misery by kings, nobles, and priests, and by them alone." [2]

Never before had Jefferson been so vehement in his denunciations of kingly and priestly usurpations, never had he been

---

[1] To Mrs. Adams, July 7, 1785. Ford, IV, 68.
[2] To George Wythe, August 13, 1786. *Ibid.*, IV, 268–269.

so positive of the necessity of preserving American civilization from any foreign influences. But again this is not with him an *a priori* view, it is the result of his observations more than of his theories.

He was confirmed in his hatred of the French régime by his conversations with Latude, who "comes sometimes to take family soup with me, & entertains me with anecdotes of his five & thirty years imprisonment, all of which for having written four lines on Madame de Pompadour." [1]

In a letter to Washington already quoted, but capital for the history of his mind, he remarked that before coming to Europe he had not even begun to suspect the evils of monarchical government; what he saw there brought home to him the conviction that "as long as a single fibre of it would remain in America, the scourge that is rendering existence a scourge to 24 out of 25 parts of the inhabitants of this country might break out." [2]

As late as 1787 he was still persuaded that under pretence of governing, the ruling classes have divided the nations into two classes, wolves and sheep: "But what can the sheep do against the wolves except to submit, to suffer without any hope of ever changing the established order." [3]

His first mention of the possibility of introducing some modification in the existing order does not occur before he heard of the convocation of the Assembly of the Notables "which had not been done for one hundred and sixty years"; but this interests him only mildly at the beginning, as nothing certain could be known about the program of the Assembly.[4] A few days later he admitted to Colonel Edward Carrington that "this event which will hardly excite any attention in America is deemed here the most important one which has

---

[1] To Mrs. Maria Cosway, October 12, 1786. Ford, IV, 323.
[2] November, 1786. *Ibid.*, IV, 328.
[3] To Edward Carrington. January 16, 1787. *Ibid.*, IV, 357.
[4] To J. Jay, January 9, 1787. Memorial Edition, VI, 45.

taken place in their civil life during the present century."
But his only real interest in it was that Lafayette had finally
been put on the list and was the youngest of the Notables but
one.[1] He felt that it was his duty to attend the first meeting
of the Notables, and still more to pay his call to the new minister Montmorin — the only thing that detained him in Paris,
and when he wrote to John Adams and Jay to describe the
inaugural session opened by the king, he restricted himself to
a dry recital of facts. With a prince of the blood at the head
of each committee, he did not expect great results from the
convocation and was skeptical about the efficiency of the members.[2] Just as he was leaving Paris for his long extensive trip
to the South of France, he thought, however, of sending a last
word of advice to Lafayette whose republican ideas he evidently
feared. It was a counsel of prudence. Whatever may have
been his sympathies for the republicans, in his opinion France
was not ready for a complete change in her system of government.

Least of all was she ready for a democratic experiment.
Consequently Jefferson, the American patriot, the enemy of
England, the alleged hater of aristocracies, advised his friend
"to proceed step by step, towards a good constitution, keeping
the good model of your neighboring country before your eyes.
Though that model is not perfect, yet, as it would unite more
suffrages than any new one which could be proposed, it is better
to make that the object.

"You see how we Republicans are apt to preach", he said
in conclusion; but his letter was more than a sermon; it contained also the advice of a shrewd and very practical politician
who recommended that every possible effort be made to give the
king what he wanted in the way of personal expenses. "If
every advance is to be purchased by filling the royal coffers

<hr />

[1] January 16, 1787. Memorial Edition, VI, 56.
[2] February 23, 1787. *Ibid.*, VI, 99.

with gold, it will be gold well employed. The King who means so well, should be encouraged to repeat those Assemblies." [1]

That was all he could say, and even so he had probably said too much, for it was a risky thing for a diplomat to write about or to discuss at all.   Jefferson was certainly guilty of trespassing on a province that constituted an essential part of the internal politics of the kingdom.   And yet the charge of plotting against the existing government cannot be laid at his door. As long as he remained in France, and I believe, even after he came back to America, he carefully refrained from giving any encouragement to those of his French friends who held radical views. He was caught in the torrent and, as we shall see later, did not always observe the reticence of an old-fashioned diplomat; but whatever influence he exerted was exerted in order to maintain rather than to overthrow the existing order of things.

During his trip he observed the condition of the peasants and, much to his surprise, found among them a smaller degree of poverty than he had expected; but if he made observations and entered many minute facts in his diary, he did not come to any conclusion nor did he seem to have been interested by the state of mind of the people. He had judged them once for all, he knew that they were priest-ridden and lord-ridden and did not see how any real reform might originate from them.   Once, however, but only once, did he indicate that he had paid serious attention to the work before the Assembly.   Writing to Lafayette's aunt, Madame de Tessé, in the evident expectation that she would communicate his ideas to the proper persons, he drew up an almost complete plan of administrative reforms: To have frequent meetings of the Assembly of Notables; the Assembly to be divided into two houses — the Noblesse and the Commons; the Commons to be taken from those chosen by the people for provincial administrations; the number of deputies for the Nobility to be reduced.   These two Houses so

[1] February 28, 1787. Memorial Edition, VI, 101.

elected "would make the King great and the people happy." And the next sentence expresses very cleverly, too cleverly perhaps, that this innocuous reform would in fact be a sort of revolution, the name of which would be avoided. "They would thus put themselves in the track of the best guide they can follow (the king); they would soon overtake it, become its guide in turn, and lead to the wholesome modifications wanting in that model, and necessary to constitute a rational government." What he had in mind at the time was a sort of government following very closely the lines of the British, not as an ideal but as a temporary measure; for before the eyes of his friends he held another prospect. But for the present that was the maximum they could wisely expect; "should they attempt more than the established habits of the people are ripe for, they may lose all, and retard indefinitely the ultimate object of their aim." [1]

Commerce more than politics absorbed all his attention when he came back from his trip. He found time, however, to send to Madison his first estimate of the king and queen, a most unflattering portrait of poor Louis XVI.

The King loves business, economy, order, and justice, and wishes sincerely the good of his people; but he is irascible and rude, very limited in his understanding, and religious, bordering on bigotry. He has no mistress, loves his queen, and is too much governed by her. She is capricious like her brother, and governed by him: devoted to pleasure and expense; and not remarkable for any other vices or virtues. Unhappily the King shows a propensity for the pleasures of the table. That for drink has increased lately, or, at least, it has become more known.[2]

It was not until August that he summed up in a letter to Monroe the great improvements in the constitution of the French effected by the Assemblées des Notables. He was sur-

[1] March 20, 1787. Memorial Edition, VI, 105.
[2] To James Madison, June 20, 1787. *Ibid.*, VI, 134.

prised at the great explosion of joy, which he thought unwarranted; for after all, even the unexampled boldness of the enemies of the régime was nothing but the "follies of nations in their dotage." [1] Yet writing to John Jay the next day he took a more serious view of things and declared "It is evident, I think, that a spirit of this country is advancing towards a revolution in their constitution. There are not wanting persons at the helm, friends to the progress of this spirit. The Provincial Assemblies will be the most probable instrument of effecting it." [2]

But it is primarily from the American point of view that he continues to be interested, and he becomes more and more convinced that, "with all its defects, and with all those of our particular governments, the inconveniences resulting from them, are so light in comparison with those existing in every other government on earth that our citizens may certainly be considered as in the happiest political situation which exists." [3] With more intimate friends he was far more violent and outspoken, as in the letter he wrote the same day to Colonel Humphreys. It is seldom he indulges in these outbursts of passionate invective, so seldom that it may be wondered whether his expression is not stronger than his thought:

From these events, our young Republic may learn useful lessons, never to call on foreign powers to settle their differences, to guard against hereditary magistrates, to prevent their citizens from becoming so established in wealth and power, as to be thought worthy of alliance . . . in short to besiege the throne of heaven with eternal prayers, to extirpate from creation this class of human lions, tigers, and mammoths called Kings; from whom, let him perish who does not say, "good Lord deliver us!" [4]

He had caught something of the general fever, and he drew a vivid picture of Paris with crowds surrounding the "Parlia-

[1] August 5, 1787, Memorial Edition.   VI, 235.   [2] *Ibid.*, VI, 247.
[3] To Washington, August 14, 1787.   *Ibid.*, VI, 276.
[4] August 14, 1787.   *Ibid.*, VI, 279.

ment House", stopping carriages in the queen's livery, indulging in *bons mots*, caricatures, "collecting in mobs, and yet the King, long in the habit of drowning his cares in wine, plunges deeper and deeper. The Queen cries, but sins on", and the only practical result one can see is that "all tongues in Paris and in France have been let loose." [1]   The same note is given six weeks later in a letter to John Jay. "The King goes for nothing. He hunts one half of the day, is drunk the other, and signs whatever he is bid." [2]   Even the reforms, the most important from the point of view of the French, seem to him insignificant, and when the edict on the Protestants appears, it is cruelly analyzed by the American minister:

It is an acknowledgement that Protestants can beget children, and that they can die, and be offensive unless buried. It does not give them permission to think, to speak, or to worship. . . . What are we to think of the condition of the human mind in a country, where such a wretched thing as this throws the State into convulsions, and how must we bless our own situation in a country, the most illiterate peasant of which is a Solon, compared with the authors of this law.[3]

When he wrote his "Autobiography", Jefferson used very extensively not only the notes he had taken when in Paris but the press copies of his correspondence, and on the whole gave an accurate picture of the events that immediately preceded the French Revolution — those he had witnessed before his departure from Paris, in October, 1789. But, true as the picture may be, it is not progressive, and here we aim not to trace again the main episodes of the French Revolution, but the development of Jefferson's mind, his reaction towards the events. Most of all we must seek to find out from contemporary evidence whether the old accusation launched by Gouverneur Morris,

[1] To John Adams, August 30, 1787. Memorial Edition, VI, 287.
[2] October 8, 1787. *Ibid.*, VI, 338.
[3] To William Rutledge, February 2, 1788. *Ibid.*, VI, 417.

seized upon eagerly by Jefferson's enemies, and since repeated again and again, is in any way justified.

We have already seen that, with a corrupted court, a weak king, a selfish and ignorant queen, the only remedy he recommended at first was for the French not to reconquer their liberties by force and by a revolution, but gradually to buy them from the king. Yet he foresaw that the nobility would make a sort of alliance with the people, that is to say the *tiers état*, in order to get money from them, and he held the rather cynical view that "Courtiers had rather give up power than pleasures; they will barter, therefore, the usurped prerogatives of the King, for the money of the people. This is the agent by which modern nations will recover their rights." [1] This is written, not to Jay in a confidential letter, but to a French liberal of his acquaintance, and that practical piece of advice cannot be called philosophical. Altogether the results reached by the Assemblée des Notables were small and the king terribly slow to see the light. So for a long time Jefferson refused not only to encourage but even to admit that he was witnessing the beginnings of a true revolution. Writing to Rutledge in July, 1788, he declared "That the struggle in this country is, as yet, of doubtful issue. It is, in fact, between the monarchy and the parliaments. The nation is no otherwise concerned, but as both parties may be induced to let go some of its abuses, to court the public favor. The danger, is that the people deceived by a false cry of liberty, may be led to take sides with one party, and thus give the other a pretext for crushing them still more." [2] Writing to Cutting a few days later he was more optimistic. Most of the late innovations had been much for the better; a convocation of the States-General could not be avoided; "it will produce a national assembly meeting at certain epochs, possessing at first a negative on the laws, but which will grow into the right of

---

[1] To De Moustier, May 17, 1788.   Memorial Edition, VII, 13.
[2] July 18, 1788.   *Ibid.*, VII, 81.

original legislation. Much could be hoped from the States-General and it was also to be hoped that all this will be effected without convulsion." [1]

Such was his confident expectation. He foresaw "that within two or three years this country will be in the enjoyment of a tolerably free constitution, and that without its having cost them a drop of blood." [2]

To Carmichael he described his own attitude as that of a bystander, not otherwise interested, but entertaining a sincere love for the nation in general and a wish to see their happiness promoted, "keeping myself clear of the particular views and passions of individuals." [3] Had he felt differently he would not have taken into his confidence a man for whom he felt no particular friendship; but, at that date at least, he could make that statement without departing from the exact truth. As far as contemporary evidence is concerned, it does not seem that he ever urged his friends forward, but on the contrary he always advised them to play a waiting game, and to keep from having recourse to violence. About the middle of that year, 1788, he toned down his severe estimate of the king, to whom he attributed "no foible which will enlist him against the good of his people." [4] Calonne had been removed and Necker called in as Director General of finance; things were looking decidedly better, a convocation of the States-General had been decided upon; the issue depended largely on three possible solutions: whether the three orders would meet separately; whether the clergy and the nobility would form a house and the Commons a second one; or finally whether the three orders would meet in one house which would give the majority to the Commons. The choice was really thought incumbent upon the king, who thus had the power to place the people on his side if he was wise

---

[1] July 24, 1788. Memorial Edition, VII, 87.
[2] To Colonel Monroe, August 9, 1788. *Ibid.*, VII, 113.
[3] August 12, 1788. *Ibid.*, VII, 124.
[4] To Cutting, August 23, 1788. *Ibid.*, VII, 131.

enough to prefer to have on his side twenty-three millions and a half instead of the other half million.[1]

At the end of 1788, with the convocation of the States-General announced for the beginning of the following year, he was still very optimistic, but he had not departed from his cautious and reserved recommendations. The States could not succeed if they asked too much, for the Commons would frighten and shock the court and even alarm the public mind. If any durable progress was to be accomplished, it would have to be by degrees and successive improvements. Such probably would be the course followed, unless an influence unaccountable, impossible to measure, and yet powerful entirely changed the situation: "The fact that women visit alone persons in office, solicit in defiance of laws and regulations, is an extraordinary obstacle to the betterment of things, unbelieveable as it may be to the inhabitant of a country where the sex does not endeavour to extend itself beyond the domestic line." [2]

He did not even believe that any real reform could be accomplished beyond fixing periodical meetings of the States-General and giving them the right to participate in the legislation and to decide on taxes. They did not seem to be unanimously in favor of the *habeas corpus;* as for the freedom of the press, — "I hardly think the nation itself ripe to accept it." [3]   This was his prophecy at the beginning of 1789, and during the first month of the year he had no occasion to express new views, since everybody was in the provinces "electioneering, choosing or being chosen."   With his experience of Assemblies, however, he could not help wondering how any result could be accomplished with a body which was to include some twelve hundred persons and moreover to consist of Frenchmen, among whom are always more speakers than listeners.[4]   In a letter to Thomas

---

[1] To Short, November 2, 1788. Memorial Edition, VII, 159.
[2] To Washington, December 4, 1788. *Ibid.*, VII, 228.
[3] To Doctor Currie, December 20, 1788. *Ibid.*, VII, 259.
[4] To Shippen, March 11, 1789. *Ibid.*, VII, 291.

Paine we find the first intimation that Jefferson began to be influenced by the political thinkers of France or rather to discover in them a certain quality of thought and presentation that make their work of some use for the American people. They were at any rate much preferable to the Englishman, who "slumbering under a kind of half reformation in politics and religion, is not excited by anything he sees or feels, to question the remains of prejudice. The writers of this country, now taking the field freely and unrestrained, or rather involved by prejudice, will rouse us all from the errors in which we have been hitherto rocked." [1] Taken in itself and without the context this sentence would tend to indicate in Jefferson an almost unreserved approval of the doctrines of the radical reformers and of the very spirit of the French Revolution, but as is so often the case with him, the real meaning is hidden in the last part. It was not so much in their theoretical views he was interested as in the fact that "their logical presentation, might be used in America to overcome the last resistance to the establishment of a true republican régime free from any vestige of monarchical order." But that he hoped that such radical reforms could succeed in France is not indicated. His complete thought is far better expressed in the letter written the next day to Humphreys:

The writings published on this occasion are, some of them, very valuable; because, unfettered by the prejudices under which Englishmen labor, they give a full scope to reason, and strike out truths, as yet unperceived and unacknowledged on the other side of the channel. . . . In fine, I believe this nation will, in the course of the present year, have as full a portion of liberality dealt out to them, as the nation can bear at present, considering how uninformed the mass of their people is.[2]

On the other hand, to believe that they would be able to establish a truly representative and free government was certainly inconceivable to him at this date. To the last moment

[1] March 17, 1789. Memorial Edition, VII, 317.   [2] *Ibid.*, VII, 321.

he hoped that some sort of an agreement would be possible between the nobility and the Commons, for he had decided very early that no confidence should be placed in the clergy. He was looking forward to a close coöperation between the younger part of the nobility and the Commons, who, working together with the king, would seek the support of the people and accomplish important reforms. No fundamental change however could be expected, since the French refused to show any interest in the most vital question of trial by jury.

But as soon as the States-General were opened he realized that he had been too optimistic. Since the *"Noblesse"* would not yield and wanted their delegates to do their dirty work for them, the only manly stand to take for a man like Lafayette, who although of liberal opinion had solicited and obtained a mandate from the nobility, was to go over wholly to the *tiers état*. The opening of the States-General was as imposing as an opera but it was poor business,[1] and even at that time Jefferson placed his confidence in the king who grew astonishingly in his estimation during this year : "Happy that he is an honest, unambitious man who desires neither money nor power for himself; and that his most operative minister (Necker), though he has appeared to trim a little, is still, in the main, a friend to public liberty." [2]

As the deadlock continued, the three orders sitting separately without being able to settle the "great parliamentary question whether they would vote by orders or by persons", Jefferson favored more and more the only solution which, in his opinion, could prevent complete failure, — a triumph of despotism or a sort of civil war :

This third hypothesis which I shall develop, because I like it, and wish it, and hope it, is that as soon as it shall be manifest that the

[1] To Lafayette, May 6, 1788. Memorial Edition, VII, 334. To Carmichael, May 8, 1788. *Ibid.*, VII, 337.
[2] To John Jay, May 9, 1789. *Ibid.*, VII, 345.

committees of conciliation, now appointed by the three chambers, shall be able to agree in nothing, the Tiers will invite the other two orders to come and take their seats in the common chamber. A majority of the Clergy will come, and the minority of the Noblesse. The chamber thus composed, will declare that the States General are now constituted, will notify it to the King, and propose to do business.[1]

At this juncture, Jefferson, in his anxiety to effect a satisfactory compromise, broke all diplomatic precedence; he could not and did not wish to write a French Declaration of Independence; but he could at least propose some form of government which would recognize the fundamental rights of the French citizen while preserving the appearance of the old monarchy. He therefore drew up a "Charter of Rights for the King and Nation" and sent it, not only to Lafayette, but also to Rabaud de Saint Etienne, a prominent defender of the newly reinstated Protestants. In view of the developments that took place later, Jefferson's proposal does not seem revolutionary. At that time, however (June 3, 1789), it went much farther than the Court was willing to go. No appeal to abstract principle and no mention of rights was made. The main provisions consisted of an annual meeting of the States-General, which alone had the right to levy taxes and to appropriate money; the abolishment of all privileges, a sort of *habeas corpus*, the subordination of the military to the civil authority and liberty of the press. In order to induce the king to accept these new charters, all debts already contracted by him became the debts of the nation, and he was to receive a sum of eighty million livres to be raised by a loan. Thus Jefferson was attempting to put into effect the advice he had several times given his French friends: to buy their liberty from the king rather than bring about a revolution. I leave it to others to judge of the morality of the expedient. Certainly it was not in accord with

[1] To Crevecœur, May 20, 1789. Memorial Edition, VII, 368.

the old battle cry of Patrick Henry. But once more Jefferson was consistent in so much as he had always maintained that what was good for America was not necessarily good for France. Moreover, he knew there was no need to stir up the spirit of the Assembly by inflammatory declarations. More than any incitement to take radical steps they needed a dose of cool common sense.

Unfortunately the man at the helm (Necker) "had neither skill nor courage; ambition was his first passion, virtue his second, his judgement was not of the first order not even of the second", and the ship continued to drift in the storm. On June 18, 1789, Jefferson wrote a long letter to Madison, to indicate the situation of the different parties after the Commons had proclaimed themselves the National Assembly on the fifteenth. His characterization even to-day seems remarkably clear and disinterested. He sided decidedly with the Commons who had in their chamber almost all the talents of the nation;

They are firm, bold, yet moderate. There is, indeed, among them, a number of very hot-headed members; but those of most influence are cool, temperate and sagacious. . . . The Noblesse on the contrary, are absolutely out of their senses. They are so furious, they can seldom debate at all. . . . The Clergy are waiting to profit by every incident, to secure themselves, and have no other object in view.

Jefferson, however, paid tribute to the *curés* who, throughout the kingdom, formed the mass of the clergy: "they are the only part favorably known to the people, because solely charged with the duties of baptism, burials, confession, visitation of the sick, instruction of the children, and aiding the poor, they are themselves of the people, and united with them." [1] The letter to Jay of June 24 is a day-by-day recital of the succession of events, the suspension of the meetings of the National

[1] To Madison, June 18, 1789.   Memorial Edition, VII, 386.

Assembly, the *serment* of Jeu de Paume on the twentieth, the *séance royale* of June 23 and the refusal of the *tiers état* to deliberate separately.

Jefferson could not help admiring the tenacity of the Assemblée Nationale, but at the same time estimated that they were going too far and had formed projects that were decidedly too ambitious. "Instead of being dismayed with what has passed, they seem to rise in their demands, and some of them to consider the erasing of every vestige of a difference of order as indispensable to the establishment and preservation of a good constitution. I apprehend there is more courage than calculation in this project." [1]

A letter of Lafayette to Jefferson dated Versailles, July 4, contains an interesting postscriptum: "Will you send me the bill of Rights with your notes." A subsequent letter is even more pressing: "To-morrow I propose my bill of rights about the middle of the sitting; be pleased to consider it again and make your observations." As Lafayette introduced his "Déclaration Européenne des droits de l'homme et du citoyen" on July 11, 1789, the latter may be dated July 10. I had the good fortune to find in the Jefferson papers not one text but two of the Declaration.

One of the versions probably antedated by several months the meeting of the National Assembly. Jefferson had it in his hands as early as the beginning of 1789 and he even sent a copy of it to Madison on January 12.[2] The second text, far more important, was annotated by Jefferson in pencil. Although the handwriting is faint, it is perfectly legible. The emendations and corrections he suggested are quite characteristic, and are studied more in detail in the text I have published elsewhere.[3]

---

[1] To John Jay, June 24–25, 1789. Memorial Edition, VII, 395.
[2] *Ibid.*, VII, 268.
[3] " Letters of Lafayette and Jefferson." Paris, Baltimore, 1929.

Some of the modifications suggested by Jefferson do not require any comment; they are mere verbal changes such as the substitution of "*tels sont*" for "*tels que.*"   But as Lafayette had enumerated among the essential rights of man "*le soin de son honneur*" and "*la propriété*", Jefferson put both terms in brackets, thus indicating that they should be taken out.   The elimination of the first term is probably due to the fact that Montesquieu had indicated that "*honneur*" is the main principle on which rests monarchical government and is easily understandable.   The elimination of the "*droit de propriété*" can only be explained if we refer to the theory of rights already discussed and by which was established a distinction between the natural rights and the civil rights.   Lafayette accepted the first correction but not the second; he was too much under the influence of his physiocratic colleagues even to understand the legalistic and historical point of view of his American friend. The project he submitted to the Assembly, as well as the three "Déclarations des droits de l'homme", consequently followed on this point the Virginia Bill of Rights rather than the Declaration of Independence.

In a similar way, Lafayette had listed the powers constituting the government in the following order: "*exécutif, législatif et judiciaire*", and refused to follow the order suggested by Jefferson's "*législatif, exécutif, judiciaire.*"   This was more than a mere question of arrangement; there was evidently in the minds of both Jefferson and his French friend a question of hierarchy and almost subordination; if it is a mere nuance, the nuance was very significant.   The last paragraph deserves even more careful consideration.   In the January version it read: "*Et comme le progrès des lumières, et l'introduction des abus nécessitent de temps en temps une revision de la constitution* . . . ."   The second edition annotated by Jefferson expressed the same idea in much more definite terms: "*Et comme le progrès des lumières, l'introduction des abus et le droit des géné-*

rations qui se succèdent nécessitent la révision de tout établissement humain, il doit être indiqué des moyens constitutionnels qui assurent dans certain cas une convocation extraordinaire de représentants dont le seul objet soit d'examiner et modifier, s'il le faut, la forme du Gouvernement." This mention of the *"droit des générations qui se succèdent"* seems a typically Jeffersonian idea. The same theory will be found fully developed in a letter to Samuel Kercheval written in 1816 and dealing with the revision of the Constitution of Virginia. It was expressed originally in a letter to James Madison, written from Paris on September 9, 1789. Curiously enough, Jefferson declared then that this theory had never been proposed before : "The question whether one generation of men has a right to bind another, seems never to have been started on this or on our side of the water. Yet it is a question of such consequence as not only to merit decision, but places also the fundamental principles of every government." [1] It is true that this special point was not retained in the "Déclaration des droits de l'homme" as finally adopted by the Assemblée Nationale in its sessions of August, 1789, although it was proposed by Montmorency and reappeared as the last article of the "Déclaration" of the Convention Nationale of May 29, 1793. But one may wonder how Jefferson could overlook the fact that the same principle was embodied in Lafayette's "Declaration." It is very unlikely that he would have claimed credit for the idea if it had been originated by his friend. A more acceptable explanation would be to admit that having suggested to Lafayette a theory which was not retained by the committee, he felt perfectly free to state that "the question had never been started."

The American plenipotentiary was not an eye-witness of the famous scenes of the fourteenth of July, or as he calls it "the tumult of Paris", but he learned about it fully from M. de Corny, and wrote to Jay a long and interesting account (July 19)

---

[1] Memorial Edition, VIII, 454.

of the capture of La Bastille, the return of the king to Paris and the presentation of the national cockade.[1]

In the meantime he was placed in a very embarrassing situation by his French admirers. The prestige of the author of the Declaration of Independence was such that the committee in charge of a plan of constitution thought they could do no better than to call into consultation the Minister of the United States. Champion de Cicé, Archbishop of Bordeaux and chairman of the committee, sent him an urgent appeal to attend one of the first meetings, so that they might profit by the light of his reason and experience.[2] Jefferson, after mentioning the invitation, relates the incident in his "Autobiography" as follows: "I excused myself on the obvious considerations that my mission was to the King, as chief magistrate of the nation, that my duties were limited to the concerns of my own country, and forbade me to intermeddle with the internal transactions of that, in which I had been received under a specific charter." This may be the sense he wished to convey to Champion de Cicé but the actual letter is far less categorical. Contrary to his custom he wrote it himself, although it is in French, alleging that the dispatches for America took all his time and adding that the committee would lay themselves open to criticism if they invited to their deliberations a foreigner accredited to the head of the nation, when the very question under discussion was a modification and abridgement of his powers. But he assured the archbishop of his most sincere and most passionate wishes for the complete success of the undertaking, which was certainly stretching diplomatic proprieties to the limit.

The deliberations of the committee went on without Jefferson's official assistance; but shortly after the project of the constitution was presented, the deputies came to a deadlock

---

[1] To J. Jay, July 19, 1789. Memorial Edition, VII, 409 and to James Madison July 22. *Ibid.*, VII, 424.

[2] Manuscript. Library of Congress, July 20, 1789.

on the veto power to be given to the king. After some stormy meetings, Lafayette conceived the idea that the house of the Minister of the United States was the only place near Versailles where some tranquillity could be obtained. He consequently invited eight of his friends to take dinner at the house of Jefferson, and having no time to consult him on the matter, scribbled a note in great hurry to ask Jefferson to make the necessary preparations for the unexpected guests : "Those gentlemen wish to consult with you and me ; they will dine to-morrow at your house, as mine is always full." [1]

Jefferson has given a somewhat embellished account of the memorable dinner in his "Autobiography." The mention of it in a letter to John Jay a few weeks later is less florid and probably more accurate.[2] The members of the committee discussed together their points of difference for six hours, and in the course of the discussion agreed on mutual sacrifices. Writing from memory, at the age of seventy-seven, Jefferson added : "I was a silent witness to a coolness and candor of argument, unusual in the conflicts of political opinion ; to a logical reasoning, and chaste eloquence, disfigured by no gaudy tinsel of rhetoric or declamation, and truly worthy of being placed in parallel with the finest dialogues of antiquity, as handed to us by Xenophon, by Plato and Cicero." [3]

Whether Jefferson remained a silent witness during these six hours is not so improbable as it would seem. It may well be doubted whether his knowledge of French was sufficient to enable him to participate in an animated discussion with eight Frenchmen. Under the circumstances silence was as much a necessity as a virtue. But when the American minister woke up the next morning he realized that it was impossible to keep the thing secret and that the French Government had

---

[1] Jefferson Papers. Library of Congress, probably August, 1789.
[2] September 20, 1789. Memorial Edition, VII, 474.
[3] "Autobiography", I, 156.

every right to blame him for lending his house for a discussion of French internal politics. Unpleasant as it was, the only thing to do was to make a clean breast of it. He went at once to Montmorin to tell him "with truth and candor how it happened that my house had been made the scene of conferences of such a character." — "He told me," Jefferson continued, "that he already knew everything which had passed," which is the stock answer of the professional diplomat, whether he wishes to appear well-informed or wants to draw some further information from his interlocutor. Jefferson opened his heart, and if Montmorin did not know everything before giving audience to the American minister, there was little he did not know after hearing his account of the dinner.

With this curious incident, Jefferson ends his account of the French Revolution. During the year, he had complained on several occasions that his French friends seemed unable to realize the importance of insisting on trial by jury in criminal cases. He finally persuaded one of the "abbés" to study the question thoroughly and on that occasion indicated exactly how he stood in matters of government. All told, his views had not changed much, and at that time he would not have accepted without reservations and qualifications the famous principle of "government by the people." There was still in his mind, if not in all his formulas, a tacit admission that all the people could not unreservedly participate in all branches of government. Nothing could be clearer than the distinctions he established and nothing could be less demagogical.

"We think, in America, that it is necessary to introduce the people into every department of government, as far as they are capable of exercising it; and that this is the only way to insure a long-continued and honest administration of its power." Then he proceded to define, point by point, the extent to which the people could safely be allowed to participate in the executive, legislative, and judiciary branches of the government.

1. They are not qualified to exercise themselves the executive department, but they are qualified to name the person who shall exercise it. With us, therefore, they choose this officer every four years. 2. They are not qualified to legislate. With us therefore, they only choose the legislators. 3. They are not qualified to *judge* questions of *law*, but they are very capable of judging questions of *fact*. In the form of juries, therefore, they determine all matters of fact, leaving to the permanent judges to decide the law resulting from those facts.[1]

Thus spoke the champion of democracy at the beginning of the French Revolution, after spending five years in Paris and supposedly permeating his mind with the wild theories of the French philosophers. And what he said of the people on this occasion did not apply to the French people alone, for he made it clear that it was the political theory applied "in America." It was essentially the theory of government by experts which he already had in mind when he proposed the reorganization of the College of William and Mary. In 1778, as well as in 1789, Jefferson did not hesitate to proclaim that if the source of all power was in the people, the people could not exercise their power in all circumstances, that they had to delegate their authority to men really qualified, retaining only the right to select them. This may not be the common acceptation of the term "Jeffersonian democracy", but I have a strong suspicion that on the whole Jefferson never changed much in this respect. He certainly never stood for mob rule, nor for direct government by the masses, and he knew too much about the delicate and complicated wheels of government to believe that the running of such a tremendous machine could be intrusted to untrained hands.

As for the French, he trusted them even less, and never believed, as long as he remained in France, that they were prepared for self-government. He refused to consider that a real

[1] To M. l'Abbé Arnoud, Paris, July 19, 1789. Memorial Edition, VII, 422.

revolution had started before his eyes or was even in sight. "Upon the whole," he wrote to Madison shortly before his departure from Paris, "I do not see yet probable that any actual commotion will take place; and if it does take place, I have strong confidence that the patriotic party will hold together, and their party in the nation be what I have ascribed it." Up to the last moment he held the belief that the king, "the substantial people of the whole country, the army, and the influential part of the clergy, formed a firm phalanx which must prevail."[1] The analysis of the situation sent to Jay just as he was about to leave Paris does not indicate even the possibility of establishing a republic, since the only parties he distinguished were:

> . . . the aristocrats, comprehending the higher members of the clergy, military, nobility, and the parliaments of the whole kingdom; the moderate royalists who wish for a constitution nearly similar to that of England; the republicans who are willing to let their first magistracy be hereditary, but to make it very subordinate to the legislature, and to have that legislature consist of a single chamber.[2]

Jefferson was not the man to indulge in effusions even when he was deeply moved and throughout his mission in France he deliberately refrained from any expression of personal feelings. But the love and friendship of the French for the United States was so general and so genuine, it formed such a contrast with the cold and tenacious enmity of Great Britain, that the American minister was won and conquered by it and had to come to the conclusion that "nothing should be spared to attach this country to us. It is the only one on which we can rely for support, under every event. Its inhabitants love us more, I think, than they do any other nation on earth. This is very much the effect of the good dispositions with which the

[1] To Madison, August 28, 1789. Memorial Edition, VII, 448.
[2] To John Jay, September 19, 1789. *Ibid.*, VII, 467.

French officers returned." [1]   Everybody is familiar with the closing lines of Jefferson's account of his mission to France: "So, ask the traveller inhabitant of any nation, in what country would you rather live? — Certainly, in my own, where are all my friends, my relations, and the earliest and sweetest affections and recollections of my life.   Which would be your second choice?   France."

These lines were written at the twilight of his life, when his memory took him back to the wonderful days he had lived in Paris, while the old régime was shedding the last rays of its evanescent glory.   Less known, but far more revealing of his true feelings at the time, is a passage in one of his letters to James Madison.   It is one of the very few times, and as a matter of fact, the first time when he declared that the nations of the world had to abandon their old code of selfishness and that a new principle of international life had to be recognized. For there is only one standard of morality, one code of conduct between nations as between individuals.

It is impossible — he wrote — to desire better dispositions towards us than prevail in this Assembly.   Our proceedings have been viewed as a model for them on every occasion; and though in the heat of debate, men are generally disposed to contradict every authority urged by their opponents, ours has been treated like that of the Bible, open to explanation, but not to question.   I am sorry that in the moment of such a disposition, anything should come from us to check it.   The placing them on a mere footing with the English, will have this effect.   When of two nations, the one has engaged herself in a ruinous war for us, has spent her blood and money to save us, has opened her bosom to us in peace, and received us almost on the footing of her own citizens, while the other has moved heaven, earth, and hell to exterminate us in war, has insulted us in all her councils in peace, shut her doors to us in every part where her interests would admit it, libelled us in foreign nations, endeavoured to poison them against the reception of our most precious commodities;

[1] To James Madison, January 30, 1787.   Memorial Edition, VI, 70.

to place these two nations on a footing, is to give a great deal more to one than to the other, if the maxim be true, that to make unequal quantities equal, you must add more to one than the other. To say, in excuse, that gratitude is never to enter into the motives of national conduct, is to revive a principle which has been buried for centuries with its kindred principles of the lawfulness of assassination, poison, perjury, etc. All of these were legitimate principles in the dark ages which intervened between ancient and modern civilization, but exploded and held in just horror in the eighteenth century. I know but one code of morality for men, whether acting singly or collectively. . . . Let us hope that our government will take some other occasions to show, that they proscribe no virtue from the canons of their conduct with other nations.[1]

[1] To James Madison, August 28, 1789. Memorial Edition, VII, 448.

BOOK FOUR

Monocrats and Republicans

CHAPTER I

THE QUARREL WITH HAMILTON

FOR more than two years Jefferson had repeatedly expressed the wish to be allowed to return to his native country, at least for a short visit. When he finally received official notification that his request had been granted, he departed from Paris rather abruptly and even without taking leave of his best friends. "Adieus are painful," he wrote to Madame de Corny, "therefore I left Paris without bidding one to you." [1] This is a naïve and quite significant confession of the difficulty he experienced in maintaining his puritanical restraint and impassibility at that time. He went with his two daughters from Le Havre to Cowes, and waited there till October 14 for favorable winds. After a rapid crossing on the *Montgomery* they sighted the "Capes" on November 13, and barely escaped being shipwrecked in the bay. Although damaged by fire and stripped of part of her rigging, the ship was able to reach Norfolk, and Jefferson promptly set out for Richmond and Monticello, stopping however on the way at Eppington with the Eppes. It was there that he received two letters from President Washington, one dated October 13, the other November 30, asking him to accept the post of Secretary of State in the newly formed cabinet. The President's letters were most flattering and indicated that he had been "determined, as well by motives of private regard, as a conviction of public propriety" to nominate him for the office.

Jefferson at first experienced the natural repugnance of a man who had put his heart into an important undertaking and

[1] "Trois amitiés françaises de Jefferson", p. 188.

was asked suddenly to abandon it. He was better acquainted
with the situation in Paris than any man he could think of: it
had taken him several years of constant work and patient efforts
to bring the French officials over to his views. His best friends
were in the new government and would help him to obtain
for the United States better commercial terms and a more
satisfactory debt settlement. Let us add that for a philosophical observer France offered the most fascinating spectacle,
and Jefferson did not feel that life in New York could bring
him the same social and intellectual pleasures as Paris. Quite
significantly he wrote to Washington: "as far as my fears, my
hopes, or my inclination enter into this question, I confess that
they would not lead me to prefer a change." On the other
hand, he did not make a categorical refusal, in case he should
be "drafted", and the President formally nominated him.

Nothing else was done in the matter until Madison visited
him at Monticello and acquainted him with the situation.
But even Madison could not win his consent,[1] and the President had to assure Jefferson that the duties of his office would
probably not be quite so complicated and hard to execute
as he might have been led at the first moment to imagine.[2]
It was not a command, but while the President left him
free to decide he expressed a strong hope and wish that
Jefferson would accept. So, on February 14 he sent his letter
of acceptance.

In the meantime he had married Martha to Thomas Mann
Randolph, Junior, "a young gentleman of genius, science, and
honorable mind", who afterwards filled "a dignified station in
the General Government, and the most dignified in his own
State."[3] Although Jefferson had wished for such a marriage,
he had left Martha free to make her own choice, as he explained
in a letter to Madame de Corny: "Tho' his talents, disposi-

---

[1] Madison to Washington.　January 4, 1790.
[2] Washington to Jefferson.　January 21.　　[3] "Autobiography", p. 161.

tion, connections, fortune, were such as would have made him my first choice, yet according to the usage of my country, I scrupulously suppressed my wishes, that my daughter might indulge in her own sentiments freely." [1]   The marriage took place on April 2, 1790, and on the next day Jefferson set out for New York to take his place in the Cabinet.   He reached Philadelphia on the twelfth.   There he stopped to pay his respects to the man "he has succeeded but not replaced", old Doctor Franklin then on the sick bed from which he never arose.   "My recent return from a country in which he had left so many friends, and the perilous convulsions to which they had been exposed, revived all his anxieties to know what part they had taken, what had been their course, and what their fate.   He went over all in succession with a rapidity and animation almost too much for his strength."   It was on this occasion that Franklin put in his hands a paper containing an account of his negotiations with Lord Howe to prevent a war between the colonies and their mother country, papers which, unfortunately, Jefferson entrusted later to William Temple Franklin, who "delayed the publication for more than twenty years." [2]   Jefferson arrived in New York on the twenty-first, took his lodgings at the City Tavern, and finally rented a small house in Maiden Lane.

Congress was in session and business had accumulated on the desk of the new secretary: he plunged at once into work. All his colleagues had already taken charge of their respective departments: Colonel Alexander Hamilton was in charge of the Treasury, General Henry Knox of the War Department, Edmund Randolph, Attorney-general.   Those were the only departments thus far created and among them the four secretaries divided all the different attributions of the executive power.   With them he was to sit in Cabinet meetings pre-

---

[1] "Trois amitiés françaises de Jefferson", p. 195.   February 28, 1790.
[2] "Autobiography."   Memorial Edition, I, 103.

sided over by Washington until his retirement from office, in December, 1793.

The distinction usually established between domestic and foreign politics is obviously an arbitrary one and does not correspond to reality. This was particularly true of an age when the attributes of the Secretary of State were far less specialized than in our day. Even if he had been inclined to neglect the questions of internal administration — to give himself entirely to foreign affairs — Jefferson would have been constantly reminded of the existence of many other problems of equal importance to the future of the nation by his colleagues and the President himself. In addition, it was Washington's ordinary practice not only to discuss all important measures in a Cabinet council, but often to request each member of his official family to give his opinion in writing on these questions. Such documents as have been preserved constitute a most precious source of information for the history of the period; they are usefully supplemented by the notes that Jefferson took at the time and transcribed "twenty five years or more" afterwards for the use of posterity. The three volumes "bound in marbled paper" in which Jefferson copied these notes, taken on loose scraps of paper, are the famous "Anas" which he collected to justify himself against the accusations that biographers of Washington — such as Marshall — had already launched against him. Although there is no reason to believe that Jefferson deliberately altered the old records, it is certain that they were edited, that many scraps of papers were discarded, although not destroyed, and that a "critical" edition of the "Anas" would not be without interest. They are preceded by an introduction in which, more than twenty-five years later, Jefferson gave an estimate of his former opponents, Hamilton and John Adams. This final judgment can in no way be used in discussing events that took place between 1790 and 1793, and it contains no indication worth retaining about

Jefferson's attitude at that time towards his colleagues and the Vice President. The man who wrote this introduction in February, 1818, was really another Jefferson. He may tell us that he arrived in the midst of a bitter contest, "But a stranger to the ground, a stranger to the actors on it, so long absent as to have lost all familiarity with the subject, and as yet unaware of its object, I took no concern in it." [1] It must be admitted at the outset that such is not the impression one can gather from the correspondence.

That the financial structure of the Continental Congress had collapsed and that immediate remedies were necessary Jefferson knew as well and probably better than any other member of the Cabinet. He had not the expert knowledge of Hamilton, but more than once he had had to deal with financial questions, and when in Paris had displayed considerable skill in dealing with the members of the Committee of Commerce. He had prepared schedules for the payment of the French and Dutch loans and discussed finances with Dutch bankers in Amsterdam. Furthermore, his governorship of Virginia during the war had acquainted him with the question of State debts. If he could be tricked and made to hold the candle, as he said, there was no man who could resist the superior genius and Machiavellism of the arch financier of the United States. As a matter of fact, if he was hoodwinked, he was not at the beginning, at least, a blind or an unwilling victim.

Following the financial reorganization defined by the Constitution and the appointment of a Secretary of the Treasury, according to the Act of 1789, Hamilton prepared for the period under consideration four documents: Report on Public Credit, January 9, 1790; Report on a National Bank, December 5, 1790; Report on the Establishment of a Mint, May 1, 1791; Report on Manufactures, December 5, 1791.

[1] Memorial Edition, I, 274.

The first subject for consideration was the national debt. The foreign debt was unquestionably a matter of national honor and had to be paid in full, according to the terms of contract: with the arrears of interest it amounted to $11,710,000. The domestic debt was estimated at $27,383,000 for the principal, $13,030,000 for accrued interest and $2,000,000 for unliquidated debt. After some opposition it was finally decided that holders of certificates would receive their face value with interest. But there remained the question of States debts which was hopelessly confused and destined to lead to a bitter controversy. The reorganization plan proposed that repayment could be made in a more orderly way through some sort of a central organization rather than through the States, and outlined the famous "Assumption" by which the Federal Government would "assume", with a discount to be determined, the debts incurred by the several States during the course of the war. It naturally meant that additional revenue had to be raised by Federal measures and consequently distributed between all the States, whose debts varied in nature and amount from State to State, some of which having already proceeded to a semi-reorganization, while others, having not suffered from the war, were financially in good condition. The opposition came naturally from the Southern States, whose population was smaller in comparison with the Northern States.

The opponents of the measure objected very strenuously at first, arguing that it would give an unfair advantage to those that had contracted debts too freely during the war, and would penalize those who had already set their financial house in order; and also that it would be a usurpation of powers not conferred by the Constitution to the Federal Government.

First defeated in Congress, the "Assumption" was finally adopted under circumstances now to be related. Jefferson's unofficial representative in Congress, Madison, had already strenuously opposed the measure proposed by the Secretary of the Treasury. When Jefferson arrived in New York to take possession of his office, the battle had been going on for some time, and four days later he wrote to T. M. Randolph that "Congress is principally occupied with the treasury report. The assumption of the State debts has been voted affirmatively in the first instance, but it is not certain that it will hold its ground through all the changes of the bill when it shall be brought in." [1] There is little doubt that Madison had already acquainted him with his views of the situation, but it is also probable that Jefferson paid small heed to them for the time being. He suffered for several weeks from severe headaches, he had to write many letters of farewell to his French friends, and the accumulation of reports and papers he found on his desk required all his attention.

In June, however, he expressed to George Mason his doubts that the "Assumption" would be finally adopted. But, far from siding with the out-and-out opponents of the measure, he thought it would be wiser to compromise, so he added, "my duties preventing me from mingling in these questions, I do not pretend to be very competent to their decision. In general, I think it necessary to give as well as take in a government like ours." [2]

As a matter of fact, it was already patent that an almost irreconcilable difference of opinion on the matter existed between Hamilton and the Virginians, and, a week later, Jefferson himself invited the Secretary of the Treasury to take dinner at his house with a few friends in order to hold an informal conference; for he thought it impossible that "reasonable men, consulting together coolly, could fail, by some mutual sacrifices of opinion to form a compromise which was to save the Union." Jefferson has related the scene in the "Anas", but a somewhat different account is given in his letter to James Monroe, written

---

[1] March 28, 1790. Memorial Edition, VIII, 9.
[2] June 13, 1790. *Ibid.*, VIII, 36.

June 20, 1790, from New York, in which he outlined the compromise. He mentioned that two considerations had impelled him to discuss it; first the fact that if some funding
bill were not agreed to, the credit of the United States at Amsterdam would collapse and vanish and each State be left alone
to take care of itself. Although he was not enthusiastic about
the means to be employed and foresaw that the United States
would have difficulties in raising the necessary money by Federal taxation instead of letting the States raise it themselves,
he accepted the solution with open eyes: "In the present instance, I see the necessity of yielding to cries of the creditors
in certain parts of the Union; for the sake of the Union, and to
save us from the greatest of all calamities, the total extinction
of our credit in Europe." More than any member of the Cabinet he was aware of the imminence of this danger. On the
other hand, and in order to give some satisfaction to the Southern States, it would be agreed that Congress would be transferred to Philadelphia for a period of twelve to fifteen years,
and thereafter, without further declaration, to Georgetown.
This was clearly a "deal", and Jefferson knew it so well that
he denied that it was one. "The Pennsylvania and Virginia
delegates have conducted themselves honorably, on the question of residence. Without descending to talk about bargains,
they have seen that their true interests lay in not listening to
the insidious propositions made, to divide and defect them, and
we have seen them at times voting against their respective
wishes rather than separate." Whether the word bargain
had been used or not is immaterial. Gentlemen sitting around
a table after the cloth has been removed and the punch bowl
brought in can come to an understanding "à demi mot."[1] Nothing official had been done yet, but writing to Dumas, the financial agent at Amsterdam, Jefferson, in order to maintain the
credit of the country, put his best foot forward and solemnly

[1] June 20, 1790. Memorial Edition, VIII, 43.

declared "that there is not one single individual in the United States, whether in or out of office, who supposes they can ever do anything which might impair their foreign contracts." With respect to domestic paper, Dumas could rest assured that "justice would be done" and, although the question was terribly complicated, it was "possible that modifications may be proposed which may bring the measure, yet into an acceptable form."[1]

With Gilmer, he was more frank and indicated clearly that among the possible ways in which the conflict in Congress might yet terminate, the best probably would be "a *bargain* between the eastern members who have it so much at heart, and the Middle members who are indifferent about it, to adopt these debts without modification, on condition of removing the seat of government to Philadelphia or Baltimore." The third solution, which Jefferson preferred, would have proposed to divide the total sum between all the States in proportion to their census, and to establish the national capital first and temporarily at Philadelphia, then, and permanently at Georgetown.[2] This was not an ideal solution; it was a compromise which would at least present the advantage of giving new life to the agriculture and commerce of the South. The main objection, however, still remained, for the Federal Government would have to raise the imposts and overburden that source of revenue, but it seemed that "some sacrifice was necessary for the sake of peace."[3] Once again, but not for the last time, Jefferson saw himself in a dilemma. He was too far-sighted not to understand that the individual States would have to abandon some of their rights and a portion of their sovereignty in order to acquire more financial stability, and that more power would be concentrated in the hands of the Federal Government. On the other hand, he was no less firmly convinced

[1] June 23, 1790. Memorial Edition, VIII, 47.
[2] To Gilmer, June 27, 1790. *Ibid.*, VIII, 53.   [3] *Ibid.*, VIII, 63.

that a secession would unavoidably result from a rejection of the "Assumption", and he was ready to sacrifice his most cherished preferences on the altar of the Union.

On August 14, Jefferson could announce to Randolph that Congress had separated

the day before yesterday, having reacquired the harmony which always distinguished their proceedings before the two disagreeable questions of assumption and residence were introduced. . . . It is not foreseen that anything so generative of dissention can arise again, and therefore the friends of the government hope that this difficulty once surmounted in the States, everything will work well. I am principally afraid that commerce will be over loaded by the assumption, believing that it would be better that property should be duly taxed.

He discussed for the first time the exact ways and means in a letter to Gouverneur Morris on November 26, 1790, and indicated that additional funds would be provided by a tax on spirituous liquors, foreign and homemade, that the whole interest would be raised by taxes on consumption. . . . "Add to this what may be done by throwing in the aid of western lands and other articles as a sinking fund, and our prospect is really a bright one." [1]

It is perfectly true that the letter to Morris was to a great extent for publicity purposes, yet we do not find in it the slightest mark of disapproval of the tax itself, nor do we find it in a letter written to De Moustier [2] in which, on the contrary, Jefferson mentioned the advantages of duties on consumption, which fall principally on the rich; for it is "a general desire to make them contribute the whole money we want, if possible." It was not until February that doubts began to percolate into his mind, and he inquired from Colonel Mason "what was said in our country (Virginia), of the fiscal arrangements

[1] November 26, 1790.   Memorial Edition, VIII, 107.
[2] December 3, 1790.   *Ibid.*, VIII, 109.

now going on." But he did not yet take the question really
to heart:

Whether these measures be right or wrong abstractedly, more
attention should be paid to the general opinion. However, all
will pass, — the excise will pass — the bank will pass. The only
corrective of what is corrupt in our present form of government will
be the augmentation of the numbers in the lower House, so as to get
more agricultural representation, which may put that interest above
that of the stock-jobbers.[1]

This is the first indication of a rift between Jefferson and
Hamilton.

Yet Jefferson was willing to yield more ground in order to
avoid an open break. The Bank Bill of Hamilton had passed
the Senate without difficulty; in the House it had been opposed
on constitutional grounds by Madison but had finally obtained
a majority. When the bill was sent to the President, Washington, unwilling to do anything unconstitutional, asked both
the Attorney-general Randolph and Jefferson to give their
opinion on the matter in writing. The report written on this
occasion by the Secretary of State is a psychological document
both interesting and revealing.

Jefferson started out by enumerating the different measures included in the Bank Bill, pointing out *en passant* that
they were intended to break down the most ancient and fundamental laws of several States, such as those against mortmain,
the laws of alienage, the rules of descent, the acts of distribution, the laws of escheat and forfeiture, the laws of monopoly.
He then demonstrated to his own satisfaction that power to
establish such an institution was neither specifically declared
nor implied in any article of the Constitution. The only general statement that could be construed as authorizing it was a
mention "to make all laws *necessary* and proper for carrying
into execution the enumerated powers." Finally he under-

---

[1] February 4, 1791. Memorial Edition, VIII, 123.

took to prove that the bank might be convenient but was in nowise necessary. The conclusion was obvious after these very closely knitted pieces of legal reasoning: "Nothing but a necessity inevitable by any other means can justify such a prostitution of laws, which constitute the pillars of our whole system of jurisprudence." The President's veto could clearly be used in that case, since that was the buckler provided by the Constitution to protect it against the invasions of the legislature.

Jefferson could and perhaps should have stopped there. But he was far from certain that Hamilton's views would not prevail, and in that case he would have committed himself irrevocably. This he did not wish to do. He consequently provided at the end a way of escape for himself as well as for the President:

It must be added, however, that unless the President's mind on a view of everything which is urged for and against this bill, is tolerably clear that it is unauthorized by the Constitution; if the pro and the con hang so even as to balance his judgment, a just respect for the wisdom of the legislature would naturally decide the balance in favor of their opinion. It is chiefly for cases where they are clearly misled by error, ambition, or interest, that the Constitution has placed a check in the negative of the President.

This was very adroit, almost too adroit. It was the answer of a master politician. Whether it was absolutely straightforward is a very different question. Jefferson, who so often accused others of being "trimmers", was undoubtedly open to such an accusation himself.

With the opinion of Randolph and Jefferson before him, the President asked Hamilton, as sponsor of the bill, to present his rejoinder in writing. On the twenty-third he submitted his famous "Opinion as to the Constitutionality of the Bank of the United States" in which he developed the doctrine of "implied powers."

Now it appears — said Hamilton — to the Secretary of the Treasury that this general principle is inherent in the very definition of government and essential to every step of the progress to be made by that of the United States, namely: That every power vested in a government is in its nature sovereign, and includes, by force of the term, a right to employ all the means requisite and fairly applicable to the attainment of the ends of such power, and which are not precluded by restrictions and exceptions specified in the Constitutions, or not immoral, or not contrary to the essential ends of political society.

As a matter of fact, the question at the bottom of the controversy was the question of State rights; but, curiously enough, it is indicated only incidentally in Jefferson's opinion. He was not ready to join issues on that question, much more clearly brought forward by Madison in his speeches before the House, when he said:

I consider the foundation of the Constitution as laid on this ground: That all powers not delegated to the United States, by the Constitution, nor prohibited by it to the United States, are reserved to the States or to the people (XIIth amendment). To take a single step beyond the boundaries thus specifically drawn around the power of Congress, is to take possession of a boundless field of power, no longer susceptible of definition.[1]

This was exactly the question, for to accept Hamilton's theory was to open the way to countless encroachments of the Federal Government on State rights. Washington's administration had come to its most momentous decision for the future of the government of the United States. This was really the parting of the ways. Jefferson knew it and saw it; it was obvious that, with a centralized financial organization, a central political organization would develop. All sorts of practical considerations may be brought in and nice legal points drawn, but the fact remains that when the representatives of the different

[1] "Writings", VI, 19–43.

States not only permitted but were eager to see the Federal Government assume the responsibility of State debts, they sold their birthright for the not unconsiderable sum of $21,500,000. Perhaps it was the only possible solution at the time. Perhaps Jefferson showed wisdom and political sense in not getting up and fighting to the last ditch. He registered as strong a protest as he could without burning his bridges. He knew from the temper of the House that there was no hope of making them accept any other solution. He knew that against the strongly organized Federalists he could not muster any well-disciplined troops. He feared the immediate dissolution of the Union and temporized; but all the rest of his life was to be spent in trying to recover the ground lost on that day.

Jefferson was soon to realize how poorly equipped and seconded he was when he had to take up the battle practically single-handed.

In the spring of 1791 Madison had loaned him a copy of Thomas Paine's pamphlet, "The Rights of Man", written in answer to Burke's denunciation of the French Revolution. When the owner of the pamphlet requested that it be returned, for it was the only copy at his disposal and he intended to have it reprinted in Philadelphia, Jefferson courteously returned it, and added a short note in which he expressed his satisfaction that such a valuable work would appear in America: "I am extremely pleased to find it will be reprinted here, and that something is at length to be publicly said against the political heresies which have sprung up among us. I have no doubt our citizens will rally a second time round the standard of 'Common Sense.'" There is no indication whatever that Jefferson intended the note for publication, but the printer thought it would help the success of the pamphlet if Jefferson's letter were printed as a preface. All the peaceful intentions of the Secretary of State had come to naught. The word heresies could apply only to the Federalists, and among the Federalists to

John Adams, whose "Discourse on Davila" had been appearing in Fenno's paper. Jefferson could declare that nothing was further from his intentions than to appear as a contradictor of Mr. Adams in public; very few men would believe it and Jefferson himself realized it so well that he wrote at once to Washington to explain his position:

Mr. Adams will unquestionably take to himself the charge of political heresy, as conscious of his own views of drawing the present government to the form of the English constitution, and, I fear, will consider me as meaning to injure him in the public eye. I learnt that some Anglomen have, censured it in another point of view, as a sanction of Paine's principles tend to give offence to the British government. Their real fear, however, is that this popular and republican pamphlet, taking wonderfully, is likely at a single stroke, to wipe out all the unconstitutional doctrines which their bell wether Davila has been preaching for a twelvemonth. I certainly never made a secret of my being anti-monarchical, and anti-aristocratical; but I am sincerely mortified to be thus brought forward on the public stage, where to remain, to advance or to retire, will be equally against my love of silence and quiet and my abhorrence of dispute.[1]

His abhorrence of dispute was so real that, at this juncture, he decided to leave Philadelphia for a trip north, staying two days in New York, visiting the battlefield of Saratoga, Lake George, Lake Champlain, and coming back through the Connecticut valley. Madison accompanied him on the trip, and Mr. Bowers has advanced the hypothesis that it was during the long conversations the two friends had during a whole month alone together that the plans were formulated for establishing a separate party to defend the republican ideals. This may have been the result of the journey, but I doubt very much that such was the purpose of Jefferson when he set out from Philadelphia. A more simple explanation is that, having written his letter to Washington and made, as he thought, his position

[1] To the President of the United States. Memorial Edition, VIII, 192. May 8, 1791.

clear, he hoped that the President would not fail to communicate its contents to Adams if any unpleasant situation should develop; and he simply withdrew from the battlefield in order not to enter into a public controversy. But he counted without Adams' temper. The Vice President considered Jefferson's short sentence as a challenge and proceeded promptly to have it answered. A series of articles signed "Publicola" began to appear in the *Centinel*, denouncing not only Paine, but Jefferson himself. "Brutus" took up the cudgels in favor of Jefferson and the newspaper battle was on. The public, always eager to identify anonymous writers, did not fail to attribute to Adams the articles signed "Publicola", while to Jefferson were attributed the answers written by Agricola, Brutus, and Philodemus. When Jefferson came back from his trip the controversy was raging, and soon he began to enjoy the conflict.

On July 10 he sent to Colonel Monroe a bundle of papers showing "what a dust Paine's pamphlet has kicked up here", and he reiterated his approval of the book:

A writer under the name of Publicola, in attacking Paine's principles, is very desirous of involving me in the same censure with the author. I certainly merit the same, for I profess the same principles; but it is equally certain I never meant to have entered as a volunteer into the cause. My occupations do not permit it. Some persons here are insinuating that I am Brutus, that I am Agricola, that I am Philodemus, etc., etc. I am none of them, being decided not to write a word on the subject, unless any printed imputation should call for a printed disavowal, to which I should put my name.

On the other hand he refused to take seriously the denial that Adams "has no more concern in the publication of the writings of Publicola, than the author of the 'Rights of Man' himself." But he saw with satisfaction that Hamilton had taxed Adams with imprudence in stirring up the question and agreed that "his business was done." What was far more serious was the fury of gambling that had arisen at the opening of the bank: "the land office, the federal town, certain schemes of manufactures, are likely to be converted into aliment for that rage." [1]

In a last effort to placate Adams, however, and chiefly in order to avoid having his name dragged into a public controversy, he wrote to the Vice President "from the conviction that truth, between candid minds can never do harm." He assured him that he had not written "a line for the newspapers." He declared "with truth in the presence of the Almighty that nothing was further from his intention or his expectations than to have either his own or Adams' name brought before the public on this occasion." This was perfectly true, but at the same time he was proposing to appoint Paine Postmaster, and on July 29 he wrote to congratulate him, for, thanks to his little book, the general opinion seemed to rally against a sect high in name but small in number. "They are checked at least by your pamphlet, and the people confirmed in their good old faith." [2] The fact that Adams accepted Jefferson's explanation more gracefully than was to be expected did not prevent the fight from going on. It had already been taken out of the hands of the leaders and the controversy was raging in the papers. At this juncture Jefferson realized that the republicans were very poorly armed in the capital and that they had no paper in which their views could be expressed so as to counteract the pernicious propaganda of Fenno's paper. Thus the result brought about was the foundation of the *National Gazette*, Philip Freneau's paper, in which Jefferson had a great part. The story has never been told completely and deserves more than passing attention, since Jefferson was soon to be attacked by his enemies for the interest he took in the *Gazette*. Several documents heretofore neglected allow us to reconstruct exactly the part played by Jefferson in the undertaking, and

[1] Memorial Edition, VIII, 208. [2] *Ibid.*, VIII, 223.

particularly to settle a few questions of chronology which are not without importance.

It does not appear that Jefferson had any ulterior motives when, on February 28, 1791, he offered to Freneau, then living miserably in New York, the clerkship for foreign languages in the Department of State. "The salary indeed is very low," he wrote, "being but two hundred and fifty dollars a year; but also it gives so little to do, as not to interfere with any other calling the person may choose . . . I was told a few days ago that it might perhaps be convenient to you to accept it. If so, it is at your service." Freneau answered promptly, on March 5, that, having been for some time engaged in endeavouring to establish a Weekly Gazette in Monmouth County and having at present a prospect of succeeding in a tolerable subscription, he found himself under the necessity of declining the acceptance of this "generous unsolicited proposal." On May 15, 1791, Jefferson, writing to T. M. Randolph, expressed his discontent at the attitude of the two leading papers of Philadelphia and added:

We have been trying to get another weekly or half weekly paper set up excluding advertisements so that it might go through the States and furnish a right vehicle of intelligence. We hoped at one time to have persuaded Freneau to set up here, but failed — in the meantime Bache's paper, the principles of which were always republican improve it's matter.

Not until August 4 did Freneau write to Jefferson that, after discussing the matter with Madison and Colonel Lee, he had succeeded in making arrangements with a printer in Philadelphia and would submit proposals for the publication of a newspaper. Freneau moved to Philadelphia, was appointed clerk for foreign languages on August 16, and took oath of office the next day. There is consequently no doubt that Freneau was induced to leave New York by the double prospect of working in Jefferson's office and at the same time establishing a republican newspaper. On November 20, Jefferson sent some sample copies to Randolph and wrote again on January 22 to ask his son-in-law to find subscribers to the *Gazette*. He sent to Freneau a list of subscribers from Charlottesville (March 23, 1792) and wrote to his friends that it was the best paper ever published in America. On November 16, 1792, he announced to Randolph that Freneau's paper was getting into Massachusetts under the patronage of "Hancock, Sam. Adams, Mr. Ames, the colossus of the monocrats and paper men will either be left out or hard run. The people of that State are republican; but hitherto they have heard nothing but the hymns and lauds chaunted by Fenno."

When Freneau was vehemently accused by Hamilton of attacking members of the government while in the pay of the government, Jefferson took up his defense and wrote to the speaker of the House to point out that Freneau received a nominal salary and had even "to pay himself special translators for languages with which he was unacquainted." [1] Finally, on October 11, Freneau sent in his resignation to date from October 1, 1793. Such are the bare facts and as Freneau's paper was to play an important part in the quarrel with Hamilton, it is important to state them exactly.

The battle did not begin in earnest until the first months of 1792. But Jefferson's distaste for the financial structure erected by Hamilton increased during the summer and fall of that year. To Carmichael he grudgingly admitted that the domestic debt "funded at six per cent., is twelve and a half per cent. above par." "But," he added, "a spirit of gambling, in our public paper has seized too many of our citizens, and we fear it will check our commerce, arts, manufactures, and agriculture unless stopped." [2] To Gouverneur Morris he declared

---

[1] Jefferson Papers. Library of Congress, January 2, 1793.
[2] August 24, 1791. Memorial Edition, VIII, 229.

that the fever of gambling on government funds has seized
everybody, "has laid up our ships at the wharves, as too slow
instruments of profit, and has even disarmed the hand of the
tailor of his needle and thimble.   They say the evil will cure
itself.   I wish it may; but I have rarely seen a gamester cured,
even by the disasters of his vocation." [1]

One may wonder at this point what course of conduct was
open to Jefferson.   He might have placed his views of the
situation before Washington and tried to open his eyes to the
danger of the Republic.   He might have broken completely
with Hamilton and declared to the President that he had to
decide between the Secretary of the Treasury and the Secretary of State, but as a matter of fact his hands were tied since
he had accepted the "Assumption" and had not dared categorically to decide against the Bank Bill.   Apparently he had
reached an impasse.   But it was not in Jefferson's temperament to try to overcome insuperable obstacles or stay very
long in a blind alley.   Since experience had shown that the
general government "tended to monarchy" and this tendency
strengthened itself from day to day, the only remedy was for
the States to erect "such barriers at the constitutional line
as cannot be surmounted either by themselves or by the
General Government." [2]   An opportunity presented itself to
experiment with the idea in a proposed convocation of a
convention in Virginia to amend the Constitution.   Jefferson,
consulted on this occasion, sent to Archibald Stuart his ideas
on the modifications desirable; to lengthen the term of the
representatives and diminish their number; to strengthen the
Executive by making it more independent of the legislature.

Responsibility is a tremendous engine in a free government.   Let
him feel the whole weight of it then, by taking away the shelter of
his executive council.   Experience both ways has already established

---

[1] August 30, 1791.   Memorial Edition, VIII, 241.
[2] To John Adams, August 30, 1791.   *Ibid.*, VIII, 245.

the superiority of this measure. Render the judiciary respectable by every possible means, to wit, firm tenure in office, competent salaries, and reduction of their numbers.

This was quite characteristic of Jefferson and of his extraordinary tenacity. It was also very good strategy. Since the strengthening of the Federal Government could not be avoided, the only way to avoid a rapid absorption of local government by the Federal machine was to strengthen in a parallel way the State governments. It was an unexpected application of Montesquieu's theory of checks and balances.[1]

Soon afterwards, however, in February, 1792, Jefferson found a favorable opportunity to reveal his ideas to Washington. The occasion that offered itself was the post-office, just reorganized as an independent and self-supporting branch of the government, thus removing it from the tutelage of the Treasury Department. Jefferson at once claimed it for the Department of State, not out of any appetite for power, "his real wish" being to avail the public of every occasion, during the residue of the President's period, to place things on a safe footing. By this he meant that the usurpations of the Treasury Department should be brought to a stop. In a long conversation the next morning after breakfast Jefferson opened his heart, indicating that he would resign before long, to which Washington answered that he could not resign when there were certain signs of dissatisfaction among the public, and that none could foresee what too great a change in the administration might bring about. This was the opening awaited by Jefferson. No wonder the public was dissatisfied, but whose fault was it! There was only one source of discontent, the Department of the Treasury. Then he launched forth on a passionate indictment of the system developed by Hamilton, contrived for deluging the States with paper money instead of

[1] December 23, 1791. Memorial Edition, VIII, 275.

gold and silver, "for withdrawing our citizens from the pursuits of commerce, manufactures, buildings, and other branches of useful industry, to occupy themselves and their capitals in a species of gambling, destructive of morality, and which had introduced its poison in the government itself." He indicated that members of Congress had been gambling in stocks and consequently could no longer be depended upon to vote in a disinterested way, for they had "feathered their nests with paper." Finally Jefferson let the cat out of the bag and told the President that the public were awaiting with anxiety his decision with respect to a certain proposition, to find out whether they lived under a limited or an unlimited government. The report on manufactures which had not heretofore drawn particular attention meant to establish the doctrine that the power given by the Constitution to collect taxes to provide for the "*general welfare* of the United States, permitted Congress to take everything under their management which *they* should deem *public welfare*, and which is susceptible of the application of money." He added that his decision was therefore expected with far greater anxiety than that felt over the proposed establishment of the Bank of the United States.[1]

On May 23, Jefferson had found it impossible to have again a heart-to-heart talk with the President, and we may well imagine that Washington rather avoided giving him another opportunity to express himself again so freely with reference to the policy of the Treasury Department. The object of the letter he wrote on that day was twofold; first of all it was to persuade Washington that in spite of his so often manifested intention to retire at the end of his first term, it was his imperious duty to the nation to remain in office. There existed, in Jefferson's opinion, a real emergency and he pointed out at length the dissatisfaction of the South, the separatist tendencies appearing in that quarter, upon seeing what they con-

[1] March 1, 1792. Memorial Edition, I, 292, "Anas."

sidered an unfair share of the Federal taxes placed on their shoulders, not only in order to pay the national debt, but also to encourage the Northern industries with bounties. Rumors were circulating everywhere that new measures were on foot to increase the mass of the debts; industry was encouraged at the expense of agriculture; the legislature itself had been corrupted. The only hope of salvation lay in the coming election and in an increase in the number of representatives following the census. But everything would be in question if the President did not run. "The confidence of the whole Union is centered in you. Your being at the helm will be more than an answer to every argument which can be used to alarm and lead the people in any quarter, into violence and secession. North and South will hang together if they have you to hang on."

This incidentally does not sound like a man who was trying to organize a strong political party for his own benefit, and I cannot believe that Jefferson was as deep a politician as Mr. Bowers has made him. He was quite sincere in his desire to retire from office "after the first periodical renovation of the government." He was tired and sick at heart, and his one inclination was "bent irresistibly on the tranquil enjoyment of his family, his farm and his books." [1] On the other hand, he was firmly convinced that the coming elections might change favorably the majority in Congress. They had no chance to be held fairly, however, unless the people had an opportunity to select as President a man who would be above all suspicion, a really national figure enjoying the confidence of every man in every section of the country, such as was Washington alone. Had Washington followed his inclination at that time; had he withdrawn at the end of his first term and left the field free to other candidates, there is no way of surmising what the issue of the campaign of 1792 would have been. Truly Jefferson was right: the fate of the republic was at stake.

[1] May 23, 1792. Memorial Edition, VIII, 341.

Shortly after, Hamilton, who had not yet attacked Jefferson personally, led an offensive against Freneau who was accused by the *Gazette of the United States* of using his salary for publications, "the design of which is to villify those to whom the voice of the people has committed the administration of our public affairs." But Freneau, in Hamilton's opinion, was only the puppet whose strings were pulled by an arch plotter, and soon the *Gazette* started direct attacks against Jefferson, asserting that while a member of the Cabinet he had undertaken to undermine the government. Freneau, in an affidavit, denied that Jefferson had any connection with his paper or had dictated or written a single line in it, and at the same time hinted that, on the contrary, the authorship of many articles published in Fenno's *Gazette* could clearly be attributed to Hamilton. This denial had precisely the value of any such statement issued during political campaigns. It was literally true that Jefferson had never written a line in Freneau's paper, but he had an opportunity to see Freneau every day, since "clerk for foreign languages" had to report to him. He was requesting all his friends to subscribe to Freneau's papers, he was following anxiously the progress of the *Gazette* in all parts of the Union, and one word from him would have stopped all attacks against Hamilton. In fact, Freneau's paper was just as much Jefferson's paper as if the Secretary of State had written all the articles in it and had owned all the stock.

Hamilton's attacks, however, had a very important and unexpected result. Whether Jefferson had serious political ambitions or not, he was not the man to come out in the open and proclaim himself the leader of a new party. Of a retiring disposition, fearful of public criticism although thirsty for public praise, he was not ready at that time to assume the part and the duties of a political chief. But the savage attacks of the Federalists attracted public attention to him, he was represented so often by them as the champion of republicanism, that discontented republicans began to rally round him and Jefferson was thus invested with the leadership of the new party as much by his enemies as by his friends.

During the summer of 1792, when he was at Monticello, he received from Washington a letter in which the President expressed his distress at the dissensions that had taken place within the government, and once more attempted to bring about a reconciliation between the two secretaries (August 23). Jefferson answered in a long letter. This time his temper had been thoroughly aroused. He had seen articles signed "An American" in Fenno's *Gazette*, accusing him on three counts: "with having written letters to his friends in Europe to oppose the present constitution; with a desire of repudiating the public debt; with setting up a paper to decry and slander the government." Jefferson had no difficulty in proving the first two accusations absolutely untrue. On the third charge he admitted and even boasted of having given a poet a miserable appointment at a salary of $250 a year, while Hamilton had filled the administration with his creatures. He protested in the name of Heaven that "I never did, by myself, or any other, directly or indirectly, write, dictate, or procure any one sentence of sentiment to be inserted in *his*, or any other gazette, to which my name was not affixed or that of my office." He confessed, however, that he had always taken it for granted, from his knowledge of Freneau's character, "that he would give free place to pieces written against the aristocratical and monarchical principles these papers had inculcated." He again protested against Hamilton's insinuation that Freneau had received his salary before removing to Philadelphia, and on this point he is supported by the evidence published above. In a very dignified way he assured Washington that he would refrain from engaging in any controversy while in office and that he wished to concentrate all his efforts on the last of his official tasks. He added, however, that he reserved the right to answer later, for, he said: "I will not suffer my retirement to be clouded by the slanders of a man whose history, from the moment at which history can stoop to notice him, is a tissue of machinations against the liberty of the country which has not only received and given him bread, but heaped honors on his head."

Jefferson has sometimes been reproached for having attacked in the "Anas" a dead enemy, but this was no posthumous attack. In one sentence he had expressed not only condemnation of Hamilton's policies but all the scorn of a Virginian, of the old stock, for the immigrant of doubtful birth, who was almost an alien. He knew full well the weight that such a consideration might have on the mind of Washington; it was a subtle but potent appeal to the solidarity of the old Americans against the newcomer. Truly, Jefferson was no mean adversary, and the rapier may be more deadly than the battle-ax. Having thus parried and thrust, he expressed the pious wish that the coming elections would probably vindicate his point of view and that it would not be necessary to make a further appeal to public opinion. He was tired and wished to retire from office at the earliest opportunity, and certainly no clique would receive any support from him during the short space he had to remain in Philadelphia. Monticello was calling him and his most earnest hope was that he would be permitted to forget all political strife in a bucolic retirement.[1]

On his way back to Philadelphia he stopped at Mount Vernon (October 1, 1792) and found Washington still undecided whether he would be a candidate for a second term. The General was not certain that the emergency was such that he must sacrifice his personal preferences. He had consulted Lear about opinion in the North; Jefferson could tell him something about the South. When he was assured that he alone could save the Republic, it was his turn to argue that Jeffer-

[1] September 9, 1792. Memorial Edition, VIII, 408.

son ought to remain in office as long as he himself would be President. Washington said that until very recently he had been unaware that such personal differences existed between the Secretary of State and the Secretary of the Treasury. The old General gently reminded Jefferson that the best way to counteract the action of Hamilton was to remain in office, in order "to keep things in their proper channel, and prevent them from going too far." Finally the President refused to accept wholly the pessimistic forecasts of Jefferson and declared: "That as to the idea of transforming this Government into a monarchy, he did not believe there were ten men in the United States whose opinions were worth attention, who entertained such a thought." He refused to take seriously Jefferson's accusation that Hamilton would have said that "this Constitution was a shilly-shally thing, of mere milk and water, which could not last, and was only good as a step to something better." That as far as corruption in the legislature was concerned, the term was probably too severe; it was simply a manifestation of "interested spirit"; it was what could not be avoided in any government, unless we were to exclude from all office particular descriptions of men, such as the holders of the funds. "For the rest he only knew that before the funding operations he had seen our affairs desperate and our credit lost, and that this was in a sudden and extraordinary degree raised to the highest pitch." With the common sense and poise that were his outstanding qualities, Washington refused to inquire into the ultimate motives of Hamilton. The Secretary of the Treasury had rescued the finances of the country from bankruptcy; he was a good, efficient, and personally honest administrator, and it was Washington's hope that he would be able to keep with him two useful collaborators whom he could not easily replace.

Shall I confess that, in my humble opinion, and in spite of the contrary judgment of several American historians, Washington was probably right. The quarrel between Hamilton and Jefferson is undoubtedly of considerable importance in the history of political parties in the United States. I am not so certain that it exerted so tremendous an influence on the destinies of the nation. Whatever may have been the ambitious schemes of Hamilton, the theoretical preferences of John Adams, it is difficult to see how any one could have succeeded at that time in establishing overnight an hereditary monarchy in the United States. Such a "*coup d'état*" is always a possibility in the old countries of Europe, all of them more or less centralized and controlled from a national capital; but in 1793 there was no national capital in America, loyalty to the Federal Government was scarcely nascent, citizens had not been accustomed to look to Congress for bounties, assistance, and subsidies. The vastness of the country would have offered insuperable obstacles, even to the genius of a Bonaparte. No real danger existed because, as Montesquieu would have said, a monarchy was not in the nature of things, and both Hamilton and Jefferson would have realized it, if they had not been caught in the maelstrom of political and personal passions.

When Jefferson left Mount Vernon, Washington was still undecided whether he would accept a second term, but Jefferson had determined that he would not stay in office any longer than he could help; and on November 8, he wrote to Humphreys to send all further communications not to him personally, but to the Secretary of State, by title and not by name. News of election was coming slowly, winter had already begun in the northern States. But the news that did arrive was reassuring and Jefferson was able to write on November 16, "the event has been generally in favor of republican, and against the aristocratical candidates." By the beginning of December, the reëlection of Washington being conceded, it appeared that the election of the Vice President "had been seized as a proper one for expressing the public sense on the doctrine of the monocrats." It was already apparent that Adams would be reëlected in spite of a strong vote against him, but Jefferson discounted the significance of the election and attributed it to "the strength of his personal worth and his services, rather than to the merits of his political creed."[1] It seemed that the anti-Federalists had gained control of the lower House and this was a most significant victory.

Then as more news of the election came, telling of the victory of the republicans or, as they were called by derision, the Jacobins, other news arrived from France. The army of the Duke of Brunswick had been forced to retreat and had failed in crushing the republican army of France. "This news," wrote Jefferson, "has given wry faces to our monocrats here, but sincere joy to the great body of the citizens. It arrived only in the afternoon of yesterday, and the bells were rung and some illuminations took place in the evening."[2] Four days later the conviction that a disaster had overcome Brunswick had made great progress, although no other news had been received, and Jefferson had anxiously awaited the arrival of ships from France. But the tide had turned and he wrote to Mercer: "The monocrats here still affect to disbelieve all this, while the republicans are rejoicing and taking to themselves the name of Jacobins which two months ago was fixed on them by way of stigma."[3] The first victory of the republicans coincided with the first victory of the Revolution against the coalition of kings. The French Revolution itself had become a domestic issue and was to inject more passion into the strife between the monocrats and the republicans.

---

[1] To Thomas Pinckney, December 3, 1792. Memorial Edition, VIII, 443.
[2] To Doctor George Gilmer, December 15, 1792. *Ibid.*, VIII, 444.
[3] *Ibid.*, VIII, 445.

CHAPTER II

JACOBIN OR AMERICAN?

ONE of the first duties of Jefferson in taking charge of foreign affairs was to explain to his French friends, who on the other side of the Atlantic had been accustomed to look up to him as a guide and counsellor, the reasons which had determined his choice to remain in America. To Madame de Corny, the Duchesse Danville, the Duc de La Rochefoucauld, Madame d'Houdetot, he wrote gracefully worded notes, in the best style of the society of the time. In France, among other things, he had learned how to turn a charming compliment. More official but still very graceful is the letter he sent to Montmorin to take formal leave of the French Court and at the same time introduce himself in his new capacity. But besides the compliments, there appears in the letter a reaffirmation that the best foundation for international friendship lay in satisfactory commercial relations. "May this union of interests forever be the patriotic creed of both countries." [1] The new Secretary of State had not forgotten that the most important questions relative to Gallo-American commerce had not yet been settled, and that it would be no negligible part of his duties to carry out the principles he had always defended when in Paris.

To Lafayette, closer to his heart than any other Frenchman, he explained more fully his view of the situation and stated once more the principles which would direct him in his policy towards France:

Wherever I am, or ever shall be, I shall be sincere in my friendship to you and to your nation. I think with others, that nations are

[1] April 6, 1790. Memorial Edition, VIII, 19.

to be governed with regard to their own interests, but I am convinced that it is their interests, in the long run, to be grateful, faithful to their engagements, even in the worst of circumstances, and honorable and generous always. If I had not known that the head of our government was in these sentiments, and that his national and private ethics were the same, I would never have been where I am.[1]

This was more than a banal compliment. To the homely wisdom of Doctor Franklin that honesty is the best policy, Jefferson had added a new element. He had combined in one formula two principles which often seem contradictory and which at any rate are difficult to reconcile. Not a mere idealist, nor simply a practical politician, he was, during the rest of his political life, to make persistent efforts to propagate that gospel of practical idealism which remains to this day one of the fundamental tenets of Americanism. In that respect, party lines count little, and Lincoln was quite as much a disciple and a continuator of Jefferson as Woodrow Wilson.

On the other hand, it cannot be denied that in many circumstances it would take more than superhuman virtue and intelligence rightly to operate that ideal combination and maintain an equal balance between national selfishness and philosophical idealism. When it came to practice, Jefferson showed himself just as canny as any European diplomat and never neglected an opportunity to further the interests of his country. This appeared in the very first letters he sent to Europe after taking charge of the foreign policies of the United States.

Communications were slow at the time. Jefferson was kept regularly informed of developments in France by Short, his former secretary, left in charge in Paris, who sent him weekly letters; but they averaged eleven weeks and a half in transit, while of his answers "the quickest were of nine weeks and the longest of near eighteen weeks coming." Information through

[1] April 2. Memorial Edition, VIII, 11.

the British papers took about five or six weeks to reach America but was not to be relied upon, and Jefferson gave definite instructions to Short for "news from Europe is very interesting at this moment, when it is so doubtful whether a war will take place between our two neighbors." [1]

This was indeed at the time his main preoccupation. War between Spain and England seemed not only possible but probable, and Jefferson saw in it an opportunity to press the claims of the United States to the navigation of the Mississippi. The question was not "the claims of Spain to our territory north of the thirty first degree and east of the Mississippi (they never merited the respect of an answer), but the navigation of the Mississippi and that was not simply to recognize the American rights on the river." Navigation "cannot be practiced without a port, where the sea and river vessels may meet and exchange loads, where those employed about them may be safe and unmolested." The right to use a thing comprehends a right to the means necessary to its use, and without which it would be useless. Jefferson added that he could not answer that "the forbearance of our western citizens would last indefinitely, and that a moment of impatience, hazard or other considerations might precipitate action on their part." On the other hand, the United States were in no position to antagonize openly even weak Spain, and in case nothing should develop Carmichael was instructed to bide his time:

You will be pleased to observe, that we press these matters warmly and firmly, under this idea, that the war between Spain and Great Britain will be begun before you receive this; and such a moment must not be lost. But should an accommodation take place, we retain, indeed, the same object and the same resolutions unalterably; but your discretion will suggest, that patience and persuasion must temper your conferences, till either of these may prevail, or some other circumstances turn up, which may enable us to use other

[1] July 26, 1790. Memorial Edition, VIII, 65.

means for the attainment of an object which we are determined, in the end, to obtain at every risk.[1]

Naturally this is no worse than the ordinary run of instructions sent at that time to diplomatic agents by other foreign secretaries, and Jefferson's policy was no more underhanded than the policies of any other nation of the Old World. It cannot be said, however, that it rested upon higher and nobler moral principles. Perhaps America had no diplomatic tradition at that time, but she was not deficient in tactics, and neither Jefferson nor his agents were exactly innocent tools in the hands of wily European diplomats.

But this is not all. Jefferson unfolded his whole plan in a letter to Short written a week later. In case of a war between England and Spain, France would be called into the war as an ally on the side of Spain. She would have a right to insist that Spain should do everything in her power to lessen the number of her potential enemies and to eliminate every cause of friction with the United States. "She cannot doubt that we shall be of that number, if she does not yield our right to common use of the Mississippi, and the means of using and securing it." The point made by the United States was that "they should have a port near the mouth of the river, so well separated from the territories of Spain and her jurisdiction, as not to engender daily disputes and broils between us." Such a claim was not an arbitrary one, but resulted from the configuration of the land. "Nature has decided what shall be the geography of that in the end, whatever it might be in the beginning, by cutting off from the adjacent countries of Florida and Louisiana, and enclosing between two of its channels, a long and narrow slip of land, called the Island of New Orleans." Jefferson conceded that the idea of ceding that territory might be disagreeable to Spain at first, because it constituted their principal settlement in those parts, with a population of ten thou-

---

[1] To Carmichael, August 2, 1790. Memorial Edition, VIII, 70.

sand white inhabitants, but "reason, and events, however, may, by little and little, familiarize them to it." The idea, however, might seem excessive to Montmorin, particularly as it was thought that France had not entirely given up the project of recovering the country along the Mississippi. But fortunately the National Assembly seemed opposed to conquest and the subject might be broached merely in general terms at the beginning. Furthermore, Lafayette could be used once more as an intermediary without officially compromising the United States.[1]

Finally Gouverneur Morris was told to warn England that should they entertain any design against any Spanish colony, the United States would contemplate a change of neighbors with extreme uneasiness. While the United States would remain neutral if "they execute the treaty fairly and attempt no conquests adjoining us," Jefferson added, "it will be proper that these ideas be conveyed in delicate and friendly terms; but that they be conveyed, if the war takes place; for it is in this case alone, and not till it be begun, that we should wish our dispositions to be known."[2] That question being disposed of satisfactorily, at least in theory, for after all, the war did not break out, Jefferson abandoned temporarily his plans to obtain New Orleans. How he resumed them and pushed them to a successful conclusion ten years later is too well known to need recalling here.

It is not until February 4, 1791, that Jefferson expressed in writing his hope to see a republican form of government established in France. This was in direct contradiction with all the advice and counsel he had given to his French friends when he was in Paris, with his repeated affirmations that the French were not ready for self-government, and with the conclusions contained in his letter written to Jay in the summer of 1789. None of the developments that had taken place in France was of such

---

[1] To Short, August 10, 1790. Memorial Edition, VIII, 79.
[2] To Gouverneur Morris, August 12, 1790. *Ibid.*, VIII, 85.

a character as to change Jefferson's attitude on the matter. But in the meantime, he had come to the conclusion that the fate of the republican government in the United States depended largely on the failure or success of the French Revolution. If it proved impossible for the French to establish a stable form of self-government, if they could not withstand the attacks of their foreign enemies, the conclusion would inevitably be drawn in America that there was an inherent defect and weakness in all republican governments. Thus the French Revolution had already become an international issue, for the cause of liberty could not remain secure for any length of time in America if it were crushed in Europe. On that particular point Jefferson himself was very explicit :

I look with great anxiety for the firm establishment of the new government in France, being perfectly convinced that if it takes place there, it will spread sooner or later all over Europe. On the contrary, a check there would retard the revival of liberty in other countries. I consider the establishment and success of their government as necessary to stay up our own, and to prevent it from falling back to that kind of half-way house, the English constitution. It cannot be denied that we have among us a sect who believe that to contain whatever is perfect in human institutions ; that the members of this sect have, many of them, names and offices which stand high in the estimation of our countrymen. I still rely that the great mass of our community is untainted with these heresies, as is its head. On this I build my hope that we have not labored in vain, and that our experiment will still prove that men can be governed by reason.[1]

On receiving the news that the National Assembly of France had gone into mourning over the death of Franklin, Jefferson sent to its President one of those letters worded in the "felicitous style" which he had perfected in France. His feelings were sincere, he had great respect and affection for the Doctor, but he

[1] To Colonel Mason, February 4, 1791.   Memorial Edition, VIII, 123.

knew what was expected of him, and with great skill, without promising anything, or using any expression that might be taken as a definite promise and turned against him later, he made a vague but satisfactory appeal to a sort of international friendship, praising the Assembly for having set the first example and brought "into our fraternity the good and the great wherever they have lived or died." He ended with a reaffirmation of the good dispositions of his government towards France: "That these separations may disappear between us in all times and circumstances, and that the union of sentiment which mingles our sorrows on this occasion, may continue long to cement the friendship and interests of our two nations, is our constant prayer." [1]

This openly declared sympathy for France and his hopes for a new form of government did not in the least obscure his views on the commercial difficulties between the two countries. The bone of contention was still the question of commerce with the West Indies. The National Assembly, on ratifying the consular conventions, had showed little disposition to admit the right of the United States to send consular agents to the West Indies. In his opinion the word "*États du roi*" did not mean merely France, but all colonial possessions of France as indicated in the translation "French dominions." He was not ready officially to press the matter so as to cause difficulties between the two nations and was willing to have the two agents already appointed, "Skipwith at Martinique and Bourne at St. Dominique", ask for a regular exequatur.[2]

He elaborated on his policy with reference to the West Indies in another letter to Short, written three months later. In it will be found expressed more discreetly, but no less firmly, the philosophy outlined already with reference to Spain and the Mississippi. He maintained first of all that the United States

[1] To the President of the National Assembly, March 8, 1791. Memorial Edition, VIII, 37.   [2] To W. Short, April 25, 1791. *Ibid.*, VIII, 185.

had no design whatever on the West Indies, for "If there be one principle more deeply rooted than any other in the mind of every American, it is that we should have nothing to do with conquest." This principle once established, he proceeded to examine the situation from a practical point of view. The regulations imposed by the French on their colonies are such that they cannot trade directly with their neighbors; for the supplies necessary to relieve their mutual wants have to be carried first to France in order to be exported either to the colonies or to the American continent. This is contrary to the natural order of things: "An exchange of surplusses and wants between neighbor nations, is both a right and a duty under the moral law, and measures against right should be mollified in their exercise, if it be wished to lengthen them to the greatest term possible." It seemed to Jefferson that such a right ought to be recognized by any unprejudiced mind; but, unfortunately, "Europeans in general have been too long in the habit of confounding force with right with respect to America." Circumstances are such that these rights cannot be pressed very strongly and "can be advanced only with delicacy", but what the United States cannot do themselves, Lafayette perhaps can present informally to his friends. He alone can make them understand that, while they are establishing a new régime for their colonial possessions of the West Indies, "in policy, if not in justice, they should be disposed to avoid oppression, which, falling on us, as well as on their colonies, might tempt us to act together." [1]

Was this a veiled threat? Not exactly. It was an extension of Montesquieu's theory of laws to international relations, an application of the theories of the French economists on free trade. But even supposing that the theory itself had some remote French origin, to a large extent it was new and typically American. Only former colonies which had won their complete

[1] See also my edition of the "Letters of Lafayette and Jefferson", chapter III. Paris, Baltimore, 1929.

independence could maintain that, in matters of trade, the colonies were completely independent of the metropolis, and that commercial and geographical considerations should outweigh political regulations. The United States were strongly inclined to use every favorable opportunity to make this principle obtain in their relations with their neighbors, and what was a far more dangerous thing, they considered this policy both "a right and a duty under the moral law." It was not political imperialism to be sure, but in our days it certainly would be called commercial imperialism under a moral disguise. At that time, it was really a theory far in advance of both the theory and practice of any European nation, and it is very doubtful whether Jefferson would have found justification for it in any of the authorities on the law of nations he had consulted with reference to the navigation of the Mississippi.[1]

There is no doubt that Jefferson fully realized all the implications of his doctrine, for he submitted it to the President before sending it to Short in cipher; but he insisted that, if the contents of his letter were permitted to leak out at a favorable opportunity, "the National Assembly might see the impolicy of insisting on particular conditions, which, operating as grievances on us, as well as on their colonists, might produce a concert of action."[2]

The news of the flight of the king was for him another evidence of the "fruits of that form of government, which heaps importance on idiots, and which the Tories of the present day are trying to preach into our favor." Then he added significantly: "I still hope the French revolution will issue happily. I feel that the permanence of our own leans in some degree on that; and that a failure there would be a powerful argument to prove there would be a failure here."[3]

---

[1] To W. Short, July 28, 1791. Memorial Edition, VIII, 217.
[2] July 30, 1791. *Ibid.*, VIII, 225.
[3] To Edward Rutledge, August 25, 1791. *Ibid.*, VIII, 234.

Meanwhile his actions were far more cautious than his theories would lead one to believe. When the Santo Domingo Assembly placed their situation before the Government of the United States, asking for ammunition, arms, and provisions to be charged against the money owed France by the United States, Jefferson answered that although the United States had with them "some common points of union in matters of commerce" he could not do anything without the approbation of Ternant. When the colonists asked him what would be the attitude of the United States in case they became independent, Jefferson did not conceal the fact that they would lay themselves open to any attack by a strong nation and that their interest, as well as the interests of the United States, was to see them retain their connection with their mother country; and he finally decided to give them such small supplies from time to time "as will keep them from real distress, and to wait with patience for what would be a surplus, till M. Ternant can receive instructions from France. . . . It would be unwise in the highest degree, that the colonists should be disgusted with either France or us."[1]

He was soon to be deprived, however, of direct news from France, for Short was transferred from Paris to the Hague and Gouverneur Morris appointed Minister Plenipotentiary to France.[2] He had to explain his policy to the new minister, which he did on March 10, 1792, this time insisting that nothing in the conduct or the views of the United States should cause any apprehension to the French Government and that he should allay all fears on that score.[3] But with Lafayette he still insisted that if he did not mention the point again, it was largely because he considered that it had been won:

We have been less zealous in aiding them, lest your government should feel any jealousy on our account. But, in truth, we as

---

[1] To Short, November 24, 1791. Memorial Edition, VIII, 261.
[2] To Short, January 28, 1792. *Ibid.*, VIII, 297.
[3] March 10, 1792. *Ibid.*, VIII, 311.

sincerely wish their restoration and connection with you, as you do yourselves. We are satisfied that neither your justice nor their distresses will ever again permit their being forced to seek at dear and distant markets those first necessaries of life which they may have at cheaper markets, placed by nature at their door, and formed by her for their support.[1]

It was not until the latter part of 1792 that reiterated letters from Morris, describing the situation and asking for instructions, forced Jefferson to make a very important declaration on relations that could be transacted with revolutionary governments. There again he displayed the resourcefulness of a good lawyer combined with the idealism of a political philosopher. Having no hint of the form of government that the French were to adopt, he thought it necessary to lay down certain principles to direct the conduct of the American plenipotentiary in Paris. They were substantially as follows: The permanent principle of the United States was to recognize any government "which is formed by the will of the nation substantially declared." If the government to be formed by the French presented such a character, there was no reason to doubt that the United States would grant recognition, and Morris could proceed without further ado to transact with them "every kind of business." On the other hand, the government established might present an entirely different complexion and in that case the recognition might be more doubtful; but even then it was to be considered as a *de facto*, if not a *de jure* government, and it was the duty of the American minister to discuss some matters with them in order to obtain concessions "reforming the unfriendly restrictions on our commerce and navigation." [2] The question as to Morris' safety was left entirely to him to determine and could not very well be the object of precise instructions.

Two weeks later, Jefferson himself had an opportunity to

<hr>

[1] To Lafayette, June 16, 1792. Memorial Edition, VIII, 381.
[2] November 7, 1792. *Ibid.*, VIII, 437.

make a practical application of his policy.   Although they had received no formal authority from the National Assembly, the United States were willing to contribute aids from time to time to Santo Domingo, and were placing at their disposal for December the sum of forty thousand dollars.   But Jefferson insisted that such moneys as were thus obtained were to be spent in America where supplies could be had cheapest, "and where the same sum would consequently effect the greatest measure of relief to the colony."   Incidentally, it was spent also for the greatest benefit of the American merchants, and strengthened the commercial connection between the islands and the American continent, a point not to be mentioned to the French envoy, but well worth keeping in mind.[1]

At the beginning of 1793, Jefferson was not only inclined to treat favorably the new French Government but resented strongly any criticism of it.   When he discovered that in several letters his friend and disciple Short had censured the proceedings of the French Jacobins, Jefferson, fearing that he had been corrupted by aristocratic friendships, undertook to set him right on the matter.   He took the following view of the situation:

The contest had been between the Feuillant patriots favoring a free constitution with an hereditary executive and the Jacobins who thought that expunging that office was an absolute necessity.   The Feuillants had their day and their experiment had failed miserably. The nation was with them in opinion and had finally won.   Certainly in the struggle many guilty persons fell without the forms of trial and innocents with them.   But altogether they are to be considered as soldiers who have fallen during a battle; their memory will be embalmed by truth and time.

Meanwhile the only thing to consider was that the liberty of the whole world depended on the issue of the contest:

Was ever such a prize won with so little innocent blood?   My own affections have been deeply wounded by some of the martyrs to this

[1] November 20, 1792.   Memorial Edition, VIII, 441.

cause, but rather than it should have failed I would have seen half the earth desolated; were there but an Adam and an Eve left in every country, and left free, it would be better than as it is now.

Short was then severely rebuked for having expressed in conversations sentiments offensive to the French patriots. He was reminded that there were in the United States "some characters of opposite principles hostile to France, and fondly looking to England as the staff of their hopes. Their prospects have certainly not brightened. . . . The successes of republicanism in France have given the *coup de grace* to their prospects, and I hope to their projects." This was to be kept in mind by Short, and, as Jefferson intended to retire at an early date, he called his attention to the fact that not knowing who his successor would be and into whose hands his further communications would fall, he had better be prudent and not let his "too great sensibility to the misfortunes of some dear friends obscure his republicanism." [1]

In a communication to Gouverneur Morris, Jefferson was more reserved but no less insistent upon the principle that the French Government was a government *de jure* as well as *de facto*:

We surely cannot deny to any nation that right whereon our own government is founded, that every one may govern itself according to whatever form it pleases, and change these forms at its own will; and that it may transact its business with foreign nations through whatever organ it thinks proper, whether King, Convention, Assembly, Committee, President, or anything else it may choose. The will of the nation is the only essential thing to be regarded. Such being the case, the United States not only should continue to pay the installment on the debt but use their utmost endeavors to make punctual payments. Urged by the strongest attachment to that country, and thinking it is even providential that moneys lent to us in distress could be repaid under like circumstances, we had no

[1] January 3, 1793. Memorial Edition, IX, 9.

hesitation to comply with the application, and arrangements are accordingly taken, for furnishing this sum at epochs accommodated to the demands and our means of paying it.

This was the doctrine of national gratitude reaffirmed and illustrated, but naturally relations could not be placed on an entirely sentimental basis. Morris was instructed at the same time "to use and improve every possible opportunity which may occur in the changeable scenes which are passing, and to seize them as they occur, for placing our commerce with that nation and its dependencies, on the freest and most encouraging footing possible." [1]

A week later news of the execution of the king arrived at Philadelphia. For the fate of Louis XVI, Jefferson felt and expressed little personal regret. He never held the monarch in high esteem : furthermore, the example set by France might teach a good lesson to other autocrats and "soften the monarchical governments, by rendering monarchs amenable to punishment like other criminals, and doing away with that rage of insolence and oppression, the inviolability of the King's person." [2] Here again it is evident that domestic considerations were uppermost in Jefferson's mind. Never could one correct too vigorously those who wished to establish a monarchy in the United States. Whether he was justified or not, Jefferson sincerely believed that the American republic was in danger, and his attitude at that time reflects his fear of the monocrats more than any real sympathy for the French Terrorists.

Thus spoke Jefferson, the party man, and he made no mystery of his sentiments either in his conversations or in his private letters. The Secretary of State, however, could not easily afford to adopt publicly the same attitude. Early in February Colonel W. S. Smith had brought the intelligence that the French Minister Ternant, whose royalist opinions shocked the

[1] To G. Morris, March 12, 1793. Memorial Edition, IX, 37.
[2] To ——, March 18, 1793. *Ibid.*, IX, 45.

French sympathizers in Philadelphia, would be recalled and Citizen Genet would be sent in his place by the Republic. It was already known that Genet would bring very advantageous propositions to the United States, for he would come

with full powers to give us all the privileges we can desire in their countries, and particularly in the West Indies; that they even contemplate to set them free the next summer; that they proposed to emancipate South America, and will send forty-five ships of the line there next spring, and Miranda at the head of the expedition; that they desire our debt to be paid them in provisions, and have authorized him to negotiate this.[1]

On the other hand it was to be feared that Genet would remind the American Government of the existence of the Treaty of 1778, by which the United States agreed to give distinct advantages to French privateers and to guarantee the integrity of the French West Indies. It was not until April that it was known war had been declared between France and England. Were the United States going to be dragged into the European convulsions and would they have to side openly with their former ally? Acting on the information received from Colonel Smith, Jefferson quickly wrote to Carmichael and Short, asking them to refrain from mentioning the Louisiana question to Spain, and chiefly to be very careful not to "bind us to guarantee any of the Spanish colonies against their own independence, nor indeed against any other nation." Jefferson believed that there was a possibility of seeing France encourage the Spanish colonies to revolt and would not have objected "to the receiving those on the east side into our confederation." This was an eventuality not to be lightly dismissed, and once more Jefferson's uppermost preoccupation was not to please the French Revolutionists but to further the interests of his country.[2] But before deciding upon any course of action it was

---

[1] "Anas", February 20, 1793.
[2] To Messrs. Carmichael and Short, March 23, 1793. Memorial Edition, IX, 55.

advisable to temporize and to find out from what quarter the wind was about to blow. The only thing to do for the present was to wait and to avoid any unpleasant complications with the powers at war; and first of all to see to it that the United States should enjoy the rights and privileges of a complete neutrality. Jefferson began sending instructions to that effect to Samuel Shaw, consul at Canton, China.[1] Two days later he wrote even more explicitly to Dumas: "We wish not to meddle with the internal affairs of any country, nor with the general affairs of Europe. Peace with all nations, and the right which that gives us with all nations are our objects. It will be necessary for all our public agents to exert themselves with vigilance for securing to our vessels all the rights of neutrality, and from preventing the vessels of other nations from usurping our flags." [2]

As the cabinet met only one month later (April 18) at the request of Washington to discuss the proclamation of neutrality, it is not without importance to call attention to the date and the text of that letter. Winning Jefferson over to the position finally adopted by the American Government could not present insuperable difficulties since he had already outlined the same policy even before consulting with the President, and on his own initiative had sent instructions to the agents.

When the Cabinet met to consider the emergency, and the several secretaries were invited by Washington to submit their opinions in writing, the course to be followed was officially agreed upon and Washington issued the famous Proclamation of Neutrality on April 22, — the very same day the new minister from France landed at Charleston. Jefferson did not lose any time notifying the American agents abroad of the policy of the United States, repeating substantially the instructions already

[1] March 21, 1793. Memorial Edition, IX, 49.
[2] To C. W. Dumas, March 23, 1793. *Ibid.*, IX, 57.

sent to Dumas one month before.[1]   At the same time Ternant was officially notified that credits opened in favor of the West Indies had to be stopped;[2] as the emergency had passed and a regular government had been established in France, money could be appropriated from the regular installments paid on the debt.

According to a letter written to Monroe,[3] Jefferson saw with a secret pleasure, the monocrat papers publish the most furious philippics against England, and the old spirit of 1776 rekindled from Charleston to Boston.   He expressed the pious wish that "we may be able to repress the spirit of the people within the limits of fair neutrality."   But he revolted against what he considered a subservient attitude to England on the part of Hamilton.   It is one of the few occasions in which he departed in a letter (I do not count the "Anas") from his judicial attitude : "In the meantime," he said, "Hamilton is panick struck, if we refuse our breech to every kick which Great Britain may choose to give it.   In order to preserve even a sneaking neutrality a fight is necessary in every council for our votes are generally two and a half against one and a half."

Jefferson's private opinion might have favored the French Revolution, as it undoubtedly did.   I do not see, however, that in any important circumstance he departed from the strict line of neutrality which he had traced for the country.

He sent instructions to Thomas Pinckney [4] to the effect that, in order to avoid any violation of neutrality, passports could be issued to vessels only in American ports ; that "in other lands American citizens were free to purchase and use any foreign built vessels, as those were entitled to the same protection as home built vessels."   That all vessels belonging to citizens of the United States loaded with grain to the port of one of the

[1] To E. P. Van Berckel, April 23, 1793.   To Morris, Pinckney and Short, April 26, 1793.   Memorial Edition, IX, 68–69.

[2] April 27, 1793.   Ibid., IX, 70.

[3] May 5, 1793.   Ibid., IX, 75.   [4] May 7, 1793.   Ibid., IX, 79.

belligerents could not be stopped by the other belligerent if going to an unblockaded port.

Then Genet, still at Charleston and before being regularly accredited, took upon himself to outfit privateers and to commission them. "The British ship *Grange*, while lying at anchor in the bay of Delaware, within the territory and jurisdiction of the United States, was taken possession of by the *Embuscade*, a frigate of the French Republic, brought to port where she was detained as a prize and the crew kept prisoners." [1] Ternant was asked to detain the vessel, waiting for a decision to be taken concerning the representations of the British minister, Hammond. But it will be seen in Jefferson's letter to Hammond [2] that he did not hesitate to grant that the capture of the *Grange* was not "warranted by the usage of nations, nor by the existing treaties between the United States and France", nor, Jefferson added, "by any law of the land." On the other hand he maintained that agents of the French Government were free to purchase "arms and military accoutrements" with an intent to export them to France, and that citizens of the United States could sell such articles, being duly warned, however, that they were subject to confiscation should they fall into the hands of a belligerent.

Indeed, it took all the calamitous blunders of Genet to turn Jefferson against him. From Charleston, where he had landed, to Philadelphia, his march had been a triumph. The citizens of Philadelphia, hearing that the President might refuse to receive him, had even decided to give him an ovation and to meet him at Gray's Ferry. He delivered his credentials on May 18, and at once communicated the object of his mission in a style which now appears grandiloquent, but simply reflected that enthusiasm for America which was running so high in France at the time. "In short," wrote Jefferson to Madison, "he offers

---

[1] To Ternant, May 3, 1793. Memorial Edition, IX, 74.
[2] May 15, 1793. *Ibid.*, IX, 89.

everything, and asks nothing."[1] This was too good to be true, and too wonderful to last long.

Less than three weeks later (June 5) Jefferson had to send to Genet strong representations on his attitude and pointed out several breaches of neutrality, particularly in the arming of French privateers in American ports, stating rather stiffly that it was "the *right* of every nation to prohibit acts of sovereignty from being exercised by any other nation within its limits and the duty of a neutral nation to prohibit such as would injure one of the warring powers."

But in a letter to Hammond he stated that the measures could not be retrospective. In the first days of the war, French citizens, duly commissioned by the authorities of their country, had captured British vessels. It was impossible for the United States to rescue those vessels from the captors. All that could be done was to prevent the repetition of such an incident and to order the departure of all French privateers from the ports of the United States. It was fine legal reasoning, not without some of that hairsplitting for which Jefferson reproached Randolph. Whether Randolph had a hand or not in the reaching of that decision is another question. Jefferson indorsed it in transmitting it both to Hammond and Genet.

Another proposition of Genet did not meet with more favorable approval. The Republic was hard pressed for money, and the new plenipotentiary had been requested to make every possible effort "to obtain payment in one lump sum of all the annuities coming to France, taking the debt in produce if necessary, or changing it into bonds to be sold to the public." To this Jefferson was unequivocally opposed, although he referred the President to Hamilton. He recommended payment in advance of the installments due for the year, but strongly objected to changing the form of the debt.[2] He wrote, furthermore, to Gouverneur Morris to acquaint him with the situation and to request him "to prevent any such proposition in the future from being brought forward." [1]

As a matter of fact, although Jefferson expressed pious and fervent wishes for the success of the French, I cannot see that he officially did much to further their cause. He was not even pleased by the agitation and propaganda in their behalf carried on in America by enthusiastic patriots. This appears very clearly in a letter to his son-in-law, Thomas Mann Randolph, which, better than any official document, indicates his state of mind at the end of June, 1793:

> The French have been guilty of great errors in their conduct towards other nations, not only in insulting uselessly all crowned heads, but endeavoring to force liberty on their neighbors in their own form. They seem to be correcting themselves on the latter point; the war between them and England embarrasses our government daily and immensely. The predilection of our citizens for France renders it very difficult to suppress their attempts to cruise against the English on the ocean, and to do justice to the latter in cases where they are entitled to it. [2]

Monroe had sent him a long dissertation on the proclamation of neutrality which he judged both "unpolitick and unconstitutional"; for, if the President "possesses the right to say we shall be neutral, he might say we should not be." [3]

To this Jefferson answered that his friends' apprehensions were somewhat exaggerated, for the United States being at peace with England, the so-called proclamation of neutrality — which, by the way, did not contain the word neutrality — did nothing but maintain a *status quo*. This was a fine legal distinction, not very convincing, but very characteristic of Jefferson's state of mind at that time and of his reluctance to favor

[1] June 13, 1789.   Memorial Edition, IX, 123.
[2] Jefferson Papers.   Library of Congress, June 24, 1793.
[3] *Ibid.*   Library of Congress, June 27, 1793 and Writings of J. Monroe, I, 261.

the French side. Had he ever wished to do it, the attitude of the French envoy would have soon forced him to adopt a different policy.

The case of Citizen Genet is too well known to require elaborate treatment. Less than six weeks after his arrival in Philadelphia, Jefferson had given him up as hopeless and dangerous:

Never in my opinion, was so calamitous an appointment made, as that of the present minister of France here. Hot headed, all imagination, no judgment, passionate, disrespectful & even indecent towards the President in his written as well as verbal communications, talking of appeals from him to Congress, from them to the people, urging the most unreasonable & groundless propositions, & in the most dictatorial style.[1]

The case of the *Little Sarah*, a British prize, taken to Philadelphia and refitted as a privateer by Genet's orders, brought the matter to a head. Genet was warned that the vessel could not sail; he refused to give definite assurances that it would not be ordered to sea. Washington was away at the time, and Knox and Hamilton proposed mounting a battery of cannon to prevent the sailing of the vessel, a measure strongly opposed by Jefferson, determined to avoid at all cost measures tantamount to a declaration of war. The *Little Sarah* and the *Democrat* escaped, and Washington in vehement words manifested his disapproval of the weakness shown on this occasion. The least the American Government could do was to ask that Genet be recalled, and it was so decided at a meeting of the Cabinet on August 3. In a long letter intended for the French Government, but sent to Gouverneur Morris and communicated to Genet himself, Jefferson drew up a terrible indictment of the French minister. Hamilton and Knox were decidedly in favor of stronger measures and of deciding then and there upon the "*renvoi*" of Genet. Jefferson, following his constant policy, was

[1] To J. Madison, July 7, 1793. Ford, VII, 436.

against a measure that could be construed as the recognition that a state of war existed between the two countries. This has been sometimes interpreted as evincing partiality to France on his part, but entries in the "Anas" under August 20 and August 23 demonstrate beyond any doubt that he was also guided by his uppermost desire to promote the interests of his country.

There was at least some reason to believe that Genet's conduct would not receive the support of his Government, and on the other hand he had brought over with him certain proposals worth considering for a treaty referring to the commerce with the West Indies. Although the Cabinet had never considered the question formally, Jefferson estimated the matter of such importance that he had taken it upon himself to discuss it with Genet in several conversations. To leave the friendly overtures of the French Republic without any answer would not only be insulting but highly unpolitic, since the Executive might be accused "of neglecting the interests of the United States." Under these circumstances some means had to be found of sparing the feelings of the French Government, so as not to lose entirely the chances of concluding a treaty so advantageous to the United States. As Secretary of State, Jefferson had to find a satisfactory formula. This was to ask the French Government to recall Genet, but at the same time to appoint his successor and to renew to this successor the powers granted originally to Genet. Such was the tenor of his letter to Morris, a very clever solution to a very difficult situation. As for Genet himself, he was to be tolerated until the arrival of his successor.

Unfortunately the "citizen" did not know how to keep quiet or when to quit. Not a dishonest man in ordinary life, not even an unintelligent man, he was the greatest bungler ever sent by a friendly nation to another. When he arrived in May, 1793, he had public opinion largely in his favor. Members of Congress and of the government, except possibly Hamilton, were not hostile to France; the French envoy could have obtained distinct advantages for his country if he had proceeded slowly and with ordinary caution. Two months later he had succeeded in turning against himself and against the country he represented the whole of public opinion, in sowing germs of distrust never to be eradicated, in fixing and crystallizing all sorts of prejudices and unfavorable generalizations about France.

Jefferson had made all possible efforts to keep the disaffection of the American Government toward the French minister as much under cover as possible. But Citizen Genet threw down the gauntlet by publishing part of his official correspondence, thus forcing an appeal to the people and running the risk of arousing the "disgusts" Jefferson had so much wished to avoid.[1] A week later, he had to admit to Madison that Genet's conduct "has given room to the enemies of France to come forward in a style of acrimony against that nation which they never dared to have done. The disapprobation of the agent mingles with the reprehension of his nation and gives a toleration to that which it never had before."[2]

By a strange irony of fate, one of the last acts of Jefferson as Secretary of State was a final protest against Genet's attitude. Six months before he had been notified that he could not be received by the Executive and that all communications from him had to be made in writing. Deciding to appeal to Congress over the head of the President, Genet had copies of his instructions printed, demanding that they should be laid before both houses. A more stupid and childish step could hardly be imagined. Jefferson, requested by the President to draw up an answer to Genet, wrote at first a scathing denunciation of the French minister which was probably thought too strong, for it is marked "not inserted" on the manuscript:[3]

[1] To James Madison, August 25, 1793. Memorial Edition, IX, 211.
[2] To Madison, September 1, 1793. *Ibid.*, IX, 211.
[3] Jefferson Papers. Library of Congress, 15832.

The terms in which you permit yourself in this and some other of your letters to speak of the President of the U. S., and the influence and impressions you venture to ascribe to him, are calculated to excite sentiments which need no explanation. On what grounds of truth they are hazarded, how to reconcile them to decorum, to the respect due to the person and character of our chief magistrate, and to the nation over which he presides and that too from the representative of a friendly people, are questions left to your mature reflection.

The letter which was finally sent, more moderate in its terms, was nevertheless a formal reminder of diplomatic proprieties:

Your functions as the missionary of a foreign mission here, are confined to the transactions of the affairs of your nation with the Executive of the United States; that the communications, which are to pass between the Executive and Legislative branches, cannot be a subject for your interference, and that the President must be left to judge for himself what matters his duty or the public good may require him to propose to the deliberations of Congress. I have therefore the honor of returning you the copies sent for distribution.[1]

That very same day Jefferson resigned his office into the hands of Washington, assuring him that in his retirement he was taking with him "a lively sense of the President's goodness, and would continue gratefully to remember it." [2]

---

[1] December 31, 1793. Memorial Edition, IX, 277.
[2] December 13, 1793. *Ibid.*, IX, 279.

CHAPTER III

MONTICELLO — AGRICULTURE AND POLITICS

WHEN Jefferson left Philadelphia for what he sincerely believed would be definite retirement from the field of politics, he felt weary, tired, and already old. He had transacted all the business of his office with a minimum of clerical assistance, attending himself to all the details not only of foreign but also of domestic affairs, sometimes translating documents which he did not trust Freneau with, preparing reports for the President, digging in his manuals of international law, Wolfe, Puffendorff, Vatel, and Grotius. The actual labor was enormous, the variety of subjects amazing; many times during the course of a day he had to shift from one subject to another. Under fire all the time, harassed by the Federalist papers, consulted by the leaders of the party which was beginning to form, he had not broken down under the strain, but was in urgent need of complete rest and agricultural quietude. He had packed books and furniture in advance and sent everything to Monticello; his letter to Genet written, he set out for Virginia without even waiting for the justification that would result from the order to publish his correspondence with the French minister.

At that time a vague idea that he could turn a new leaf and start a new life may fugitively have crossed his mind. He had respectfully but profoundly admired Madame de Corny when he was in Paris. News from her had come through Mrs. Church; Mr. de Corny had died; Madame de Corny left a widow in very limited circumstances had retired to Rouen.[1]

---

[1] Angelica Church to Jefferson, August 19, 1793. Chinard, "Trois Amitiés Françaises", p. 155.

It seems that he entertained the hope that she might decide to move to America and in that case he would have liked to see her at Monticello: "Madame de Cosway is in a convent . . . that she would have rather sought the mountain-top. How happy should I be that it were *mine*, that you, she, and Madame de Corny would seek." But he had seen too many of these brilliant French women in Philadelphia to believe that a Parisian could ever become accustomed to the simplicity of Monticello and to its lack of entertainments, and he made the suggestion very timidly: "I know of no country where the remains of a fortune could place her so much at her ease as this, and where public esteem is so much attached to worth, regardless of wealth; our manners & the state of society here are so different from those to which her habits have been formed, that she would lose more perhaps in that scale." After all, he had not changed so much since he had declared his flame to Belinda, almost in the same terms, twenty years earlier. This was the typical Jeffersonian way of presenting his own wishes, of letting the others decide after he had stated the pros and cons; clearly he was not made to win personal triumphs, either in love or in politics.

Of politics he was utterly sick. He pictured himself spending the rest of his days in bucolic occupations. "The length of my tether is now fixed for life from Monticello to Richmond," he wrote to Gates. "My private business can never call me elsewhere, and certainly politics will not, which I have ever hated both in theory and practice." [1]

Writing to Mrs. Church, he had gone into more details.

I am to be liberated from the hated occupations of politics retire into the bosom of my family, my farm, & my books. I have my house to build, my family to form, and to watch for the happiness of those who labor for mine. I have one daughter married to a man of science, sense, virtue and competence; in whom indeed I have noth-

[1] Jefferson Papers. Library of Congress, February, 1794.

ing more to wish. They live with me. If the other shall be as
fortunate in the process of time, I shall imagine myself as blessed as
the most blessed of the patriarchs.[1]

At Monticello he found Martha and her husband, Thomas
Mann Randolph, and induced the young couple to stay with
him. Maria was now a tall girl, vivacious and witty, who
would soon find a suitor. Devoting himself entirely to his
family and domestic cares, Jefferson plunged into the reorganization of his estate left to an overseer for more than ten years,
and granted so little attention to politics that he did not even
subscribe to any newspaper, being quite content with those
published at Richmond. "I think it is Montaigne who has
said that ignorance is the softest pillow on which a man can
rest his head," he wrote to Edmund Randolph. "I am sure it
is true as to everything political, and shall endeavor to estrange
myself to everything of that character." [2] Since that time
there have been in American politics many instances of politicians who left for a hunting party, or retired to their farms in
order to avoid responsibility. This was not the attitude of
Jefferson; his was no temporary retirement while waiting for
the storm to blow itself over. Had he chosen to remain in
Philadelphia, as he had been asked to do by Washington, he
would have at least checked Hamilton's personal influence and
counterbalanced in Washington's mind the advice and counsels
of his enemy. His party had been reorganized and the republicans had just obtained a majority in the new Congress, but his
principles were far from being secure. He indicated it himself
in the same letter to Randolph when he wrote:

I indulge myself on one political topic only, that is, in declaring
to my countrymen the shameless corruption of a portion of the
Representatives to the first and second Congresses, and their implicit
devotion to the Treasury. I think I do good in this, because it

---

[1] "Amitiés françaises", p. 161.
[2] February 3, 1794.   Memorial Edition, IX, 279.

may produce exertions to reform the evil on the success of which the form of the government is to depend.

Shortly after coming back to Monticello, he discovered, somewhat to his dismay, that the rank and file of the good people of the country did not pay much attention to the political battle which was still raging in Philadelphia. He went to "court" at Charlottesville at the beginning of February and was amazed to find that his neighbors had not heard of Madison's speeches in Congress or even of the recall of Genet.

I could not have supposed — he wrote to Madison — when at Philadelphia that so little of what was passing there could be known even at Kentucky as is the case here. Judging from this of the rest of the Union, it is evident to me that the people are not in a condition either to approve or disapprove of their government, nor consequently to influence it.[1]

This would tend to give confirmation to the supposition I timidly ventured in the last chapter. Neither the inflammatory speeches made in Congress, nor the foundation of democratic clubs, nor the newspaper battle between different editors had been able to rouse the people of the country. In America, as in every other country, the rural population, at that time the majority of the population, remained passive and took little interest in discussions that did not immediately affect their interests. Then, too, as in our days, the press was able to modify and to influence to some extent public opinion, but did not express it. Editors were years in advance of the slow-moving masses in their prognostications. It takes a national emergency, a violent crisis or a well-organized political machine to coalesce the great majority of a people and force them to see beyond the limited horizon of their village, their county or their State. This is so even now, and it was certainly so a century and a half ago, when the parochial and provincial spirit was still stronger than the national spirit.

[1] Jefferson Papers. Library of Congress, February 15, 1794.

Since this was realized by Jefferson, it is difficult to under-stand how he did not come to the conclusion that his clear duty was to go back to Philadelphia and do his utmost to educate an apathetic people. But he was not the man to enjoy strife and struggle; he was too sensitive of personal criticism and attacks, too timid also to care to exchange blows with an opponent. He was the type of man who likes to play chess by correspondence, to suggest solutions, but not the one "to knead the dough", as the French say, and to take an active part in the daily game of politics.

From his retirement he found time to answer letters from Madison and Monroe. Before leaving Philadelphia, he had transmitted to the House of Representatives a Report on the Privileges and Restrictions of the Commerce of the United States.[1] It was incumbent upon Madison to draw from it specific recommendations. Jefferson pointed out in a dis-passionate way the obstacles put by Great Britain to the growth of American commerce, her lack of reciprocal treatment, her prohibitions and restrictions. He ended by indicating that France had, of her own accord, proposed negotiations for improving the commercial relations between the two countries by a new treaty on fair and equal principles; that her internal disturbances alone had prevented her from doing it, though the government had repeatedly manifested reassuring disposi-tions. On the contrary, "in spite of friendly advances and arrangements proposed to Great Britain, they being already on as good a footing in law, and a better in fact, than the most favored nation, they have not, as yet, discovered any disposi-tion to have it meddled with." As a remedy, pending the conclusion of treaties, Jefferson laid down five principles to protect American commerce and retaliate in so far as would not hurt the interests of the American people, although at the beginning trade might suffer from it. A storm broke out in

[1] December 16, 1793. Memorial Edition, III, 261-283.

Congress, and once more Jefferson became the target of the Federalists.

He was not uninformed of these developments, for Madison and Monroe sent him several letters at short intervals at the beginning of March; nor did he leave his lieutenants without directions. He still hoped that a war could be avoided; but he could not conceive that it would be possible in any event to let Great Britain seize the French West Indies: "I have no doubt that we ought to interpose at a proper time, and declare both to France and England that these islands are to rest with France, and that we will make a common cause with the latter for that object." Having thus outlined these policies, he relapsed into his ataraxy, affirming that he had not seen a Philadelphia paper until he had received those inclosed by Madison. The patience of Monroe must have been taxed to the breaking point when, after sending to his chief a long letter full of detailed information, he received in answer an equally long letter replete with agricultural disquisitions — "on such things as you are too little of a farmer to take much interest in."[1]

The supposed leader of the Republicans was not more encouraging in his letters to Madison when he wrote a month later: "I feel myself so thoroughly weaned from the interest I took in the proceedings there, while there, that I have never a wish to see one [a newspaper], and believe that I shall never take another paper of any sort. I find my mind totally absorbed by my rural occupation."[2] Yet the old fame flared up occasionally, as when he learned that Hamilton was being considered to succeed Pinckney who would be recalled from England: "a more degrading measure could not have been proposed," he wrote to Monroe. In regard to Hamilton, he foresaw an

[1] Jefferson Papers. Library of Congress, March 3, and March 11, 1794.
[2] April 3, 1794. Memorial Edition, IX, 281 and Manuscript Library of Congress, March 16.

investigation on the Treasury and had wanted to withdraw before it took place.[1]

But he fell back into the same detached attitude of mind, when he wrote to Washington the next day: "I return to farming with an ardor which I scarcely knew in my youth, and which has got the better entirely of my love of study. Instead of writing ten or twelve letters a day, which I have been in the habit of doing as a thing of course, I put off answering my letters now, farmer-like, till a rainy day."

As a matter of fact, I doubt very much whether he had reached any such equanimity. For if he was unwilling to reënter public life, he was not averse to giving his opinion and advice in critical circumstances. While Madison's resolutions were still before Congress, news arrived in Philadelphia of the seizure of American ships in the Caribbean, under the Order in Council of November 6. Indignation was running high and democratic societies held patriotic meetings throughout the country. War seemed imminent, and although Jefferson preferred to contemplate the tranquil growth "of his lucern and potatoes", he still felt indignant when thinking "of these scoundrels" (the British). Yet he believed that war should be avoided and wrote to that effect to Tench Coxe:

We are alarmed here with the apprehension of war; and sincerely anxious that it may be avoided; but not at the expense either of our faith or honour. . . . As to myself I love peace, and I am anxious that we should give the world still another useful lesson, by showing to them other modes of punishing injuries than by war, which is as much a punishment to the punisher as to the sufferers.[2]

To Washington he wrote two weeks later a most amusing letter, starting with a dissertation on crop rotation and "a certain essence of dung, one pint of which would manure an acre according to Lord Kaims", but not forgetting, in a negligent

---

[1] April 24, 1794. Jefferson Papers, Library of Congress.
[2] May 1, 1794. Memorial Edition, IX, 285.

way, to slip in at the end a piece of political advice: "to try to extricate ourselves from the event of a war; at the same time to try to rouse public opinion in Great Britain and the only way to do it being to distress their commerce." But he added once more, "I cherish tranquillity too much to suffer political things to enter my mind at all." [1] This was nothing but the non-intercourse policy then debated by the government and of which Jefferson had evidently heard. When his letter reached the President, a solution had already been adopted and Jay had sailed for England on the mission which was to end with his signing the famous or infamous treaty. The summer went on without any new letter from Jefferson. A letter of the Secretary of State, asking him whether he would not consider lending a hand to the President in the present emergency, found him in bed "under a paroxysm of rheumatism which had kept him for ten days in constant torment." Then he emphatically added,

No circumstance will evermore tempt me to engage in any thing public. . . . It is a great pleasure to me to retain the esteem and approbation of the President, and this forms the only ground of any reluctance at being unable to comply with every wish of his. Pray convey these sentiments, and a thousand more to him, which my situation does not permit me to go into.[2]

This was the very time when the Whisky Boys of Eastern Pennsylvania revolted against the excise laws of Hamilton which fell on them harder than on any other part of the rural population, for they could not market their grain for lack of transportation facilities and their only means of living was distilling it into whisky. Individual acts of resistance to the agents of the excise culminated in August, 1794, in an armed convention denouncing the law and defying the government on Braddock Field, in spite of the moderating influence of the young Jeffersonian, Albert Gallatin. Not only was the militia

[1] May 14, 1794. Memorial Edition, IX, 287.
[2] September 7, 1794. *Ibid.*, IX, 291.

called but the President and Hamilton went to visit the camp at Carlisle. The insurrection ended without bloodshed, but the side of the insurrectionists was taken up in the large cities by the Democratic societies in which the Irish element was largely represented — hot-headed people, recently come from an oppressed land, who felt an ingrained spirit of revolt against soldiers and men in uniform, — until dressed in a uniform themselves. The immediate effect of the Hamiltonian policy was to amalgamate rural population and urban groups of mechanics and small operatives in a hostile attitude towards the aristocratic government. Hamilton thought the time had come to crush the vanguard of the Jeffersonian troops, and Washington, who had an inveterate hatred of anything smacking of disorder and mob rule, lent a favorable ear. He wrote a stinging denunciation of the Democratic societies in his yearly message to Congress.

This time Jefferson was aroused, although personally he had never had anything to do with Tammany in New York nor any of the Democratic societies in Philadelphia. He fairly exploded in a letter to James Madison: the denunciation of the Democratic societies was "one of the extraordinary acts of boldness of which we have seen so many from the faction of monocrats." How could one condemn the Democratic societies and let alone the Society of the Cincinnati, "a self-created one, carving out for itself hereditary distinctions, lowering over our Constitution eternally." It was an inexcusable aggression. With regard to the transactions against the excise law, he refused to take seriously the "meeting of Braddock field", and ridiculed the mobilizing of an army against men who were not thinking seriously of separating, "simply consulting about it." — "But to consult on a question does not amount to a determination of that question in the affirmative, still less to the acting *on such determination*," he advised. A fine legal distinction which Jefferson forgot at the time of the Burr conspiracy! But "the first and only cause of the whole trouble was the infernal excise law." The first error was "to admit it by the Constitution"; the second, to act on that admission; the third and last will be to "make it the instrument of dismembering the Union." In conclusion he advised Madison to stay at his post, "to take the front of the battle" for Jefferson's own security, and once again he reaffirmed that he would not give up his retirement for the empire of the universe.[1]

On April 23, 1795, he wrote to James Madison to refuse categorically any resumption of office high or low. That was already his firm resolution when he had left Philadelphia and it was even stronger then, since his health had broken down during the last eight months: "My age requires that I should place my affairs in a clear state. The question is forever closed with me." To propose his name would only mean a division of votes in the party and that was to be avoided before everything.[2] To Giles he repeated that his days "were busy with now and then a pious ejaculation for the French and Dutch, returning with due despatch to my clover, potatoes, wheat, etc."[3] In the meantime Jay had returned with the treaty surrendering practically all the claims of the United States, placing the country in a position of constant inferiority with reference to England, opening the Mississippi to the British trade and forbidding American vessels to carry molasses, sugar, and cotton to any ports except their own. It was laid in special session before the Senate on June 8, ratified on June 24, and sent to the President without the contents being known to any one. It would have remained secret if Thomson Mason of Virginia had not taken a copy of it to Bache, who published it the next day in the *Aurora*. It was a most humiliating and scarcely defensible transaction: Jay had been outgeneraled at every step by Grenville and, in a way, betrayed by Hamilton.

[1] December 28, 1794. Memorial Edition, IX, 293.
[2] April 27, 1795. *Ibid.*, IX, 301. [3] April 27. *Ibid.*, IX, 305.

But although it was distinctly a Federalist victory, it offered good campaign material for the Republicans.[1]

On August 30, Jefferson sent to Thomas Mann a sort of apologia, telling him how, "while all hands were below deck, every one at his own business and the captain in his cabin attending to the log book a rogue of a pilot had run the ship into an enemy's port." Not that he wanted to express any opinion of his own but, "metaphor apart, there is much dissatisfaction with Mr. Jay and his treaty. . . . For my part, I consider myself now but as a passenger leaving the world and its government to those who are likely to live longer in it."[2]

With H. Tazewell he was more outspoken : a glance at the treaty had been enough to convince him that the United States would be much better without any treaty than with a treaty of that sort. "Acquiescence under insult is not the way to escape war," and he could only hope that the Executive's sense of public honor and spirit would be awakened. To Madison he gave the benefit of his advice. There was no leader in the camp of the Republicans to take advantage of the situation ; rioting in the streets could not influence favorably the judgment of Washington, who had not yet signed, and there was always Hamilton, who had retired to be sure, but was "a host in himself" ; the Federalists were in a defile, but "too much security will give time to his talents and indefatigableness to extricate them." He ended with an appeal to Madison : "We have had only middling performances to oppose to him. In truth, when he comes forward, there is nobody but yourself who can meet him. . . . For God's sake take your pen, and give a fundamental reply to Curtius and Camillus."[3]

With real perspicacity Jefferson had put his finger on the fundamental weakness of the Republicans. They were only the

[1] See S. F. Bemis. "Jay's Treaty." New York, 1923.
[2] August 30, 1795. Memorial Edition, IX, 307.
[3] September 21, 1795. *Ibid.*, IX, 309.

yeomanry; they counted a number of very honest and distinguished men; some of them were even brilliant in debates and could flatter themselves that they were victorious, as long as the Federalist chieftain did not appear in person on the battlefield. When he did, however, they had no outstanding man with the same capacity for work, the same ability to marshal facts, to present cogent arguments and to use biting sarcasm.   Jefferson alone, with his great felicity of expression and his mastery of style, could have opposed successfully the Federalist leader, but, as he wrote to Rutledge: "after five and twenty years' continual employment (in the service of our country), I trust it will be thought I have fulfilled my tour, like a punctual soldier and may claim my discharge." [1]

That he would have been a redoubtable opponent, had he chosen to be so, appears in a letter he sent at the time to William B. Giles.   The treaty once ratified by the Senate and signed by the President, it was thought that the House, on which fell the duty of making the necessary appropriations for the enforcement of the different articles, might possibly pass in their turn on the merits of the document.   Randolph had been requested by the President to give his opinion on the subject and did it in one of those written consultations which Jefferson had so often been asked to prepare himself, when in the official family of Washington.   To Giles, who was to attack the treaty in the House with Gallatin and Madison, Jefferson sent an elaborate and cruel dissection of Randolph's opinion:

The fact is that he has generally given his principles to one party, and his practice to the other, the oyster to one, the shell to the other. . . .   On the precedent now to be set will depend the future construction of our Constitution, and whether the powers of legislation shall be transferred from the President, Senate, and House of

[1] November 30, 1795.   Memorial Edition, IX, 313.

Representatives to the President and Senate, and Piamingo or any other Indian, Algerine, or other chief.[1]

Clearly he was getting back into his stride and when thoroughly aroused, as he had been once or twice in his career, he could also hit back or rather pierce with rapid thrust of the rapier. And yet he was not really thinking of reëntering the arena, for at the same time he was offering to George Wythe to superintend an edition of the laws of Virginia, of which he had made as complete a collection as he could, "either the manuscripts crumbling into dust or printed."[2] Yet he had an eye upon the budding geniuses of the Democratic party. Soon he realized the value of Albert Gallatin, who had undertaken a thorough analysis and demolition of Hamilton's administration :

Hamilton's object from the beginning was to throw them into forms which would be utterly undecypherable. . . . If Mr. Gallatin would undertake to reduce this chaos to order, present us with a clear view of our finances, and put them in a form as simple as they will admit, he will merit an immortal honor. The accounts of the United States ought to be, and may be made as simple as those of a common farmer, and capable of being understood by common farmers.[3]

With such sentences, simple and easily remembered, such felicity of expression and of thought, one can make a lasting impression on the people, without addressing directly the Indians of Tammany Hall or participating in whisky riots. One can also throw suspicion of intentional dishonesty on one's adversaries, coin mottoes which, repeated in a political campaign, fix themselves easily in the unsophisticated minds of the common people. But it does not ensue necessarily that Jefferson was an arch plotter, pulling the strings and laying plots to explode years later. He was quite sincere in his dislike of

[1] March 21, 1796. Memorial Edition, IX, 329.
[2] January 16, 1796. *Ibid.*, IX, 319.
[3] To James Madison, March 6, 1796. *Ibid.*, IX, 323.

Hamilton's budgets, for the simple reason that he did not understand them himself. The master financier and expert was beyond Jefferson's comprehension; in many respects he was even far ahead of his own time, while Jefferson, in matters of finance at least, remained all his life an eighteenth-century man. But the young Swiss-American who had made his mark in the whisky insurrection must have felt himself elated at Jefferson's approval. By such appropriate compliments and encouragements, great tacticians create and foster party and personal loyalty, and Jefferson was a past master in this difficult art.

As he had encouraged Gallatin, he encouraged Giles, kept in touch with him and through him sent a word of congratulation to a new Republican recruit, Doctor Leib: "I know not when I have received greater satisfaction than on reading the speech of Doctor Leib in the Pennsylvania Assembly.   He calls himself a new member.   I congratulate honest republicanism on such an acquisition, and promise myself much from a career which begins on such elevated ground." [1] He reminded him that Democratic societies were proscribed in England and that it would be interesting to know the terms of the bill proposed by Pitt against them.   Gallatin again called for his commendation for a speech printed in Bache's *Aurora*, the sole organ of the Republicans since Freneau had discontinued his *Gazette:* "It is worthy of being printed at the end of the *Federalist*, as the only rational commentary on the part of the law to which it relates." [2]   Then Jefferson raved over the indignities heaped upon the country by the treaty, over the point made by the Federalists that the House had nothing to say in the matter, and in his fury he even went so far as to treat Washington more severely than he had ever done before.   "Curse on his virtues," he exclaimed; "they have undone his country."   This political advice was naturally buried under rural news: "Mercury at

twenty degrees in the morning.   Corn fallen at Richmond to
twenty shillings."   But this bucolic note stopped short and the
political thermometer was consulted again and indicated that
"Nicholas was sure of his election, R. Joue and Jo. Monroe, in
competition for the other vote of the county."

Three weeks later Jefferson dug in his files to send Madison
more ammunition, showing clearly that, at least in one case,
Washington himself had recognized formerly the authority of
the legislature, that is to say both branches of the House, when
it came to ratifying the treaty with the new Emperor of Morocco.[1]   Then he wrote to his former neighbor, Philip Mazzei, a
letter which was to cause him more difficulties than any of the
previous acts of his career.   He thought that he could and
should give news of the country to this curious character, who
had come to Virginia as a vine-grower to engage in agricultural
experiments but who was also the former agent of the Duke of
Tuscany and of Stanislas of Poland, a Grimm "*au petit pied*",
a literary correspondent and a philosopher.   In all fairness to
Jefferson a preliminary remark is here necessary.   He was apt
in conversation to take his cue from his interlocutors rather
than to force on them any topic, and he was apt also to speak
in the same tone and same diapason.   In his letters he instinc-
tively yielded to the same tendency, changing his tone and style
according to his correspondent.   Writing to an Italian he
adopted a flowery, metaphoric, and emphatic manner not often
found in his letters, and in his desire to flatter the Tuscan ear
of his friend, he overshot the mark and overemphasized what
he would have stated much more moderately to an American :

Against us are the Executive, the Judiciary, two out of three
branches of the Legislature, all the officers of the government, all
who want to be officers, all timed men who prefer the calm of despotism to the boisterous sea of liberty. . . .   It would give you a fever
were I to name to you the apostates who have gone over to these

[1] April 9, 1790.   Memorial Edition, IX, 334.

heresies, men who were Samsons in the field and Solomons in the council, but who have had their heads shorn by the harlot England. . . .

But these men had not realized the great strength of the party then coming into being: "We have only to awake and snap the Lilliputian cords with which they have been entangling us during the first sleep which succeeded our labors." Then came the customary mention of his health, even more mournful than usual: "I begin to feel the effects of age. My health has suddenly broken down, with symptoms which give me to believe that I shall not have much to encounter of the *tedium vitae*." [1] Little did he believe when he indulged in this rhetorical outburst that Mazzei would give the letter to an Italian paper, that it would be translated from the Italian into French, from French into English and finally appear in America.

For Jefferson was eager to remain on good personal terms with Washington, even if he strongly disapproved of his policies, and this appeared when a few months later he denied having communicated to Bache's *Aurora* the questionnaire on the *Little Sarah*, and he seized the occasion to assure Washington once again of his affectionate sentiments. But he was already thinking of protecting himself, for in the same letter he asked the President to send him copies of the opinions presented by Hamilton and Randolph as "they had his opinion and he never had been able to obtain copy of theirs." And significantly he added, "Though I do not know that it will ever be of the least importance to me, yet one loves to possess arms, though they hope never to have occasion for them." [2]

The summer was apparently entirely occupied in agricultural and scientific pursuits. La Rochefoucauld-Liancourt, the former president of the National Assembly, at whose house Jefferson used to visit when in Paris to meet the *"républi-*

---

[1] April 24, 1796. Memorial Edition, IX, 335.
[2] June 19, 1796. *Ibid.*, IX, 339.

cains", was then traveling through the United States and stopped at Monticello for a week. The Duke has left us a most valuable description of Jefferson's establishment and the country around it. He praised the house "which will deserve when completed to be ranked with the most pleasant mansions in France and in Europe." He admired the view from the hill: for "Mr. Jefferson's house commands one of the most extensive prospects you can meet with." But his eye was that of a refined and overcivilized Frenchman of the eighteenth century accustomed to limited horizons, limited forests, to a certain balance between the woods, the rivers and the lands inclosed with hedges, to a nature stamped, modified, remolded by centuries of human labor. The contrast between the "moderate French landscapes" and the unlimited vistas in which plowed fields occupied a negligible space, impressed him almost painfully.

It was a magnificent view, but too vast; and rather than look at the scene as it presented itself, he preferred to call on fancy "to picture to us those plains and mountains such as population and culture will render them in a greater or smaller number of years." He looked with some suspicion at the numerous agricultural experiments of Jefferson, who seemed "to have derived his knowledge from books." He was not alone in this opinion. In any farming country, innovations are looked upon askance and we are not surprised to learn that "his system is entirely confined to himself; it is censured by some of his neighbours, who are also employed in improving their culture with ability and skill, but he adheres to it, and thinks it founded on just observation." Finally came the picture of the master himself and life at Monticello, worth preserving and reproducing.

In private life, Mr. Jefferson displays a mild, easy and obliging temper, though he is somewhat cold and reserved. His conversation is the most agreeable kind, and he possesses a stock of information not inferior to that of any other man. In Europe he would hold a distinguished rank among men of letters, and as such he has already appeared there; at present he is employed with activity and perseverance in the management of his farms and buildings; and he orders, directs and pursues in the minutest detail every branch of business relative to them. I found him in the midst of the harvest, from which the scorching heat of the sun does not prevent his attendance. His negroes are clothed, and treated as well as white servants could be. As he cannot expect any assistance from the two small neighboring towns, every article is made on his farm; his negroes are cabinet-makers, carpenters, masons, bricklayers, smiths, etc. The children he employs in a nail factory, which yields already a considerable profit. The young and old negresses spin for the clothing of the rest. He animates them by rewards and distinctions; in fine, his superior mind directs the management of his domestic concerns with the same abilities, activity, and regularity which he evinced in the conduct of public affairs, and which he is calculated to display in every situation of life. In the superintendence of the household he is assisted by his two daughters, Mrs. Randolph and Miss Maria, who are handsome, modest, and amiable women. They have been educated in France.

It is pleasant to have the direct testimony of a foreigner and a philosopher on the way Jefferson treated his slaves. But how can we believe that a man who could supervise all the details of the agricultural and industrial life around Monticello and endure the harvest sun was absolutely broken down in health? If he had ever been, Jefferson certainly was picking up. It seems probable that he did not discuss politics with the noble traveler. Perhaps he heard another recital of the excesses of the French Revolution, — a painful subject and one that did not serve any purpose; far better was it to exchange views on crop rotation, sheep raising, dung and manure, clover and potatoes and to demonstrate the new plow he had invented with a mold board of least resistance, which was to bring him some years later the "*grande médaille*" of the Agricultural Society of Paris.[1]

[1] To Jonathan Williams, July 3, 1796. Memorial Edition, IX, 347.

The first mention of the coming presidential election occurs in a letter to Monroe of July 10, 1796. The treaty had finally passed, but the party of the monocrats was shaken to its very foundation, "Mr. Jay and his advocates are treaty-foundered." The result was not doubtful. Even if a monocrat were elected, he would be overborne by the republican sense of his constituents. "If a republican, he will, of course, give fair play to that sense and lead things into the channel of harmony between the governors and the governed. In the meantime, patience!" He mentions that in order to operate a division and to split the Virginia vote, *they* had unsuccessfully endeavored to run Patrick Henry for vice president and would probably fall back on Pinckney, "in which they regard his southern position rather than his principles." But curiously enough the presidential nominees or preferences are not even mentioned. Could Monroe really believe that *Hamlet* was going to be played without Hamlet, and that the election of a vice president was the only thing that mattered? This omission was far more significant than any expressed preference. If Jefferson mentioned no candidates, it was simply because he already knew at that date that his faithful lieutenants in Congress were thinking of him as the only logical candidate, the only one who had not participated actively in the last three years' fierce debates in Congress, the only one who had not officially and openly taken a definite position, and consequently would be entirely free to make whatever concessions were necessary to reëstablish harmony in the divided camps of the voters. The result of the election was certainly in doubt; but at a time when foreign affairs were the dominant question, when in spite of the Jay treaty England was multiplying almost unbearable insults, when the nation was deeply humiliated, and even the Federalists resented the terms of the treaty, there were only two men of the first rank in America who had maintained the prestige of the United States before foreign nations and had shown themselves to be able negotiators: the man who with Franklin had put his signature to the Treaty of Peace, and the man who had concluded treaties of commerce with the nations of Europe; Adams and Jefferson.

A strange campaign it was, in which the champion of the Republicans seemed to remain completely silent. The middle of December came, and Jefferson had not yet manifested any desire to run, nor had he made any declaration concerning his program. He had to come out however when, on the night of the sixteenth, he received a letter from Madison informing him that there was no longer any doubt about the logical choice of the Republicans and that Madison would decline to be candidate. Jefferson took up his pen at once to define his position to his friend. He hoped that Adams would be elected; and in that case he would be satisfied with the second place although he would prefer the third, that is, his rejection, since he would be free to remain at home. It was desirable, however, in case of a tie, that Madison be instructed to request on his behalf that Mr. Adams should be preferred. Some of the reasons he gave were highly honorable, the best being that Mr. Adams was his senior and had always "ranked" him in public life, either in France or in America. Other reasons he did not indicate: one was evidently that the situation had never worn so gloomy an aspect since the year 1783 and that Jefferson did not believe he could steer clear of the present difficulties.[1]

Ten days later he wrote more at length to Rutledge. No news had come from Philadelphia, but he protested that he had no political ambition: "Before my God, I shall from the bottom of my heart, rejoice at escaping." Scrutinizing himself, he found that the unmerited abuse he had been subjected to still rankled; he was convinced that "no man will ever bring out of that office the reputation which carries him into it." The honeymoon would be as short in that case as in any other, and its

---

[1] December 17, 1796. Memorial Edition, IX, 351.

moments of ecstasy would be ransomed by years of torment and hatred.   Frankly he had no heart for the job.   Nor was this a declaration of philosophical principles, but another instance of his political foresight, and a simple admission of facts, for not only had Franklin been bitterly attacked after his death, but Washington himself was not immune from public abuse, and such would be the fate of Adams.

Jefferson was quite sincere when he declared: "I have no ambition to govern men; no passion which would lead me to delight to ride in a storm."   In advance, he repeated the *suave mari magno* of the old poet and hoped that he would not be elected, his only wish was that the newspapers would permit him " to plant his corn, beans, peas, etc. in hills or drills as he pleased, while our eastern friend will be struggling with the storm which is gathering over us, perhaps be shipwrecked in it! This is certainly not a moment to covet the helm."   If this was not a sincere and true statement, then language certainly has been given to man to conceal his thought.   If Jefferson was thirsty for power at that time he was more Machiavellian than Machiavelli himself.   But in spite of the inferences of ill-intentioned historians, I do not see that there is the slightest ground to doubt Jefferson's sincerity . . . except that he accepted finally the vice presidency, as he clearly hinted he would if it were offered to him.[1]   He ended with a picturesque and energetic phrase and said in French what he could not say in English.   He had not forgotten the words he had heard in the streets of Paris and perhaps in some salons after dinner, but certainly not in the mouth of Madame de Tessé or Madame de Corny: "*Au diable les bougres!*"

The next day he started writing to John Adams: he had not received any direct news of the election, but from his own calculations he had every reason to believe that barring a "trick worthy of your arch-friend of New York, Hamilton", Adams

[1] To Rutledge, December 27, 1796.   Memorial Edition, IX, 353.

would be elected. In that eventuality he wished to send his best wishes, and had only one hope to express, that Adams would be able to avoid the war. A friendly, sincere letter which Adams never saw. As Jefferson was going to send it, came Madison's letter of the seventeenth, announcing the complete results of the election.

It caused a certain amount of surprise to Jefferson; the vote had come much nearer an equality than he had expected, and, as he wrote a week later to Volney, "the difference between sixty-eight and seventy-one votes is little sensible." The presidency would have been decidedly distasteful to him; the vice presidency was something different and he could not in his own mind decide whether he "had rather have it or not have it." Then he went into a curious piece of philosophizing which marks him as very different from eighteenth-century philosophers and eighteenth-century optimists. More of a realist in politics than he is given credit for, he showed himself once more a disciple of Hobbes in his vision of society:

I do not recollect in all the animal kingdom a single species but man which is eternally and systematically engaged in the destruction of its own species. What is called civilization seems to have no other effect than to teach him to pursue the principle of *bellum omnium in omnia* on a larger scale, and in place of the little contests of tribe against tribe, to engage all quarters of the earth in the same work of destruction. When we add to this that as to the other species of animals, the lions and tigers are mere lambs compared with men alone, that nature has been able to find a sufficient barrier against the too great multiplication of other animals and of man himself, an equilibrating power against the fecundity of generation. My situation points my views chiefly to his wars in the physical world: yours perhaps exhibit him as equally warring in the moral one. We both, I believe, join in wishing to see him softened.[1]

[1] To Madison, January 1, 1797. Memorial Edition, IX, 357.

For the first time Jefferson was going to occupy a position of prestige in the American Government and to become President of the Senate, second only to the President, the "heir apparent", as Adams had termed himself during the preceding administration. Far from rejoicing over the honor, he expressed his reluctance to attend elaborate ceremonies for the inauguration, and he did his best to wriggle out of them. He asked whether it would not be possible for him to be notified of his election by mail instead of being waited upon by a special delegation from the Senate; then he looked up the Constitution and decided that he could just as well take oath of office in Charlottesville as in Philadelphia, and that it was hardly worth the trouble, since Congress was to adjourn at once, to undertake the long journey over muddy roads for such an ordeal. Finally he set out for Philadelphia. He had reëntered public life for twelve more years and little suspected that it would be so long before he could come back to dear Monticello and resume his agricultural experiments.

CHAPTER IV

"THE DICTATES OF REASON" AND PURE AMERICANISM

WHEN Jefferson arrived in Philadelphia to attend the inauguration of the new President, he had not seen Adams for four years and only insignificant communications had passed between them, since Madison had thought it proper to suppress the letter written by Jefferson at the end of December, not knowing "whether the rather difficult temper of Mr. Adams would not construe certain passages as a personal criticism." [1] With Adams, however, the first impulse was often the best. At the time he felt in a very conciliating mood; he even indulged in the hope that it would be possible to announce a sort of political armistice and to bring about a union of the different parties.

The two old friends had a cordial interview. Both of them, years later, wrote accounts of this historical meeting; though differing in a few details they agreed as to Adams' intention of burying the hatchet and beginning anew. He offered to send Jefferson to Paris as special envoy, insisting that he alone had the confidence of the French and would be able to bring about an arrangement. Jefferson being both unwilling and unavailable, Madison's name was mentioned, but nothing was decided as both knew that Madison had refused such an offer when tendered by Washington.

In his inaugural address Adams discreetly sounded a note of reconciliation. He praised the Constitution, declared that it was "better adapted to the genius, character, situation and rela-

[1] James Madison to Jefferson, January 15, 1797. "Works", VI, 303.

tions of this nation and country than any which had ever been proposed or suggested"; he added, much to the disgust of the Federalists, that he did not think of "promoting any alteration in it but such as the people themselves in the course of their experience should see and feel to be necessary or expedient"; finally, he seemed to desert the Federalist camp when he averred that, since he had seen the Constitution for the first time, "it was not then, nor had been since, any objection to it in his mind that the Executive and Senate were not more permanent."

Not without good reason had Hamilton failed to show any enthusiasm over the candidacy of Adams, and the Hamiltonians had some ground for declaring that the speech "was temporizing" and "was a lure for the favor of his opponents at the expense of his sincerity." Two days later Jefferson and Adams attended a dinner offered by Washington to the new administration. When they left the house they started walking home together and the name of Madison being mentioned, Adams declared that objections to the nomination had been raised. The President and the Vice President had come to Fifth Street, where their roads separated; they took leave of each other and the subject was never mentioned again. It was really the parting of the ways after a timid effort toward reconciliation. Adams in the meantime had called together his Cabinet and the Cabinet, as he himself admitted afterwards, had proposed to resign *en bloc* if he insisted on Madison's nomination.

For the "incongruous portrait gallery" that constituted the Cabinet inherited by Adams from Washington, we may refer to the vivid picture of Mr. Bowers: "Ali Baba among his Forty Thieves is no more deserving of sympathy than John Adams shut up within the seclusion of his Cabinet room with his official family of secret enemies" may seem to some a rather severe characterization. The least that can be said, however, is that it was a Cabinet hand-picked by Hamilton and that neither Pickering, Wolcott nor McHenry were the best minds Adams could have chosen in his party. But there again the term party is inaccurate; if Adams had, in some respect, Federalist tendencies, he was not a party man or a party leader. The irritable, impulsive, patriotic, peevish old New Englander was too individualistic to belong to any party; he was not the man either to rally the hesitating, to uphold the vacillating, or to encourage and educate the blind. Curiously enough, he has found very few defenders. Severely treated by the friends of Jefferson, he has not been spared by the admirers of Hamilton. He stands alone, one of the most complicated and contradictory figures in American history — a pure patriot, whose patriotic work is almost forgotten, a catholic spirit who loved to play with ideas and paradoxes, a contrary mind, but in my opinion more widely read than any of his American contemporaries, not excepting Jefferson. A man who spent his life by the side of the severe and haughty "New England Juno", but who had more ideas in his brain than any sultan of the Arabian Nights had favorites in his harem.

He had taken the helm at the climax of external difficulties. Complicated and delicate as were the problems of domestic administration, they were overshadowed by the difficulties with France. The misunderstandings, the incidents repeated on both sides, had accumulated with such an effect that, at the beginning of 1797, war with France seemed to be almost unavoidable. Though Jefferson had very little to do with it, it is not out of place to recall the main facts.

Genet had unfortunately his American parallel in Gouverneur Morris. As witty and devoid of ordinary morals and honesty as Talleyrand himself, elegant, refined, and corrupt, Gouverneur Morris had been, since his arrival in Paris, the toast of French aristocrats. His activities in favor of the king and his partisans were not unknown to the French, and when Genet was sent to America he had been requested to present discreetly the situation to the American Government. Genet had made no official representation, but he discussed Morris' attitude in a private conversation with Jefferson, and Washington, apprised of the facts, had seen the necessity of acting.

Monroe, on the contrary, had attempted to resume the Jeffersonian tradition. A disciple of the former minister, a true Liberal, and friendly to the French Revolution, he had been enthusiastically received at once, in spite of the many difficult problems he had to present to the government. But the Jay treaty had proved a bitter pill to swallow, and the Directory had made strong representations to the American minister: America was accused of having violated the treaties of Alliance and Commerce, and when Monroe was recalled, the Directory not only refused to receive the successor that had been appointed but even ordered him to leave the French territory at once.

Without entering into the merits of the question, we may say that Jefferson was still decidedly for peace, although somewhat doubtful of Adams' intentions. Shortly after the inauguration he analyzed his position as follows:

I sincerely deplore the situation of our affairs with France. War with them, and consequent alliance with Great Britain, will completely compass the object of the Executive Council, from the commencement of the war between France and England; taken up by some of them from that moment, by others more latterly. I still, however, hope it will be avoided. I do not believe Mr. Adams wishes war with France; nor do I believe he will truckle to England as servilely as has been done. If he assumes this front at once, and shows that he means to attend to self-respect and national dignity with both the nations, perhaps the depredations of both on our commerce may be amicably arrested. I think we should begin first with those who first began with us, and, by an example on them, acquire a right to re-demand the respect from which the other party has departed.

An ideal policy, but hardly enforceable with a man of Adams' temperament and with the Cabinet he had inherited. Immediately after taking oath of office, Jefferson had repaired to Monticello and was getting acquainted with his duties as presiding officer of the Senate; in January he asked his old master George Wythe to send him all possible information on parliamentary procedure "whether in books or scraps of paper",[1] and he was working on his "Parliamentary Manual." Early in April news of the refusal of the Directory to receive Pinckney arrived in Philadelphia, Adams proclaimed at once a day of fasting and prayer and called an extraordinary session of Congress for May 15. It was to be feared that a declaration of war would be the order of the day, for "the President did not need the assistance of Congress to continue in peace."[2]

As soon as he reached Philadelphia, Jefferson studied the situation and summed it up in a letter to Elbridge Gerry even before the opening of Congress. He had already come to the conclusion that a rapprochement between Adams and himself would prove impossible. There was really no way to convince Adams that Jefferson had not coveted the first place and did not nourish some rancor at his alleged failure to obtain it. Furthermore, it was quite certain that the Hamiltonians would do everything in their power to poison the mind of the President. This was most unpleasant but of little import to politics. Jefferson considered himself part of the legislative and not of the executive, and he had not even the right to be heard in consultation. It was his duty as well as his inclination to sit back, without trying to meddle in any way with the conduct of government.

On the other hand, he had not given up the right of expressing an opinion as a private citizen on matters of importance to the nation, and after stating that he had no concern in the present

---

[1] January 22, 1797. Memorial Edition, IX, 370.
[2] April 9, 1797. *Ibid.*, IX, 380.

situation, he launched out on a long *exposé* of the political situation as he saw it on the eve of the special session. With reference to foreign relations his wish and hope was that "we should take our stand on a ground perfectly neutral and independent towards all nations." This was particularly true with respect to the English and the French, but more easily said than done, since the English, not satisfied with equal treatment, wanted special privileges. Then Jefferson drew up a very impressive picture of the hold on the United States maintained by Great Britain through her commerce. Without domestic industries the United States had to go to England; she was the workshop of America. Goods were largely transported in English bottoms; British merchants, some of them fictitiously naturalized, were in every American port and in all the cities and towns of the interior, occupying strategic positions. The British also were dominating American banks and American finance and, through finance, could exert a powerful influence on American political life. Finally, they were accused of attempting to break the Union by advocating in their subsidized press a scission between the North and the South. If difficulties came to such a point that the only way to avoid a secession was to go to war with Europe, Jefferson, much as he abhorred war, was willing to become embroiled with Europe. He still hoped, however, that it would be possible to find some means to keep out of European quarrels and in the meantime gradually to free America from all foreign influence, "political, commercial, or in whatever form it may be attempted."

One might say that this was no original point of view to develop. It was to a certain extent the policy advocated by Washington in his Farewell Address. Curiously enough, it was not absolutely remote from Hamilton's theory, for these two men who, temperamentally, could never come together, held about the same view of the situation. That England had the larger share of American commerce and that English manufactures had a sort of monopoly of the American market had been repeatedly pointed out by Hamilton. And on this Jefferson agreed completely. If one objected to that condition, the obvious remedy according to the Hamiltonian doctrine was, not to take measures to exclude English goods from the market, but to encourage American manufactures so as to enable them to compete with imported products. In this Jefferson differed from Hamilton, but while complaining of the situation, he did not propose any remedy, except perhaps to protect American inventors and thus stimulate them to establish new manufacturing plants. One must admit that at this point he let his "philosophy" interfere with realities.

As a matter of fact, he was thoroughly opposed to the development of manufacturing plants, to the creation of large industrial cities housing thousands of salaried workers. As we have said, his vision of America was a sort of Arcadia where every man would live on his own farm, off the products of his own land. In some respects it may seem perfectly absurd, and yet it was very natural and to a certain extent quite logical. It was purely and simply the extension of the Monticello type of organization to the whole country. La Rochefoucauld-Liancourt had been struck by the fact that Monticello was practically a self-supporting economic unit. Jefferson was raising his own horses and just enough sheep to provide the wool spun by the women slaves to clothe the workers and sometimes the masters. On the plantation lived smiths, carpenters, cabinet makers, brick makers, and layers; some grain was sold, some nails were manufactured and sold to the neighbors. Selling comparatively little, buying practically nothing, Jefferson's estate came as close to being a sort of Robinson Crusoe island as was possible in a modern country. Thus the Virginia planter had come to develop a philosophy of society not unlike the ideal society described by Rousseau in the "Nouvelle Héloise" and more feudal than he himself realized, since, after all, if serfdom had been abolished, it rested essentially on slavery. He was unequivocally against great agglomerations, although he had not visited any of the large industrial cities of England except London; but at least he knew London and Paris, he had lived in Philadelphia and New York, and he felt that it was not good for men to herd too closely together. Work in factories was both unhealthy and immoral, for in congested centers of population there developed a spirit of discontent aggravated by the fact that industrial workers, who generally did not own a particle of land, were footloose, unattached, and free to move from one city to another at any time; they constituted a restless and dangerous element. It mattered little that, for the present, they gave their support to the Republicans and had joined the Democratic clubs; Jefferson knew too well that they would be easily influenced in their views by a good orator, by passions of the moment, and could not be relied upon in an emergency.

It would be easy to point out the close resemblance of certain features of this ideal of Jefferson with the theories of the Physiocrats. Such a parallelism, however, can be easily exaggerated and to a great extent is very misleading. Whether all riches came from the soil, or were the product of labor in any form, or both, Jefferson did not know and did not care. He was no more a disciple of Quesnay than of Adam Smith, simply because he was not an economist but a sociologist. Hamilton, who was an economist of the first rank, was primarily interested in the development of production and in the circulation of wealth, and paid little attention to the social modification that an industrialization of the country would probably bring about. Jefferson, on the contrary, was solely interested in protecting and preserving a certain pattern of civilization which was essentially an agricultural pattern — the only safe foundation for the political and private virtues of vital importance in a democracy. Manufactures meant surplus production, which meant, in turn, the necessity of exporting. If America became a great industrial nation, she would have, sooner or later, to export her surplus production and in turn to import many products from Europe. But if the country maintained extensive trade connections with Europe she would be necessarily caught in the maze of international politics. Her commercial interests would clash with the interests of Europe, and this would ultimately result in wars or at least in a constant threat of war. It would also mean the building of a strong navy to protect American commerce, perhaps the establishment of a permanent army; at any rate, the immediate consequence would be an enormous increase in taxes, the necessity of resorting to internal taxation, the burden of which would fall on the backs of the farmers. Numerous tax collectors would have to be appointed; Federal employees and officials ready to act at the beck and call of the Government would swarm all over the country. State rights and individual rights would be restricted and invaded, and liberty would exist only in name. On the other hand, foreign commerce was not to be entirely suppressed. Commerce was a natural and desirable thing with one's neighbors. Geographically the West Indies had closer connections with America than with Europe, and it was in that direction that the United States could develop their trade. This was a natural law and a natural right, and any obstacle put to the natural flow of trade between the islands and the American continent was unjust and to be fought persistently.

Such seems to have been at that time the political and social dream of Jefferson. Like most dreams of the sort it was perfectly logical, even if impossible to realize. But, as a matter of fact, it was far more admissible than the ideal he was to propose four years later in his inaugural address, following the lead of Washington: "peace, commerce with all nations, entangling alliances with none." He was far more clear-sighted when he came to the conclusion that America could not combine political aloofness and commercial and economic relationship. This formula was a desperate and none too successful attempt to coalesce two contradictory principles and ideals, and for the last hundred and thirty years America has been striving to achieve this impossible program. Such a position has always seemed most absurd and unintelligible to Europeans, with the result that America has often been accused of hypocritical conduct in her foreign affairs, and more indulgent historians have repeatedly confessed their puzzlement and inability to understand her. The consequences of this incestuous union of Jeffersonian political aloofness and Hamiltonian industrial and commercial development are still apparent to-day. They were conspicuous in the position taken by President Wilson during his first administration; they reappear again and again in all American declarations referring to the League of Nations, mandates, and reparations. One of the first results was necessarily to embroil America in all European wars and to raise again and again the question of neutrality.

It is doubtful however whether, even in 1797, Jefferson would have consented to carry to an extreme the realization of his bucolic dreams. He knew full well that America had commercial aspirations that could not be suppressed; all one could do was not to encourage them as Hamilton wanted to do and, in the meantime, to reduce political connections to a minimum.

At the end of the short session of Congress in which measures relative to Europe had been debated, Jefferson wrote to Rutledge: "as to everything except commerce, we ought to divorce ourselves from them all." But this system would require "time, temper, wisdom, and occasional sacrifice of interests; and how far all of these will be ours, our children may see, but we shall not."[1] Such has been the hope and the endeavor of America ever since that time; with what success it is for others to judge.

[1] June 24, 1797. Memorial Edition, IX, 408.

Adams' speech had been a warlike one. That the Government of the United States had been insulted by the French Directory was no "matter of doubt." Pinckney, sent as successor to Monroe, had not been received by the Government, and Monroe had been informed that the Directory "would no longer recognize nor receive a minister plenipotentiary from the United States, until after a reparation of the grievances demanded of the American Government, and which the French Republic had a right to expect." Pinckney himself had been notified that his presence in Paris was illegal and that he could not stay in the country. No wonder that Adams declared that: "Such attempts ought to be repelled with a decision which shall convince France and the world that we are not a degraded people, humiliated under a colonial spirit of fear and sense of inferiority, fitted to be the miserable instruments of foreign influence, and regardless of national honor, character and interest."

On May 23 the Senate sent an address to the President, indorsing his views by a vote of seventeen to eleven. The fight was to take place in the House and in the newspapers. "Foreign influence is the present and just object of public hue and cry", wrote Jefferson to Thomas Pinckney.[1] As always happens when the cry of wolf is raised, "the most guilty and foremost and loudest in the cry", those who were denouncing French influence, were to a large extent English propagandists and not of the best type. But news from France was infrequent and slight and, at the beginning of June, Jefferson waited anxiously for the daily arrival of Paine and Monroe from whom he expected a true account of the situation. Then came the news of Bonaparte's latest victories and the announcement that the preliminaries of peace were signed between France and Austria. This was the only thing which could and did cool the fury of the British faction. "The victories of the Rhine

[1] May 29, 1797. Memorial Edition, IX, 389.

and Italy, peace with Austria, bankruptcy of England, mutiny in her fleet, and the King's writing letters recommending peace" — all that constituted a string of events nothing less than miraculous.[1]

At this juncture Jefferson made a momentous political move. He wrote a long letter to Colonel Aaron Burr to take him into his confidence. The Vice President was beginning to gather up the loose threads: "Some general view of our situation and prospects, since you left us, may not be unacceptable. At any rate, it will give me an opportunity of recalling myself to your memory, and of evidencing my esteem for you." What could this mean in ordinary language if not that he counted on him to counterbalance Hamilton's influence in New York and present the views of the chief to the leaders of the party. First of all he called his attention to the fact that the Republican party was losing ground in the House as well as in the Senate, and that the majority was in the hands of "five or six individuals of no fixed system at all, governed by the panic or the prowess of the moment, who flap as the breeze blows against the Republican or the aristocratic bodies."

For the present, the danger of going to war was less disquieting. Bonaparte's victories had brought many to their senses and some were complaining that Congress had been called together to do nothing. "The truth is, there is nothing to do, the idea of war being scouted by the events of Europe; but this only proves that war was the object for which we were called." It had been a close call, and France might have declared war against the United States if the Ancients had not pronounced against it. "Thus we see two nations who love one another affectionately, brought by the ill temper of their executive administrations, to the very brink of a necessity to imbue their hands in the blood of each other."

But leaving aside all sentimental considerations, Jefferson

[1] June 15, 1797. To James Madison, Memorial Edition, IX, 397.

undertook to demonstrate that such a war would have, as a result, the immediate occupation of Louisiana by France, and with Louisiana again a Gallo-American colony, the danger would indeed be great. Such were "some of the truths that ought to penetrate into the Eastern States", and Burr was no doubt intrusted with the mission to preach the true doctrine of republicanism in his district.[1]

Four days later Jefferson announced with infinite joy to Elbridge Gerry that he had been appointed to go as envoy extraordinary, jointly with General Pinckney and Mr. Marshall, to the French Republic. Once more he insisted upon the necessity of coming to some sort of an arrangement with Europe. War against England or France could only result in civil war in America and probably secession. The fate of the United States was at stake.[2]

Congress was to adjourn on the twenty-eighth of June and Jefferson was already looking forward to the rural quiet of Monticello, where he could "exchange the roar and tumult of bulls and bears for the prattle of his grandchildren and senile rest." His quiet however was disturbed by an unexpected incident. Early in August he sent an urgent call to Madison to come to Monticello with Monroe in order to consult with them on an urgent matter. The letter written to Mazzei the preceding year had come back, translated from the French, and was used as a political weapon against Jefferson and the Republicans. Public repudiation of the letter was impossible, since he had really written it, although the translation had garbled the meaning of some important sentences. To remain silent under fire and accept as true the accusations hurled against him was equally difficult. His friends alone could help him out of the difficulty. He finally decided to ignore the whole matter as he had already been advised to do by his Philadelphia friends, but

---

[1] June 17, 1797. Memorial Edition, IX, 400.
[2] June 21, 1797. *Ibid.*, IX, 405.

the letter preyed on his mind and this was not an incident to be easily forgotten.   It was during the summer and fall of that year that certain principles were definitely crystallized in his mind.

Deploring the fact that both factions had been incensed by political considerations and political hatred rather than by a true judgment of the situation and what he had called in a letter to Rutledge "the dictates of reason and pure Americanism", he then reached for himself certain conclusions which were to direct his political conduct during the rest of his career. He was thoroughly sickened by the insults passing in the press. Men of his own party he could not severely condemn for this, nor could he take from their hands the weapons used to defeat the enemy, but he was also loath to approve of their tactics.   In Democratic societies, established in large cities, he placed very little confidence; they were fighting on his side, at least for the present, and were vociferous enough; but to a large extent they were made up of office hunters.   They did not and could not constitute a trustworthy bulwark for Republican institutions. Fortunately events had proved that there existed in the country a large body of people sincerely attached to republican principles; these had been slumbering and their leaders had almost steered the ship into a foreign port, but they could be enlightened and made to manifest their true sentiments; for all reforms "must be brought about by the people using their elective rights with prudence and self-possession, and not suffering themselves to be duped by treacherous emissaries."   "It is the sober sense of our citizens that we are safely and steadily conducting from monarchy to republicanism, and it is by the same agency alone that we can be kept from falling back." [1] As to foreign questions, the fact that their intrusion into American life had divided the nation against itself proved conclusively that the only safe course to follow was to sever the last

[1] To Colonel A. Campbell, September 1, 1797. Memorial Edition, IX, 419.

bonds that connected America with Europe and "to place our foreign connections under a new and different arrangement." [1] The time had come for America to proclaim her independence in all foreign matters, for " we owe gratitude to France, justice to England, subservience to none."

It was in coining these fine political maxims that Jefferson was at his best. As had happened so often during his life, he refused to be carried away by popular passions raging in Philadelphia, New York, and Boston. From the "mountain top" of Monticello he was able to judge dispassionately the sordid struggles of party politics. He was no party boss, not even a party leader; if he had any ambition at that time, it was to become a national leader and the exponent of what he himself had called in his letter to Rutledge "pure Americanism."

Congress had been called for November 13, but the Vice President felt no inclination to hurry back to Philadelphia and reënter the scene of strife. He did not leave until December 4 and found, as he had expected, that Congress was marking time, waiting for news from Paris. Madison he kept informed minutely of all the changes that had taken place during the summer, of the progress of republicanism in Vermont and New York, and of all the small talk of politics, interesting only as showing how eagerly Jefferson kept his finger on the pulse of the country. He had an ulterior motive in sending to Madison papers and pamphlets recently published in Philadelphia; it was that "the paragraphs in some of these abominable papers may draw from you now and then a squib." Matters seemed to be on the mend; the latest official intelligence from Paris was that the envoys "would find every disposition on the part of the Government to accommodate with us." [2] The session dragged on. Jefferson's melancholy statement that the Senate

[1] June 24, 1797. Memorial Edition, IX, 409.
[2] January 3, 1798. *Ibid.*, IX, 431.

was divided "twenty-two and ten and will probably forever be", was not helped by Adams' declaration that:

No republic can ever be of any duration, without a Senate, and a Senate deeply and strongly rooted, strong enough to bear up against all popular storms and passions. The only fault in the Constitution of our Senate is, that their term of office is not durable enough. Hitherto they have done well, but probably they will be forced to give way in time.[1]

The only important proposition before Congress was "the bill of foreign intercourse and the proposition to arm our foreign vessels"; but both parties seemed to be afraid to press the matter. Everything was in suspense "as the ensuing month will probably be the most eventful ever yet seen in modern Europe." If Bonaparte's projected invasion of England succeeded the tables would turn; in the meantime the official ball given on Washington's birthday offered to Philadelphia society a pretext for engaging in hot controversies. Business was bad and bankruptcies multiplying. Congress was thinking of appropriating some money for national defense so as to furnish convoys to vessels going to Europe and to provide for the protection of smaller vessels of the coast trade. Adams had decided to reorganize his Cabinet. Wolcott would remain in office, but it seemed that McHenry was to go and Pickering was very doubtful whether he would stay.[2]

Meanwhile dispatches from the American envoys had arrived; they were being deciphered and the President hesitated upon the advisability of communicating them in full to Congress. Then, on the nineteenth, came Adams' message declaring that "it was incumbent on him to declare that he perceived no ground of expectation that the objects of their mission could be accomplished on terms compatible with the safety, honor, or the essential interest of the Nation."

[1] February 22, 1798. Memorial Edition, IX, 444.
[2] March 15, 1798. *Ibid.*, X, 6.

On the twenty-first Jefferson wrote to Madison that "a great change has taken place in the appearance of our political atmosphere"; the "insane message" had had great effect but there was still a possibility that, if all members were present, the war measures would be defeated by one voice in the House. What was to be done in that case? The only possible solution was to make a bid for time and wait for the results of Bonaparte's expedition against Great Britain. Jefferson's plan therefore was to propose an adjournment of Congress "in order to go home and consult their constituents on the great crisis of American affairs now existing." "To gain time is everything with us." In this letter Jefferson made one of his few material errors, so strange on the part of a man in his position, and hardly to be explained unless we suppose that the wish was father to the thought. "We relied," he said, "with great security on that provision which requires two-thirds of the Legislature to declare war. But this is completely eluded by a majority's taking such measures as will be sure to produce war." Certainly there was no such article in the Constitution, unless Jefferson in his excitement interpreted the ratification of treaties by two-thirds of the Senate to imply also that a declaration of war should have such a majority.[1] A week later he was convinced that "the question of war and peace depends now on a toss of cross and pile. If we could gain but one season we should be saved."[2] It was to these Fabian tactics that the Republicans were to bend all their efforts in order to avoid a formal declaration of war.

In the meantime the dispatches of the envoys were made public and the famous X.Y.Z. case came to light. Debate was hot in Congress on the Sprigg resolution declaring that "under existing conditions it is not expedient for the United States to resort to war against the French republic."[3] Adams then decided to communicate the letters from Paris.

[1] March 21, 1798. Memorial Edition, X, 9.
[2] To Madison, March 29, 1798. *Ibid.*, X, 17.   [3] March 27, 1798.

No more terrible blow could have been inflicted upon the friends of peace. Jefferson heard the news on April 3, but as it was still undecided whether they could be made public, he refrained from discussing them with Madison until the sixth. His first impressions were "very disagreeable and very confused." Yet he tried, as was his wont, to see both sides of the question. With the story of the abortive negotiations was interwoven

. . . some base propositions on the part of Talleyrand, through one of his agents, to sell his interest and influence with the Directory towards soothing difficulties with them, in consideration of a large sum (fifty thousand pounds sterling); the arguments to which his agent resorted to induce compliance with this demand were unworthy of a great nation (could they be imputed to them), and calculated to excite disgust and indignation in the Republicans particularly, whom they so far mistake, as to presume an attachment to France and hatred to the Federal party and not to the love of their country, to be their first passion.

In the papers, as communicated, Adams had substituted for the names given by the envoys — Hottinger, Bellamy, and Hauteval — the initials X.Y.Z., hence the name given at once to the incident.

Whether the French bankers really represented Talleyrand is absolutely immaterial; the result on American public opinion alone is to be considered here. According to Jefferson, the public's first reaction was one of astonishment;[1] furious indignation followed very quickly. Sprigg's resolution was naturally discarded as not appropriate; war seemed the order of the day. The last resort left to the remaining Republicans was to avoid open hostilities with the French Republic and, not being able to prevent a vote of credits for armaments, to insist that they should be granted specially for internal defense and preparation.[2] A more mature consideration of the letters

[1] To Madison, April 12, 1798. Memorial Edition, X, 27.
[2] April 12, 1798. *Ibid.*, X, 28.

convinced Jefferson that the door to negotiation was not absolutely closed.[1] But popular indignation was too strong; riotous scenes took place in the streets of Philadelphia, addresses from all parts of the country came to Adams, urging him to stand for national honor and the Federalist press fanned the flames. The few faithful Republicans grew discouraged and one by one drifted out of Philadelphia. "Giles, Clopton, Cabell, and Nicholas have gone," wrote Jefferson on April 26, "and Clay goes to-morrow. Parker has completely gone over to the war party. In this state of things they will carry what they please. One of the war party, in a fit of unguarded passion, declared sometime ago they would pass a Citizen Bill, an Alien Bill, and a Sedition Bill."[2] Madison, although urged to take up his pen "for heaven's sake and not desert the public cause altogether", remained silent in Virginia. Jefferson felt that the first and second measures were directed against his close friend Volney,[3] who had been somewhat imprudent. That the republican press would be muzzled for "the war hawks talk of septembrizing, deportation and the examples for quelling sedition set by the French executives. All the firmness of the human mind is now in a state of requisition."[4]

It is remarkable, and not the smallest achievement of Jefferson, that he kept a cool head in the midst of this turmoil. Insulted every day in the press and in public meetings, lampooned and caricatured, he had to remain silent because of his official position and could not protest to the government. No stranger political situation could be imagined than this, — a man recognized as the head of a party opposed to the government, yet next to the President in rank, without power to defend himself and to enter into polemics, ostracized, and, as he admitted himself, "insulated in every society", forced to listen

[1] April 12, 1798. Memorial Edition, X, 29.
[2] To Madison, April 26, 1798. *Ibid.*, X, 31.
[3] See Chinard, "Volney et l'Amérique." Paris, Baltimore, 1923.
[4] To Madison, April 26, 1798. Memorial Edition, X, 33.

to the reading of the most detestable things such as the Alien Bill, and still not indulging in bitterness. A comparison of his letters with those written by Adams and Hamilton at the same time would constitute the most extraordinary tribute to his self-mastery. He persisted in seeing some faint hope and refused to give up the ship.

First there was a possibility that when the merchants would see that actual war meant War Tax, Land Tax, and Stamp Tax, these measures would constitute sedatives to cool their ardor. The present session had already cost two hundred thousand dollars and that was only a beginning. Furthermore, there was also a possibility that, if an actual declaration of war could be prevented during the summer, the coming election would reën-force the republican party. Volney had decided to go back to France with a few other aliens who had chartered a boat, without waiting for the enactment of the Alien Bill. Many of them were much irritated, but Volney at least was "thoroughly impressed with the importance of preventing war, whether considered with reference to the interests of the two countries, of the cause of Republicanism, or of man on a broad scale." [1]

Isolated though he was in Philadelphia, from his room in the Philosophical Society of which he was president, Jefferson persisted in hoping against hope. One thing however was to be avoided at all cost. If the situation became such that the Northern States, Connecticut and Massachusetts particularly, clearly dominated the situation, it was far better to submit temporarily and endure even detestable measures than to break the Union. The beginning of the disaggregation could not be stopped; a realignment of States conducing to new secessions would finally be the result. Men must quarrel, and "seeing, therefore, that an association of men who will not quarrel with one another is a thing which never yet existed, from the greatest confederacy of nations down to a town meeting or a

[1] To Madison, May 31, 1798. Memorial Edition, X, 43.

vestry; seeing that we must have somebody to quarrel with, I had rather keep our New England associates for that purpose, than to see our bickerings transferred to others." [1]

This was a most important declaration and shows to what length Jefferson was willing to go in order to avoid the only irremediable catastrophe. Whatever may have been his weaknesses and shortcomings, his inconsistencies and contradictions, the man who, in the hectic atmosphere of Philadelphia, was able to put aside his own interests, the interests of his party, his social and political ideals to think nationally, was indeed a great American. We may even venture to say that he was at the time the only great American in the country.

When Marshall came back from France — much to his surprise, as a war hero and as an avenger of national honor — the Republicans began to take a less pessimistic view of the situation. After all, the situation was not so desperate as they had been led to believe; Gerry had remained in Paris, and negotiations could be resumed. The show of honesty made by the envoys in Paris was most gratifying to national honor and gave the public a feeling of triumph over the corrupt practices of European diplomacy. But with the return of Marshall a new campaign broke out against Jefferson. Doctor Logan on his own initiative had gone to Europe in the interest of peace, but had gone mysteriously and without telling any one of his intentions. It was soon assumed that he had been sent on an unauthorized and unofficial but highly objectionable mission by the Jacobins "to solicit an army from France, instruct them as to their landing, etc.", and Jefferson was again accused of being the arch plotter. Nothing could be more ridiculous, for the poor doctor was simply one of those idealistic pacifists who sometimes do more harm than good, but whose intentions are not open to suspicion.

[1] To John Taylor, June 1, 1798. Memorial Edition, X, 45.

But popular passions once aroused cannot be silenced in a day and the efforts of the friends of peace were weak and inefficient. On April 14 a bill was passed on second reading by the Senate, declaring the treaties with France void and nonexistent. Adams made it known that he would refuse Gerry's request that other envoys be sent. If Congress remained in session in a city where war hysteria had reached a paroxysm, extreme measures were unavoidable. The only remedy was to adjourn as soon as possible, for "to separate Congress now, will be withdrawing the fire from under a boiling pot." [1]   Congress did not separate, however, without authorizing the President to increase the navy, to expend two hundred fifty thousand dollars for fortifications, to purchase eight hundred thousand dollars' worth of arms and ammunition, to raise an army of ten thousand troops and to equip vessels to seize and bring to port any armed vessels which had attacked American vessels or might be found "hovering on the coast of the United States for the purpose of committing depredations on the vessels belonging to the citizens thereof." On July 6 were passed the famous Alien Bills, and on the fourteenth, as a sort of defiance to the principles of the French Revolution, Congress adopted the "Sedition Law", giving power to the government "to prosecute persons or to prevent the circulating or saying of any utterance against the Government of the United States, or either House of the Congress of the United States, or the President of the United States."

[1] To Madison, June 21, 1798.   Memorial Edition, X, 49–53.

POLITICAL LEADER AND STRATEGIST

WHEN Jefferson went home after the adjournment of Congress he remained completely silent for two months. But the newspaper war went on in Philadelphia with more virulence than ever: attacks against the arch plotter and the defender of the French Jacobins were multiplied, prosecutions were begun in Massachusetts under the Sedition Act and for a time Jefferson himself seems to have feared for his own safety. To Samuel Smith, who had sent him a clipping in which he was vehemently accused, he answered that he had "contemplated every event which the Maratists of the day can perpetrate, and I am prepared to meet every one in such a way, as shall not be derogatory to the public liberty or my own personal honor." He naturally denied that he had in any way plotted with Bache, the editor of the *Aurora*, or Doctor Leib; then he went on to define once more his position. He had acted on the same principles from the year 1775 to that day, and he was convinced that these principles were those of the great body of the American people. He was for peace certainly, not only with France but also with England. He was aware that both of them "have given and are daily giving, sufficient cause of war; that in defiance of the laws of nations, they are every day trampling on the rights of the neutral powers, whenever they can thereby do the least injury, either to the other." But he still maintained that the best policy was and would have been "to bear from France for one more summer what we have been bearing from both of them these four years." With England the United States had chosen peace; with France they had chosen war; to what extent the Government was supported by the majority of the people was a thing to be seen in the coming elections. He ended with a note of Christian forgiveness for Fenno and Porcupine, who "covered him with their implacable hatred." "The only return I will ever make them, will be to do them all the good I can, in spite of their teeth." [1]

This was almost too godly to be true; but if we remember that his letters were intercepted and read by Adams' police, as he repeatedly complained, and that letters sent to him were opened on their way to Monticello, we may wonder whether he did not write these lines for the eye of the censor, and with his tongue in his cheek. That he really believed at the time in the existence of a monarchical conspiracy appears from a letter to Stephens Thompson Mason.[2]

The Alien and Sedition bills were just a beginning. If the people did not revolt against them, the next step would be to persuade Congress that the President should continue in office for life, reserving to another time the transfer of the succession to his heirs and the establishment of the Senate for life.

This was a very accurate prophecy of the course that events were to follow, not in America, but in France, and this shows at least that Jefferson had an exact understanding of the gradual steps through which a republican government might become an empire. But France had Bonaparte, while neither Adams nor Washington ever had the inclination or the power to bring about such a change in America. Yet when one thinks of the military ambitions of Hamilton, of his real opposition and scorn for republican government, it would perhaps be unfair to dismiss these apprehensions as absolutely groundless. Whatever the case may have been, Jefferson thought the time had come to erect a strong barrier against the encroachments of the Federal Government. Towards the end of the same month, the

---

[1] August 22, 1798. Memorial Edition, X, 61.
[2] October 11, 1798. *Ibid.*, X, 62.

two Nicholas brothers, George and Wilson C., discussed with Jefferson at Monticello a plan to put to work the Republicans, who, finding themselves useless in Congress, had retired from the field. A plan was finally adopted to arouse the State legislatures; during these meetings were drawn up the famous "Resolutions" that George Nicholas was to present to the legislature of Kentucky, and which Madison was to bring before the Virginia Assembly.[1]

The exact authorship of the "Resolutions" remained a matter of doubt until Jefferson more than twenty years later acknowledged his participation in a letter to the son of George Nicholas.[2] It was well for Jefferson's peace of mind that he remained behind the scenes on this occasion and let Madison take the responsibility of the recommendation, which he did not allow to pass without modifying the original text to a considerable degree. The Kentucky resolutions have been the subject of many discussions, and Madison himself used a great deal of ink and time to explain the true import of the measures he had sponsored before the Virginia Assembly. They will become much more intelligible when studied in the light of the theory we have already discussed and by which the social compact is considered as a *pactum foederis* and not a *pactum subjectionis*.[3] It was simply the reaffirmation that in forming a society neither men nor States abdicate entirely their sovereignty but reserve a specified part of their natural rights set forth in a Bill of Rights — an essential foundation on which to build a constitution. Such is clearly the meaning of the first resolution :

1. *Resolved.* That the several States composing the United States of America are not united on the principle of unlimited submission to their general Government; but that, by a compact under the style and title of a Constitution for the United States,

---

[1] To Madison, November 17, 1798. Memorial Edition, X, 62.
[2] December 11, 1821. *Ibid.*, XV, 351.   [3] See pp. 80–82.

and of amendments thereto, they constituted a general Government for special purposes — delegated to that Government certain definite powers, reserving, each State to itself, the residuary mass of right to their own self-government; and that whensoever the general Government assumes undelegated powers, its acts are unauthoritative, void, and of no force; that to this compact each State acceded as a State, and is an integral party, its co-States forming, as to itself, the other party: that the Government created by this compact was not made the exclusive or final judge of the extent of the powers delegated to itself; since that would have made its discretion, and not the Constitution, the measure of its powers; but, that, as in all other cases of compact among powers having no common judge, each party has an equal right to judge for itself, as well of infractions as of the mode and measure of redress.

Not only was Jefferson perfectly consistent in repeating almost word for word in this Resolution the doctrine of natural rights and State rights reached early in his career, but the last lines foretold the theory he was to defend against Marshall during his presidency. By denying that the parties to the Federal compact had a common judge, he refused in advance to consider the Supreme Court as the guardian, interpreter, and defender of the Constitution. This principle once asserted, Jefferson endeavored to prove that the Sedition Bill, the Alien Bill and other measures adopted by Congress at the instigation of the Federalists constituted an infringement of State rights, since they did not deal with matters specifically reserved to Congress and since it was provided that "the powers not delegated to the United States by the Constitution, nor prohibited by it to the States are reserved to the States respectively or to the people." This was at the same time an attempt to prove the unconstitutionality of the recent legislation and an endeavor to define more exactly the powers of the Federal Government. The Eighth Resolution, the longest, proposed the establishment of a committee of correspondence to communicate the resolutions to the different legislatures and enunciated the doctrine of nullification, namely that the State had the right to consider as nonexistent such laws as might be passed in defiance of the Constitution. Naturally the Law of Sedition and the Alien Bill came under that category.

Strong as the language of the Resolutions may have been, it was not Jefferson's intention to promote a rebellion of certain States against the Federal Government and to provoke a secession. They contained a strong affirmation that the subscribers to the Resolutions were sincerely anxious for the preservation of the Union. As a matter of fact, in Jefferson's intention they were a piece of political strategy and he had no desire to push the matter too far. A letter he wrote to Madison on the subject is particularly significant on that score: "I think we should distinctly affirm all the important principles they contain, so as to hold to that ground in future, and leave the matter in such a train as that we may not be committed absolutely to push the matter to extremities, and yet may be free to push as far as events will render prudent."[1]

In other words, it was what the French call a gesture, the act of a lawyer reserving certain points in a trial before a tribunal and the right to present conclusions. It was not the act of a revolutionist and for the time being at least, although adopted in a modified form both by Kentucky and Virginia, it remained a gesture and a simple protest against Federalist usurpations.

The end of the fall came, and Jefferson relapsed once more into his cautious silence. One letter only, written from Monticello to John Taylor, is found in the files for that period.[2] This time Jefferson was more optimistic; the ardor of the Federalists for war seemed to have cooled down and the people began to realize that national pride was a very expensive article, that wars had to be paid for: "the Doctor is now on his way to cure it, in the guise of the tax gatherer."

[1] November 17. Memorial Edition, X, 63.
[2] November 26, 1798. *Ibid.*, X, 63.

At the end of the month, the Vice President set out for Philadelphia to attend the opening of the third session of the Fifth Congress. Adams' address was anxiously awaited. Much to the surprise and disgust of the war party, if it could not be called conciliatory, it was far less provocative than the address of the twenty-first of June preceding. He protested against the decree of the Directory constituting "an unequivocal act of war" and maintained that "to invigorate measures of defence" was the true policy of the United States. But while he thus reiterated some of his previous statements, the tone was far less truculent. President Adams, while frowning threateningly, held behind his back the olive branch and was ready to extend it. The conclusion was one of these milk-and-water statements, that curious balancing of two positions so often found in American State papers relating to foreign affairs :

But in demonstrating by our conduct that we do not fear war in the necessary protection of our rights and honor, we shall give no room to infer that we abandon the desire of peace. . . . An efficient preparation for war can alone insure peace. It is peace that we have uniformly and perseveringly cultivated, and harmony between us and France may be restored at her option.

Then came the really important part : "The United States Government could not think of sending another minister . . . unless given positive assurances that he would be received. It must therefore be left with France (if she is indeed desirous of accommodation) to take the requisite steps."

Apparently an innocuous statement, but yet it was a new note ; as it was known that Adams had received some communications from Gerry and was to make these communications known, it was supposed that a real change and a change for the better was about to take place in the relations between the two countries. Therefore Jefferson could mention in the speech "a moderation unlike the President", and he also knew that Vans

Murray, the American minister at the Hague, had informed his Government "that the French Government is sincere in their overtures for reconciliation and have agreed, if these fail, to admit the mediation offered by the British Government." [1]

In the meantime the fight in Congress was merrily going on, with that peculiar circumstance that both leaders remained behind the scenes. To the Kentucky Resolutions, followed by much milder representations from other State legislatures, Hamilton opposed his instructions sent to Dayton, and since published in his "Works." If they had fallen into Jefferson's hands he would have found in them ample grounds for his fears. The Federalist leader was of the opinion that his party was losing ground, and the late attempt of Virginia and Kentucky to unite the State legislatures in a direct resistance to certain laws of the Union, could be considered in no other light than as an attempt to change the Government. Under the circumstances, and considering that "the enemies of the Government were resolved, if it shall be practicable, to make its existence a question of force", Hamilton had devised a certain plan to be executed by the Federalist troops in Congress. The measures came under four heads: establishments which will extend the influence and promote the popularity of the Government; provision for augmenting the means and consolidating the strength of the Government; arrangements for confirming and enlarging the legal powers of the Government; laws for restraining and punishing incendiary and seditious practices. The detail of the recommendations showed a perfectly well-concerted plan to concentrate all powers in the hands of the Federal Government.

One of the most remarkable proposals was perhaps the project of subdividing the larger States into several small States containing no less than a hundred thousand persons each, as these new units would be "better adapted to the purposes of

[1] To James Madison, January 3, 1799. Memorial Edition, X, 67.

local regulations and to the preservation of the Republican spirit." It is not without interest here to note that the Federalist leader proposed the very measures which had been adopted in France when the old provinces were divided into *départements*. In the case of the Federalists, as in the case of the Constituents, the purpose was the same : a concentration of all powers into the hand of a central authority and the suppression of local government. Other recommendations were an extension of the judiciary with a Federal judge at the head of each district ; the appointment of conservators or justices of peace, who were to supervise the energetic execution of the laws and to promote "salutary patronage"; a stronger army; improvement of roads; powers given to the Government to call out the militia to suppress unlawful combinations and insurrections; power given to Congress to build canals through the territory of two or more States, that "all seditious writings levelled against any officers whatever of the U. S. shall be cognizable in the courts of the United States."

If the administrative reorganization advocated by Hamilton had been effected, it would have made the United States not far different from the France of Napoleon and, such being the plans of the Federalists, it cannot be said that Jefferson's fear was entirely exaggerated.

One of the first victories of the Federalists was to pass the famous Logan Law (January 30) forbidding any citizen of the United States to commence or carry on any verbal or written correspondence or intercourse with any foreign government, or any officer thereof in relation to any disputes or controversies with the United States. Doctor Logan's intentions had been of the best. He had seen members of the French Directory in Paris and had brought with him "non-equivocal proofs of the pacific dispositions of the French Government towards the United States " and particularly the Statement of Merlin that "*la liberté des États-Unis nous a coûté trop de sang pour qu'elle ne nous soit pas chère.*" [1] None of these activities could be called treacherous, and in normal times would not have been noticed. But behind Logan, Jefferson was aimed at, and he was perfectly aware, as he wrote to Madison, that "the real views in the importance they have given to Logan's enterprise are mistaken by nobody." [2] Yet he thought he had to justify himself to his friends, and sent a long letter on the subject to Gerry. Far more important than his defense was a declaration of the principles he did not fear to avow. "They are unquestionably," he said, "the principles of the great body of our fellow-citizens." It was really the program of the Democratic Party and the most luminous exposition of the Jeffersonian doctrine ever made.

I do then, with sincere zeal, wish an inviolable preservation of our present federal Constitution, according to the true sense in which it was adopted by the States . . . and I am opposed to the monarchising its features by the forms of its administration, with a view to conciliate a first transition to a President and Senate for life, and from that to an hereditary tenure of these offices . . . I am for preserving to the States the powers not yielded by them to the Union, and to the legislature of the Union its constitutional share in the division of powers; and I am not for transferring all the powers of the States to the General Government, and all those of that Government to the executive branch. I am for a government rigorously frugal and simple, applying all the possible savings of the public revenue to the discharge of the national debt; and not for a multiplication of officers and salaries merely to make partisans . . . I am for relying, for internal defence, on our militia solely, till actual invasion . . . and not for a standing army in time of peace, which may overawe the public sentiment; nor for a navy, which by its own expenses and the eternal wars in which it will implicate us, will grind us with public burthens, and sink us under them. I am for free commerce with all nations; political connections with none;

---

[1] Madison to Jefferson, June 26, 1799. Jefferson Papers. Library of Congress.
[2] January 16, 1799. Memorial Edition, X, 69.

and little or no diplomatic establishment . . . I am for freedom of religion, and against all manoeuvres to bring about a legal ascendency of one sect over another : for freedom of the press, and against all violations of the Constitution to silence by force and not by reason the complaints of criticism, just or unjust, of our citizens against the conduct of their agents. And I am for encouraging the progress of science in all its branches ; and not for raising a hue and cry against the sacred name of philosophy. . . .[1]

Jefferson ended with a paragraph in which he solemnly proclaimed the integrity of his American nationalism, although he admitted that he was a well wisher to the success of the French Revolution and still hoped that it would succeed ; but he added at once : "The first object of my heart is my own country. In that is embarked my family, my fortune, my own existence. I have not one farthing of interest, nor preference of any one nation to another, but in proportion as they are more or less friendly to us."

The man who drew up that program in the midst of an unprecedented political strife and the riotous scenes of the streets of Philadelphia was a political leader of the first rank. The letter to Gerry is more than a letter from one individual to another ; it transcends the circumstances of the moment. It is the result of mature reflection ; the conclusions reached by Jefferson after almost thirty years of political life. It is really the first program of his party and the first complete definition of Government and of Americanism ; for it was distinctly American. I fail to perceive in it the influence of any foreign political thinker except in so far as such principles as freedom of the press, separation of the Church and the State may have been ideas common to a great majority of political thinkers of the eighteenth century. Even if Jefferson's request to Gerry to keep the communication absolutely secret was obeyed, there is little doubt that we have here the gist of the communication

[1] To Elbridge Gerry, January 26, 1799. Memorial Edition, X, 77-78.

made orally by Jefferson to his friends and to the leaders of the Republicans in Congress.

For the moment the letter contained a strong appeal to Gerry to place every evidence at his disposal before the public, since the Government refused to do it, and to publish in full the report on his mission. He alone could save the situation by coming forward independently. But even if Gerry acceded to this wish, some one else would have to present a brief synopsis of the evidence and draw up a judicial arraignment of the administration. At this juncture Jefferson thought of his old master Pendleton, at whose feet he had sat in Williamsburg, and with whom he had worked in the revision of the statutes of Virginia. He alone could give the "*coup de grâce*" to the ruinous principles and doctrines; he alone could recapitulate all the vexations and disgusting details of the Stamp Act and the Direct Tax. A small handbill would be printed and they could "disperse ten or twelve thousand copies under letter covers, through all the United States, by the members of Congress when they return home." [1] To make Pendleton's coöperation more certain, Jefferson even drew up the plan of the indictment and inclosed all the necessary documents.

February was for Jefferson a period of hectic activity. During all the first part of the month he multiplied his entreaties to Pendleton to gird up his loins and enter the fight. If he still refused to write for the press he was not averse to communicating to the editors papers written by his friends, and he begged these for expressions of opinion to be sent to the press.

The engine is the press. Every man must lay his purse and his pen under contribution. As to the former it is possible I may be obliged to assume something for you. As to the latter, let me pray and beseech you to set apart a certain portion of every post day to write what may be proper for the public. Send it to me while here,

[1] January 29, 1799, Memorial Edition, X, 87 and Jefferson Papers, Library of Congress, February 14, 1799.

and when I go away I will let you know to whom you may send, so that your name shall be sacredly secret.[1]

The propaganda was beginning to bear its fruits. John Ogden was writing from Litchfield that "many publications in the *Aurora* have reached Connecticut, within four weeks, which have opened the eyes of the dispassionate" and he was asking for more pamphlets.[2] But a week later Ogden was arrested and to Jefferson he sent a letter "From Lichtfield Goal (sic) at the suit of Oliver Wolcott Esq", to affirm that "prison has no horror to the oppressed, inspired and persecuted." To Aaron Burr in New York Jefferson wrote very affectionately and very familiarly to acquaint him with the state of public affairs.[3] To Monroe he was sending pamphlets, asking him to distribute them where they would do most good, adding as usual "Do not let my name be connected in the business." He never tired of repeating that the proper argument to strike the voters was the enormous increase in the budget of the United States: a loan authorized for five millions at eight per cent., another of two millions to follow and that was just a beginning. All these measures were accepted by Congress in the teeth of Gerry's communications with Talleyrand, showing the French Government willing to continue the negotiations.

Then on February 18 came "the event of events." While all the war measures were going on, while the Government of the United States was blockading the French West Indies and French vessels were captured, while there were in several instances cases of actual warfare, the President had had in his hand for several weeks letters exchanged between Pichon, the French chargé at the Hague, and Vans Murray, declaring that the French Government was ready to receive "whatever plenipotentiary the Government of the United States should

[1] To Madison, February 5, 1799. Memorial Edition, X, 95.
[2] John Ogden to Jefferson, February 7, 1799. Jefferson Papers. Library of Congress.
[3] February 11, 1799. *Ibid.*

send to France to end our differences and that he would be received with the respect due to the representative of a *free, independent, and powerful nation.*" Adams, almost on the eve of the adjournment of Congress, had decided, as it seems, against the advice and without the knowledge of his Cabinet, not only to communicate the Vans Murray-Pichon papers, but to recommend that Murray be appointed as plenipotentiary to France. The Federalists in the Senate were appalled and at first did not know what to do.[1] But they were not lacking in strategy; not daring to come out openly, they appointed on the President's recommendation, not only Murray but Oliver Ellsworth and Patrick Henry, the last two "not to sail from America before they should receive from the French Directory assurances that they should be received with the respect due to the law of nations, to their character, etc."

This, as Jefferson noticed at once, was a last effort to postpone the patching-up of difficulties and also a last effort to provoke the French, since they had already given such an assurance to Murray.[2] "The whole artillery of the phalanx was played secretly on the P. and he was obliged himself to take a step which should parry the overture while it wears the face of acceding to it," he wrote to Madison.[3] But the war party was defeated, the Federalists had received a fatal blow; victory already was in sight when Congress adjourned at the beginning of March.

Then Jefferson repaired to Monticello, while in the back counties assessors clashed with farmers, troopers with small-town editors, while Duane was flogged in the street after being dragged from his office by militiamen. But he was not idle, although for some mysterious reason several of the letters he published during the summer have never been printed. He

---

[1] To Madison, February 19, 1799. Memorial Edition, X, 111.
[2] To Bishop James Madison, February 27, 1799. *Ibid.*, X, 122.
[3] Jefferson Papers. Library of Congress, February 26, 1799.

received many visitors, wrote to friends, proclaimed his faith in ultimate victory for "the body of the American people is substantially Republican, but their virtuous feelings have been played on by some fact with more fiction. They have been the dupes of artful manoeuvres and made for a moment to be willing instruments in forging chains for themselves." [1]   He encouraged Bache and Venable to publish a gazette, for unfortunately "the people of Virginia were not incorruptible and offices there as elsewhere were acceptable", so that the situation was neither safe nor satisfactory.   To William Greene he wrote a truly splendid letter on "progress" in which he expressed his belief "with Condorcet, that man's mind is perfectible to a degree of which we cannot as yet form any conception", and predicted limitless discoveries in the field of science.   The present convulsions could only be temporary, for it was impossible, he maintained, that "the enthusiasm characterizing America should lift its parricidal hand against freedom and science. This would be such a monstrous phenomenon as I cannot place among possible things in this age and in this country."

At the same time he was not unmindful of keeping in complete harmony the heterogeneous elements of the party just being formed.   He strove to placate Callender who, jealous of Bache, was writing epileptic letters to complain of the whole universe, and asking at the same time that Jefferson should send him some money, as he was short of funds.[2]   John Taylor, who was planning to declare void and unconstitutional laws adopted by Congress, and to call together a convention to appoint a dictator, had to be told to "forbear to push on to this ultimate effort." [3]   Much preferable was the work undertaken by Randolph in presenting a legal refutation of the Federalist

[1] Jefferson Papers. Library of Congress. To Bishop Madison, March 12, 1799.
[2] *Ibid*. Callender to Jefferson, August 10, 1799. From Richmond.
[3] *Ibid*. Marked received December 11, undated.

attitude towards the foundation of law, and the similar document on which Wilson Nicholas was working.[1]

All this time Jefferson was haunted by the fear that his letters would fall into the hands of his enemies. To the few communications he wrote during the later part of the summer, he did not even dare to put his signature, "the omission of which has been rendered almost habitual with me by the necessity of the post office; indeed the period is now approaching during which I shall discontinue writing letters as much as possible, knowing that every snare will be used to get hold of what may be perverted."[2] He came to the point that on Monroe's advice he had to refuse to see Madison in order to "avoid the appearance of a collusion between them."[3]

At the beginning of December he was back in Philadelphia for the session of Congress and soon after was able to send reassuring news to Monroe who had become one of his "grand electors." Those who persist in thinking him a dreamy idealist must read the letters he wrote between January and May, 1800; not only did he keep his hand on the pulse of the country, but he calculated the changes of the Republicans in every State and figured out to a unit the possible number of votes they would receive in the coming election. He knew the situation too well not to admit that he was the natural choice of the Republicans even before any census was held, and very early in January acknowledged it to Monroe:

Perhaps it will be thought I ought in delicacy to be silent on the subject. But you, who know me, know that my private gratification would be most indulged by that issue, which should leave me most at home. If anything supersedes this propensity, it is merely the desire to see this government brought back to its republican principles. Consider this as written to Mr. Madison as much as yourself;

[1] August 18, 1799. Memorial Edition, X, 125.
[2] Jefferson Papers. Library of Congress. To Callender, undated, unsigned.
[3] To Madison, November 22, 1799. Memorial Edition, X, 133.

and communicate it, if you think it will do any good, to those possessing our joint confidence, or any others where it may be useful and safe.[1]

He was undoubtedly sincere in disclaiming any ambition, but under the circumstances he was bound to observe a certain reticence, being the President of the Senate, next to Adams in the Government and yet Adams' adversary in the next election. But in his letters he made no pretense of false modesty and frankly mentioned time and again what he called "our ticket." Yet he was not the man who could ever give all his energy to a single task, and absorbing as were his political preoccupations he showed during the summer of 1800 as much versatility as ever. He took up again the transformation of William and Mary College, this time to make a real university of the old institution. He wrote to Priestley to send him a good plan of reorganization and a few weeks later to Du Pont de Nemours who composed for him his "Plan of a National Education." [2] With Colonel Benjamin Hawkins he discussed the desirability of studying the language and customs of the Indians, while there was still time.[3] He was thinking of compiling a volume on the "Morals of Jesus" and discussed religion with Bishop Madison who intended to write a book to prove that the Christian religion, "rightly understood and carried into full effect, would establish a pure Democracy over the world. Its main pillars are — Equality, Fraternity, Justice, Universal Benevolence." [4]

At the same time he was keeping close watch on the news coming from France and on political developments in Congress. Rumors circulated that a new revolution had taken place in Paris and that Bonaparte was at the head of it. This was a

---

[1] January 12, 1800. Memorial Edition, X, 136.
[2] Priestley's answer, never hitherto published, will be found in my volume on "Jefferson and the Physiocrats."
[3] March 14, 1800. Memorial Edition, X, 110.
[4] Jefferson Papers. Library of Congress, February 11, 1800.

wonderful opportunity to test out by actual experience the disadvantage of a directory or executive committee as compared with a single executive in a republic.[1] From what he knew of the French character, he did not believe that a monarchy could be reëstablished in France, for "If Bonaparte declares for Royalty, either in his own person, or that of Louis XVIII, he has but a few days to live. In a nation of so much enthusiasm, there must be a million Brutuses who will devote themselves to death to destroy him." But a few days later he had come to the conclusion that it was probably what Bonaparte had done, and what had been done in France could probably be done in America when our Bonaparte, surrounded by his comrades in arms, may step in to give us political salvation in his way." One thing was certain, however: Bonaparte had clearly demonstrated that he had no brains, no creative and constructive mind; and, with the pride of a man who was engaged in a stupendous experiment, Jefferson pitilessly criticized the Napoleonic reconstruction of France: "Whenever he has meddled we have seen nothing but fragments of the old Roman government stuck into materials with which they can form no cohesion; we see the bigotry of an Italian to the ancient splendor of his country, but nothing which bespeaks a luminous view of rational government."[2]

To his friend Samuel Adams, who had written him at the end of January, he repeated the same judgment in less striking but perhaps even harsher terms:

I fear our friends on the other side of the water, laboring in the same cause, have yet a great deal of crime and misery to wade through. My confidence has been placed in the head not in the heart of Bonaparte. I hoped he would calculate truly the difference between the fame of a Washington and a Cromwell. Whatever the views may be, he has at least transferred the destinies of the

---

[1] To Henry Innis, January 23. Memorial Edition, X, 143.
[2] To T. M. Randolph, February 2, 1800. *Ibid.*, X, 151.

republic from the civil to the military arm. Some will use this as a lesson against the practicability of republican government. I read in it a lesson against the danger of standing armies.[1]

No more patent demonstration could be desired of the fact that in his judgments of the French Revolution, Jefferson was at all times influenced by the possible effects that European examples might have on the American crisis. The precedent established by Bonaparte was a very dangerous one and might put similar ambitions into the head of an unscrupulous schemer. Whether he really believed or not that there was such an immediate danger for America, and that Hamilton had really such intentions, is an entirely different question. Probably he did not himself know. He only felt that a permanent army would constitute a permanent temptation and consequently a permanent danger, for he had only limited faith in the virtue of individual man, although he continued to believe in the wisdom of the collectivity.

Domestic matters and other more immediate preoccupations were no less worthy of attention. He followed very closely every measure proposed in the House on the coming elections, on the voting procedure to be adopted, and anxiously studied the political forecasts. The situation was decidedly on the mend. This appears clearly in the attitude of the Federalists towards him, not only in public but also in private. For Madison he wrote a very elaborate review of the comparative strength of the two parties in all the States of the Union; he saw that the key States were Pennsylvania, Jersey and New York, the other States being equally divided, and he concluded that "Upon the whole the issue was still very doubtful." But officially one had to maintain a confident attitude.[2]

When April came, he thought that it would be desirable for the Republicans to come out with a public declaration, stating

---

[1] February 26, 1800. Memorial Edition, X, 153.
[2] To Madison, March 8, 1800. *Ibid.*, X, 157-159.

their program and their ideals. "As soon as it can be depended on," he said, "we must have a Declaration of the principles of the Constitution, in the nature of a Declaration of Rights, in all points in which it has been violated."[1]

If the plan had been put to execution we would have had the first presidential "platform" as early as 1800, and Jefferson would thus have hastened the formation of distinct political parties. But more commonplace measures were not to be neglected. Discussing the situation in North Carolina, still a very doubtful State, he advised that "the medicine for that State must be very mild and secretly administered. But nothing should be spared to give them true information." We would like Jefferson better if he had shown more discrimination in the choice of the men selected to disseminate this true information. For at that time, at least, he was still employing Callender in Richmond — an amusing scoundrel not much better than Cobbet, the Peter Porcupine of the Federalists. But Callender was a useful tool, who was doing his utmost to publish the second volume of the *Prospect* and to catch up with Federalist propaganda. One could condone much in a man then writing: "I had entertained the romantic hope of being able to overtake the Federal Government in its career of iniquity. But I am now satisfied that they can *act* much faster than I *can write* after them."[2]

Fortunately he had the approval and indorsement of much more respectable characters. Samuel Adams had already written him; then it was John Dickinson, the Revolutionary hero, who wrote, when sending his thanks for a copy of the late "Resolutions of the Legislature of Virginia": "It is an inestimable contribution to the cause of Liberty . . . How incredible was it once, and how astonishing is it now, that every

---

[1] To P. N. Nicholas, April 7, 1800. Memorial Edition, X, 163.

[2] Jefferson Papers. Library of Congress. Callender to Jefferson, February 10 and March 15, 1800.

measure and every pretense of the stupid and selfish Stuarts, should be adopted by the posterity of those who fled from this madness and tyranny to the distant wilds of America." [1]

Such letters, the congratulations of George Wythe, who urged him to publish the "Manual of Parliamentary Practice", those of Pendleton, who consented to revise the final text and to "freely cast his mite into the treasury", were indeed balm on the wounds made by the fierce attacks of the Federalist press. [2]

The end of the session was approaching and the most earnest desire of the Federalists was to adjourn as soon as possible, for fear that the envoys to France should announce the conclusion of a treaty. Their power seemed on the wane, but Jefferson was still very doubtful of ultimate victory. To Livingston he wrote that his knowledge of the art, industry, and resources of the other party did not permit him to be prematurely confident. The tide had turned, to be sure, and the Federalists were losing ground constantly, but the main question whether "that would insure a Republican victory was still undecided and it might take one or two elections more." [3]

Congress adjourned on May 14. During the session congressional caucuses had nominated for the Federalists John Adams, and General Charles Cotesworth Pinckney of South Carolina; the choice of the Republicans could only be Jefferson, and for candidate to the vice presidency they selected Aaron Burr of New York.

In the course of the summer, Adams and his wife moved to the new Federal City laid out by Major Lenfant, which boasted of one tavern, the Capitol, the President's house, and a few boarding houses, — a capital in the midst of the woods, in a veritable wilderness of trees, with impassable paths, — a town unable to lodge Congress except at Georgetown, which was

---

[1] March 18, 1800. Jefferson Papers. Library of Congress.
[2] *Ibid.*
[3] April 30, 1800. Memorial Edition, X, 163.

connected with the new city by a clay road. Jefferson, according to his custom, had hurried back to his "farm" and was apparently absorbed by his domestic occupations, his children, and grandchildren.

During the whole campaign he remained almost absolutely silent, not daring to write, because his letters might have been intercepted and used against him, receiving few visitors and reading without comment the newspapers filled with the insults and abuse of the Federalists. He broke his silence on few occasions, but these occasions are worth studying in some detail. In a letter to Monroe, written from Eppington, he discussed the best plans for assisting Callender, then jailed under the Sedition Act, who "should be substantially defended whether privately or publicly" and whose case should be laid before the legislature.[1] These efforts did not avail since in August the publicist wrote from his Richmond jail that he was in very bad health "owing to the stink of the place."[2] There is not much that can be said for Callender, and Jefferson might have better chosen his friends; but when one reflects on the accusations commonly circulated against Jefferson at the time, the interest taken by the Republican leader in the pamphleteer seems less astonishing. If Callender had certainly insulted Adams and Hamilton, had not the Reverend Cotton Mather Smith accused Jefferson of "having robbed a widow and fatherless children of an estate of which he was executor?" To Gideon Granger, who had called his attention to the attacks of the clergyman, Jefferson easily justified himself and seized the opportunity to discuss with his friend a problem of general politics of far greater importance. It had very little to do with the details of the election and for his remarkable capacity to rise above contingencies Jefferson truly deserves the title of "political philosopher." To incidents which he deemed without permanent

---

[1] Jefferson Papers. Library of Congress, May 26, 1800.
[2] *Ibid.*, August 14, 1800.

significance he paid little attention, but when dealing with a phenomenon which seemed to him to indicate an important change in the orientation of national policies, he always tried to penetrate beyond the surface and reach the core of the question.

The thing that now disturbed him more than the possible victory of Adams and Pinckney was the fact that political divisions seemed to correspond to a geographical division. Not without reason had he written to Colonel Benjamin Hawkins: "those who knew us only from 1775 to 1793 can form no better idea of us than of the inhabitants of the moon." [1] The North and the South had never been in complete harmony; economically they were different and had different interests, but something new had developed during the seven or eight years just passed. There was evidently a rift in the Union; on several occasions talks of secession had been heard. These rumors did not correspond to any real danger, but if the elections proved that the Union was formed of two solid blocks of States, if the North remained Federalist and the South were Republican, the very existence of the nation would be put in question. Yet this seemed to be a probable eventuality. In these circumstances, a victory of the South would mean a defeat of the North, the country would be divided against itself and the Union would be destroyed. This was particularly to be feared if the powers of the Federal Government were enlarged. Leaving aside all question of principle as to the moral merit of the questions under dispute, Jefferson tried to show, on the one hand, that it was impossible ever to organize a centralized form of government for the simple reason that the United States were too big and covered a territory much too large. If a centralized government were established on paper, it would be necessary to have many agents of the Federal Government with extensive powers distributed over all the States, and because of their very remote-

[1] March 14, 1800. Memorial Edition, X, 160.

ness they would be beyond the possibility of continuous control. This could only mean corruption, plunder, and waste. On the other hand, since on fundamental questions it was impossible to bring into accord the North and the South, the true and only remedy was to minimize the chances of conflict and to reduce to a minimum the powers and attributes of the Federal Government. "The true theory of our Constitution is surely the wisest and best, that the States are independent as to everything within themselves, and united as to everything respecting foreign nations." Once more, therefore, he came back to the same political theory that, in forming a social compact, liberty is exchanged for security and only those rights are given up which the members of the new society have not full power to enforce. Thus his theory of State rights was not only well founded in theory but proved by practice and experience. Any other system would almost necessarily conduce to a secession. The man who wrote these lines in the summer of 1800, more than half a century before the Civil War, was certainly not an ordinary politician; his was the clear farsightedness of a great statesman and true political philosopher.

Furthermore, in the controversy which had been going on since 1793, Jefferson had been submitted to fierce criticism on every possible ground: as he wrote to McGregory, "the floodgates of calumny had been opened upon him." It had been particularly distressing to him to see that the religious issue had been injected into politics. There is no doubt that his Bill for Religious Freedom proceeded, not from hostility to religion, but from a deep and sincere conviction, reached after careful study of the evidence available that "in law" there ought to be no connection between the Church and the State and that if any had ever been established, it was due to monkish fabrications and usurpations. That he had turned against himself some of the Episcopalian clergy of Virginia was quite natural, but before he went to France these attacks were necessarily limited and did not extend beyond the borders of the State or take the aspect of a national question.

When, on the contrary, he began to be criticized for his supposed foible for the French Revolution, such attacks became far more pressing. The excesses of the Revolution were attributed to the infidel doctrines of the French philosophers; and, being "contaminated" by French political philosophy, Jefferson was naturally accused of having brought back from France its atheism. These views received confirmation when he befriended Volney and Priestley, one a confirmed atheist, as Priestley himself had demonstrated, the other a Unitarian — which in the eyes of the orthodox clergy was possibly worse. The attacks from the pulpit became more numerous, and a clergyman of New York, a close friend of Hamilton, even published a pamphlet entitled "The voice of Warning to Christians on ensuing election", in which Jefferson was accused of having answered to a certain Doctor Smith, who expressed his surprise at the condition of a church: "It is good enough for Him who was born in a manger."

Considering, on the other hand, that a large portion of the clergy were enrolled under the Federalist banner, Jefferson had come to the conclusion that the clergy had "a very favorite hope of obtaining an establishment of a particular form of Christianity through the United States; and as every sect believes its own form the true one, every one perhaps hopes for his own, especially the Episcopalians and the Congregationalists." Whether this was so absolutely untrue or impossible, as some historians seem to believe, is a question far too difficult to answer and one which probably cannot be solved. On the face of things it does seem that there was in it a grain of truth, for no human organization, whether ecclesiastical or civil, ever relinquishes voluntarily the smallest particle of power or prestige.

One thing, however, is certain : if Jefferson had said the word, the religious issue would have been injected into the campaign;

and some of his friends, believing that "Christianity was the strong ground of Republicanism", were urging him to give his consent, for it was only necessary for "Republicanism to ally itself to the Christian religion, to overturn all the corrupted political and religious institutions in the world."[1] But this was for Jefferson a forbidden subject. He had "sworn upon the altar of God eternal hostility against every form of tyranny over the mind of man"; he had formed "a view of the subject which ought to displease neither the rational Christian nor the Deists and would reconcile many to a character they have too hastily rejected"; but this was not the time or the place to discuss matters that ought to be reserved for a calm and dispassionate discussion between friends, so he refused to authorize the publication of any statement referring to his religious views.[2]

In the meantime the political campaign was going on and the Federalists' affairs were assuming a decidedly unhealthy complexion. How this happened is a story of extraordinary intrigue and machination, already told several times and still a delight to historians fond of studying political deals. To a large extent the victory of the Republicans was due to divisions in the Federalist camp and it came to pass that no other man did more than Hamilton to assure Jefferson's success. From the beginning, the former leader of the Federalists had set himself against Adams, employing every effort to have Pinckney receive the first place in the nomination. The first sign of a Federalist defeat appeared in New York State, where Burr had his headquarters and had so cleverly maneuvered things that the State went Republican at the April election. This was a personal defeat for Hamilton and also a terrible blow to the Federalists. Then Adams went into one of those fits of anger which make him such a picturesque figure; he decided that he had been

---

[1] Jefferson Papers. Library of Congress, Benjamin Rush to Jefferson, August 22, 1800. [2] September 23, 1800. Memorial Edition, X, 173.

betrayed by his Cabinet, summarily dismissed his Secretary of War, McHenry, and offered Pickering an opportunity to resign, which the Secretary of State did not choose to take. Thereupon the President informed him that he "discharged him from further service in the Cabinet." He then called into the Cabinet John Marshall of Virginia as Secretary of State and Samuel Dexter of Massachusetts as Secretary of War. From that time on, the political campaign reads as if the leaders of the Federalists had really lost their heads. Hamilton bent all his efforts towards holding another election in New York and, failing in that, towards preventing Adams from obtaining a majority. The affair culminated in the publication of a pamphlet, entitled "The true conduct and character of John Adams, Esq. President of the United States", pointing out the weakness of Adams' character. The pamphlet was intended for private distribution, but it found its way into the hands of the Republicans; Aaron Burr had parts of it printed in the *New London Bee* and the whole was soon to be given to the public. When the whole pamphlet came out, it added more fuel to the raging controversy. This is only one incident, but not the least significant, among the many so vividly related by Mr. Bowers.

The electoral colleges met in each State on December 4. Returns came in slowly to Washington but by the thirteenth it was known, in so far as could be, that the Federalists were defeated; it also appeared that there was a tie between the two Republican candidates. At this juncture Jefferson, who had remained perfectly silent, took the matter in hand and calmly assumed that he would be elected. To Robert R. Livingston, brother of Edward Livingston who was a member of Congress from New York, Jefferson wrote a letter congratulating him on his communications to the American Philosophical Society and discussing quite seriously the discovery "of some large bones supposed to be of the mammoth" in the vicinity of New York. Then, as in an afterthought, he mentioned the political situation. The matter of the election was as good as settled : "We may, therefore, venture to hazard propositions on that hypothesis without being justly subjected to raillery or ridicule." "To put the vessel on a Republican tack", they would require the entire coöperation of "men who could at once inspire the nation with perfect confidence in their honesty and talents", and Jefferson asked Livingston whether he would not assume the Secretaryship of the Navy. That in his own mind he considered the election well over appears in the sentence in which he speaks, not as a candidate but as the leader of his party, and as if no other hypothesis could enter his mind: "Though I have been too honorably placed in front of those who are to enter the breach so happily made, yet the energies of every individual are necessary, and in the very place where his energies can most serve the enterprise." [1]

The next day he wrote in the same vein to Aaron Burr to congratulate him in no uncertain terms on his election as Vice President, expressing his regrets that this distinction would prevent him from availing himself of the services of Burr in the Cabinet. He based his conclusion on the assurance he had received that South Carolina would withdraw one vote from Burr, that Smith of Tennessee would give its second vote to Gallatin. It was also surmised that the vote of Georgia would not be entire. This would leave Burr well ahead of Adams but decidedly in the second place. Jefferson indicated that several of the Federalists had expressed the hope that "the two Republican tickets may be equal" and in that case they expected to prevent a choice by the House and "let the Government devolve on a President of the Senate." Then came a gently insinuating sentence : "Decency required that I should be so entirely passive during the late contest that I have never once asked whether arrangements had been made to prevent so many from dropping votes intentionally, as might frustrate half the Republican

[1] December 14, 1800. Memorial Edition, X, 176.

wish; nor did I doubt till lately that such had been made."
In the last paragraph, Jefferson, refusing even to consider that
Burr might aspire to the presidency, indicated that he considered the matter as settled and firmly put Burr where he
belonged:

While I must congratulate you, my dear Sir, on the issue of this
contest, because it is more honorable, and doubtless more grateful to
you than any station within the competence of the chief magistrate,
yet for myself, and for the substantial service of the public, I feel
most sensibly the loss we sustain of your aid in the new administration. It leaves a chasm in my arrangements, which cannot be
adequately filled up.

If we put things together, the letter of Jefferson certainly
meant first that the time had come to make some "arrangements" to thwart the schemes of the Federalists; second, that a
tie was almost certain, and finally that it was up to Burr to
declare that he was not running for the presidency.

This conclusion is all the more probable because three days
later, writing to John Breckenridge, Jefferson did not mention
again Georgia and Tennessee, but declared that "we are brought
into a dilemma by the probable equality of the two Republican
candidates." Then he added: "The Federalists in Congress
mean to take advantage of this, and either to prevent an election altogether, or reverse what has been understood to have
been the wishes of the people, as to the President and Vice-
President; wishes which the Constitution did not permit them
specially to designate." [1] Nothing could be clearer; it was to
some extent the situation of 1796, but reversed as to the candidates, and Jefferson expected that Burr would do the right
thing by him.

This, however, was not so obvious to Burr himself. The
letter he sent in reply to Jefferson must have been most disappointing in this respect. The colonel side-stepped the issue,

[1] December 18, 1800. Memorial Edition, X, 183.

refused to come out frankly and did not write a single line that could be constructed as an acceptance of Jefferson's point of view. On December 31, Jefferson wrote to Tench Coxe to express his opinion that an agreement between the two higher candidates was their only hope "to prevent the dissolution of the Government and a danger of anarchy, by an operation, bungling indeed and imperfect, but better than letting the Legislature take the nomination of the Executive entirely from the people." [1]

This could have been construed as a hint to Burr to give up his unavowed hopes of becoming President. But Burr, who was in New York, could not easily be communicated with and kept his sphinxlike silence. January passed without Jefferson's finding any necessity of writing any political letters. With Hugh Williamson he discussed the range of temperature in Louisiana and whether the turkey was a native bird: [2] with William Dunbar the temperature, Indian vocabularies and the origin of the rainbow.

In February, however, he again wrote to Burr. He had been informed that certain individuals were attempting "to sow tares between us that might divide us and our friends." He assured Burr that he had never written anything that could be regarded as injurious by his running mate; the only time that he had discussed his conduct was in a letter to Breckenridge written on December 18, in which he had expressed the conviction that the wishes of the people were that he and not Burr be President. That was a pure statement of fact at which no man could take offense. This time, Burr apparently did not answer at all, and while the House was preparing for the balloting, Jefferson discussed with Caspar Wistar the bones found in the State of New York, "the vertebra, part of the jaw, with two grinders, the tusks, which some have called the horns,

---

[1] Memorial Edition, X, 188.
[2] January 10, 1800. *Ibid.*, X, 188.

the sternum, the scapula, the tibia and fibula, the tarsus and metatarsus, and even the phalanges and innominata." [1]

On the morning of the election and before going to the Capitol he wrote to Tench Coxe: "Which of the two will be elected, and whether either, I deem perfectly problematical: and my mind has long been equally made up for either of the three events." This was on a Wednesday. After the result of the election had been officially announced, the House retired to proceed to the election of the President. Ballots were taken, Jefferson receiving eight States, Burr six, nine being necessary to a choice. The House stayed in continuous session till eight o'clock the next morning, taking twenty-seven ballots without any change in the results; members of the House dozing between ballots, snatching a bit of sleep whenever they could, all of them admiring the fortitude of Joseph N. Nicholson who, although sick in bed, had been brought to the House and rested in a committee room, voting at each ballot. The House adjourned until eleven o'clock on Friday and then took two successive ballots without being able to break the deadlock. On Saturday three ballots were taken without any change in the alignment, and they adjourned until Monday. In the meantime passions were raging. The Federalists had been told in no equivocal terms that, should they attempt to have the Government devolve to some member of the present administration, "the day such an act would pass, the Middle States would arm" and that "no such usurpation would be tolerated even for a single day."

On the other hand, Jefferson had been approached by the more sensible heads of the Federalists, and apparently by Gouverneur Morris, who stopped him as he was coming out from the Senate Chamber, and had offered to influence one member of Vermont, provided he would declare: "1. that he would not turn all the Federalists out of office; 2. that he

[1] February 3. Memorial Edition, X, 197.

would not reduce the navy; and 3. would not wipe off the public debt." To which Jefferson answered that he would not become President by capitulation and would not make any declaration. Then he went to see Adams, who seemed ready to approve of the choice of Jefferson as President and who told him that he could have himself elected by subscribing to conditions analogous to those indicated by Morris. Finally he was visited in his room by Dwight Foster, senator from Massachusetts, who also reiterated the same offer. These are, undoubtedly, some of the maneuvers he mentioned on Sunday, the day of rest, in a letter he wrote to Monroe : "Many attempts have been made to obtain terms and promises from me, I have declared to them unequivocally, that I would not receive the government on capitulation, that I would not go into it with my hands tied." [1]

On Sunday and Monday parleyings went on, caucuses were held, and no change was yet apparent. But on Tuesday morning an agreement was reached. It was described by Jefferson himself as follows :

"Morris of Vermont withdrew, which made Lyon's vote that of his State. The Maryland Federalists put in four blanks, which made the positive ticket of their colleagues the vote of the State. South Carolina and Delaware put in six blanks, so there were ten states for one candidate, four for another, and two blanks." And the speaker of the House, Theodore Sedgwick, one of Jefferson's bitterest enemies, was forced to announce his election.

The letter he wrote to Monroe the same day is not a pæan of triumph. The long-disputed victory, the irreducibility of a large portion of the Federalists, made him fearful lest the fight would soon renew. Furthermore, Adams had at once started making new appointments, naturally without consulting his successor; Bayard was nominated plenipotentiary to the French Republic, "Theophilus Parsons, Attorney General of the

[1] February 15, 1801. Memorial Edition, X, 201.

United States in the room of C. Lee, who, with Keith Taylor *cum multis aliis* are appointed judges under the new system. H. G. Otis is nominated a District Attorney." [1]

On his side, Jefferson wrote at once to Henry Dearborn to offer him the Secretaryship of War in his Cabinet and courteously communicated with Dexter, Secretary of the Treasury, and Stoddart, Secretary of the Navy, to thank them for their offer to conduct the affairs of their departments pending the arrival of their successors. To a certain Major William Jackson whom he did not know and who had written him to express the fear that he would discriminate against commerce, he answered that he "might appeal to evidences of his attention to the commerce and navigation of our country in different stations connected with them."

This was an evident allusion to his mission to France and to the activity he had displayed in defending the commercial interests of the United States. He resented particularly the fact that he had been represented as a friend to agriculture and an enemy to commerce, "the only means of disposing of its products." [2] The true position of Jefferson on this matter has already been pointed out in a preceding chapter; but the fact that the letter was written the very day he was notified of his election is proof enough that he already intended to conciliate both the agricultural and the commercial interests of the country. To the smoothing over of old differences of opinion he bent all his efforts during the three weeks that separated him from his inauguration. Bayard having refused his appointment to France, he approached at once Robert R. Livingston, intending to give the nomination to the Senate at the first opportunity. At the same time he repeated that the great body of the Federalist troops was discouraged and truly repentant, or disposed to come back into the fold. Those who

[1] February 18, 1801. Memorial Edition, X, 203.
[2] *Ibid.*, X, 206.

were so inclined should be received with open arms for "If we can once more get social intercourse restored to its pristine harmony, I shall believe we have not lived in vain; and that it may, by rallying them to true Republican principles, which few of them had thrown off, I sanguinely hope." [1]

He resigned from the Chair of the Senate on the twenty-eighth, and made the necessary preparations for the inauguration. The ceremonies were to be very simple but dignified. John Marshall, Chief Justice of the Supreme Court, was asked by Jefferson himself to administer the oath, and on March 4, 1801, the new President was inaugurated, while John Adams, mourning for his son, too tired, too bruised, to find courage to attend the inauguration of his successor, was starting on his way to New England.

[1] To Thomas Lomax, February 25, 1801.   Memorial Edition, X, 211.

BOOK FIVE

The Presidency

CHAPTER I

"ALL REPUBLICANS, ALL FEDERALISTS"

THE battle over, Jefferson's first and only desire seems to have been to bring about a reunion of the former political opponents. He had hardly been elected when he declared that he was not the choice of one party, but that the analysis of the last ballot showed clearly that "the former federalists have found themselves aggregated with us and that they are in a state of mind to be aggregated with us." [1]

And this, much to the surprise and disappointment of the militants who had fought the hard battle with him and for him, was the keynote of his inaugural speech. Throwing overboard his former defense of the French Revolution, he did not hesitate to attribute the political storm which the ship had just weathered to the baneful influence of European disturbances:

During the throes and convulsions of the ancient world, during the agonizing spasms of infuriated man, seeking through blood and slaughter his long-lost liberty, it was not wonderful that the agitation of the billows would reach even this distant and peaceful shore; that this should divide opinions as to measures of safety. But every difference of opinion is not a difference of principle. We have called by different names brethren of the same principles.

Then came the final and definitive formula: "We are all republicans — we are all federalists."

In more than one sense this was the most characteristic and the most masterly of Jefferson's political utterances. The battle of Capitol Hill was ended, the last streamers of smoke had

[1] To Thomas Lomax, February 25, 1801. Memorial Edition, X, 210.

floated away and America had found herself: "a rising nation, spread over a wide and fruitful land, traversing all the seas with the rich productions of her industry, engaged in commerce with nations who feel power and forget right, advancing rapidly to destinies beyond the reach of mortal eyes."

This was not written simply for effect and for the public eye. To Monroe, Jefferson had declared that the policy of the new administration would not be a policy of reprisals. The victory had been won partly through the repentance of former Federalists who had seen their error, and during the awful suspense of the week of the eleventh to the seventeenth of February, had feared that the country would become a prey to anarchy. These he welcomed back into the fold; the leaders, of course, were irreconcilable, but the majority were to be forgiven, and few removals from office were to be made on the ground of political divergences of opinion. "Some, I know, must be made. They must be as few as possible, done gradually, and bottomed on some malversation or inherent disqualification." [1]

Of the thousands of Federal officers in the United States, the President estimated that not twenty would have to be removed, while in two or three instances, officers removed by Mr. Adams for refusing to sign addresses were to be restored. Jefferson realized that by so acting and "stopping thus short in the career of removal" he would give offense to many of his friends, and he added with some melancholy: "That torrent has been pressing me heavily, and will require all my force to bear up against; but my maxim is "fiat justitia, ruat cælum." [2]

All this sounds perfectly sincere and true. Even the most superficial consideration of Jefferson's life would convince any one that he was not a man of vindictive character. By nature a pacifier and a harmonizer, nothing would have been farther from his program than to revive the old fires and to prolong party

[1] March 7, 1801. Memorial Edition, X, 218.
[2] To Doctor Benjamin Rush, March 24, 1801. *Ibid.*, X, 241.

strifes. But if it takes only one to declare war, it takes two to make peace, and the defeated party was in no peaceful mood. Hamilton was removed from the scene, and the form of government was apparently definitively settled by the election of Jefferson, but the Federalists had not given up every hope; they were still strongly intrenched and the battle went on during all of Jefferson's administration. It was not so spectacular as the fight with Hamilton, for the chief protagonist, John Marshall, lacked the dramatic qualities of the former leader of the Federalists; but it was no less momentous and no less important for the destinies of the United States.

When it came to actual removals, however, difficulties arose immediately. Whether in all cases Jefferson was rightly advised or inspired is open to question. The wisdom of appointing Samuel Bishop, a man of "sound understanding, pure integrity and unstained character", as collector of New Haven may be doubted, and there was something undeniably worth considering in the protest of New Haven merchants, that a man seventy-seven years old was unfit for such an office. The incident in itself was paltry, but the letter written by the President in answer to the protest put once again into light that curious mixture of theoretical idealism and practical political sense so remarkable in Jefferson. After all, the Federalists had begun with filling every office with their partisans and it was necessary to reëstablish a just balance, even if some individuals had to suffer. If the rights of the minority could not be ignored, the majority had its rights also and could not submit to the monopoly claimed by the Federalists: "Total exclusions," concluded the President, "call for prompt corrections. I shall correct the procedure; but that done, return with joy to that state of things, when only questions concerning a candidate shall be, is he honest? Is he capable? Is he faithful to the Constitution?"[1] In other

[1] To Elias Shipman and others, July 12, 1801.

words, Jefferson was not ready to proclaim the principle so frankly avowed later "to the victor belong the spoils." His principle was and remained absolutely different. But he considered that he was confronted by a situation which had to be remedied without any delay, and in his behavior he reminds one in some way of the French publicist who, although theoretically opposed to the death penalty, declared, "*Que messieurs les assassins commencent!*" Certainly this is not the pure and exalted morality of the political philosopher, but neither is it the cynical attitude of the political "boss", and one may wonder how many men who have occupied high offices would stand better than Jefferson in this respect if documents were available and could be subjected to the same scrutiny.

The fact remains, however, that during the battle from which he had come out victorious, Jefferson had to employ and sometimes associate with men whose character was not absolutely spotless. The presence of Aaron Burr in the government was already a thorn in his side. It was also particularly unfortunate that he had given aid and assistance to Callender, whose scurrilous attacks against Adams went far beyond a legitimate discussion of public utterances and actions of a man at the head of the government. Callender had been sentenced under the Sedition Act to a term in jail and liberated by Jefferson with all the other victims of the act when he took office. It was even more unfortunate that the pamphlet of Callender, "The Prospect Before Us", was reprinted under a modified title as the "History of the Administration of John Adams" more than a year after the new administration had taken hold of things. It was also regrettable that the son of John Adams should have been removed from office after the election. Soon after the death of Jefferson's younger daughter, Mrs. Adams, who had befriended the little girl when she arrived in London all alone in 1787, wrote to the bereaved father to express her sympathy. Jefferson took the opportunity to reassert his personal friendship for John Adams. He could not help mentioning, however, that one act of Adams' administration he had to consider as personally unkind, his last appointment to office of Jefferson's most ardent political enemies.[1] This letter called for an answer, and Mrs. Adams was not a woman to miss an opportunity to express her husband's views and her own on the removal of Federal judges and particularly of John Quincy. Thus Jefferson was led to write a final letter in which he expressed more clearly than he had done anywhere else his opinion on the judiciary and on the place it should occupy in the general scheme of government. To understand this letter fully it is necessary to go back to the beginnings of Jefferson's administration.

The original draft of Jefferson's message to Congress, December 8, 1801, contained a paragraph which, after more mature reflection, the President decided to omit "as capable of being chicaned, and furnishing something to the opposition to make a handle of." [2] In it Jefferson held the theory that the three powers existing in any government had been distributed among three equal authorities, constituting each a check on one or both the others. The President asserted that each of these three branches of the government had a right " to decide on the validity of an act according to its own judgment and uncontrouled by the opinions of any other department." According to this theory, even if opposition developed among different departments, no permanent ill could ensue, since at the next election the people were at liberty to refuse to reëlect those whose interpretation seemed erroneous.

Jefferson's disapproval of the Sedition Act had been known for a long time; he had a right to assume that his election meant

[1] June 13, 1804. Memorial Edition, XI, 28.
[2] A. J. Beveridge: "Life of Marshall", II, 51–53 and Appendix.

that the people approved of his position and to make this declaration:

On mature deliberation, in the presence of the nation, and under the tie of the solemn oath which binds me to them and to my duty, I do declare that I hold that act in palpable and unqualified contradiction to the constitution, considering it then as a nullity, I have relieved from oppression under it those of my fellow citizens who were within the reach of the functions confided to me.

In its final form the message was far less provocative. It simply contained the statement that "the judiciary system . . . and especially that portion of it recently enacted, will, of course, present itself to the contemplation of Congress." But the Federalists and particularly Marshall were not placated by this apparent moderation; they knew that the assault against the judiciary was about to begin. The debate between Federalists and Republicans had already been transferred to another ground.

No better account of it can be found than the chapters written on the subject by Albert J. Beveridge in his "Life of Marshall." It must be remembered, however, that Beveridge's account was necessarily colored by his own political views, as were the views of most historians of the subject.[1] One of the first episodes of the battle was the repeal of the Judiciary Act passed in 1801 by the Federalists, in order to reorganize the Supreme Court and to increase the number of Federal judges. This was immediately followed by the impeachment of Judge Pickering, the deposition of Judge Addison by the Senate of Pennsylvania, and the famous decision given by Marshall on "Marbury versus Madison." These incidents were of unequal importance and significance. It was recognized by Pickering's friends and family that the judge was half-demented and for several years had been unable to fulfill his duties. But since

---

[1] "Life of Marshall", II, 51–222; McMaster, "History of the People of the United States", Vol. III.

the Act of 1801 had been repealed, no one seemed to have authority at the time to remove the judge from office. The Pickering case simply provided the Republicans with an opportunity to test out their favorite contention, that impeachment was unrestricted and could be enforced against any officer of the government deemed undesirable by two thirds of the Senate.

Of far greater importance was the decision of Marshall in "Marbury versus Madison." The senior member of the Supreme Court formulated on this occasion a doctrine on the powers of the Court which, although never written in the Constitution, was to obtain final recognition and which to this day had remained one of the many unwritten laws of the land. Another most curious situation this, so disconcerting to historians and observers trained in the principles of Roman law, but often recurring in American politics and administrative life. The case itself was of no importance. Marbury was one of the "midnight judges" whose commission, signed by Adams, had been withheld by Madison, on the theory that the powers of the former President to make appointments had really expired, not on the third of March, 1801, at midnight, but on the day his successor was elected. It was maintained by the administration that the commission not having been delivered Marbury had no right to take office and to sit on the bench. Marbury had appealed to the Supreme Court, but the sessions of the Court being suspended for fourteen months by Congress, Marshall had at first no opportunity to declare himself publicly on the matter.

When he finally passed on the case, the Chief Justice saw at once that his hour had come, and gave his definition of the powers of the Court in its relation to the executive and the legislative. Curiously enough, as Beveridge remarked, the matter had never before come up and would have remained undecided for a long time, if this particular juncture had not made it a question of paramount importance for the destinies of the country. Briefly summed up, the theory of Marshall, shorn of its legal phraseology, was this: The happiness of the American people rested on certain principles embodied in the Constitution. These principles could not be altered by legislation; if, however, the legislative passed a law evidently contrary to the Constitution, there must be for the individual some recourse, some means of asserting his rights. In cases where Congress adopts laws contrary to the Constitution, these laws must be void. On this principle Jefferson and Marshall were in complete agreement. But from that point on they differed widely. The next question was to determine where does the power rest to declare a law unconstitutional? With the Executive and even with the States, Jefferson had first declared in his draft of 1801. With the Supreme Court, answered Marshall; for this is essentially a judicial function. Under this construction, the Constitution remains the supreme law of the land, but it is within the powers attributed by the Constitution to the judiciary, for the Supreme Court to decide on the constitutionality of an act passed by the legislature. Thus the Court is not placed above the Constitution, but its judges stand as the keepers and interpreters of the superior law of the country.

Jefferson did not engage directly in a controversy with Marshall and held his peace. But, as he was wont, he seized another opportunity to express his views on the subject, and he did it in his letter written to Mrs. Adams on September 11, 1804. In this, he maintained that "nothing in the Constitution has given the judges a right to decide for the Executive, more than to the Executive to decide for them. Both magistrates are equally independent in the sphere of action assigned to them." Judges believing a law to be constitutional have a right to pass sentences. But "the Executive believing the law to be unconstitutional were bound to remit the execution of it; because that power has been confided to them by the Constitution."

What he did not say on this occasion, but repeated on many others, was that, the ultimate source of authority resting in the people, it was for the people to decide at the next election in case a conflict of interpretation should arise between any of the three branches of the government. In case of a conflict between the judiciary and the legislative, however, impeachment proceedings could be initiated and judges removed in a regular and, according to him, perfectly constitutional way.

It must be recognized here that the position taken by Jefferson was perfectly logical, far more logical than the interpretation given out by Marshall. Whether Jefferson's theory would have worked out satisfactorily is quite another matter. It is only too evident that perfectly logical constructions do not always fit the complexity and contradictions of human affairs. The system of democracy which was Jefferson's ideal at that time might have worked in the case of a New England town meeting; it would have been more difficult to apply to the government of a State. In the case of a large and growing federation of States, it would have injected into presidential and congressional elections constant elements of discord and bitterness. Thus the cost of liberty would not have been eternal vigilance, but eternal strife and political dissensions.

It may even be doubted whether Jefferson would ever have entertained such an extreme theory if at that time he had not been moved by immediate considerations. He had come to see in the judiciary, as it was constituted after the appointments made by Adams, an institution endangering the very life of the Republic. As for Marshall, who had hurled a challenge at the executive and the legislative branches of the government, it had to be ascertained whether some means could not be found to remove him from office.

That such was the ultimate intent of the Republican leaders was understood generally when proceedings were started to impeach Judge Chase of the Supreme Court. As in the case of

Pickering, the Republicans had carefully selected the card they intended to play. Was he not the very man who had sentenced Fries to the gallows and Callender to jail, who had been relentless in his application of the Sedition Act and in the prosecution of Republicans? He had finally, and this was the immediate ground for his impeachment, bitterly criticized from the bench the repeal of the Federal judiciary act, and predicted that the country would be enslaved by mob tyranny and that soon "they would all establish the worst kind of government known to man."

The impeachment proceedings took place in the Senate room elaborately decorated for the occasion with a display of crimson, green, and blue cloth draping the rows of benches and the sections reserved for the heads of departments, foreign ministers, members of the House, and the general public. The Senate convened to hear the case on February 4, 1805, and for almost a month all other business was practically suspended. But it was far more than the fate of a single judge which was going to be decided. On the decision of the Senate hung not only the future of the Constitution but probably the fate of the Union. For New England had already on several occasions threatened secession; the North resented what was already termed "Virginia tyranny", and it was to be feared that these feelings of disaffection might be strengthened. It was also the most exciting ceremony the new capital had yet witnessed, and the formalities of the proceedings, the effort to clothe them with dignity and solemnity, presented a strange contrast with the uncouth appearance of the city itself, with its ramshackle boarding houses, its muddy streets, and surrounding wilderness.

The debates provided a rare occasion for an extraordinary display of American eloquence. This is not one of the least surprises to a student of American civilization, to discover the taste of the people as a whole for oratory and the remarkable gift of American orators for long speeches, even in the early days. Scarcely less surprising was the capacity of American audiences to listen patiently for long hours and with apparent interest to discussions and debates. It seems as if the gift attributed by Cæsar to the Gauls of old had been transferred to the new continent and to a people racially much different. Oratory was to a certain extent a new art, for few occasions were offered in the colonial times for long political speeches; but even in the early days of the Revolution, born orators appeared and since that time have filled the legislative halls with an inexhaustible flow of eloquence. This is said without the least irony and merely as another illustration of the danger of generalizing when discussing national characteristics. To the point these speeches were, perhaps, but they were not short by any means. A careful study of the development of the American school of oratory would certainly repay a specialist in the history of public speaking.

During the session, the oratorical stars were Luther Martin of Maryland, who spoke for Chase, and John Randolph, who summed up the case for the administration. It appeared, however, when the final vote was taken, that Jefferson had not been able to keep his party in hand. There were thirty-four senators, of whom nine were Federalists and twenty-five Republicans. Twenty-two votes were necessary to convict, but the administration was able to muster only sixteen for impeachment, and on one count Chase was proved unanimously "not guilty." For the time being John Marshall was safe, and the acquittal of Chase was undoubtedly a personal defeat for the President.

This wound to his *amour-propre* was compensated by the success of the last election. Jefferson had been reëlected without opposition; the strength of the Federalists as a separate party had dwindled to the vanishing point, and only three days separated him from the beginning of his second term. But everybody understood that the matter at issue had not been settled and that another test would have to be made. The very day Chase was acquitted, John Randolph introduced a resolution proposing an amendment to the Constitution, to the effect that "The judges of the Supreme Court, and of all other courts of the United States, shall be removed by the President on the joint addresses of both Houses of Congress requesting the same, anything in the Constitution of the United States notwithstanding." This was referred to a committee and, as Congress had only three more days to sit, it was decided by sixty-eight votes against thirty-three that the motion would be made the order of the day for the first Monday in December.

The assault against the judiciary constitutes one of the most striking episodes of Jefferson's first administration and has received its due share at the hands of American historians. It must not be forgotten, however, that even in other respects the President had no easy sailing. The friend of Priestley, Thomas Cooper, Volney, and Thomas Paine continued to be represented in the press and in the public as the champion of infidelity. The President could not engage in any controversy in order to justify himself but, according to his favorite methods, he encouraged his friends to hit back, and he became more and more convinced that the intrusion of the churches into politics was one of the worst evils that could befall any country. He soon came to the conclusion that many members of the clergy were unworthy to speak in the name of the great teacher; that the Christian doctrine had degenerated in their hands, and that no true religion could long exist when it was intrusted to the priests. Hence the many expressions of his preference for the Quakers so often found in his correspondence.

The mild and simple principles of the Christian philosophy would produce too much calm; too much regularity of good, to extract from its disciples a support from a numerous priesthood, were they not to sophisticate it, split it into hairs, and twist its texts till they cover the divine morality of its author with mysteries, and require the

priesthood to explain them.   The Quakers seem to have discovered
this.   They have no priests, therefore no schisms.   They judge of
the text by the dictates of common sense and common morality.[1]

The indignation of the Federalists and the clergy reached a
paroxysm when it was discovered that the President had not
only invited Paine to come to America but had even promised
him passage on a public vessel.   For Paine was no longer
remembered as the eloquent political writer who in prophetic
accents had celebrated the uniqueness of America's position in
the world.   He was the detestable atheist who had participated
in the bloody excesses of the French Revolution — a wretch
unworthy of being thus honored by a Christian nation.   Once
more religion was injected into politics.   The President was
bitterly reproved by the New England clergy for having refused
to proclaim days of fasting and thanksgivings as his predecessors had done, and Jefferson, who would have preferred
to let sleeping dogs lie, had to come out and explain his position on an alliance between "Church and State, under the
authority of the Constitution." [2]

That Jefferson, who was so restive under public criticism,
suffered even more than he dared admit appears in many
passages of his letters.   "Every word of mine," he wrote to
Mazzei, "which they can get hold of, however innocent, however orthodox, is twisted, tormented, perverted, and like the
words of holy writ, are made to mean everything but what they
were intended to mean." [3]   The whole subject is not an easy
one to treat and cannot be discussed here; but it would be
very difficult to reach a fair estimate of internal politics during
Jefferson's first administration if that element of hostility were
entirely left out.   We can only express the hope that some day
it will receive due attention.   An investigation of the New

[1] To Elbridge Gerry, March 29, 1801. Memorial Edition, X, 251.
[2] To the Attorney-general, January 1, 1802. *Ibid.*, X, 305.
[3] July 18, 1804. *Ibid.*, XI, 38.

England papers and Church publications of the time would undoubtedly bring to light many hidden currents of hostility.

But, in spite of these difficulties, the new administration went ahead with a program of political reforms of great moment. No tradition for the respective duties of the Cabinet members and their relation to the President had yet been established. Under Washington's administration letters sent to the President were referred by him to the departments concerned to be acted upon, and letters sent to the department heads were submitted to the President with a proposed answer. Generally they were sent back with his approbation; sometimes an alteration was suggested, and when the subject was particularly important it was reserved for a conference. In this manner Washington always was in accurate possession of all facts and proceedings in all parts of the Union. This procedure had been impossible to follow during Adams' administration, owing to the long and habitual absences of the President from the seat of government, and little by little the department heads had assumed more and more responsibility, with the result that the government had four different heads "drawing sometimes in different directions." This usurpation of powers and this maladministration Jefferson meant to end. In a very courteous, but very firm manner, he reminded the members of the Cabinet that the President had been intrusted with a certain set of duties incumbent upon him and for which he was responsible before the public, and that he considered it necessary to return to the procedure followed by Washington. What had been an informal custom was to become a regular and official routine; it entailed an enormous expenditure of time on the part of the President, a great flexibility of mind, and a necessity of adapting himself to many different problems in the course of one day. To a large extent, Jefferson is responsible for placing on the shoulders of the chief executive the enormous load under which several Presidents have broken down.

This was not the most conspicuous reform introduced by Jefferson in the plan of government, yet it was one of the most important. Of no less consequence was the reform of the financial system of the United States. The privilege of the bank had still several years to run, but many other modifications could be introduced at once. Hamilton had multiplied the number of internal taxes and at the same time the number of Federal office-holders in order to strengthen his hold on the government. These had to be done away with, as well as the abominable excise taxes which had created so many difficulties under the preceding administrations. They were at best a temporary expedient, to be resorted to only in case of war, and the Federal Government had to make an effort to return to the more orthodox system of bringing its expenditures within the limits of revenue raised by taxes on importations. This was perfectly consistent with Jefferson's theory of the State rights and the general functions of the Federal Government. To substitute economy for taxation, to reduce the debt as rapidly as possible, to keep down the expenses for the navy and the army, — such was the policy of the new administration, and in his second annual message on December 15, 1802, Jefferson could point out with pleasure that "in the department of finance the receipts of external duties for the last twelve months have exceeded those of any former year." To care for the Louisiana Purchase, Gallatin recommended a loan of $11,250,000, running for fifteen years and carrying a six per cent. interest. But in his fourth message the President declared that "the state of our finances continues to fulfill our expectations. Eleven million and a half dollars received in the course of the year ending on the thirtieth of September last, have enabled us, after meeting all the ordinary expenses of the year, to pay upward of $3,600,000 of the public debt, exclusive of interest." Thus it was amply demonstrated that the financial structure of the Federal Government had not been endangered by a departure from

Hamilton's policies. It is worth noting also that Jefferson's party, at that time, stood for a strong tariff, while the last Federalists advocated internal taxes. In that respect, at least, it is hardly possible to say that the present-day Democrats continue the Jeffersonian policies.

This system, however, presented many advantages in the eyes of Jefferson. In his first message he had made one of those many declarations, so often found in official documents of the sort, by which men in public life are wont to define their policies in almost sibylline terms, so as to express their own aspirations and satisfy the members of their party without arousing undue antagonism in an influential minority. "Agriculture," he had written, "manufactures, commerce, and navigation, the four pillars of our prosperity, are the most thriving when left most free to individual enterprise." But at once he had added: "Protection from casual embarrassments, however, may sometimes be reasonably interposed. If in the course of your observations or inquiries they should appear to need any aid within the limits of our constitutional powers, your sense of their importance is a sufficient assurance they will occupy your attention." This second statement could only mean one thing, that the President was not ready to depart entirely and radically from Hamilton's policy of giving encouragement to manufactures. But there is no doubt that in his opinion America was to remain essentially an agricultural nation. He still had before him the vision of a large country in which every citizen would live on his own land and from this land derive most of his subsistence instead of congregating in large cities. It was a Vergilian vision magnified a million times; it was based also to a large extent on his own experience at Monticello where he had proved that it was possible to manufacture tools, to bake bricks, to make furniture, and to maintain a comparatively large family on the products of the soil. He was not ready to antagonize openly those who dreamed of another future for

America, and he did not believe that he had a right to do so, since his duty was to carry out the wishes of the people.

Jefferson was not the man to take the lead in these matters, but he was not the man either to oppose any measure to encourage manufactures and commerce that Congress would deem proper to adopt. On this point he had not varied since the letter he had written from Paris to Hogendorp. His preference for "an agricultural condition" remained largely theoretical, sentimental, and personal. He may be considered as the leader of an agrarian party, he may have felt in sympathy with the French Physiocrats, but when it came to practice he acted very much like Du Pont de Nemours himself who, in spite of his theories, spent all he had to establish a tannery and a powder mill near Wilmington, and at the end of his days proposed to the American Government a "Plan for the Encouragement of Manufactures in America." If it is true that during Jefferson's administration industrial and agricultural interests clashed for the first time in America, I fail to see that the President made any effort to favor agriculture at the expense of industry.

When the end of his first term approached, Jefferson did not need any coercion to remain in the saddle for another period of four years. It had already been decided that Aaron Burr would not and could not again be a candidate, and George Clinton was chosen as running mate of Jefferson. Never in the history of the United States was an election so little contested: Jefferson obtained one hundred sixty-two electoral votes while his opponent could only muster fourteen. The Republican Party had really become the National party and the President had been able to achieve political unity.

CHAPTER II

PROTECTIVE IMPERIALISM AND TERRITORIAL EXPANSION

THE famous Inaugural Message of Jefferson gave more space to questions of domestic politics than to foreign problems, but it contained a clear definition of America's attitude towards Europe — a short and terse statement in which the President reiterated the principles which had guided him when Secretary of State. These were the same principles that underlay the foreign policies of the United States from the early days of the Revolution. They had already appeared in the Plan of Treaties drawn up by Adams in 1776; they had been solemnly proclaimed by Washington in his Farewell Address; and they still direct to a large extent America's attitude in her dealings with foreign nations on the American continent as well as abroad.

These principles were presented by Jefferson as being essentially the result of natural conditions for which the Americans themselves were not responsible : "Kindly separated by nature and a wide ocean from the exterminating havoc of one quarter of the globe; too high-minded to endure the degradations of others; possessing a chosen country, with room enough for our descendants to the hundredth and thousandth generation", there was only one course for the American people to follow : "commerce and honest friendship with all nations — entangling alliances with none."

Thanks to the Republican victory, America no longer had to pay any attention to the political convulsions which were tearing the vitals of the Old World. The American experiment no longer depended on the issue of the French Revolution. The

Argosy had weathered the storm; America had become the sole arbiter of her destinies, she had become, Jefferson proclaimed, "a standing monument and example for the aim and imitation of the people of other countries; and I join with you in the hope and belief that they will see, from our example, that a free government is of all others the most energetic; that the inquiry which has been excited among the mass of mankind by our revolution and its consequences, will ameliorate the condition of man over a great portion of the globe."

Such a declaration should not be mistaken for a manifestation of a missionary spirit by which Jefferson was never moved and which was absolutely abhorrent to his nature. America was not to engage in any crusade. She was not to preach a new gospel of liberty to the oppressed peoples of the earth. She had proclaimed no *Déclaration européenne des droits de l'homme et du citoyen*, as the French Revolution had ambitiously done. She was not sending overseas to the shackled nations a call to throw off the yoke and liberate themselves. Such declarations would have seemed to Jefferson idle and dangerous. Every people had to work out their own salvation; any attempt by America to help and encourage them would only embroil her in difficulties which would retard her own development. She could best serve the cause of humanity by standing aloof and simply existing as an example which others, if they had eyes to see, could not fail sooner or later to imitate. It was essentially the doctrine which has been so often expounded by the non-interventionists every time America has been invited to coöperate with Europe.

This doctrine therefore was not the expression of a passing mood; it constituted one of the fundamental principles of Americanism and had a permanent value, because, as Montesquieu would have said, it was the result of "the nature of things", and not a deduction drawn from an *a priori* principle. On the other hand, it contained a new and interesting affirmation of the unquestionable superiority of the American people over all the peoples of the earth, not only morally but intellectually; and this was not forgotten either, for the "high-mindedness" of Jefferson was echoed and reflected more than a hundred years later in the "too proud to fight" of Woodrow Wilson. Taken in itself, this statement was no worse than so many statements made in political speeches; all peoples like to be told and to believe that they are a chosen people. But it must be confessed that Jefferson drew very dangerous conclusions from that uniqueness of America's position.

One of the earliest and frankest expressions of that naïve and almost unconscious imperialism appears in an unpublished letter to Doctor Mitchell. After discussing every possible subject under heaven, from frosts to mammoth bones and electricity, Jefferson concluded with this disquieting statement: "Nor is it in physics alone that we shall be found to differ from the other hemisphere. I strongly suspect that our geographical peculiarities may call for a different code of natural law to govern relations with other nations from that which the conditions of Europe have given rise to there." [1]

This idea was reiterated in a letter written to Short more than a year later. In it Jefferson laid down the principle, the moral foundation of American imperialism — a curious mixture of common sense, practical idealism, and moralizing not to be found perhaps in any other people, but more permanently American than typically Jeffersonian. To any sort of arrangement with Europe he was irreducibly opposed: "We have a perfect horror at everything connecting ourselves with the politics of Europe." In order to protect America from the wiles of the European diplomats, the best course was "in the meantime, to wish to let every treaty we have drop off without renewal. We call in our diplomatic missions, barely keeping up those to the most important nations. There is a strong

[1] Jefferson Papers. Library of Congress, June 13, 1800.

disposition in our countrymen to discontinue even these; and very possibly it may be done." Jefferson admitted that the neutral rights of the United States might suffer; they would undoubtedly suffer temporarily, and one had to accept this as an unavoidable evil. But it would be only temporary: "We feel ourselves strong and daily growing stronger . . . If we can delay but for a few years the necessity of vindicating the laws of nature on the ocean, we shall be the more sure of doing it with effect. The day is within my time as well as yours; when we may say by what laws other nations shall treat us on the sea. And we will say it." [1]

Nor was this imperialism purely theoretical. It was susceptible of immediate applications and it manifested itself openly in a letter written to James Monroe a few weeks later. The people of Virginia were most anxious to get rid of a band of malefactors guilty of insurgency, conspiracy, and rebellion. Had they been whites, the solution would have been easy enough, but it happened that they were colored people and they could not reasonably be sent to the northern boundary, or be provided with land in the Western Territory. Could these undesirables be pushed into the Spanish sphere of influence? To this solution Jefferson was unequivocally opposed and for reasons worth considering: "However our present situation may restrain us within our own limits," he wrote to Monroe, "it is impossible not to look forward to distant times, when our rapid multiplication will expand itself beyond those limits, and cover the whole northern, if not the southern continent, with a people speaking the same language, governed in similar forms, and by similar laws; nor can we contemplate either blot or mixture on that surface." [2]

Truly enough, Jefferson said at the beginning of the letter that publication of his views might have an ill effect in more

---

[1] To W. Short, October 3, 1801. Memorial Edition, X, 288.
[2] November 24, 1801. *Ibid.*, X, 294.

than one quarter. I shall not even advance the theory that Jefferson's foreign policies constituted a systematic effort to put such a program into effect. But that such aspirations and ambitions existed in his mind and influenced him to a certain extent cannot be denied, and they should not be overlooked in any discussion of his attitude during the negotiations that led to the purchase of Louisiana.

Many of Jefferson's contemporaries, and not a few American historians, have harshly criticized him for buying Louisiana from France, when no clause in the Constitution authorized the acquisition of new territory. On the French side, not only historians but even Bonaparte's brother considered that the cession, without the previous consultation of the Chambers, of a colony recently recovered by France was an act arbitrary and unconstitutional. Both principals have been condemned and praised by posterity, but there is no doubt that the full responsibility for the transaction rests not upon the peoples of France and America, but on the President of the United States and the Premier Consul. It was remarkable that two great minds, so divergent in their views and principles, should meet on a common ground instead of clashing. On neither side was it a triumph of idealism, but of that enlightened self-interest which, according to Jefferson, directs the actions of men as well as of nations.

Nor were they entirely unsupported by the public opinion of their respective countries. I have already indicated in a preceding book [1] that a friendly conspiracy seems to have been organized in France in order to induce the First Consul, and chiefly Talleyrand, to acquiesce in the cession. At any rate, it appears from several letters of Volney that the Ideologists were anxious to avoid an open conflict with the United States and, at the same time, to promote a measure which, in their opinion, would insure the growth and prosperity of the Republican

[1] "Volney et l'Amérique." Paris and Baltimore, 1923.

Promised Land. Volney, himself one of the "*voyageurs*" of the Directory, had made a trip to the West and come back fully convinced that France could never hope to develop an empire in the Mississippi Valley. The few scattered French colonists who remained isolated in the Middle West were condemned to be gradually absorbed by the influx of American pioneers and to disappear before the rising flood of American colonization. The question of the lower valley of the Mississippi was different, to be sure, but if the United States were thwarted in their development, if they were hemmed in on every side by powerful neighbors, the theory of Montesquieu that only small nations could adopt the republican system of government would seem vindicated. It was not only the fate of the United States which was at stake, but the fate of the doctrine of popular government, and it was the duty of all liberals to bend every effort to make more secure the prosperity of America.

On the other hand, as we have already seen in previous chapters, while Jefferson was satisfied to leave Louisiana in the hands of Spain, at least temporarily, he had always watched for a favorable opportunity to unite the Spanish colonies to the main body of the United States. It was not so much desire of expansion and imperialism as the conviction that colonies were only pawns in the game of European politics; that they could change hands at any time according to the fortunes of war; that there existed consequently a permanent danger of seeing France recover some day her former colonies or, still worse, to have them fall into the hands of the British. With England, or possibly France, on the northern border, in the Floridas, on the Gulf, and in the valley of the Mississippi, the old dream of European domination of the North American continent would revive. The United States would be placed in the same position as the old colonies with reference to France. A clash could not be avoided; the issue would have to be fought out, until one of the adversaries should remain in full and undisputed possession of the whole northern part of the New World.

Although the Treaty of San Ildefonso, by which France was to recover and occupy Louisiana at the first favorable opportunity, was intended to remain secret, rumors that some deal had been concluded greatly disturbed the American Government. As early as March, 1801, Rufus King had been informed in London that such a cession was contemplated and learned that General Collot intended to leave for Louisiana with a considerable number of followers. On June 1, King called his Government's attention to the fact that the cession of Louisiana "might enable France to extend her influence, and perhaps her dominion, up the Mississippi; and through the Lakes even up to Canada." The information caused great concern to the British Government, and Lord Hawkesbury had acquainted the American minister with the rumors. At that time, King, who was evidently familiar with the views of Jefferson on the matter, had answered by quoting Montesquieu that "it is happy for trading powers, that God has permitted Turks and Spaniards to be in the world, since of all nations they are the most proper to possess a great empire with insignificance." The purport of this quotation being, he wrote, that, "we are contented that the Floridas remain in the hands of Spain, but should not be willing to see them transferred, except to ourselves." It was a double-edged answer, since it set at nil any hope the British might have had of occupying Louisiana and the Floridas; and at the same time it constituted a very accurate statement of the position maintained by Jefferson when Secretary of State in all his dealings pertaining to the Spanish colonies.

This policy was clearly defined in the general observations communicated by the President to Charles Pinckney, minister in Madrid (June 9, 1801) and in the instructions given to Livingston, hastening his departure for France (September 28,

1801).   Jefferson did not know yet what part of the Spanish colonies was to be ceded to France and was more preoccupied with the eventuality of the cession of the Floridas.   The solution preferred for the present was clearly the *status quo*.   Should the cession have irrevocably taken place, the rights to the navigation of the Mississippi were to be safeguarded, and if possible France should be induced "to make over to the United States the Floridas, if included in the cession to her from Spain, or at least West Florida, through which several of our rivers (particularly the important river Mobile) empty themselves into the sea."   Finally, if the cession had never been contemplated, Livingston was instructed to induce France "to favor experiments on the part of the United States, for obtaining from Spain the cession in view."

The die was cast; for the first time the United States took the position that the time had come for them to control the territory extending between their States and the Gulf of Mexico, and to insure the peaceful and unquestioned rights of navigation on the Mississippi.   From the point of view of international law or *droit des gens*, Madison reiterated the doctrine of Jefferson, that it was a natural law that the States should have access to the sea; and in this particular instance he hinted at another principle — the application of which to the old territories of Europe would be far-reaching — namely that the nation possessing a certain river was entitled also to the mouth of the river.   But this again was probably in his opinion one of these "natural laws" which applied to America only.   At the end of November, Rufus King sent to Madison a copy of the treaty between the Prince of Parma and Lucien Bonaparte, signed at Madrid, March 31, 1801, and in December he had the opportunity of mentioning the possibility of France paying her debts by ceding Louisiana back to the United States, which only brought the curt answer that "none but spendthrifts satisfy their debts by selling their lands."

Livingston, in a letter to Rufus King, took the view that the cession would be disastrous not only to the United States but to Spain and England, since the French would not fail to contract alliance with the Indians and to renew relations with "the peasantry of Canada", rendering the possessions of Britain very precarious. He could only hope that King would do his utmost to "induce the British ministry to throw all the obstacles in their power in the way of a final settlement of this business, if it is not already too late."

The British ministry refused to take the hint. Unwelcome as the passing of Louisiana into French hands might be considered they were not disposed to endanger the success of the negotiations shortly to be begun at Amiens, and Rufus King was told that the subject would not even be mentioned by Lord Hawkesbury.[1] Evidently England never intended to draw the chestnuts out of the fire for the sole benefit of the United States, and Livingston alone was left to face the situation. The letter he wrote on his own initiative, unable as he was to consult the home government, was somewhat blunt in tone. He called attention to the fact that the arrival in Louisiana or Florida of a large body of French troops could not fail to alarm the people of the Western Territory. He conceded that no protest could be made under the sixth article of the Treaty of 1778, since it had been superseded by the agreement of September 30, 1800; but he maintained that even in the absence of a formal treaty the clause expressed a very desirable policy, that at least the United States wished to know exactly the boundaries of the territory ceded by Spain. At the same time, he discreetly added that "the government of the United States desired to be informed how far it would be practicable to make such arrangements between their respective governments as would, at the same time, aid the financial operations of France, and remove, by a strong and natural boundary,

[1] King to the Secretary of State, January 1, 1802.

all future causes of discontent between her and the United States."

These different reports, and particularly Livingston's letter to King, of December 30, created some perturbation in the mind of Jefferson, and on March 16, Madison wrote the American minister in Paris "that too much circumspection could not be employed." The great danger was that any sort of a combination with Great Britain would have to be paid later in kind or in territory. While Madison sent recommendations to Pinckney and to Livingston, the clear wish of Jefferson was to keep out England as much as possible. It was at that time that the President decided to take a hand directly in the negotiations. At the beginning of April, 1802, Du Pont de Nemours had written Jefferson that political as well as commercial considerations made it imperative for him to go to France for a short visit. Jefferson saw at once a possibility to use Du Pont as in the past he had employed Lafayette, and asked him to come to Washington to become acquainted "with certain matters that could not be committed to paper." [1]

Very significantly he added: "I believe that the destinies of great countries depend upon it, such is the crisis now existing." As Du Pont answered that he could not possibly see the President before sailing, Jefferson decided to explain his point of view fully in a long letter and at the same time he expressed himself even more forcibly in a letter to Livingston which he asked Du Pont to read before sealing it.

The two letters complete and explain each other. First of all, Jefferson rejected as a very imperfect solution the granting free access to the sea to the territories situated on the left bank of the Mississippi. He bluntly declared that although America had a more natural and instinctive friendship for France than for any other nation, it was quite certain that the national characteristics of the two peoples were so divergent that they

[1] Jefferson Papers. Library of Congress, April 21, 1802.

could not live peacefully side by side for any length of time. Even the cession by France of the Floridas and New Orleans would be only a palliative which might delay but not suppress the unavoidable conflict.[1]   The only solution was for France to give up entirely the rights she had acquired under the Treaty of San Ildefonso and to return to the *status quo*.   Any attempt by Bonaparte to send soldiers to Louisiana would be considered as a *casus belli*, and the President wrote significantly : "Peace and abstinence from European interference are our objects, and so will continue while the present order of things in America remains uninterrupted."   If, on the other hand, France insisted upon taking possession of Louisiana, it was the declared intention of Jefferson to come to an agreement with England, then to launch an expedition against New Orleans, to occupy the territory claimed by France, so as to prevent any new European nation from setting foot on the continent.   That this policy of non-colonization should apply to South America as well as to the northern continent was evidently in the mind of the President, since he declared that after the annihilation of the French fleet, two nations — America and Great Britain — would rule the sea, and the two continents would be practically "appropriated by them."

The threat was so formidable that Du Pont refused to believe that it was seriously meant.   He saw at once that if such representations were made to the First Consul, even with proper diplomatic precautions, they would be looked upon by him as a challenge that could not be ignored.   "Give up that country, or we shall take it", is not at all persuasive.   "We will defend it", is the answer that comes naturally to any man. Furthermore, the old Physiocrat predicted that if the United States ever followed such a policy, they would lose their prestige as a democratic and peaceful nation.   Jefferson would thus play into the hands of the militaristic faction which ambitioned

[1] Jefferson Papers. Library of Congress, April 25, 1802.

the conquest of Mexico; if, on the contrary, Mexico were to be emancipated, it might become a dangerous neighbor for the United States. He consequently urged Jefferson to accept what he considered as a much more sensible program, namely a compromise which would insure free access to the sea to "the territories of the Cumberland, the Wabash and both banks of the Ohio." Finally he warned the President against entering into such an alliance with England, since England would never permit the United States to become a naval power of first importance. If, however, the United States insisted on having a free hand in the South, was it not possible, in view of the impending war between France and England, to permit France to recover Canada instead of Louisiana, and to tell Bonaparte: "Give us Louisiana and at the first opportunity we shall restore Canada to you"?

Even if that were refused, if nothing could remove Jefferson's objection to the establishment of a French colony on the northern continent, there was still a possibility of giving satisfaction to both parties concerned without unduly irritating the national pride of either. This was simply for America to buy from France her claim on the Southern territory. True to his training and doctrine, Du Pont had devised a commercial solution to a political problem. The question of Louisiana was to be treated as a business, with a political background to be sure, but essentially on business terms.

The answer of Jefferson has unfortunately disappeared and was probably destroyed by Du Pont; but another letter of the old Physiocrat permits us to reconstruct its contents. Jefferson contended that the United States had no money and could not afford to pay any important amount for such a purchase. To which Du Pont answered that purchasing would be infinitely more economical than going to war:

The sum offered and accepted will not exclude any compensation for all or part of the sum which might be paid to you under the treaty. To agree on the price is the important thing. To arrange for the forms of payment, to charge against it legitimate reductions is only a secondary matter, which will take care of itself. All the rest of your instructions is easy to follow, and I shall follow them exactly.

Then proving himself to be as good a prophet as a philosopher Du Pont added that Bonaparte would be more attracted by a frank and complete proposal than by a compromise: "I hope it will succeed because Bonaparte is a man of genius, and his character is much above ordinary ideas." [1]

It is not entirely to the credit of Jefferson that, when he was thus declaring to Du Pont that the United States could not afford to negotiate on such a basis, Madison, on May 1, 1802, was writing to Livingston, asking him to ascertain precisely the price at which the Floridas, "if included in the cession would be yielded to the United States."

The whole story of the negotiations as it appears in the Jefferson papers and in the documents published in the Annals of Congress would be worth retelling in detail. The evasions of the French minister Talleyrand, the reticences of the Spanish ambassador as to the true extent of the cession, the attempts of Rufus King to determine the British Government to throw their influence on the side of the United States, the blundering efforts of Livingston to place the case of his Government before the eyes of Bonaparte, form one of the most complicated and fascinating diplomatic mazes in which the inexperienced and not highly skillful agents of the United States tried to find their way. Livingston, who thought himself very adroit, was particularly unfelicitous in his tone. The conclusion of the memoir he wrote on August 10 and had printed for distribution to the French Government may give an idea of his style:

In reasoning upon this subject, I have confined myself to such observations as obviously presented themselves, without seeking

[1] May 12, 1802. Manuscript, Library of Congress.

any of those subtleties which may serve to mislead the judgment. I have candidly exposed the plainest facts, in the simplest language. If ever they are opposed, it will be by a contrary course. Eloquence and sophistry may reply to them and may obscure them; but time and experience will evince their truth.

Such a language may have seemed to the American minister candid and honest, but addressed to Bonaparte and Talleyrand it was very undiplomatic, to say the least. One cannot help feeling, on reading the documents, that had Livingston wished to break off negotiations he would not have expressed himself otherwise, and it is difficult to share the opinion of Henry Adams, who claimed for the American minister most of the credit for bringing the negotiations to a successful conclusion.

By the end of the summer 1802, it appeared that, before going any further, France intended to take possession of Louisiana, and Du Pont knew only too well that such a step would cause an irresistible outburst of public opinion in the United States. He kept in constant touch with Livingston, giving counsels of moderation and patience. He even proposed the project of a treaty which in his opinion would give temporary satisfaction to the United States while being acceptable to France. This plan included the cession of New Orleans and the Floridas, reserving for French vessels the same treatment as for American shipping; France to keep all the territories on the right bank of the Mississippi, but the navigation of the river to be free to both nations. Finally the United States were to pay the sum of six million dollars for the territories described in the first article.[1]

In the meantime things were moving fast in America. The suspension of the right of deposit by the Spanish authorities was taxing the none too strong endurance of the inhabitants of the western territory, and the war party was making great

[1] Jefferson Papers. Library of Congress. Du Pont de Nemours to Jefferson, October 4, 1802.

progress.   Madison wrote on November 27, 1802, that should the Spanish intendant "prove as obstinate as he has been ignorant or wicked, nothing can temperate the irritation and indignation of the Western country, but a persuasion that the energy of their own government will obtain from the justice of that of Spain the most ample redress." [1]

In his message to Congress read on December 15, the President included a short paragraph pregnant with significance:

The cession of the Spanish province of Louisiana to France, which took place in the course of the late war, if carried into effect, makes a change in the aspect of our foreign relations which will doubtless have just weight in any deliberation of the Legislature connected with that subject.

This sentence could have only one meaning: that if France took possession of Louisiana, appropriations would be in order to prevent her from establishing herself permanently in the territory.   It was a direct threat of war.   The President had apparently given up any hope of reaching an agreement and was yielding to the war party.

On December 17 it was, on motion of Randolph:

Resolved, That the President of the United States be requested to cause to be laid before this house such papers as are in the possession of the Department of State as relate to the violation on the part of Spain, of the Treaty of Friendship, Limits, and Navigation, between the United States and the King of Spain.

Jefferson complied with this request on December 22, averring that he "was aware of the obligation to maintain, in all cases, the rights of the nation, and to employ, for that purpose, those just and honorable means which belong to the character of the United States." [2]

There is no doubt that the President himself had lost patience and that the United States were rapidly drifting towards overt

[1] Annals of Congress, p. 1059.   [2] Ibid., p. 286.

acts that could only have war as a consequence. On January 4, it was moved in the House that the President be requested to communicate all the information at his disposal on the reported cession of Louisiana. Then quite unexpectedly, on January 11, Jefferson sent to the Senate a message recommending that James Monroe be appointed special envoy to France with full powers, " jointly with Mr. Livingston to enter into a treaty or convention with the First Consul of France, for the purpose of enlarging and more effectually securing, our rights and interests in the river Mississippi, and in the territories eastward thereof." The next day, the House, on recommendation of a committee which presented a lengthy report, voted an appropriation of "two million dollars to defray the expenses which may be incurred in relation to the intercourse between the United States and foreign nations."

The sudden change in Jefferson's attitude can largely be attributed to the fact that, between December 15 and January 11, he had received a letter sent from Paris by Du Pont de Nemours on October 4,[1] submitting a tentative plan for a treaty and discounting the pessimistic reports of Livingston. There is not the slightest doubt that the President was much impressed by Du Pont's letter. On January 18, Madison wrote to Pinckney:

In order to draw the French government into the measure, a sum of money will be made part of our propositions. . . . From a letter received by the President from a respectable person, it is inferred, with probability that the French government is not averse to treat on those grounds; and that such a disposition must be strengthened by circumstances of the present moment.[2]

Finally Jefferson himself wrote to Du Pont that his letter had been received with particular satisfaction, because while it held up terms that could not be entirely yielded, "it proposed

---

[1] Jefferson Papers. Library of Congress, marked received December 31.
[2] Annals of Congress. Appendix, p. 1065.

such as a mutual spirit of accommodation and sacrifice may bring to some point of union." [1]

The President indicated, however, that the action of Spain in suspending the rights of deposit had rendered imperative an immediate settlement: "Our circumstances are so imperious as to admit of no delay as to our course; and the use of the Mississippi so indispensable, that we cannot hesitate one moment to hazard our existence for its maintainance." Despite this more conciliatory tone, the President did not recede from the position he had taken previously with Du Pont. He repeated that the country was in no position to offer such a sum as mentioned by Mr. Du Pont (six million dollars) in order to insure the purchase of the said territory.

In this, Jefferson was to some extent guilty of double-dealing with his friend, or at least of not laying all his cards on the table. The instructions given to Monroe and Livingston on March 2, 1803, specified that "should a greater sum (than two million dollars) be made an ultimatum on the part of France, the President has made up his mind to go as far as fifty millions of *livres tournois*, rather than to lose the main object." Incidentally, this passage explains how Monroe and Livingston could feel authorized to accept the proposal to purchase the whole territory for sixty million francs. They were not so bold as is commonly supposed, since they were empowered by the President to go as far as fifty million for part only of Louisiana. Whether Jefferson had the constitutional right to promise such a sum without formal approval of Congress is quite another matter. It is only fair, however, to recall here that, due to the difficulty of communicating between Washington and Paris and the urgency of the situation, it was an absolute necessity to give considerable leeway to the plenipotentiaries and to provide for every possible emergency. But it must also be remembered that had not Jefferson taken at that precise time

[1] Jefferson Papers. Library of Congress, February 1, 1803.

the responsibility of engaging the resources of the United States, neither Livingston nor Monroe would have felt authorized to sign a transaction involving six times the sum voted by the House of Representatives. The blame or praise, whatever it may be, must in final analysis fall entirely on Jefferson.

It is not without some interest to notice here that Livingston was entirely unaware of the value of Du Pont de Nemours' plan. Unable to pin down Talleyrand or Lebrun, he soon came to the conclusion that it was impossible to treat and that he might as well leave Paris. "I see very little use for a minister here, where there is but one will; and that will governed by no object but personal security and personal ambition; were it left to my discretion, I should bring matters to some positive issue, or leave them, which would be the only means of bringing them to an issue." [1] He maintained to the last minute that Du Pont de Nemours had given the French government "with the best intentions, ideas that we shall find hard to eradicate, and impossible to yield to",[2] and on hearing that Monroe had been appointed, following receipt of Du Pont's letter, he answered that he was much surprised that Du Pont should talk "of the designs of this court, the price, &c., because he must have derived these from his imagination only, as he had no means of seeing anybody here that could give him the least information." [3]

Who was the better informed of the two it is not easy to decide. But by a curious coincidence, while Livingston was writing this in Paris, the ink was hardly dry on the instructions to Monroe which contained this striking paragraph: "It is to be added that the overtures committed to you coincide in great measure with the ideas of the person through whom the letter of the President of April 30, 1802, was conveyed to Mr.

---

[1] To James Madison, January 24, 1803. Annals of Congress, p. 1066.
[2] To the Secretary of State, March 24, 1803. *Ibid.*, p. 1083.
[3] To Madison, March 3, 1803. *Ibid.*, p. 1083.

Livingston, and who is presumed to have gained some insight into the present sentiments of the French Cabinet." [1]

The very same day Du Pont was able to write Jefferson that he had several times seen Talleyrand and Lebrun and that the French Government had decided to give every possible satisfaction to the United States. On April 6, he added, without giving any detail, that good progress had been made; but that he had not told everything to Livingston.

There is little doubt that the letter of Du Pont made Jefferson delay any strong measure in the Mississippi Valley affair and stayed the hand of the God of War. If negotiations had been broken off at that point, it was the intention of the British government "to send an expedition to occupy New Orleans." [2] What the consequences of such an action would have been can easily be surmised.

The rest of the story lies outside of our province, since Jefferson had nothing to do directly with it. Barbé-Marbois has told the dramatic scene of Easter Sunday, April 10, 1803, when Bonaparte called in two ministers and gave the first indication that he considered the whole colony lost and that it might be better to give it up entirely. The next morning the First Consul requested Marbois to act as plenipotentiary and to see Livingston at once. When Monroe arrived, a preliminary understanding had been reached. The treaty was concluded on May 4 and signed four days later, although it was antedated and marked April 30.

The question of deciding whether Jefferson had foreseen the possibility of acquiring the whole territory of Louisiana and had given to Monroe instructions to that effect has provided his biographers, whether friendly or unfriendly, with a nice bone to pick. It seems here that a distinction must be established between the wishes of the President and what he considered

[1] March 2, 1803. Annals of Congress, p. 1098.
[2] King to Livingston, May 7, 1803. *Ibid.*, p. 1803.

within the range of actual possibilities.   From his letters to
Lafayette and Du Pont de Nemours, it is easily perceived that
he was unequivocally opposed to the reinstatement of France
on any part of the continent.   On this point he never varied.
On the other hand, he had soon become convinced that France
would never relinquish such an enormous territory without a
compensation that the United States could not afford to pay.
He limited his plans very soon to the acquisition of the two
Floridas, which he supposed had been made part of the transaction, so as to give the United States access to the Gulf, while
taking a strong position on the Mississippi River.   In his letter
to Du Pont de Nemours dated February 1, 1803, he reiterated
that the United States wanted and needed the Floridas, that
"whatever power, other than ourselves, holds the country east
of the Mississippi, becomes our natural enemy."   But further
he did not go.   On February 27, 1803, he wrote to Governor
Harrison a letter which seems to settle the question : "We
bend our whole views to the purchase and settlement of the
country on the Mississippi, from its mouth to its northern re-
gions, that we may be able to present as strong a front on our
western as on our eastern border, and plant on the Mississippi
itself the means of its own defence."   As for the Indians, they
were either "to be incorporated with us as citizens of the United
States, or removed beyond the Mississippi."   Finally the letter
written on July 29 to Livingston and Monroe is as definite a
statement as can be desired and ought to set the controversy
at rest :

When these (your instructions and commission) were made out,
the object of the most sanguine was limited to the establishment
of the Mississippi as our boundary.   It was not presumed, that more
could be sought by the United States, either with a chance of success,
or perhaps without being suspected of a greedy ambition, than the
island of New Orleans and the two Floridas. . . .   Nor was it to
be supposed that in case the French government should be willing to

part with more than the territory on our side of the Mississippi, an arrangement with Spain for restoring the territory on the other side, would not be preferred to a sale of it to the United States. . . . The effect of such considerations was diminished by no information, or just presumptions whatever.[1]

Whatever may have been Jefferson's satisfaction on hearing the news, he did not write himself to the commissioners to congratulate and thank them in the name of the nation. He was not the man to make grand gestures. The Virginian could be as self-restrained as any New Englander, as appears from a letter to Horatio Gates in which the two envoys are mentioned: "I find our opposition very willing to pluck feathers from Monroe, although not fond of sticking them into Livingston's coat. The truth is, both have a just proportion of merit; and were it necessary or proper, it would be shown that each has rendered peculiar services and of important value."[2] More than that he did not say, and probably said very little more to Monroe, his friend and "*élève*" when he came back from France.

Congress had been called for October 17, to ratify the treaty; but before that date, Jefferson sent letters and questionnaires all around in order to gather any possible information on the limits, geography, resources and condition of the inhabitants of the newly acquired territory. In a letter to Breckenridge (August 12, 1803), he expressed himself more freely than to any other correspondent. First of all he admitted that he was somewhat disappointed at having being unable to secure the Floridas. But it was only a delayed opportunity; sooner or later Spain would engage in some war, and the realistic politician added: "If we push them strongly with one hand, holding out a price in the other, we shall certainly obtain the Floridas, and all in good time." For the present, the United States, without claiming possession of the Spanish territories, would act pretty freely: "In the meantime, without waiting

[1] Annals of Congress, p. 1167.   [2] July 11, 1803. Memorial Edition, X, 402.

for permission, we shall enter into the exercise of the natural right we have always insisted on with having a right of innocent passage through them to the ocean. We shall prepare her to see us practice on this, and she will not oppose it by force."

He had already heard many objections to the treaty; of all of them he disposed summarily. He did not take seriously the danger mentioned by the Federalists of seeing a fringe of States, different in interest from the original States, form along the Mississippi and threaten the homogeneity of the Union. If it came to the worst, it would be better for the United States to have as neighbors along the western border a Federation of States inhabited by a people of the same blood than a Spanish or French dominion. Then Jefferson prophetically outlined the development of the West as he foresaw it. The inhabited part of Louisiana was to become a new State as soon as possible. Above Pointe Coupée, the best procedure was probably to move the Indians across the river and to fill the vacant territories with white colonists. "When we shall be full on this side, we may lay off a range of States on the western bank from the head to the mouth, and so, range after range, advancing compactly as we multiply."

As to the constitutionality of the purchase, he admitted there was no article of the Constitution authorizing the holding of foreign territory, and still less contemplating the incorporation of foreign nations into the Union. "The executives, in seizing the fugitive occurrence which so much advances the good of their country, have done an act beyond the Constitution." They were justified in doing it, however, just as much as a guardian has the right to invest money for his ward in purchasing an adjacent territory and saying to him when of age: "I did this for your good; I pretend to no right to bind you; you may disavow me, and I must get out of the scrape as I can: I thought it my duty to risk myself for you." This is another instance when Jefferson the lawyer discarded what he called "meta-physical subtleties" to look squarely at the facts and to do his duty as he saw it, "as a faithful servant."

The third annual message of the President was read before Congress on October 17. Written in simple language like all the State papers of Jefferson, it contained a graceful word for "the enlightened government of France", and pointed out soberly the advantages that would accrue to the United States from the purchase:

While the property and sovereignty of the Mississippi and its waters secure an independent outlet for the produce of the western States, and an uncontrolled navigation through their whole course, free from collision with other powers and the dangers to our peace from that source, the fertility of the country, its climate and extent, promise in due season important aids to our treasury, an ample provision for our posterity, and a wide-spread field for the blessings of freedom and equal laws.

The President avoided any specific recommendation on the measures to be adopted to incorporate into the Union the recently acquired territories, resting on the wisdom of Congress to determine the "measures which may be necessary for the immediate occupation and temporary government of the country; for rendering the change of government a blessing to our newly adopted brethren; for securing to them the rights of conscience and of property; for confirming to the Indian inhabitants their occupancy and self-government." The Senate ratified the treaty after a two-day discussion, the members voting strictly on party lines. It came before the House on the twenty-second. The discussion was hot and more prolonged; doubts as to the French title to the purchase were raised; doubts as to the constitutionality of the measure. The treaty proper was ratified on October 25, and on November 3 acts were passed authorizing the issue of bonds in order to pay France.

A letter of Jefferson to Livingston contains the epilogue of the negotiations. It is another very interesting instance of the way Jefferson knew how to handle men. Pichon, the French minister, had been instructed by his Government to secure a clause to the ratification providing "against any failure in time or other circumstances of execution on the part of the United States." Jefferson took the matter in hand himself and demonstrated to Pichon that in case the French Government insisted upon such a proviso, the United States would insert a similar clause of protestation "leaving the matter where it stood before." He insisted that it was to throw on the good faith of both nations a doubt most unpleasant to an honest man to entertain, and concluded that he had "more confidence in the word of the First Consul than in all the parchment we could sign." What could the Frenchman do except to bow politely and acquiesce, and "like an able and honest minister (which he is in the highest degree) he undertook to do what he knew his employers would do themselves, were they spectators of all existing circumstances, and exchange the ratifications purely and simply." "So," concluded Jefferson, "this instrument goes to the world as an evidence of the candor and confidence of the nations in each other, which will have the best effects."

A last point remained to be settled. It was suspected that Spain had entered a formal protest against the whole transaction, "since the First Consul had broken a solemn promise not to alienate the country to any nation." On that point Jefferson refused to express any opinion : "We answered that these were questions between France and Spain which they must settle together ; that we derived our title from the First Consul and did not doubt his guarantee of it." Meanwhile measures were provided to take formal possession from Laussat after he should have received the territory from Spain. "If he is not so disposed *we* shall take possession and it will rest with the Government of France, by adopting the act as their own, then to settle the latter with Spain."[1] In order to provide for any eventuality, the governor of the Mississippi was ordered to move down with General Wilkinson all his troops at hand to take formal possession.

Thus the transaction fraught with so many dangers came to what Jefferson called in a letter to Priestley (January 29, 1804) "a happy denouement", thanks "to a friendly and frank development of causes and effects in our part and good sense enough in Bonaparte to see that the train was unavoidable and would change the face of the world."

If Jefferson took liberties with the Constitution in the matter of the purchase, he was equally broad-minded in his construction of the treaty.   One of the articles provided that the inhabitants of the territories ceded by France "will be incorporated into the Union and admitted as soon as possible according to the principles of the Federal Constitution to the enjoyment of all the advantages and immunities of the citizens of the United States" (Article III).   This was precisely what Jefferson was firmly resolved not to do.   Theoretically, and according to his often expressed views on self-government, he should have taken steps to admit immediately the newly acquired territory into the Union and to allow the inhabitants to decide on a constitution.   Practically, he considered that they were unfitted for self-government and, although he did not formally declare it at the time, he was convinced that self-government could not succeed with a population mainly French and Spanish.   The letter he wrote on the subject to Du Pont de Nemours is almost disarming in its naïveté :

We are preparing a form of government for the Territory of Louisiana. We shall make it as mild and free, as they are able to bear, all persons residing there concurring in the information that they were neither gratified, nor willing to exercise the rights of an elective government. The immense swarm flocking thither of

[1] Memorial Edition, X, 424.

Americans used to that exercise, will soon prepare them to receive the necessary change.[1]

It was impossible to state more clearly that representative government could not be granted to Louisiana as long as the inhabitants remained essentially French. Only when checked and controlled by the "immense swarm" of American pioneers and colonists spreading all over the territory could they be admitted to the immunities and advantages of American citizens. This attitude of Jefferson, which seems in flagrant contradiction with his theories, can astonish only those who see in him a world prophet of the democratic faith; while his only ambition was to build an American democracy, on strictly American principles, for the sole benefit of American citizens, true heirs and continuators of the old Anglo-Saxon principles.

But his vision of a greater America extended even beyond the limits of the Louisiana Purchase. In January, 1803, just one week before Monroe's appointment as special envoy to Paris, he had sent a message to Congress to recommend that a sum of twenty-five hundred dollars be appropriated to send "an intelligent officer with a party of 10 or 12 men to explore even to the Western Ocean and to bring back all possible information on the Indian tribes, the fauna and flora of the region." The intelligent officer was Merriwether Lewis, private secretary to the President, who was to engage in this "literary pursuit" in a region claimed by Spain. It was calmly assumed, however, that "the expiring state of Spain's interests there" would render such a voyage a matter of indifference to this nation. Jefferson made the expedition his own concern; he drew up the most detailed instructions for the mission. He even wrote for Lewis "a letter of general credit" in his own hand and signed with his name, by which the captain was authorized to draw on "the Secretaries of State, the Treasury of War, and of the Navy of the United States according as he might find his draughts

[1] Jefferson Papers. Library of Congress, January 19, 1804.

would be most negotiable, for the purpose of obtaining money or necessaries for himself and men." [1] Practically unlimited resources were placed at the disposal of the expedition. Jefferson kept his former secretary minutely informed of the new possibilities opened up by the negotiations with France, writing him on July 4, 11, 15, November 16 and January 13. On January 22, he sent new instructions: the United States had "now become sovereigns of the country" Lewis was going to explore; it was no longer necessary to keep up the pretense of a "literary pursuit", and the President felt authorized in proposing to the Indians the establishment of official connections, and in declaring frankly to them that "they will find in us faithful friends and protectors." So Jefferson was no longer thinking of the Mississippi as the ultimate frontier of the United States. He already foresaw the time when the Empire would extend from the Atlantic to the Pacific.

Besides providing the United States with almost unlimited possibilities of growth, the Louisiana Purchase had eliminated the immediate danger of a conflict with France, and the chances of remaining at peace with Europe had considerably increased. "I now see nothing which need interrupt the friendship between France and this country," wrote Jefferson to Cabanis. "We do not despair of being always a peaceable nation. We think that peaceable means may be devised of keeping nations in the path of justice towards us, by making justice their interest, and injuries to react on themselves. Our distance enables us to pursue a course which the crowded situation of Europe renders perhaps impracticable there." [2]

There remained, however, a danger point in the policies of the British navy with regard to contraband. The United States had now to make a strenuous effort to bring the British to abandon their "right" to search neutral vessels on the high

---

[1] July 4, 1803. Memorial Edition, X, 398.
[2] July 12, 1803. *Ibid.*, X, 404.

seas in order to impress British sailors found on those vessels, and to use American ports as cruising stations. Not only was this attitude of Great Britain contrary to justice but it was also contrary to these natural laws on which rested Jefferson's system of Americanism; above all, they were most obnoxious and detrimental to American commerce, for "Thornton says they watch our trade to prevent contraband. We say it is to plunder under pretext of contraband." [1]

Meanwhile the President was receiving the most pessimistic accounts from Monroe, lost in the maze of European intrigues, and almost losing faith in the future security of the United States. One of his letters of the spring of 1804 had mentioned the possibility of a dark plot against America. France and England might forget their old differences and operate a reconciliation at the expense of the United States; they would form a combination to divide between them the North American continent, France repossessing Louisiana, while England would reannex the United States to the British dominions. A mad scheme if ever there was one, and it is very much to be doubted that it was ever contemplated by any responsible Frenchman. Jefferson's confidence in the remoteness of the American continent was not disturbed for a minute by these alarming reports. He excused Monroe on the ground that a person placed in Europe was very apt to believe the old nations endowed with limitless resources and power. Everything was possible, even a return of the Bourbons; but "that they and England joined, could recover us to British dominion, is impossible. If things are not so, then human reason is of no aid in conjecturing the conduct of nations." Still the policy of watchful waiting was more than ever in order. Every point of friction was to be eliminated, one of the first measures being to accept the "Louisianais" to full citizenship and thus bring to an end the patronage of France. Another step was to enforce strictly the rule against

[1] To Madison, August 25, 1803. Memorial Edition, X, 412.

British cruisers in American harbors, so that "each may see un-equivocally what is unquestionably true, that we may be very possibly driven into her scale by unjust conduct in the other." [1]

Thus was fixed not in theory but in practice a policy of neutrality fraught with risks. The most apparent danger was that both belligerents might turn against the United States. But of that Jefferson was not afraid, as an alliance between the two hereditary enemies seemed inconceivable. In the meantime proper preparations were to be made to insure the security of the American flag.

The message of October 17, 1803, contained an earnest appeal to "complete neutrality." Neutrality of fact the Government was decided to observe, and most of all to view in a disinterested way the carnage in Europe.

How desirable it must be, in a government like ours, to see its citizens adopt individually the views, the interests and the conduct which their country should pursue, divesting themselves of those passions and partialities which tend to lessen useful friendships and to embarrass and embroil us in the calamitous scenes of Europe.

Then came a passage which sounds strangely familiar to those of us who have lived through the last fourteen years:

Confident, fellow citizens, that you will duly estimate the importance of neutral dispositions toward the observance of neutral conduct, that you will be sensible how much it is our duty to look on the bloody arena spread before us with commiseration indeed, but with no other wish than to see it closed, I am persuaded you will cordially cherish these dispositions in all communications with your constituents.

A nation neutral in speech and neutral in thought, willing to intervene only to help the victims of the war or as an arbiter between the belligerents, such was at that time the ideal of Jefferson as it was to be for several years the ideal of Woodrow Wilson, and to a large degree the permanent ideal of the United States during their whole history.

[1] To James Madison, August 15, 1804.　Memorial Edition, XI, 45.

CHAPTER III

"SELF-PRESERVATION IS PARAMOUNT TO ALL LAW"

WHEN, on the fourth of March, 1805, Jefferson began his second term, he had a right to review with some complacency the achievements of his first administration. To foreign affairs he scarcely granted a short paragraph, but he pointed out with great details the suppression of unnecessary offices, the reduction of taxes, the fact that the Federal Government was almost entirely supported by duties levied on importations, so that "it may be the pleasure and pride of an American to ask, what farmer, what mechanic, what laborer, ever sees a tax-gatherer of the United States?" The Louisiana Purchase had increased enormously the potential riches of the country and removed a very dangerous source of conflict. The right bank of the Mississippi was to be settled by "our own brethren and children" and not by "strangers of another family."

Of great interest was the long passage given to Indian affairs. Jefferson's sympathy for the red men dated from the early days of his youth, when he had seen the chiefs stop at the house of his father on their way to Williamsburg. He had handsomely stood in defense of them in the "Notes on Virginia." Now he was regarding them with the commiseration their history began to inspire:

Endowed with the faculties and the rights of men, breathing an ardent love of liberty and independence, and occupying a country which left them no desire but to be undisturbed, the stream of over-flowing population directed itself on these shores, without power to divert, or habits to contend against, they have been overwhelmed by the current, or driven before it.

This was certainly a very regrettable situation, but the idea of questioning the right of an overflowing population to occupy scarcely populated territories did not for a moment enter Jefferson's mind. To deny such a right would have been not only detrimental to the very existence of the United States, but also a denial of the "right" of "our Saxons ancestors" to settle in England. Furthermore, the President was confronted with a certain set of facts and not with a theory. The territory of which the Indians had so long enjoyed undisturbed possession was growing narrower every day. With the recent acquisition of Louisiana, it was to be foreseen that they would not be able to roam freely much longer in the vast territories extending west of the Mississippi. They were now "reduced within limits too narrow for the hunter's state." The only thing they could do was to submit to new economic conditions, to settle down and become farmers, and it was the duty of the government "to encourage them to that industry which alone can enable them to maintain their place in existence, and to prepare them in time for that state of society, which to bodily comforts adds the improvement of mind and morals."

The President had no patience with

. . . the interested and crafty individuals among them who inculcate a sanctimonious reverence for the customs of their ancestors; that whatsoever they did, must be done through all time; that reason is a false guide, and to advance under its counsel, in their physical, moral, or political condition, is a perilous innovation; that their duty is to remain as their Creator made them.

The attitude of these reactionaries among the Indians gave Jefferson an opportunity to hit at one stroke the medicine men and the clergymen who were attacking him fiercely.

In short, my friends, among them is seen the action and counteraction of good sense and bigotry; they, too, have their anti-philosophers, who find an interest in keeping things in their present state, who dread reformation, and exert all their faculties to maintain the ascendency of habit over the duty of improving our reason, and obeying its mandates.

The New England and New York clergymen who had stood with the Federalists knew exactly where they belonged.

But if the President was unwilling to let the attacks to which he had been subjected pass entirely unnoticed, he maintained at the same time that no official steps must be taken to repress in any way freedom of speech and freedom of the press. In more emphatic terms than ever before, he reasserted the fundamental doctrine he had defended against all comers for more than twenty-five years:

During this course of administration, and in order to disturb it, the artillery of the press has been levelled against us, charged with whatsoever its licentiousness could devise or dare. These abuses of an institution so important to freedom and science, are deeply to be regretted, inasmuch as they tend to lessen its usefulness, and to sap its safety; they might, indeed, have been corrected by the wholesome punishments reserved and provided by the laws of the several States against falsehood and defamation; but public duties, more urgent press on the time of public servants, and the offenders have therefore been left to find their punishment in the public indignation.

Thus were the Callender and the Federalist pamphleteers handed over to the public to be dealt with, according to the merits of their cases.

The address ended with a new appeal to harmony, with the hope that truth, reason and well-understood self-interest might enlighten the last opponents of true republicanism. It ended also with a sort of prayer which may or may not have expressed the religious beliefs of Jefferson at the time:

I shall need the favor of that Being in whose hands we are, who led our forefathers, as Israel of old, from their native land, and planted them in a country flowing with all the necessaries and comforts of life; who has covered our infancy with his providence, and our riper years with his wisdom and power, and to whose goodness I ask you to join me in supplications.

Jefferson had not forgotten that twenty years before he had proposed that the seal of the United States should represent the Children of Israel led by a pillar of light. As much as the Puritans he was convinced that the American people was a chosen people, that they have been gifted with superior wisdom and strength, and this belief was just as much part of his creed of Americanism as it was the more openly expressed doctrine of more recent presidents of the United States.

With these brilliant and reassuring prospects before his eyes, Jefferson entered his second term. Little did he believe at that time that the four years before him were to be the most agitated and most distressing of his long career. The man whose fondest hope was to "secure peace, friendship and approbation of all nations" was to begin a series of police operations against the Barbary pirates of the Mediterranean and was confronted, at a time, with the possibility of a war with Spain, a war with England and a war with France. His philosophical toga was torn to shreds by the thorns strewn along the tortuous paths of international relations. At home he had to use all his ingenuity and resourcefulness to keep together disaffected elements in the Republican Party, to withstand the attacks launched in Congress by John Randolph of Roanoke, the impulsive, erratic and dangerous leader of the discontented Republicans. The man who had framed the Kentucky resolutions and had stood as the advocate of States rights was reproached with using his influence with Congress to pass the Embargo Act, "more arbitrary, more confiscatory" than any measure ever proposed by the Federalists. The man who had protested against the sedition bills had to repress the seditious attempts of the former Vice President of the United States. It seemed as if an evil genius had taken a malicious pleasure in making every effort to test the President in every possible way, and to confront him with the necessity of renouncing his most cherished principles. Jefferson did not come out of the ordeal without scars and deep wounds; but whatever may have been his deficiencies and his faults, whatever sins he may have committed, he kept his faith in the ultimate wisdom of public opinion and never tried to suppress by coercion the criticism to which he was subjected.

As a matter of fact, the roseate view of the situation presented by Jefferson in his second Inaugural Address was hardly warranted by facts. Even before the close of the first term, Randolph, who had been the standard bearer of the Republicans in the House, had shown signs of discontent. He had supported the "Remonstrance of the people of Louisiana", protesting that one of the essential provisions had been violated and that they should be admitted at once to "all the rights, advantages and immunities of citizens." On the other hand, Aaron Burr, even while remaining in office, had already paved the way for the dark and romantic machinations which were to culminate with his trial before Marshall at Richmond.

The story of Burr's conspiracy deserves a special place among American "*causes célèbres*." It has been told many times, and very vividly, but only the pen of Alexandre Dumas could do justice to it. Many efforts have been made to whitewash the memory of the chief conspirator, to throw most of the odium on Wilkinson and on Jefferson who, according to his enemies, would have gone out of his way to obtain the condemnation of a man who could not be proved guilty of any overt act, although there is no doubt that he had originated some of the most reprehensible schemes against the safety of his country. But Americans always had a foible for soldiers of fortune, for adventurers who dreamed of conquering new empires; for in them they see the magnification of the frontier spirit which for so long constituted one of the "pillars" of American civilization.

By an extraordinary trick of heredity, this adventurer, who should have been a Spanish conquistador, this arch plotter who had the insinuating ways of the Florentine, the tortuous and complicated mind so often considered as a privilege of the Europeans, was the great-grandson of Jonathan Edwards and of pure New England descent. He had fought bravely and enthusiastically in the Revolutionary War, he was a lawyer of no mean achievement; but his thirst for popularity, applause and success was beyond imagination, and this Machiavellic politician lacked in an extraordinary degree common sense and political vision. Had he withdrawn from the run for the presidency in time, had he gracefully accepted the second rank in December, 1800, he would have had a great political career before him. But to the last minute he refused to say the word that was expected from him; he accepted without protest the votes of the Federalists and was considered as a traitor to his party even before he took office. As early as January, 1804, he had gone to Jefferson and, after complaining that the President did not show him the same friendship as before, he had offered to resign at once if he were appointed to some foreign embassy. After Burr had left without obtaining any definite answer, Jefferson put down on paper a complete account of the conversation and dryly concluded:

I should here notice, that Colonel Burr must have thought that I could swallow strong things in my own favor, when he founded his acquiescence in the nomination as Vice-President, to his desire of promoting my honor, the being with me; whose company and conversation had always been fascinating with him etc.[1]

Disappointed in this respect, Aaron Burr turned his eyes towards New York, where he had worked so successfully during the preceding election. The post of governor happened to be vacant, and in February Burr was chosen by the discontented

[1] "Anas", January 26, 1804.

Republicans of the State to run for governor. It seems quite
certain that, if he had been elected, the movement for secession
already strong in New England would have received a new
impetus and that a desperate effort would have been made to
shake off "the rule of Virginia."   When, after a savage campaign marked by invectives, brawls and riots, Burr was finally
defeated, he could and did rightly attribute his failure to
Hamilton who, from the very beginning, opposed his candidacy.   A personal encounter was decided and the two adversaries met on the bank of the Hudson, pistol in hand, in a duel to
the death.   It has always been said that Hamilton did not take
aim and fired first.   Burr fired deliberately and Hamilton,
fatally wounded, fell to the ground, to die the next day.

Found guilty of murder by a grand jury, and in fact already
a fugitive from justice, Burr hid at first in Georgia and there
concocted the most extraordinary plan to effect a separation
of the western part of the United States with the help and
financial assistance of England.   Although evidence was not
procurable at the time of his trial, there is no doubt that he
thought the scheme feasible; that back in Washington, and
when he was presiding over the impeachment proceedings of
Judge Chase, the Vice President of the United States was
prudently sounding the delegates of the western States, in-
gratiating himself to them and that the wildest dreams of empire
were haunting his feverish imagination.

As soon as the session was over, Colonel Burr started out for a
tour of the western States and, on an island of the Ohio, met by
chance the philosopher-planter Blennerhasset, the innocent
victim of his plots.   Leaving Blennerhasset, Burr went to
Cincinnati, Frankfort, Nashville.   He met Andrew Jackson,
the uncouth son of the frontier, and Wilkinson, the general in
charge of the western territory.   After a visit to New Orleans,
where he was greatly elated by the discontent of the population,
he went back to Saint Louis to discuss the situation with

Wilkinson. Whether he still adhered to the original plan of separating the western from the eastern States is to a considerable degree doubtful. His immediate object seems rather to have been to lead an expedition of adventurers against Mexico, in case the war that was threatening between the United States and Spain should break out. It must be admitted that the plan in itself was not particularly objectionable to the Government, but it soon appeared that this scheme too had to be given up. After vainly attempting to secure assistance from the British Government, Burr, changing from conqueror to farmer, undertook to buy, with Blennerhasset, a grant of several hundred thousand acres on the Washita River, in Northern Louisiana, in order to establish there a model colony.

The rest of the story is well known. Rumors of a conspiracy grew in the West without disturbing at first the security of the Federal Government. Burr, summoned to appear before the district attorney of Frankfort, surrendered himself, but was twice discharged and continued his preparations for the settlement of Washita. Jefferson did not move until he received from Wilkinson a confidential message purporting to be the transcription of a ciphered letter sent by Burr. The President was so alarmed that he issued at once a proclamation, warning the people that a conspiracy had been discovered and directing the arrests of the conspirators and the seizure of "all vessels, arms and military stores." Wilkinson, eager to show his loyalty to the Government, arrested "without warrant" several emissaries of Burr. One of them was released, but two, Bollman and Swartwout, were sent out by sea to Baltimore and thence to Washington, where they were kept in the military barracks. In a special message to Congress, Jefferson apprised the Senate and the House of the facts "touching an illegal combination of private individuals against the peace and safety of the Union, and a military expedition planned by them against the territories of a power in amity with the United

States, with the measures pursued for suppressing the same."
(January 22, 1807)

Shortly after Marshall, in Washington, had refused to indict
Bollman and Swartwout on the count of "levying war" against
the United States, Burr was finally arrested and taken under
military escort to Richmond, there to be delivered to the
civil authorities after Marshall had signed a special warrant
(March 26, 1807). After long skirmishes between the prosecution and the defense, legal moves and countermoves, Burr was
indicted under two counts, — treason and high misdemeanor.
On the first charge the jury rendered a verdict to the effect that
"We of the jury say that Aaron Burr is not proved guilty under
this indictment by any evidence submitted to us; we therefore
find him not guilty."

This was a most unusual and illegal form of rendering a
verdict and the jury evidently intended to emphasize the fact
that the evidence submitted did not warrant a conviction,
although they reserved their opinion as to the real guilt of
Colonel Burr. Marshall overruled objections to the form of
the verdict which threatened a reopening of the case and
decided that it would be recorded as "not guilty." Burr was
soon recommitted on the second count and declared not guilty
by a second jury. Upon which a third charge was brought in by
the prosecution and Burr summoned to appear at the session of
the Circuit Court of the United States to be held at Chillicothe
in January, 1808. He never appeared and his bond was forfeited;
it is more than doubtful that he would have been convicted.

A serious discussion of the merits of the case would necessi-
tate a minute analysis of all the evidence placed before the jury
and cannot be undertaken here. Several attempts have been
made to rehabilitate Aaron Burr's memory, although certain
facts are so patent that they cannot be overlooked by the most
indulgent biographers. It is a curious bend of the popular
mind that the greatness of the conspiracy seems an excuse and

attenuation of the most evident guilt. There was something apparently heroic in the ambition of that man who wanted to carve for himself an empire in the wilderness and to plunder the treasures of the mysterious Southwest. Then, by contrast, the obstinacy of Jefferson in using every means in his power and in the power of the Federal Government in order to obtain a conviction, has been represented as a display of pettiness unworthy of the chief of a great nation. Nor is this tendency restricted to the impulsive and emotional masses; it creeps into the accounts of the trial given by the most judicial historians, and I am not certain that it is entirely absent from Beveridge's treatment of the Richmond proceedings.

Legally speaking, it is difficult to find fault with the findings of Marshall, with the definitions he gave of "treason" and "overt act", with his sifting of the evidence and, except in one or two cases, with his behavior during the trial. On the other hand, Jefferson has been accused of having unduly interfered by sending detailed instructions to the district attorney, by coaching him on several occasions, and by attempting directly and indirectly to arouse public opinion against a man who was on trial for his life, but who finally could not be convicted on any count. After such an interval of time, it is easy to find fault with the conduct of the Executive, and it cannot be denied that he acted in a very high-handed manner, condoned acts which were technically illegal and maintained without sufficient proofs of Burr's guilt that there was not "a candid man in the United States who did not believe some one, if not all, of these overt acts to have taken place." [1]

On the other hand, if we try to place ourselves in the atmosphere of the time, it is equally easy to find explanations that to a large extent justify Jefferson's attitude. It must be remembered that the President was not unaware of Burr's intention "to form a coalition of the five eastern States, with New York

[1] To W. B. Giles, April 20, 1807. Memorial Edition, XI, 187.

and New Jersey, under the new appellation of the Seven Eastern States."[1] If Burr's machination with the English minister to effect a separation of the western States were still unknown, there was little doubt about his plans. All of Burr's ambitious schemes failed miserably, but it is perfectly natural that the Government should have been seriously alarmed at the time. They did not know of Wilkinson's shameful deals with Spain, but they had every reason to believe that a man who had already plotted a secession of the western territory and happened to be in charge of that territory and in command of the Federal army was scarcely to be depended upon in an emergency. For years the West had been very restive, New Orleans was full of discontented Creoles, and if war had not been officially declared with both England and Spain, it was felt that it could break out at any time. None of these considerations could be brought out before the jury, but they amply warranted some action of the Executive. The first step taken by Jefferson was to warn the people of the existence of a conspiracy. If we remember again that Aaron Burr was at that time roaming at will in a part of the country sparsely settled, where he counted many friends, where communications with Washington were slow and rare, it is difficult to see how the President could have done less.

After the conspirators were arrested the situation changed entirely. They had been delivered to the civil authorities, they were to appear before a regular court and given trial by jury; they no longer constituted a public danger. It must be admitted that Jefferson himself declared to his French friends, Lafayette and Du Pont de Nemours, that Burr never had a chance to succeed and "that the man who could expect to effect this, with American material must be a fit subject for Bedlam."[2] This is hard to reconcile with the statement

[1] To Gideon Granger, March 9, 1814. Memorial Edition, XIV, 113.
[2] To Lafayette, July 14, 1807. *Ibid.*, XI, 277.

which comes immediately after, that "the seriousness of the crime demands more serious punishment", and particularly with the instructions sent to George Hay. One may suspect that Jefferson saw in the trial of Burr an opportunity to test the loyalty of the Chief Justice to the Constitution and to the Government and allowed himself to be carried away by political preoccupations which had nothing to do with Colonel Burr. This appears clearly in one of the letters to Giles :

> If there has ever been an instance in this or the preceding administrations, of federal judges so applying principles of law as to condemn a federal or acquit a republican offender, I should have judged them in the present case with some charity. All this, however, will work well. The nation will judge both the offender and judges for themselves.[1]

This was reiterated in the instructions sent to George Hay after the first acquittal of Burr, that no witness should be permitted to depart

> . . . until his testimony has been committed to writing, either as delivered in court, or as taken by yourself in the presence of Burr's counsel. . . . These whole proceedings will be laid before Congress, that they may decide, whether the defect has been in the evidence of guilt, or in the law, or in the application of the law, and that they may provide the proper remedy for the past and the future.

The intention to scrutinize the documents to uncover any bias of Marshall and use any such evidence against the Chief Justice is even openly admitted : "I must pray you also to have an authentic copy of the record made out (without saying for what) and to send it to me; if the Judge's opinions make out a part of it, then I must ask a copy of them, either under his hand, if he delivers one signed, or duly proved by affidavit." [2] Who could deny after reading this that Jefferson's intention was to push vigorously the attack against the judiciary, and to

---

[1] To William B. Giles, April 20, 1807.   Memorial Edition, XI, 187.
[2] To George Hay, September 4, 1807.   *Ibid.*, XI, 360.

institute impeachment proceedings against Marshall on the slightest justification? Thus the trial of Burr became a test of strength between the executive and the judiciary, between the President and the Chief Justice; it was fought out in the courtroom the more fiercely as the two antagonists were kinsmen and brought into it the obstinacy and animosity of Southern feudists.

Marshall came out as the stanch and unshakable champion of legality, and Jefferson did not refrain from using the arguments and reasonings resorted to by the Federalists when the Sedition Act was passed. There was little excuse for a man of his legal training in believing that Burr could be convicted and punished for his "intentions" to commit a crime, and the prosecution failed to bring in sufficient proof of Aaron Burr's guilt. It would have been more dignified and more consistent with Jefferson's theories if, after the conspirator was made powerless, the President had remained silent. That, however, he could not do. Early in October, he called back Attorney-general Robert Smith in order to prepare a selection and digestion of the documents respecting Burr's treason and, in his message to Congress, on October 27, if he did not use the word treason, he still accused Burr of "enterprise against the public peace." He assumed responsibility and claimed credit for the measures that had permitted "to dissipate before their explosion plots engendering on the Mississippi." He laid before Congress the proceedings and evidence exhibited on the arraignment of the principal offenders. Finally, he concluded that Burr's acquittal was evidence that there was something wrong somewhere, and that the nation could not remain defenceless against such dangers. "The framers of our constitution certainly supposed they had guarded, as well their government against destruction by treason, as their citizens against oppression, under pretence of it; and if these ends are not attained, it is of importance to inquire by what means more effectual they may be secured."

A year later, writing to Doctor James Brown about the measures of repression taken by Wilkinson in New Orleans, Jefferson presented what he considered a full justification of his conduct:

I do wish to see these people get what they deserved; and under the maxim of the law itself, that *inter arma silent leges*, that in an encampment expecting daily attack from a powerful enemy, self preservation is paramount to all law. I expected that instead of invoking the forms of the law, to cover traitors, all good citizens would have concurred in securing them. Should we have ever gained our Revolution, if we had bound our hands by manacles of the law, not only in the beginning, but in any part of the revolutionary conflict? [1]

This was exactly the sort of reasoning that Jefferson had opposed so strenuously when advanced by his political opponents. Apparently he had completely reversed his position after getting in the saddle, which was very illogical and perhaps very damnable, but also very human. He was now, to use the vivid expression of a French statesman, "on the other side of the barricade", and he saw things in a different light. But if this episode can serve to illustrate the inconsistency of the philosopher, it constitutes also a most striking refutation of the accusations of Jacobinism so often launched against Jefferson; for only the Jacobin is perfectly consistent in all circumstances. More than thirty years had elapsed since Jefferson had copied the old maxim *fiat justitia ruat cælum* in his "Memorandum book" and he was still wont to repeat it, but it had taken him less than eight years of executive responsibility to make him admit that democracy does not work in times of emergency. It was a most dangerous admission, but one to be expected from a man in whom still lived the ruthless spirit of the frontier. Pioneer communities in which unrestricted and unlimited democracy prevails are pitiless for the outlaw who endangers

[1] October 27, 1808. Memorial Edition, XII, 183.

the life of the group, and are not stopped by "legal subtleties." In Jefferson there was more of the pioneer than he himself believed. For this very reason he was probably more completely and intensely an average American than if he had "acted up" to the letter of the law in every circumstance.

This was by far the most dramatic of the internal difficulties that Jefferson had to face during his second term. Burr's conspiracy obscured the attacks against Madison led by the former spokesman of Jefferson's party, John Randolph of Roanoke. But already, when Burr's trial was held in Richmond, "circumstances which seriously threatened the peace of the country" had made it a duty to convene Congress at an earlier date than usual. Once again, as under the administrations of Washington and Adams, foreign policies were to dominate and direct domestic policies, and once again America was to bear the penalty of all neutrals who try to keep out of the war in a world conflagration.

CHAPTER IV

"PEACE AND COMMERCE WITH EVERY NATION"

WAR is not always an unmixed curse, at least for nations who manage to remain neutral while the rest of the world is torn by calamitous conflicts. Europe's misfortune had been to some extent America's good fortune. With comparatively short intermissions, France and England were engaged in a death struggle from 1793 to 1815, and although Britannia ruled the sea, the belligerents had to resort to neutral shipping. The exports of the United States, which were valued at only nineteen millions in 1791, reached ninety-four millions in 1802, and one hundred eight millions in 1807. The imports followed approximately the same curve for the corresponding dates, jumping from nineteen millions to seventy-five millions in 1802 and reaching over one hundred thirty-eight millions in 1807. If the United States had been permitted to pursue the policy outlined by Jefferson in his messages, "to cultivate the friendship of the belligerent nations by every act of justice and of incessant kindness" (October 17, 1803), "to carry a commercial inter-course with every part of the dominions of a belligerent" (January 17, 1806), a sort of commercial millennium would have been attained and the prosperity of the United States would have been boundless. But, at least at the beginning of the nine-teenth century, neither the rights of neutrals nor international law were observed by the belligerents, and neutrals were bound to suffer as well as to profit by their privileged situation.

For his conduct of foreign affairs Jefferson has been severely taken to task, not only by many of his contemporaries but by several historians, one of the most formidable critics being

Henry Adams. During his second administration, America suffered deep humiliations which aroused the national spirit. In many occasions war could have and perhaps should have been declared; the navy, which had been reduced to a minimum under Gallatin's policy of economy, could have been expanded so as to enable the country to protect herself against foreign insults. On matters concerning national honor and national pride Americans alone are qualified to pass, and I can hold no brief for Jefferson in the matter. Perhaps it would have soothed the wounds inflicted to the *amour-propre* of the nation if war had been declared against France, or England, or both, and if America had taken part in the "bloody conflicts" of Europe. It must be said, however, that one fails to see what material advantages would have resulted for the country; in this case, as in many others, Jefferson's conduct seems to have been directed by enlightened self-interest. He was most unwilling to favor and help in any way Napoleon's ambitious schemes by declaring war against England; on the other hand, the prospect of forming a *de facto* alliance with a country which on so many occasions had deliberately insulted the United States and manifestly entertained feelings of scorn and distrust toward the young republic was equally abhorrent to him. Finally, it must not be forgotten that by keeping out of the deadly conflict in which Europe was engaged, the United States were able to lay the solid foundations of an unparalleled prosperity. While the young manhood of Europe perished on the battlefields of Napoleon, the population of America grew by leaps and bounds, passing from 5,300,000 in 1800 to 7,250,000 in 1810. While the farms and the factories of the Old World were left abandoned, immense territories were put under cultivation and new industries were developed to satisfy the demands of consumers who could no longer import manufactured products from England. The whole life of the nation was quickened and the industrial revolution hastened.

When, after Waterloo, Europe resumed her peaceful pursuits, America had freed herself of economic and financial dependence from the Old World. She had become a rich, powerful and self-supporting nation. She appeared to the impoverished peoples of the earth as an economic as well as a political Eldorado. Whether the price she paid for it was too high is a question which I may be permitted to leave for others to decide.

In his second inaugural address, the President found it unnecessary to state again the directing principles of his policies, simply declaring that he had "acted up" to the declaration contained in his first inaugural. Of foreign affairs he had little to say, except to reiterate his conviction that "with nations, as well as with individuals, our interests soundly calculated, will ever be found inseparable from our moral duties." Yet there was a passing reference to possible difficulties. War sometimes could not be avoided: "it might be procured by injustice by ourselves, or by others"; and provision ought to be made in advance for such emergencies, so as "to meet all the expenses of any given year, without encroaching on the rights of future generations, by burdening them with the debts of the past." The President foresaw that, with the rapid growth of the population and the corresponding increase in revenue raised from import taxes, it would be possible

To extinguish the native right of soil within our limits, to extend those limits, and to apply such a surplus to our public debts, as places at a short day their final redemption, and that redemption once effected, the revenue thereby liberated may, by a just repartition among the states, and a corresponding amendement of the constitution, be applied, *in time of peace*, to rivers, canals, roads, arts, manufactures, education, and other great objects within each State.

One may wonder whether at that time Jefferson realized the possible consequences of such a system. We have not to seek

very far for the exact "source" of these ideas; they were taken
bodily from Hamilton's report of manufactures. It was the
same proposal to distribute subsidies and bounties from the
Federal treasury, to encourage commerce and manufactures.
Apparently what was damnable and criminal under a Federalist administration became praiseworthy under a Republican
régime.

As a matter of fact, even during Jefferson's first term, some of
the resources of the Federal treasury had to be spent in warlike
activities. Jefferson had never been able to forget the deep
humiliation he had felt when, as a minister to the Court of
France, he had been forced to negotiate with the Barbary
pirates for the redemption of American prisoners. He had been
less than six months in office when he decided to answer the new
demands of the Barbary States by sending an American fleet to
protect American commerce in the Mediterranean. To this
incident he gave a large part of his first message (December 8,
1801), and the activities of the small squadron kept in Europe
for several years, in order to blockade the pirates in their harbors, was regularly mentioned in his subsequent messages.
The tone of some passages is well worth studying. His hope
to reduce "the Barbarians of Tripoli to the desire of peace on
proper terms by the sufferings of war" (November 8, 1804); his
determination to send to Europe additional forces, "to make
Tripoli sensible that they mistake their interest in choosing war
with us; and Tunis also, should she have declared war as
we expect and almost wish" (July 18, 1804) — all this reveals
a warlike Jefferson very different from the pacifist philosopher
he is supposed to have been in all circumstances.

It was irritating enough to bear the insults of British and
French vessels to the American flag in order to keep the United
States out of a European war. To yield to the demands of a
band of pirates who could be cowed by energetic action with a
minimum of bloodshed and expenditure, would have been an

insufferable disgrace. The Barbarians had to be beaten into submission, and the European powers who did not seem to be willing to emancipate themselves from that degrading tribute could perhaps understand at the same time that there were limits to the forbearance of the United States.

With reference to England the situation was entirely different. The United States had no fleet able to cope with the English fleet. The American coasts were unprotected and the American harbors could be bombarded from the sea without even being able to make a pretense of resisting. A large navy could not be built in a day, and even if one had been improvised, the odds would have been so uneven that many American vessels would have gone down and many lives would have been lost under the fire of the British frigates. Thus for practical reasons as well as from philanthropic motives, Jefferson bent all his efforts to the preservation of peace with the great countries of Europe.

Hardly three weeks after the signature of the treaty through which he gave up Louisiana, Bonaparte declared war against England. When he received the news, Jefferson wrote a long letter to Lord Buchan in which he defined his policy:

My hope of preserving peace for our country is not founded in the greater principle of non-resistance under every wrong, but in the belief that a just and friendly conduct on our part will procure justice and friendship from others. In the existing contest, each of the combatants will find an interest in our friendship. I cannot say we shall be unconcerned spectators of this combat. We feel for human sufferings, and we wish the good of all. We shall look on, therefore, with the sensations which these dispositions and the events of the war will produce.[1]

Thus spoke Jefferson in July, 1803, and Woodrow Wilson, who borrowed more than one page from the book of his predecessor, expressed himself in almost the same words one hundred

[1] Memorial Edition, X, 399.

and eleven years later. Thus, also, would probably speak any President of the United States should a new conflagration break out to-morrow. This, to be sure, was no proclamation of neutrality and none was needed at the time ; but had Jefferson written one, he could scarcely have expressed himself more forcibly than he did in a letter sent two days later to General Horatio Gates : "We are friendly, cordially and conscientiously friendly to England. We are not hostile to France. We will be rigorously just and sincerely friendly to both."

But this fine declaration did not make Jefferson forget the immediate interests of the United States, for the preoccupation uppermost in his mind at that time was to find out how the European situation could be used to the best advantage of his own country.

In signing the treaty France had refused to give any guarantee as to the extent of the territory ceded under the Louisiana Purchase. Whether the cession included West Florida, on the occupation of which Jefferson had been so intent, was a matter of doubt. This particular point had not been pressed during the negotiations, France, according to the old maxim *caveat emptor*, taking the position that the question lay between the United States and Spain, while the United States had never abandoned the hope that they would be able to induce Bonaparte to exert pressure on Madrid so as to enable the American Government to make the most of the transaction. Soon after the treaty was signed, the United States found themselves enmeshed in one of the most complicated intrigues of European diplomacy.

While Madison and Jefferson were negotiating in Washington with the Spanish minister Yrujo, Pinkney and later Monroe negotiated in Madrid, sometimes at cross purposes but without ever losing sight of the main object. Jefferson had renewed his old contention that the United States were entitled to "all the navigable waters, rivers, creeks, bays, and inlets lying within the United States, which empty into the Gulf of Mexico east of the River Mississippi." As Henry Adams remarked, this was a most remarkable provision, as "no creeks, bays, or inlets lying within the United States emptied into the Gulf."[1] But if Jefferson's geography was faulty, his intent was perfectly clear, and every opportunity was to be used to round out the perimeter of the United States. When in October, 1804, Monroe reached Paris to push negotiations more vigorously, the plans of the United States had crystallized. They had a beautiful simplicity: to make Spain pay the claims resulting from the shutting-up of the Mississippi by Morales, to take immediate possession of Western Florida and to obtain the cession of Eastern Florida.

With the details of the diplomatic maneuvers we are not concerned here, but rather with the remarkable proposal made by Jefferson to Madison during the summer of 1805. Spain having declared war against England, the President, fearful of being "left without an ally", thought immediately of proposing "a provisional alliance with England" (August 7, 1805). This alliance was to be conditional and would become effective only in case the United States should have to declare war against France or Spain. "In that event," wrote Jefferson, "we should make common cause, and England should stipulate not to make peace without our obtaining the objects for which we go to war, to wit, the acknowledgment by Spain of the rightful boundaries of Louisiana (which we should reduce to a minimum by a secret article) and 2, indemnification for spoliation, for which purpose we should be allowed to make reprisal on the Floridas and *retain them* as an indemnification." Jefferson added that "as it was the wish of every Englishman's heart to see the United States fighting by their sides against France", the king and his ministers could do no better than to enter into an alliance and the nation would consider it "as the price and

[1] H. Adams, II, 257.

pledge of an indissoluble friendship."[1] There is little doubt that if, at this juncture, Monroe had maneuvered more skillfully, if England had showed less arrogance in her treatment of the United States, she could have secured at least the benevolent neutrality of America. But apparently England did not care for a benevolent neutrality. After Trafalgar, she was left undisputed mistress of the ocean, she could enforce her own regulations as she pleased, and she proceeded to do so.

The presidential message of December 3, 1805, had to present very "unpleasant views of violence and wrong." The coasts of America were infested by "private armed vessels, some of them with commissions, others without commissions", all of them committing enormities, sinking American merchantmen, "maltreating the crews, abandoning them in boats in the open seas or on desert shores." The same policy of "hovering on the coast" was carried on by "public armed vessels." New principles, too, had been "interloped into the law of nations, founded neither in justice nor in the usage or acknowledgment of nations"; this was an allusion to the decision of Judge Scott in the Essex case. With Spain negotiations had not had a satisfactory issue, propositions for adjusting amicably the boundaries of Louisiana had not been acceded to, and spoliation claims formerly acknowledged had again been denied.

The President concluded that, although peace was still the ultimate ideal of the United States, there were circumstances which admitted of no peaceful remedy. Some evils were "of a nature to be met by force only, and all of them may lead to it." Finally specific recommendations were made to organize the national defense: furnishing the seaports with heavy cannon, increasing the number of gunboats, classifying the militia so as to have ready a competent number of men "for offence or defence in any point where they may be wanted", prohibition of the exportations of arms and am-

[1] To James Madison, August 27, 1805. Memorial Edition, XI, 86.

munition, — such were the chief measures contemplated by the President.

In the spring of 1806, he wrote a long letter to Alexander of Russia, who had manifested a desire to have a copy of the Constitution of the United States. This was an appeal to the Czar, insisting that special articles defining the rights of neutrals in time of war be inserted in the definitive treaty of peace sooner or later to be concluded between the European belligerents. Having taken no part in the troubles of Europe, "the United States would have no part in its pacification", but it was to be hoped that some one would be found "who, looking beyond the narrow bounds of an individual nation, will take under the cover of his equity the rights of the absent and unrepresented." [1] Unfortunately, more than ten years were to elapse before that pacification of Europe so earnestly hoped for by Jefferson came about, and only a week before the British ministry had again aggravated regulations against the neutrals by issuing orders blockading the coast of the continent (April 8, 1806).

A few weeks later, Jefferson who, yielding to the pressure of Congress, had agreed to appoint a special envoy to help Monroe negotiate a commercial treaty with England, sent William Pinkney of Maryland to London. "He has a just view of things, so far as known to him," wrote Jefferson to Monroe, but he did not deem it desirable to trust him with special instructions. For Monroe alone he reserved the complete exposition of the plans then brooding in his mind. The death of Pitt would probably mark a change in the attitude of Great Britain; the President had more confidence in Mr. Fox than in any other man in England and relied entirely on "his honesty and good sense." Then came an outline of the reasoning to be put forward by Monroe: "No two countries upon earth have so many points of common interests and friendship; and their rulers must be great bunglers indeed, if, with such disposi-

[1] April 19, 1806. Memorial Edition, XI, 103.

tions, they break them asunder." England might check the United States a little on the ocean; but she should realize that nothing but her financial limitations prevented America from having a strong navy. If France provided the money, so as to equip an American fleet, the state of the ocean would be no longer problematical. If England, on the contrary, made such a proposition, an alliance of the two largest fleets "would make the world out of the continent of Europe our joint monopoly." Then Jefferson added: "we wish for neither of these scenes — We ask for peace and justice from all nations; and we will remain uprightly neutral in fact, though leaning in belief to the opinion that an English ascendency on the ocean is safer for us than that of France."

Finally, at the end of the letter, came the most extraordinarily imperialistic proposition ever made by any nation; it was the extension of a pet theory of Jefferson to the Atlantic Ocean. As he had claimed for the United States the free navigation of all the streams originating on the territory of the United States, he was ready to claim that the great current originating from the Gulf should not be considered differently, and he wrote: "We begin to broach the idea that we consider the whole Gulf Stream as of our waters, in which hostilities and cruising are to be frowned on for the present, and prohibited so soon as either consent or force will permit us." [1]

This might be thought a visionary scheme and merely a flight of imagination, if Jefferson had not expressed the same idea in identical terms in a conversation with the French minister concerning the treaty negotiated in London by Monroe and Pinkney: "Perhaps we shall obtain the right to extend our maritime jurisdiction, and to carry it as far as the effect of the Gulph Stream makes itself felt, — which would be very advantageous both to belligerents and neutrals." [2]

[1] To Colonel James Monroe, May 4, 1806. Memorial Edition, XI, 106.
[2] Turreau to Talleyrand, December 12, 1806, in H. Adams, III, 424.

These being Jefferson's views, it would have taken a far more successful negotiator than Monroe to make the British Government accept them. The treaty finally signed by the American envoys on December 1, 1806, was far from satisfactory. As a matter of fact, the American envoys had been caught between the hammer and the anvil. To the Fox blockade of April, 1806, Napoleon had answered by the Berlin Decree at the end of November, placing the British islands in a state of blockade, declaring all merchandise coming from England subject to confiscation and refusing admission into any French port to any vessel coming either from England or her colonies. Forbidden by England to trade with France, by France to trade with England, the neutrals were placed in a sorry plight. Yet not only did Monroe in his treaty recognize the right of visit and of impressing British seamen found on board American vessels, but he gave up the American claims to indemnity for outrages committed on American commerce in 1805, and accepted the most humiliating conditions concerning American trade with the French and Spanish colonies. Finally, before Monroe could obtain the signature of the British negotiators, he had to agree to an additional article by which he promised not to recognize the decree of Berlin. In less than three weeks Jefferson received Napoleon's decree, the text of the Pinkney-Monroe treaty, and the news of Lord Howick's retaliatory order requesting that no goods should be carried to France unless they first touched at an English port and paid a certain duty.

In spite of the pressing request of the Senate, Jefferson refused to communicate the text of the treaty. The explanation publicly given by the President was that Monroe had concluded the treaty before receiving information as to the points to be insisted upon, and that a new effort would be made to obtain the modification of some particularly objectionable features. "This is the statement we have given out," he wrote to Monroe, "and nothing more of the treaty has ever been made known. But depend on it, my dear Sir, that it will be considered as a hard treaty when it is known." If it appeared to Monroe that no amendment was to be hoped for, he was authorized to come home, leaving behind him Pinkney, who by procrastination would let it die and thus would give America more time "the most precious of all things to us." [1]

New instructions were sent accordingly to the American envoys at the end of May, but the problem of the relations with England became suddenly more acute during Aaron Burr's trial.

On June 22, the *Chesapeake* of the American navy, bound for the Mediterranean, was hauled up in view of Cape Henry by the *Leopard* of the British squadron, and summons were sent to Commodore Barron to deliver some British deserters he was supposed to have on board. Upon Barron's refusal, the *Leopard* opened fire and for fifteen minutes sent broadsides into the American ship, so unprepared and unready that only one shot could be fired in answer. The American flag was hauled down, British officers boarded the ship and took four deserters; after which Captain Humphreys of the *Leopard* declared to Barron that he could proceed on his way. The *Chesapeake* limped back into port, and on the twenty-fifth, Jefferson called back to Washington Dearborn and Gallatin to consider the emergency in a meeting of the Cabinet.

What his indignation over the outrage may have been is a matter of surmise. He did not express it either privately or publicly. To Governor William H. Cabell, who had sent him a special message and report, he answered diplomatically that, after consulting the Cabinet he would determine "the course which exigency and our constitutional powers call for. — Whether the outrage is a proper cause of war, belonging exclusively to Congress, it is our duty not to commit them by doing

[1] To Monroe, March 21, 1807. Memorial Edition, XI, 167.

anything which would have to be retracted." But it is certain that, even at that time, he was not ready to recommend any radical step, for he added:

This will leave Congress free to decide whether war is the most efficacious mode of redress in our case, or whether, having taught so many other useful lessons to Europe, we may not add that of showing them that there are peaceable means of repressing injustice by making it the interest of the aggressor to do what is just and abstain from future wrong.[1]

It was scarcely necessary to call the Cabinet together; three days before the special meeting the President had already decided on a policy of forbearance and watchful waiting. The proclamation which was issued was moderate in tone, but Jefferson expressed more clearly in a letter to the Vice President, George Clinton, the reasons for his moderation.

The usage of nations requires that we shall give the offender an opportunity of making reparation and avoiding war. That we would give time to our merchants to get in their property and vessels and our seamen now afloat; That the power of declaring war being with the Legislature, the executive could do nothing necessarily committing them to decide for war in preference of non-intercourse, which will be preferred by a great many.[2]

In order to make even more certain that no precipitate step would be taken, it was decided to issue, on August 24, a proclamation calling Congress together, but not until the fourth Monday in October. It was the manifest hope of the President that by that date some satisfaction would be obtained from England with regard to the most flagrant violations of the "*droit des gens*", and that extreme measures could be avoided.

In the meantime new instructions had been sent to Monroe. "Reparation for the past, and security for the future is our motto," wrote the President to Du Pont de Nemours. Repara-

---

[1] June 29, 1807. Memorial Edition, XI, 256.
[2] July 6, 1807. *Ibid.*, XI, 258.

tion for the past, at least as far as the attack on the *Chesapeake* was concerned, would have been easy to obtain, but Canning refused persistently to make any promise for the future, or to alter the policy of Great Britain with regard to visit and impressment. For his firmness in refusing to settle the case of the *Chesapeake* independently, Jefferson has been most severely criticized by Henry Adams, whose admiration for Perceval's and Canning's superior minds is unbounded. Shall I confess that on this particular point, at least, I should rather agree with the English biographer of Jefferson, Mr. Hirst, who declares that "no second-rate lawyer was ever more obtuse than Perceval, and the wit of Canning, his foreign secretary, seldom issued in wisdom." On this occasion Great Britain was even more stupid than she had been in 1776; she missed her great opportunity to operate a reconciliation with the United States and to turn them against France, without other compensation than the pleasure of outwitting the American envoys and once more treating scornfully the younger country. The real answer of England was given in the Orders in Council of November 11, 1807, prohibiting all neutral trade with the whole European seacoast from Copenhagen to Trieste. No American vessel was to be allowed to enter any port of Europe from which British vessels were excluded without first going to England and abiding by regulations to be determined later.

In the meantime, Jefferson was pushing fast his preparations for defence. A detailed examination of his correspondence during the summer and fall of that year would justify him amply from the criticism of several American historians.[1] He still hoped for peace, or more exactly peace remained his ideal, although he had very little hope that Monroe would succeed in his negotiations. But nothing could be done as long as American ships and sailors, "at least twenty thousand men",

---

[1] See particularly his letters to Cabell, August 11, 1807, and to Dearborn, August 28. Memorial Edition, XI, 318, 342.

were on the seas, an easy prey to British vessels in case war should be declared at once. "The loss of these," wrote Jefferson quite correctly, "would be worth to Great Britain many victories on the Nile and Trafalgar." [1]

To judge of Jefferson's conduct at that time from our modern point of view would be most unfair and dangerous. He could neither cable, nor send radiograms, nor even steamships to warn American citizens in distant ports, nor give instructions to agents of the United States all over the world. It took months for news to cross the ocean and sometimes a year or more to receive an answer to a letter. The geographical isolation of the United States, their remoteness from Europe and the slowness of communications were obvious factors of the situation, yet they are too often neglected in judging the policy then followed by the President. As the year advanced, Jefferson's hope of being able to maintain peace grew fainter. There is a spirit of helplessness in a letter he wrote to James Maury at the end of November:

The world as you justly observe, is truly in an awful state. Two nations of overgrown power are endeavoring to establish, the one an universal dominion by sea, the other by land. . . . We are now in hourly expectation of hearing from our ministers in London by the return of the "Revenge." Whether she will bring us war or peace, or the middle state of non-intercourse, seems suspended in equal balance.[2]

The message to Congress, of Octorber 27, contained no specific recommendation. It was a dispassionate recital of the circumstances which had necessitated new instructions to Monroe, a promise that Congress would be informed of the result of the negotiations, news of which was expected hourly, and an enumeration of the measures taken towards the defense of the country. When the first news finally came, the President

[1] To John Page, July 17, 1807. Memorial Edition, XI, 285.
[2] November 22, 1807. *Ibid.*, XI, 397.

had already decided upon the course to follow.   On December 18, 1807, he sent to Congress one of his shortest messages :

The communications now made, showing the great and increasing dangers with which our vessels, our seamen, and merchandise, are threatened on the high seas and elsewhere, from the belligerent powers of Europe, and it being of great importance to keep in safety these essential resources, I deem it my duty to recommend the subject to the consideration of Congress, who will doubtless perceive all the advantages which may be expected from an inhibition of the departure of our vessels from the ports of the United States.   Their wisdom will also see the necessity of making every preparation for whatever events may grow out of the present crisis.

The situation was much more clearly described in a letter to General John Mason written approximately at the same time.

The sum of these mutual enterprises on our national rights — wrote the President — is that France, and her allies, reserving for further consideration the prohibiting our carrying anything to the British territories, have virtually done it, by restraining our bringing a return cargo from them; and that Great Britain, after prohibiting a great proportion of our commerce with France and her allies, is now believed to have prohibited the whole.   The whole world is thus laid under interdict by these two nations, and our vessels, their cargoes and crews, are to be taken by the one or the other, for whatever place they may be destined out of our own limits.   If therefore, on leaving our harbors we are certain to lose them, is it not better, as to vessels, cargoes and seamen, to keep them at home ? This is submitted to the wisdom of Congress, who alone are competent to provide a remedy.[1]

As in so many other instances the temptation is great to draw a parallel between Jefferson's policies and the neutrality advocated by Woodrow Wilson during his first term, and to repeat the worn-out and dangerous adage "history repeats

[1] Memorial Edition, XI, 401.   This may be simply a draft of the message written on a sheet of paper which happened to bear the name of General Mason.   See Henry Adams, IV, 168.

itself." As a matter of fact, the situation faced by Jefferson in 1808 was entirely different from that which confronted President Wilson from 1914 to 1917. America was not then a rich and powerful country with unlimited resources. The people had just emerged from a long and distressing financial crisis, for it took more than one generation to heal the wounds of a war which had lasted six years. The Federal Government was far from being as strong as it was destined to become. The navy was ridiculously inadequate, not only to go out and give battle to the English fleet, but even, to use Jefferson's expression, to keep the seaports "*hors d'insulte.*"

These facts must be kept in mind if one wishes to form a true estimate of Jefferson's conduct and character during the calamitous years of his second term. To criticize his policies is an easy feat for a modern historian, for it is natural that an American of to-day should resent Jefferson's attitude as unworthy of a great self-respecting nation. Undoubtedly the President might have sent a warlike message to Congress and war would have immediately followed, but on the whole the issue had been taken out of his hands in December, 1807. The embargo, as he justly pointed out, was no new policy and no new measure; it was simply a recognition of a situation created by both France and Great Britain. The only way out would have been a formal declaration of war, and one does not quite see what this grand gesture would have accomplished. Certainly the United States were no more in position to march into Canada in 1807 than they were in 1812, and if they had succeeded in taking possession of the British colony, it is unlikely that Great Britain would have accepted such a loss with equanimity. Furthermore, even if a formal alliance had been concluded with France, the French fleet would have been powerless to prevent the British navy from cruising on the American coast and repeating, if they had wished, the outrages that had befallen Copenhagen.

Another solution, favored by such a liberal historian of Jefferson as Mr. A. J. Nock, would have been frankly to recognize the existing situation and to leave the New England merchants free to send out their vessels at their own risk. This would have relieved to a certain extent the economic distress of the northern States, but whether it would have been more honest or more dignified than the embargo is a matter of opinion. Such a policy would have been neutral only in appearance; it would have amounted to a tacit recognition of a British monopoly of the American trade, since England was really the only country to which American ships would have been permitted to go. Granting that the embargo was "the most arbitrary, inquisitorial, and confiscatory measure formulated in American legislation up to the period of the Civil War",[1] I fail to see that the prestige of the United States would have gained much by allowing their citizens to submit to the humiliating Orders in Council of November 11, 1807. Of all policies this would have been the most evasive, most vacillating and least dignified.

It must be furthermore remembered that though he was gifted with remarkable foresight, Jefferson was in no position to guess that the conflict between England and France would last for seven more years. He believed, on the contrary, that the Titanic struggle would come, if not to a definite close, at least to a pause, within a comparatively short time: "Time may produce peace in Europe; peace in Europe removes all causes of difference, till another European war; and by that time our debt may be paid, our revenue clear, and our strength increased." [2] This reasoning reappears in many letters written by Jefferson during the last year of his administration. His correspondence during the months that separated him from rest and philosophical meditation may be devoid of dramatic

---

[1] A. J. Nock, "Jefferson", p. 266. New York, 1926.
[2] To John Taylor, January 6, 1808. Memorial Edition, XI, 413.

interest, but a thorough perusal of it would demonstrate that at no time during his long political career were his motives less interested, less partisan and more truly patriotic.

At no time, either, was he more bitterly attacked. He suffered from "the peltings of the storm" and cried out pathetically to Benjamin Rush: "Oh! for the day when I shall be withdrawn from it; when I shall have leisure to enjoy my family, my friends, my farm and books." But the defection of the Republicans in Congress, the divergence of opinions in his Cabinet, the threats of secession, the anonymous letters and the press campaign launched against him had no power to shake his strong negative resolution. Yet in all justice to him it may be seen that his policy was not entirely negative.

First of all his letters show that he never considered the embargo as a permanent cure. As early as March, 1808, writing to Charles Pinckney, the former envoy to Spain, he declared that the effect of the embargo would be "to postpone for this year the immediate danger of a rupture with England." He admitted that a time would come "when war would be preferable to a continuance of the embargo and that the question would have to be decided at the next meeting of Congress unless peace intervened in the meantime." [1] Under these circumstances the repeal of the embargo voted by Congress to take effect after Jefferson's retirement cannot be considered as a rebuke to the President. Moreover, it appears that Jefferson had given some thought to three and not two alternatives: 1, embargo; 2, war; 3, submission and tribute, — the third being exactly that advocated by Mr. Nock. In Jefferson's opinion this third solution was at once "to be put out by every American and the two first considered." [2] Writing to Thomas Leib, earlier in the year, he had already defined his position with regard to this solution, recommended by the

---

[1] March 30, 1808. Memorial Edition, XI, 23.
[2] To Governor Charles Pinckney. November 8, 1808. *Ibid.*, XII, 190.

mercantile interests : "It is true, the time will come when we must abandon it (the embargo).   But if this is before the repeal of the orders of council, we must abandon it only for a state of war.   The day is not distant, when that will be preferable to a longer continuance of the embargo.   But we can never remove that, and let our vessels go out and be taken under these orders without making reprisal."   This is itself evidence, but it has apparently escaped many historians as well as many contemporaries of Jefferson.   If the embargo is considered not as a permanent policy but as a political expedient and a political experiment, the greater part of Henry Adams' arraignment of Jefferson's political philosophy falls flat.[1]   When, on the other hand, the same writer admits that "the result was that the embargo saved perhaps twenty millions of dollars a year and some thousands of lives which the war would have consumed", we may be permitted to add that Jefferson would not have granted the principle that "the strongest objection to war was not its waste of money or even of life; for money and life in political economy were worth no more than they could be made to produce."   If this is economic history, Heaven preserve us from economic policies!   As to the accusation that "Jefferson's system was preaching the fear of war, of self-sacrifice, making many smugglers and traitors, but not a single hero", I must humbly confess that one does not see that America would have been much richer for engaging without adequate preparation or even a fair chance to defend herself in a useless and, in last analysis, probably inglorious war.

It is claimed, however, that the embargo caused an economic catastrophe :

As the order was carried along the seacoast, every artisan dropped his tools, every merchant closed his doors, every ship was dismantled. American produce — wheat, timber, cotton, tobacco, rice — dropped in value or became unsalable; every imported article rose

[1] Henry Adams, IV, chapter XII, "The Cost of Embargo."

in price; wages stopped, swarms of debtors became bankrupt; thousands of sailors hung idle around the wharves. . . . A reign of idleness began; and the men who were not already ruined felt that their ruin was only a matter of time.[1]

A very pathetic picture this, made even more pitiful by the classic quotation from the British traveler, Lambert, who visited New York in 1808 and described it as a place ravaged by pestilence. But why not quote also from another traveler, John Mellish, who spoke of the impetus given to manufactures and home industries?[2] Why forget to mention Gallatin's report of 1810, pointing out that some basic industries had been firmly established in the United States, such as iron, cotton, flax, hats, paper, printing type, gunpowder, window glass, clocks, etc. Who could deny, at any rate, that manufactures made enormous progress, thanks to the embargo, and that goods formerly imported from England began to be made in America? Even supposing that the picture drawn by H. Adams were true, it would be necessary to admit that there was another side to it and that a few artisans, at least, remained working steadily at their benches.

The last annual message of Jefferson to Congress was noncommittal on the measures to be taken. It presented first a dispassionate recital of the negotiations carried on with France and England to bring them to rescind the most offensive features of their orders and decrees. It recognized that "this candid and liberal experiment had failed." It was left to Congress to determine what course to follow:

Under a continuance of the belligerent measures which, in defiance of laws which consecrate the rights of neutrals, overspread the ocean with danger, it will rest with the wisdom of Congress to decide on the course best adapted to such a state of things; and bringing with

[1] Henry Adams, IV, 277.
[2] Walter W. Jennings, "A History of economic progress in the United States", p. 160, New York, 1926.

them, as they do, from every part of the Union, the sentiments of our constituents, my confidence is strengthened, that in forming this decision they will, with an unerring regard to the essential rights and interests of the nation weigh and compare the painful alternatives out of which a choice is to be made.

This reserved attitude Jefferson intended to maintain during the rest of his term. "I have thought it right to take no part myself in proposing measures, the execution of which will devolve on my successor. I am therefore chiefly an unmedling listener to what others say." [1] But to Doctor William Eustis he protested that "while thus endeavoring to secure, and preparing to vindicate that commerce, the absurd opinion has been propagated, that this temporary and necessary arrangement was to be a permanent system and was intended for its destruction." [2] And this seems to indicate that he was quite definite in his own mind, even if he refrained from expressing his opinion officially.

After more than a month's deliberation in Congress, Jefferson had come to believe that "Congress had taken their ground firmly for continuing the embargo till June, and then war." Quite suddenly, however, the majority, frightened by threats of secession openly made by the New England members, and fearful of the famous Essex Junto, rallied to a compromise. Neither the people nor Congress were for war, and that fact had been clearly realized very early both by the French and the British ministers; at the same time it was felt that something must be done to relieve to some extent the financial distress of the Virginia planters and New England merchants. The result was that Congress decided to remove the embargo on March 4, "non intercourse with France and Great Britain, trade everywhere else, and continuing war preparations." [3]

[1] To Doctor George Logan, December 27, 1808. Memorial Edition, XII, 219.
[2] January 14, 1809. *Ibid.*, XII, 227.
[3] To Thomas Mann Randolph, February 7, 1809. *Ibid.*, XII, 248.

On the first of March, three days before the inauguration of his successor, Jefferson signed the bill, but not without serious misgivings. The letters he wrote at that time contain even more convincing evidence that he did not expect the embargo to last much longer. To General Armstrong, the American representative in Paris, he declared on March 5 that "War must follow if the edicts are not repealed before the meeting of Congress in May." With Short, whom he had tried without success to have appointed Minister to Russia, he was more explicit if no less emphatic: "We have substituted for it (the embargo), a non-intercourse with France and England and their dependencies, and a trade to all other places. It is probable that the belligerents will take our vessels under their edicts, in which case we shall probably declare war against them." [1] Finally, to Madison himself, he wrote after reaching Monticello:

It is to be desired that war may be avoided, if circumstances will admit. Nor in the present maniac state of Europe, should I estimate the point of honor by the ordinary scale. I believe we shall, on the contrary, have credit with the world, for having made the avoidance of being engaged in the present unexampled war, our first object. War, however, may become a less losing business than unresisted depredation. [2]

Whatever may have been the opposition to the embargo and the opposition to Jefferson of disaffected Republicans, it is remarkable that he was able to keep his party in hand to the last minute and to choose his successor. Early at the beginning of his second term, he had expressed his irrevocable intention not to become a candidate for a third term. He was longing for his farm, his books, for the comforts of family life and he was not in the best of health.

Not only had he been troubled by rheumatism, but "periodical headaches" recurring at frequent intervals left him

[1] March 8, 1809. Memorial Edition, XII, 264.
[2] March 17, 1809. *Ibid.*, XII, 266.

for days unable to write and hardly able "to compose his thoughts."

The Republicans had to make a choice between three possible candidates: George Clinton, Monroe, and Madison. The strongest argument that could be advanced in favor of the first was that, according to a precedent already apparently established, the Vice President was the logical successor, the "heir apparent", as Adams had termed it, to a retiring President. Moreover, Clinton could count on the support of the New York Republicans and had aroused no strong antagonism against himself. It soon became obvious, however, that the contest lay between the two Virginians and that the Virginia dynasty would not be broken as yet. Monroe was not without support in his native State and his candidacy had been upheld by a Republican caucus held by Randolph and his friends at Richmond; but another caucus of the Assembly had given a decisive majority to Madison. On January 23, 1808, a congressional caucus held in Washington pronounced decisively for Madison as President and George Clinton as Vice President. But Randolph held aloof and with his friends published a protest against the candidacy of Madison, who had "moderation when energy was needed", whose theories of government were tainted with federalism, "when the country was asking for consistency and loathing and abhorrence from any compromise." The danger of a split in the Republican Party was indeed serious, and while Jefferson reasserted his wish not to participate in any way in the campaign, he wrote to Monroe a long letter, deploring the situation and making an obvious appeal to his party loyalty. He warned him particularly against the passions that could not fail to be aroused in such a contest, and conjured him to keep clear "of the toils in which his friends would endeavor to interlace him."

That Monroe's *amour-propre* was deeply wounded appears in the letter he wrote in answer to his "chief." He complained lengthily and bitterly of having been handicapped by the sending of Pinkney and of the criticism to which he had been subjected on account of the treaty.   Once again Jefferson had to soothe the discontent of his friend and "*élève*", which to a certain extent he succeeded in doing.   It soon appeared, however, that the question would solve itself, that neither Monroe nor Clinton was strong enough to control the Republican majority.   When the results came in, the Republicans had suffered the loss of all New England except Vermont, but Madison carried the election by one hundred and twenty-two votes, against forty-seven to C. C. Pinckney and six for Clinton. True enough, in several states the electors had been selected before the full pressure of the embargo was felt, but with such a substantial majority it is difficult to accept unreservedly Henry Adams' view that "no one could fail to see that if nine months of embargo had so shattered Jefferson's power, another such year would shake the Union itself."

BOOK SIX

The Sage of Monticello

CHAPTER I

"AMERICA HAS A HEMISPHERE TO ITSELF"

WHEN, after a long and fatiguing journey, Thomas Jefferson reached Monticello in the spring of 1809, he was in his sixty-third year and had well earned his "quadragena stipendia." But the Republic did not serve any pension to retired Presidents. For more than twelve years he had perforce neglected his domain, and his son-in-law, who had been in charge of the estate for some time, was scarcely a man to be intrusted with the administration of complicated financial interests. A large part of Jefferson's time was necessarily spent in setting things to rights; but the times were against him, and the embargo had proved more detrimental to the great landowners of the South than to the New England manufacturers. A planter whose sole revenue consisted in his crops had the utmost difficulty in providing for a large family of dependants, and a considerable number of slaves who had to be fed and clad, and most of all in keeping up appearances. Jefferson was hardly freed from public responsibilities when he had to labor under domestic difficulties which worried him even to his death bed.

Under his direction, however, Monticello became more than ever a self-supporting community; the slaves were taught all the necessary trades and when, thanks to the merino sheep brought over by Du Pont de Nemours, woolen goods of fine quality were made at Monticello, the master of the house was proud to wear clothes of homespun which, in his opinion, could rival the best produce of the English manufactures. Whole books could be written, and several have been written, on Jefferson the agriculturist, the surveyor, the civil engineer, the inventor and the architect. There is, however, another aspect of his last years which deserves more attention than it usually receives.

For thirty years Jefferson had lived almost constantly under the scrutiny of the public. His utterances had been pounced upon by eager enemies of the "cannibal press"; letters intended solely for friends had been printed, several times in a garbled form, and during his presidency he had been unable to communicate freely with his European friends for fear of having his letters intercepted. At last, he could express himself freely. He was no longer the spokesman of the country who had to ascertain the state of public opinion before writing a message or sending a communication to a foreign government. He could speak for himself, without being hindered by the ever-present danger of political repercussions, and if he did not speak much, he wrote several thousand letters, many of which are still unpublished — an overwhelming treasure for historians of the period. His physical strength was somewhat impaired, but his intellectual powers were in no way diminished; never had his mind been keener, his perception of realities clearer and his extraordinary gift of political prophecy more accurate than during the last fifteen years of his life. This is the period to study in order to understand more fully his conception of Americanism, his vision of democracy and the practical wisdom which permeated his philosophy of old age.

His valedictory letter to Madison, written from Monticello on March 17, 1809, contained a very curious admission of the inability of the United States to carry out war successfully with their present organization; "I know of no Government," he wrote, "which would be so embarrassing in war as ours. This would proceed very much from the lying and licentious character of our papers; but also, from the wonderful credulity of the members of Congress in the floating lies of the day."[1]

[1] Memorial Edition, XII, 267.

This was no passing whim of his, but a very definite and categorical understanding of the functions devolving upon the Executive in times of emergency. He had not forgotten his experience as Governor of Virginia, when he had to coax necessary measures from a reluctant Assembly; his eight years as Chief Executive of the country had only strengthened him in the opinion that "In times of peace, the people look most to their representatives, but in war to the Executive solely." He found a confirmation of this theory in the state of public opinion, when he wrote to Rodney, early in 1810: "It is visible that their confidence is now veering in that direction: that they are looking to the executive to give the proper direction to their affairs, with a confidence as auspicious as it is well founded." [1]

A few months later, writing to J. B. Colvin, he took up again the same question: "In what circumstances is it permitted for the man in charge to assume authority beyond the law?" That he was personally interested in the matter was evident, since he had exceeded his constitutional powers very recently, during the Burr conspiracy. It is nevertheless remarkable to see the champion of legality and democracy declare that:

A strict observance of the written law is doubtless *one* of the high duties of a good citizen, but it is not the *highest*. The laws of necessity, of self-preservation, of saving our country when in danger are of higher obligation. To lose our country by a scrupulous adherence to written law, would be to lose the law itself, with life, liberty, property and all those enjoying them with us; thus absurdly sacrificing the end to the means.[2]

To a certain extent this was a plea *pro domo sua*. If we remember that, during the World War, the motto of America was, for more than two years, "Stand by the President", it will be seen that Jefferson was as good a prophet as an intel-

[1] February 10, 1810. Memorial Edition, XII, 357.
[2] To J. B. Colvin. September 20, 1810. *Ibid.*, XII, 422; see also letter to Cæsar Rodney, September 25. *Ibid.*, XII, 426.

ligent observer. This admission of his may seem undemocratic, but it simply shows that the former President had a clear perception of the permanent tendencies that direct American consciousness; for no people are more disciplined and more ready to follow their chosen executive than the Americans, at least on critical occasions, and more particularly when confronted with foreign aggression.

War was still to be avoided and considered only as the *ultima ratio rei publicae.* On this point also, Jefferson was perfectly consistent, and, having shed the responsibility, he did not suddenly change his attitude. The "point of honor" was not to be estimated by the ordinary scale in the present maniac state of Europe. But America must realize at the same time that no ordinary treaty could insure her safety. A treaty with England could not even be thought of; for "the British never made an equal treaty with any nation."

With regard to France the situation was somewhat different. Some compensation was due to America for forcing Great Britain to revoke her orders in council. But what compensation? The acquiescence of Bonaparte to the annexation of the Floridas? That was no price; for "they are ours in the first moment of the first war; and until a war they are of no particular necessity." The only territory that the United States might covet was Cuba. "That would be a price, and I would immediately erect a column on the southernmost limit of Cuba, and inscribe on it a *ne plus ultra* to us in that direction . . . . Cuba can be defended by us without a navy, and this develops the principle which ought to limit our views. Nothing should ever be accepted which would require a navy to defend it."

In the meantime, Jefferson did not miss any opportunity to justify the embargo. Even after its repeal, he insisted that "enough of the non-importation laws should be preserved 1st, to pinch them into a relinquishment of impressments, and 2nd,

¹ To Madison, April 27, 1809. Memorial Edition, XII, 275.

to support those manufacturing establishments, which their orders, and our interests, forced us to make." [1]

To Du Pont de Nemours he wrote a long letter, stating in detail the advantages accrued to America from the embargo, and this point is well worth keeping in mind by those who insist on considering Jefferson as a hundred per cent. agrarian :

The barefaced attempts of England to make us accessories and tributaries to her usurpations on the high seas — he wrote to the old Physiocrat — have generated in this country an universal spirit for manufacturing for ourselves, and of reducing to a minimum the number of articles for which we are dependent on her. The advantages too, of lessening the occasions of risking our peace on the ocean, and of planting the consumer on our own soil by the side of the grower of produce, are so palpable, that no temporary suspension of injuries on her part, or agreements founded on that, will now prevent our continuing in what we have begun. [2]

So wrote the supposed agrarian to the founder of physiocracy, and this is a *prima facie* evidence that Jefferson was not a Physiocrat of the first water. As a matter of fact, on this point as on so many others, he had strong negative principles. As we have already pointed out on several occasions, Jefferson was not so much opposed to manufactures and industries as to mercantilism, and particularly to English mercantilism. This corrective ought to be taken into consideration in any estimate of the Jeffersonian democracy, and one may wonder whether some continuators of Mr. Beard are sufficiently aware of this capital distinction.

It soon appeared to Jefferson that there was no possible way out except war. Contrary to all expectations, the convulsions of Europe continued and no hope of a permanent peace was in sight. The death of Bonaparte "would remove the first and chiefest apostle of the desolation of men and morals and might

---

[1] To Madison, April 19, 1809. Memorial Edition, XII, 271.
[2] June 28, 1809. *Ibid.*, XII, 293.

withdraw the scourge of the land. But what is to restore order and safety on the ocean. The death of George III? Not at all . . . The principle that force is right, is become the principle of the nation itself." [1]

As a matter of fact, Bonaparte was little to be feared. He still had the whole world to conquer before turning his eyes towards America.

England on the contrary is an ever-present danger not to be relied upon as an ally for she would make a separate peace and leave us in the lurch. Her good faith? The faith of a nation of merchants. The *Punica fides* of modern Carthage. Of the friend of the protectress of Copenhagen. Of the nation who never admitted a chapter of morality into her political code.

Then follows a formidable indictment of the treacherous policies of England with a curious and most interesting discrimination at the end, for Jefferson observes that "it presents the singular phenomenon of a nation, the individuals of which are as faithful to their private engagements and duties, as honorable, as worthy, as those of any nation on earth, and whose government is yet the most unprincipled at this day known." [2]

All told, both nations could be tarred with the same brush "for," said Jefferson, "I should respect just as much the rules of conduct which governed Cartouche or Blackbeard as those now acted on by France or England." [3] The only difference was that France was not in a position to cause as much damage to American interests as her hereditary enemy whose claim to "dominion of the ocean and to levy tribute on every flag traversing that, as lately attempted and not relinquished, every nation must contest, even *ad internecionem*." [4]

[1] To Rodney, February 10, 1810. Memorial Edition, XII, 357.
[2] To Governor John Langdon, March 5, 1810. *Ibid.*, XII, 373.
[3] To Thomas Cooper, August 6, 1810. *Ibid.*, XII, 401.
[4] To Thomas Law, January 15, 1810. *Ibid.*, XII, 439.

This detestation of English policies and English rulers did not, however, extend to individuals. Even when war was to be declared Jefferson took care to establish what he considered as a very necessary distinction in a fine letter sent to James Maury, his "dear and ancient friend and classmate":

Our two countries are at war, but not you and I. And why should our two countries be at war, when by peace we can be so much more useful to one another. Surely the world will acquit our government from having sought it. . . . We consider the overwhelming power of England on the ocean, and of France on the land, as destructive of the prosperity and happiness of the world, and wish both to be reduced only to the necessity of observing moral duties. I believe no more in Bonaparte's fighting merely for the liberty of the seas, than in Great Britain's fighting for the liberties of mankind. . . . We resist the enterprises of England first, because they first come vitally home to us. And our feelings repel the logic of bearing the lash of George III, for fear of that of Bonaparte at some future day. When the wrongs of France shall reach us with equal effect, we shall resist them also. But one at a time is enough; and having offered a choice to the champions, England first takes up the gauntlet.[1]

Since war was declared, the only thing to keep in mind was to make it as advantageous as possible to the United States. Thanks to the Louisiana Purchase, France had been eliminated forever from the American continent, but the existence of a large British province on the northern border constituted an ever-present source of anxiety and danger for the Union. The first war aim of the United States was consequently to expel Great Britain from the North American continent, for as long as England could use her continental dominion as "a fulcrum for her Machiavellian levers" there would be no safety for the United States. On the other hand, the war could not be carried out to a successful conclusion if during the hostilities

[1] April 25, 1812. Memorial Edition, XIII, 145.

America were kept unable to export the surplus of her produce. Jefferson therefore recommended that neutral vessels be used "and even enemy vessels under neutral flag, which I should wink at", wrote Jefferson to the President.[1]

This last recommendation may seem surprising and almost treasonable, but Jefferson lived in close contact with farmers and planters, and he still remembered their attitude during the Revolutionary War and knew that "to keep the war popular we must keep open the markets. As long as good prices can be had, the people will support the war cheerfully."

Later in the year he was able to report to the President:

Our farmers are cheerful in the expectation of a good price for wheat in Autumn. Their pulse will be regulated by this, and not by the successes or disasters of the war. To keep open sufficient markets is the very first object towards maintaining the popularity of the war, which is as great at present as could be desired.[2]

To be correctly understood, this attitude of Jefferson advocating trade with the enemy requires some further elucidation. As a matter of fact, the issue was not so clear-cut as it would seem. While England was to be considered as America's enemy on the continent, she was "fighting America's battles" in Europe, for the ultimate triumph of Bonaparte would have been pregnant with dangers for the Union. He consequently advocated the exportation of grain to Great Britain:

If she is to be fed at all events, why may not we have the benefit of it as well as others. I would not indeed, feed her armies landed on our territory, because the difficulty of inland communication subsistence is what will prevent their ever penetrating far into the country. . . . But this would be my only exception, and as to feeding her armies in the Peninsular, she is fighting our battles there, as Bonaparte is on the Baltic.[3]

[1] June 29, 1812. Memorial Edition, XIII, 173.
[2] August 5, 1812. *Ibid.*, XIII, 183.
[3] *Ibid.*, XIII, 206.

But it must also be admitted that Jefferson considered that in war all is fair. He had not changed much since the remote days of the Revolution when he urged Washington to permit him to use measures of retaliation on the British prisoners. Once again he did not scruple to recommend measures sometimes used but seldom so frankly advocated. He would not have hesitated to bring the war home to Great Britain and to resort to retaliation. "Perhaps they will burn New York or Boston," he wrote to Duane. "If they do, we must burn the city of London, not by expensive fleets or congreve rockets, but by employing an hundred or two Jack-the-painters, whom nakedness, famine, desperation and hardened vice, will abundantly furnish among themselves." [1]

But the thing never to be lost sight of was the conquest of Canada and "the final expulsion of England from the American continent." It was to be a very simple expedition, "a mere matter of marching", and the weakness of the enemy was to make "our errors innocent." All these sanguine expectations were blasted to dust by the Hull disaster. Three frigates taken by "our gallant little navy" could not balance "three armies lost by treachery, cowardice, or incapacity of those to whom they were entrusted." The mediation of Russia was the only hope left, but the enemies were to remain "bedecked with the laurels of the land" — the reverse of what was to be expected and perhaps what was to be wished. [2]

Throughout the whole campaign Jefferson was unable to choose between France and England, or rather between Bonaparte and England's corrupted government. Strong as were his denunciations of English policies and crimes, he almost foamed at the mouth when he mentioned the abominable Corsican:

That Bonaparte is an unprincipled tyrant who is deluging the continent of Europe with blood, there is not a human being, not even

[1] October 1, 1812. Memorial Edition, XIII, 187.
[2] To William Duane, April 4, 1813. *Ibid.*, XIII, 231.

the wife of his bosom, who does not see. There is no doubt as to the line we ought to wish drawn between his successes and those of Alexander. Surely none of us wish to see Bonaparte conquer Russia, and lay thus at his feet the whole continent of Europe. This done, England would be just a breakfast.[1]

The "true line of interest" of the United States was consequently that Bonaparte should be able to effect the complete exclusion of England from the whole continent of Europe, in order to make her renounce her views of dominion over the ocean. As there was no longer any hope of expelling England completely from the American continent, it remained "the interest of the U. S. to wish Bonaparte a moderate success so as to curb the ambition of Great Britain." [2]

From this and many other similar passages it would follow that Jefferson was one of the first exponents of the famous policy of the balance of power. Although at war with England, America could not wish for a complete defeat of her enemy which would enable the monster to pursue his dreams of world domination. But hateful as the Corsican was, no one could wish for an English victory which would leave Great Britain the undisputed ruler of the ocean. Incidents of the war did wring from Jefferson impassioned outbursts which expressed a temporary anger, but whenever he took time to weigh the different factors in his mind, the realistic politician emerged every time.

This appears clearly in his correspondence with Madame de Staël, who had urged him on several occasions to make every effort to decide his fellow countrymen to join in the battle against the oppressors of liberty. It appears also quite significantly in his correspondence with Madison, following the burning of the White House and the destruction by the English soldiers of the first Congressional Library. His indignation

---

[1] To Thomas Leiper, January 1, 1814. Memorial Edition, XIV, 45.
[2] To John Clark, January 27, 1814. *Ibid.*, XIV, 79.

ran high when he learned "through the paper" that "the vandalism of our enemy has triumphed at Washington over science as well as the arts, with the destruction of the public library with the noble edifice in which it was deposited." "Of that transaction, as that of Copenhagen, the world will entertain but one sentiment," he wrote to Samuel H. Smith.[1] But it was characteristic of the man that he thought at once of the means of restoring the library. Books could not be procured easily from abroad and there was no other private library in the country comparable to the collection of books he had systematically accumulated for over forty years. He placed his books at the disposal of Congress "to be valued by persons named by the Library Committee, and the payment made convenient to the public." This was not a piece of business in order to retrieve his fortune, nor a disguised request for financial help, but simply the act of a public-spirited citizen unable to make an outright gift and yet unwilling to make any profit on the public treasury.

The end of the war was in sight — a war which could be considered as a draw, in which both sides had lost heavily and neither had gained anything :

It is a deplorable misfortune to us. It has arrested the course of the most remarkable tide of prosperity any nation ever experienced, and has closed such prospects of future improvements as were never before in the view of any people. Farewell all hopes of extinguishing public debt ! Farewell all visions of applying surpluses of revenue to the improvement of peace, rather then the ravages of war. Our enemy has indeed the consolation of Satan on removing our first parents from Paradise ; from a peaceable and agricultural nation, he makes us a military and manufacturing one. . . .[2]

It could truly be said that the war had failed. The best that could be expected was the *status ante bellum.* "Indemnity

<hr>

[1] September 21, 1814. Memorial Edition, XIV, 191.
[2] To William Short, November 28, 1814. *Ibid.*, XIV, 214.

for the past and security for the future which was our motto at the beginning of this war, must be adjourned to another, when, disarmed and bankrupt our enemy shall be less able to insult and plunder the world with impunity." [1]

The news that peace had been signed did not cause him any elation, it was "in fact but an armistice", and even when he wrote again to his dear and ancient friend James Maury, Jefferson was careful to note that America would never peacefully accept again England's practice of impressment on the high seas. "On that point," he wrote, "we have thrown away the scabbard and the moment an European war brings her back to this practice, adds us again to her enemies." [2]

This was repeated in a letter to his old friend Du Pont de Nemours who had asked him for his influence in order to send his grandson to the Naval Academy :

For twenty years to come we should consider peace as the *summum bonum* of our country. At the end of that period we shall be twenty millions in number, and forty in energy, when encountering the starved and rickety paupers and dwarfs of English workshops. By that time your grandson will have become one of our High-Admirals, and bear distinguished part in retorting the wrongs of both his countries on the most implacable and cruel of their enemies.[3]

Yet one would be mistaken in believing that Jefferson felt against England any deep-seated animosity, and his resentment, however justifiable, did not last long after the close of hostilities. The fine friendly letters he wrote to Thomas Law and James Maury at the eve of the war were more than mere gestures. He had many friends in England, he was imbued with English philosophy, English ideas, English law and, if he detested the rulers and the régime, he always maintained the

---

[1] To Correa de Serra, December 27, 1814. Memorial Edition, XIV, 221.
[2] To William H. Crawford, February 25, 1815. *Ibid.*, XIV, 243, and June 15, 1815. *Ibid.*, XIV, 312.
[3] December 1, 1815. *Ibid.*, XIV, 369.

same sentimental and quite natural feelings of so many Americans for the mother country as a whole:

Were they once under a government which should treat us with justice and equity — he wrote to John Adams — I should myself feel with great strength the ties that bind us together, of origin, language, laws and manners; and I am persuaded the two people would become in future as it was with the ancient Greeks, among whom it was reproachful for Greek to be found fighting against Greek in a foreign army.[1]

On the same day he wrote to the Secretary of State, James Monroe, about the proposed inscription to be engraved in a conspicuous place on the restored Capitol, and he had suggested that if any inscription was considered as necessary, it should simply state the bare facts, such as:

FOUNDED 1791. BURNT BY A BRITISH ARMY 1814. RESTORED BY CONGRESS 1817.

But a question of more importance was whether there should be any inscription at all. "The barbarism of the conflagration will immortalize that of the nation . . . . We have more reason to hate her than any nation in earth. But she is not now an object of hatred . . . . It is for the interest of all that she should be maintained nearly on a par with other members of the republic of nations." [2]

With regard to France, his correspondence with Du Pont de Nemours and Lafayette offers precious and significant testimony. Much as he loathed Bonaparte, he deplored the return of the Bourbons and the reactionary measures of the *Restauration*. His indignation ran high when he received

. . . the new treaty of the allied powers, declaring that the French nation shall not have Bonaparte and shall have Louis XVIII as their ruler. They are all then as great rascals as Bonaparte him-

---

[1] October 16, 1816. Memorial Edition, XIV, 85.
[2] October 16, 1816. *Ibid.*, XVI, 80.

self. While he was in the wrong, I wished him exactly as much success as would answer our purpose, and no more. Now that they are wrong and he in the right, he shall have all my prayers for success, and that he may dethrone every man of them.[1]

Writing to Albert Gallatin he indulged in a "poetical effusion" which shows how deeply his feelings were stirred:

I grieve for France . . . and I trust they will finally establish for themselves a government of rational and well tempered liberty. So much science cannot be lost; so much light shed over them can never fail to produce to them some good in the end. Till then, we may ourselves fervently pray, with the liturgy a little parodied; Give peace till that time, oh Lord, because there is none other that will fight for us but only thee, oh God.[2]

When all was told, and it was realized that "the cannibals of Europe were going to eating one another again and the pugnacious humor of mankind seemed to be the law of his nature", the only course for the United States to follow was to keep out of the fray as much as possible and so to direct their policy as to give no pretext for the European powers to intervene in the New World.

Already, in 1812, Jefferson had formulated his views in the most unequivocal manner, when he wrote to Doctor John Crawford:

We specially ought to pray that the powers of Europe may be so poised and counterpoised among themselves, that their own safety may require the presence of all their force at home, leaving the other quarters of the globe in undisturbed tranquillity. When our strength will permit us to give the law to our hemisphere, it should be that the meridian of the mid-Atlantic should be the line of demarkation between war and peace, on this side of which no act of hostility should be committed, and the lion and the lamb lie down in peace together.[3]

---

[1] To Thomas Leiper, June 14, 1815. Memorial Edition, XIV, 311; and to John Adams, August 10, 1815. *Ibid.*, XIV, 343.

[2] October 16, 1815. *Ibid.*, XIV, 355.

[3] January 2, 1812. *Ibid.*, XIII, 117.

The progress of the revolt of the Spanish colonies was at first to strengthen him in the position he had already taken.

Jefferson received the news without any elation.   For a long time he had known that the link between the Spanish and Portuguese colonies was growing weaker.   He doubted very much, however, that the colonies were ready for self-government.   There might have been some hope for Mexico, because of her proximity to the United States : "But the others, I fear," he wrote to Baron Alexander von Humboldt, "will end in military despotisms.   The different castes of their inhabitants, their mutual hatred and jealousies, their profound ignorance and bigotry, will be played off by cunning leaders, and each be made the instrument of enslaving the others."   The important point he made was in what followed, and Jefferson here indulged in one of his curious political prophecies, in which he so often hit the mark :

But in whatever government they will end, they will be *American* governments, no longer to be involved in the never-ceasing broils of Europe.   The European nations constitute a separate division of the globe; their localities make them part of a distinct system; they have a set of interests of their own in which it is our business never to engage ourselves.   America has a hemisphere to itself.   It must have its separate system of interests; which must not be subordinated to those of Europe.   The insulated state in which nature has placed the American continent, should so far avail it that no spark of war kindled in the other quarters of the globe should be wafted across the wide oceans which separate us from them and it will be so.   In fifty years more the United States alone will contain fifty millions of inhabitants, and fifty years are soon gone over. . . .   And you will live to see the period ahead of us; and the numbers which will then be spread over the other parts of the American hemisphere, catching long before that the principles of our portion of it, and concurring with us in the maintainance of the same system.[1]

[1] December 6, 1813.   Memorial Edition, XIV, 22.

For the present the situation was entirely different — and as he had done during the Revolution with regard to France, he advocated prudence and slowness. It was one thing for the American colonies to engage in a war with the mother country in order to preserve the liberties they had hitherto enjoyed, and again it was another entirely different thing for people who had not the faintest experience of self-government to declare their independence and suddenly to sever all connections with the past. In addition he was fully aware that the new republics would be in no condition to fight off foreign aggressors and thus would become an easy prey for the unscrupulous and greedy nations of Europe. Unable to stand on their own feet, the most natural course for South America was to fall back on Spain. Jefferson did not visualize the "*foris familiation*" of the colonies without a sort of moral protectorate of the mother country: "if she extends to them her affection, her aid, her patronage in every court and country, it will weave a bond of union indissoluble by time." [1] At the time Jefferson did not go further, and as a matter of fact he long held that this would have been the best solution for South America. As late as January, 1821, he still maintained this opinion in a letter to John Adams:

The safest road would be an accomodation to the mother country which shall hold them together by the single link of the same chief magistrate, leaving to him power enough to keep them in peace with one another, and to themselves the essential power of self-government and self-improvement, until they will be sufficiently trained by education and habits of freedom to walk safely by themselves. Representative government, native functionaries, a qualified negative on their laws, with a previous security by compact for freedom of commerce, freedom of the press, habeas corpus, and trial by jury, would make a good beginning. This last would be the school in which their people might begin to learn the exercise of

---

[1] To Don Valentino de Torunda Corunda, December 14, 1813. Memorial Edition, XIV, 31.

civic duties as well as rights.   For freedom of religion they are not yet prepared.[1]

This was the ideal solution, but "the question was not what we wish, but what is practicable." If consequently the new republics refused such a compromise, another alternative could be offered :

As their sincere friend and brother, I do believe the best thing for them, would be for themselves to come to an accord with Spain, under the guarantee of France, Russia, Holland, and the United States, allowing to Spain a nominal supremacy, with authority only to keep the peace among them, leaving them otherwise all the powers of self-government, until their experience in them, their emancipation from their priests, and advancement in information shall prepare them for complete independence.   I exclude England from this confederacy, because her selfish principles render her incapable of honorable patronage or disinterested co-operation ; unless indeed, what seems now probable, a revolution should restore to her an honest government, one which will permit the world to live in peace.[2]

This is a capital passage for it contains in germ much more than the so-called Monroe Doctrine.   What Jefferson had in mind at the time was evidently a society of nations, which the United States would have joined in order to guarantee the territorial integrity of the South American republics under a Spanish mandate.   For Brazil alone he contemplated a real and immediate independence, for "Brazil is more populous, more wealthy, and as wise as Portugal."

But in Jefferson's mind this plan was only a temporary solution.   He was firmly convinced that a time would necessarily come when all the American republics would be drawn together by their community of interests and institutions and coalescing in an American system, independent from and unconnected with that of Europe, would form a world by themselves :

[1] To John Adams, January 22, 1812.   Memorial Edition, XV, 309.
[2] To Lafayette, May 14, 1817.   *Ibid.*, XV, 117.

"The principles of society there and here, then, are radically different and I hope no American patriot will ever lose sight of the essential policy of interdicting in the seas and territories of both Americas the ferocious and sanguinary contests of Europe. I wish to see this coalition begun." [1]

Such, according to Jefferson, was to be the cardinal principle of American policies for all times to come; for, as he wrote to his friend Correa who had come back to the United States as Minister from Portugal:

Nothing is so important as that America shall separate herself from the system of Europe, and establish one of her own — Our circumstances, our pursuits, our interests, are distinct, the principles of our policy should be so also. All entanglements with that quarter of the globe should be avoided that peace and justice shall be the polar stars of American societies.[2]

On the other hand, it was not advisable for the United States to intervene directly in South America or to help the colonies to sever their bonds from the metropolis. There is little doubt that the Spanish colonies would never have thought of revolting if they had not had constantly before their eyes the example of their northern neighbors. Ill-conducted as they were, the revolutions of South America could trace their origin directly to the American revolution and the Declaration of Independence. It was so plain that Jefferson's French friends, Lafayette, Du Pont de Nemours, and Destutt de Tracy expected him to declare enthusiastically in favor of the South American republics and to use whatever influence he still had to bring about an open intervention of the United States in their favor. Their optimism only shows how little they knew their American friend and how little they understood his policy. To Destutt de Tracy he answered at the end of 1820:

[1] To W. Short, August 4, 1820. Memorial Edition, XV, 263.
[2] October 24, 1820. Ibid., XV, 285.

We go with you all lengths in friendly affections to the independence of S. America, but an immediate acknowledgement of it calls up other considerations. We view Europe as covering at present a smothered fire, which may shortly burst forth and produce general conflagration. From this it is our duty to keep aloof. A formal acknowledgement of the independence of her colonies, would involve us with Spain certainly, and perhaps too with England, if she thinks that a war would divert her internal troubles. Such a war would hurt us more than it would help our brethren of the South; and our right may be doubted of mortgaging posterity for the expenses of a war in which they will have a right to say their interest was not concerned. . . . In the meantime we receive and protect the flag of S. America in it's commercial intercourse with us, on the acknowledged principles of neutrality between two belligerent parties in a civil war; and if we should not be the first, we shall certainly be the second nation in acknowledging the entire independence of our new friends.[1]

This Jefferson pressed again even more tersely in a letter written to Monroe almost four years later. "We feel strongly for them, but our first care must be for ourselves." [2]

Surveying the whole situation from the "mountain-top" of Monticello, the philosopher wondered at times "whether all nations do not owe to one another a bold declaration of their sympathy with the one party and their detestation of the conduct of the other?" But he soon concluded: "Farther than this we are not bound to go; and indeed, for the sake of the world, we ought not to increase the jealousies or draw on ourselves the power of this formidable confederacy." After the treaty of Ghent, at the beginning of the "era of good feeling", the United States could reasonably count on a long period of peace; all their difficulties with Europe had been settled, and only one possible point of friction could be discovered. "Cuba alone seems at present to hold up a speck of war to us. Its

---

[1] Jefferson Papers. Library of Congress. December 26, 1820, and Chinard, "Jefferson et les Idéologues." Paris, Baltimore, 1925, p. 203.
[2] Jefferson Papers. Library of Congress, July 18, 1824.

possession by Great Britain would indeed be a great calamity to the United States; but such calamity could only be temporary, for in case of war on any account, Cuba would be naturally taken by the United States, or the island would give itself to us, when able to do so."

Thus Jefferson, once again, reasserted the cardinal principle of his policy — the policy of the United States since the early days of the Union:

I have ever deemed it fundamental for the United States, never to take active part in the quarrels of Europe. Their political interests are entirely distinct from ours. Their mutual jealousies, their balance of power, their complicated alliances, their forms and principles of government are all foreign to us. They are nations of eternal war. All their energies are expended in the destruction of the labor, property, and lives of their peoples . . . on our part, never had a people so favorable a chance of trying the opposite system, of peace and fraternity with mankind, and the direction of our means and faculties to the purposes of improvement instead of destruction.[1]

Thus, little by little, the famous doctrine took its final shape in the minds of both Jefferson and Monroe. Jefferson contributed to it its historical background, the weight of his experience and authority, and the long conversations he had with Monroe on the matter gave him an opportunity not only to get "his political compass rectified" but to map out for the President the course to follow. The often quoted letter written by Jefferson to Monroe on October 24, 1823, contained little more than what had passed between them when Monroe visited his estate in Virginia. It was simply a reaffirmation of the fundamental maxims of the Jeffersonian policies: — "never to entangle ourselves in the broils of Europe — never to suffer Europe to intermeddle with cis-Atlantic affairs."

After making a survey of all the circumstances, Jefferson could write in conclusion:

[1] To Monroe, June 11, 1823. Memorial Edition, XV, 455.

I could honestly, therefore, join in the declaration proposed, that we aim not at the acquisition of any of those possessions, that we will not stand in the way of any amicable arrangement between them and the Mother country; but that we will oppose, with all our means, the forcible interposition of any other form or pretext, and most especially, their transfer to any power by conquest, cession, or acquisition in any other way.

Finally, although the letters to be exchanged between the British and American governments did not properly constitute a treaty, Jefferson advised Monroe to lay the case before Congress at the first opportunity, since this doctrine might lead to war, "the declaration of which requires an act of Congress."

Whatever use has been made of the Monroe Doctrine and whether or not the "mandate" assumed by the United States has proved irksome to several South American republics, there is no doubt that it was not proclaimed without long hesitation and that its promoters did not take up this new responsibility with "*un cœur léger.*"   There is no doubt, either, that it was not considered as an instrument of imperialism.   It was primarily the extension of the doctrine of self-protection already advanced by John Adams in 1776 and since then maintained by Washington and Jefferson himself.   It was also a corollary of the theory of the balance of power which Jefferson always kept in mind.   In this he was not only followed but urged on by all his liberal friends in Europe.

I would not be sorry — wrote Lafayette in 1817 — to see the American government invested by the follies of Spain, with the opportunity to take the lead in the affairs of her independent colonies. Unless that is the case or great changes happen in the European policies, the miseries of those fine countries will be long protracted. Could you establish there a representative system, a free trade, and a free press, how many channels of information and improvement should be open at once.[1]

[1] Jefferson Papers.   Library of Congress.   December 10, 1817.

Jefferson himself was too respectful of self-government ever to think of interfering with the internal affairs of the new republics. On the other hand, he was too firmly convinced of the moral, intellectual and political superiority of his own country not to believe that a time would come when the contagion of liberty would extend to the near and remote neighbors of the United States. The unavoidable result of the Monroe Doctrine and the moral mandate of America would be ultimately to form a "Holy American Alliance" of the free peoples of the Western Hemisphere, to counterbalance the conspiracy of Kings and Lords "called the European Holy Alliance."

CHAPTER II

DEMOCRATIC AMERICA

PROTECTED against foreign entanglements and having survived the convulsions that had shattered the old structures of
Europe, America was at last free to pursue her development
along her own lines. The philosopher of Monticello could sit
back, take a more disinterested view of the situation and make
a forecast of the future of his country. He could also advise,
not only his immediate successors, but the generations to come
and take up again the part of "counsellor" which had always
suited him better than the part of the executive. He believed
too much in the right of successive generations to determine
their own form of government, to attempt to dictate in any way
the course to follow. But he was none the less convinced that
certain principles embodied in the Constitution had a permanent and universal value, and during the years at Monticello
he formulated the gospel of American democracy.

As it finally emerged from the several crises that threatened
its existence, the American Government was, if not the best
possible government, at least the best government then on the
surface of the earth. It was at the same time the hope and the
model of all the nations of the world.

We exist and are quoted — wrote Jefferson to Richard Rush — as
standing proofs that a government, so modelled as to rest continu-
ously on the will of the whole society, is a practicable government.
Were we to break to pieces, it would damp the hopes and efforts of
the good, and give triumph to those of the bad through the whole
enslaved world. As members, therefore, of the universal society of
mankind, and standing high in responsible relation with them, it is

our sacred duty to suppress passion among ourselves and not to blast the confidence we have inspired of proof that a government of reason is better than a government of force.[1]

Some dangers, however, were threatening to disturb the equilibrium of the country. The most pressing was perhaps the extraordinary and unwholesome development of State and local banks, which suspended payment in great majority in September, 1814. The deluge of paper money and the depreciation of the currency became, for Jefferson, a real obsession and strengthened him in his abhorrence of commercialism. He did not cease to preach the necessity of curbing the fever of speculation that had accumulated ruins upon ruins and the return to more sound regulations of the banks. "Till then," he wrote to John Adams, "we must be content to return, *quoad hoc*, to the savage state, to recur to barter in the exchange of our property, for want of a stable, common measure of value, that now in use being less fixed than the beads and wampum of the Indians." [2]

His banking theories, however, had scarcely any influence upon his contemporaries, and even Gallatin was little impressed by them. But the evident danger of inflation turned his mind back to the days when he had fought the Hamiltonian system and gave him once more an opportunity to pass judgment upon his opponent of the old days:

This most heteregeneous system was transplanted into ours from the British system, by a man whose mind was really powerful, but chained by native partialities to everything English; who had formed exaggerated ideas of the superior wisdom of their government, and sincerely believed it for the good of the country to make them their model in everything, without considering that what might be wise and good for a nation essentially commercial and entangled in complicated intercourse with numerous and powerful

[1] October 20, 1820. Memorial Edition, XV, 284.
[2] About the economic and banking theories of Jefferson, I can only indicate here some points more fully treated in my book on "Jefferson et les Idéologues." Paris, Baltimore, 1925.

neighbors, might not be so for one essentially agricultural, and insulated by nature, from the abusive governments of the old world.[1]

From this and many other passages it might be surmised that Jefferson still held to the old antimercantile theories that had crystallized in his mind when he was in Europe. If this were true, the contradiction between his conduct as President and his personal convictions would be so obvious that his sincerity might be questioned. As a matter of fact, on this point as on many others, he had undergone a slow evolution. He was certainly sincere when, shortly after leaving office, he wrote to Governor John Jay in order to make his position clearer:

An equilibrium of agriculture, manufacture, and commerce, is certainly become essential to our independence. Manufactures, sufficient for our own consumption (and no more). Commerce sufficient to carry the surplus produce of agriculture, beyond our own consumption, to a market for exchanging it for articles we cannot raise (and no more). These are the true limits of manufacture and commerce. To go beyond is to increase our dependence on foreign nations, and our liability to war.[2]

This can be taken as the final view of Jefferson on a subject on which he is often misquoted and misunderstood. That he was fully aware of the change that had taken place in his own mind can be seen in a declaration to Benjamin Austin, written in January, 1816. Between 1787 and that date, and even earlier, Jefferson had seen the light and realized that to discourage home manufactures was "to keep us in eternal vassalage to a foreign and unfriendly people." He had no patience with politicians who brought forth his old and now obsolete utterances to promote their unpatriotic designs:

You tell me I am quoted by those who wish to continue our dependance on England for manufactures. There was a time when

[1] To William H. Crawford, June 20, 1816. Memorial Edition, XV, 27.
[2] April 7, 1809. *Ibid.*, XII, 271.

I might have been so quoted with more candor, but within the thirty years which have elapsed, how circumstances changed. . . . Experience since has taught me that manufactures are now as necessary to our independence as to our comfort; and if those who quote me as of different opinion will keep pace with me in purchasing nothing foreign where an equivalent of domestic fabric can be obtained, without regard to the difference of price, it will not be our fault if we do not soon have a supply at home equivalent to our demand.[1]

Desirable as it was to promote the industrial development of the United States, it was no less desirable not to encourage it beyond a certain point.   Jefferson saw quite clearly that, under existing conditions, a great industrial growth of the country would have as an unavoidable result the perpetuation of slavery in the South and the even more undesirable creation of a proletariat in the North.   He had always held that slavery was a national sore and a shameful condition to be remedied as soon as conditions would permit.   He was looking forward to the time when this could be done without bringing about an economic upheaval; but all hope would have to be abandoned if slavery were industrialized and if slave labor became more productive.   As to the other danger of industrialism, it was no vague apprehension; one had only to consider England to see "the pauperism of the lowest class, the abject oppression of the laboring, and the luxury, the riot, the domination and the vicious happiness of the aristocracy."   This being the "happiness of scientific England", he wrote to Thomas Cooper, "now let us see the American side of the medal":

And, first, we have no paupers, the old and crippled among us, who possess nothing and have no families to take care of them, being too few to merit notice as a separate section of society, or to affect a general estimate.   The great mass of our population is of laborers; our rich, who can live without labor, either manual or professional, being few, and of moderate wealth.   Most of the laboring class

[1] January 9, 1816.   Memorial Edition, XIV, 387.

possess property, cultivate their own lands, have families, and from the demand for their labor are enabled to exact from the rich and the competent such prices as enable them to be fed abundantly, clothed above mere decency, to labor moderately and raise their families. They are not driven to the ultimate resources of dexterity and skill, because their wares will sell although not quite so nice as those of England. The wealthy, on the other hand, and those at their ease, know nothing of what the Europeans call luxury. They have only somewhat more of the comforts and decencies of life than those who furnish them. Can any condition of society be more desirable than this? [1]

Once more Jefferson appears as a true disciple and continuator of the Physiocrats and one might be tempted at first to agree entirely with Mr. Beard on this point. But this is only an appearance. To understand Jefferson's true meaning, it is necessary to turn to his unpublished correspondence with Du Pont de Nemours.[2]

The rapid industrialization of the United States had greatly alarmed the old Physiocrat. In his opinion there was a real danger lest the national character of the people be completely altered and the foundation of government deeply shaken. Considering the situation from the "economist's" point of view, Du Pont came to the conclusion that the development of home industries in America would necessarily bring about a permanent reduction in the Federal income, largely derived from import duties. The government could not be run without levying new taxes and the question was to determine what methods should be followed in the establishment of these new taxes. If the United States decided to resort to indirect taxation, that is to say, excise, the unavoidable result would be the creation of an army of new functionaries, as in France under the old régime, and the use of vexatory procedure for the en-

---

[1] To Thomas Cooper, September 10, 1814. Memorial Edition, XIV, 179.
[2] See my introduction to their correspondence. Baltimore, 1931.

forcement of the new system. Furthermore, according to the theories of the Physiocrats, indirect taxation was an economic heresy, since it was a tax on labor, which is not a source but only a transformation of wealth. The same criticism applied *a fortiori* to the English income tax which constituted the worst possible form of taxation.

In the controversy which arose between Jefferson and his old friend, the Sage of Monticello again took a middle course. First of all, he refused to concede that the development of industries could ever change the fundamental characteristics of the United States. They were essentially an agricultural nation, and an agricultural nation they would remain, in spite of all predictions to the contrary. Furthermore, the question was not to determine theoretically what was the best possible form of taxation, but to find out what form the inhabitants of the country would most easily bear. That in itself was a big enough problem and could not be solved in the abstract, since, according to Jefferson: "In most of the middle and Southern States some land tax is now paid into the State treasury, and for this purpose the lands have been classed and valued and the tax assessed according to valuation. In these an excise is most odious. In the Eastern States, land taxes are odious, excises less unpopular." [1]

Finally, Jefferson pointed out that his friend had neglected several important factors, one of them being "the continuous growth in population of the United States, which for a long time would maintain the quantum of exports and imports at the present level at least." Consequently, for several generations, the Government would be able to support itself with a tax on importations, "the best agrarian law in fact, since the poor man in the country who uses nothing but what is made within his own farm or family, or within the United States, pays not a farthing of tax to the general government." With the char-

[1] Jefferson Papers. Library of Congress. April 15, 1811.

acteristic optimism of the citizen of a young, strong and energetic country, Jefferson then added:

Our revenue once liberated by the discharge of public debt and its surplus applied to canals, roads, schools, etc., and the farmer will see his government supported, his children educated, and the face of his country made a paradise by the contributions of the rich alone without being called on to spare a cent from his earnings. The path we are now pursuing leads directly to this end, which we cannot fail to attain unless our administration should fall into unwise hands.[1]

This point alone should suffice to differentiate Jefferson's system from physiocracy, since the Physiocrats had adopted as their motto the famous *laissez faire laissez passer* and were certainly in favor of free trade. How far from Du Pont Jefferson remained in other particulars may be gathered from his "Introduction" and notes to the "Political Economy" of Destutt de Tracy, the translation and publication of which he supervised and directed. In it he paid homage to the founders of the science of political economy, and particularly to Gournay, Le Trosne and Du Pont de Nemours, "the enlightened, philanthropic and venerable citizen, now of the United States." But he pointed out that the several principles they had discussed and established had not been able to prevail, "not on account of their correctness, but because not acceptable to the people whose will must be the supreme law. Taxation is, in fact, the most difficult function of the government, and that against which their citizens are most apt to be refractory. The general aim is, therefore, to adopt the mode most consonant with the circumstances and sentiments of the country."

This is Jefferson's final judgment on the Economists. Another confirmation of his lack of interest in principles and theories not susceptible of immediate application may be seen in it. In matters of government, the important question, after

[1] Jefferson Papers. Library of Congress. April 15, 1811.

deciding what should be done, was to determine how much could be done under the circumstances, and if a particular piece of legislation was turned down by the public will or only reluctantly accepted, to bide one's time and wait for a more favorable occasion. Even when doubting the wisdom of a popular verdict, it was the duty of the public servant to do the public will. Thus in this correspondence are revealed the two sides of Jefferson's character, or to speak more exactly, the two parallel tracks in which his mind ran at different times.

At the bottom of his heart, he believed that many of the economic doctrines of Du Pont were fundamentally sound; but he also knew that the citizens of the United States were not ready to accept the truth of these principles, and he did not feel that, as an executive, he had the right to attempt to shape the destinies of his country according to his own preferences. Thus he laid himself open to the reproach of insincerity, or at least of inconsistency, for on many occasions one may find a flagrant contradiction between his public utterances and the private letters he wrote to his friends. For this reason, Du Pont de Nemours was never fully able to understand his American friend. This difference between the French theorician and the American statesman will appear even more clearly in the letters in which they exchanged views on democracy and discussed the conditions requisite for the establishment of a representative government.

Jefferson's opinion of the French people with regard to the form of government they should adopt had never varied since the earliest days of the Revolution. Every time he was consulted by his friends on the matter, he invariably answered that they could do no better than to follow as closely as possible the system of their neighbors and hereditary enemies, the British. This answer, which recurred periodically in his correspondence, was made particularly emphatic in 1801, when he again warned Lafayette that France was not ready to enjoy a truly republican government. He went on by categorically stating that what was good for America might be very harmful to another country and that even in America it was neither desirable nor possible to enforce at once all the provisions of the Constitution. Thus, in a few lines, he defined his policies more clearly than any historian has ever done; he analyzed that curious combination of unwavering principles and practical expediency so puzzling to those once called by Jefferson himself "the closet politicians."

What is practicable — he said — must often control what is purely theory and the habits of the governed determine in a great degree what is practicable. The same original principles, modified in practice to the different habits of the different nations, present governments of very different aspects. The same principles reduced to form of practice, accommodated to our habits, and put into forms accommodated to the habits of the French nation would present governments very unlike each other.[1]

Thirteen years later his opinion had not varied one iota. Reviewing the situation in France after the return of the Bourbons, he wrote to Du Pont de Nemours:

I have to congratulate you, which I do sincerely, on having got back from Robespierre and Bonaparte, to your ante-revolutionary condition. You are now nearly where you were at the Jeu de Paume, on the 20th of June 1789. The King would then have yielded by convention freedom of religion, freedom of the press, trial by jury, habeas corpus and a representative legislation. These I consider as the essentials constituting free government, and that the organization of the executive is interesting, as it may ensure wisdom and integrity in the first place, but next as it may favor or endanger the preservation of these fundamentals.[2]

The same note reappears constantly in the letters written by Jefferson to his French friends, but a rapid survey of his corre-

---

[1] Jefferson Papers. Library of Congress. January 18, 1802.
[2] *Ibid.* February 28, 1815.

spondence with Du Pont de Nemours may serve to make his position even more definite.

When, in December, 1815, Du Pont was invited by "the republics of New Grenada, Carthagenes and Caracas" to give his views on the constitution they intended to adopt, he drew up a plan of government for the "Equinoctial republics" and sent it for approval to the Sage of Monticello. Faithful to the principles of the Physiocrats, he had divided the population into two classes : the real citizens or landowners and the "inhabitants", those who work for a salary, possess nothing but personal property, can go any day from one place to another, and make with their employers contracts which they can break at any time. These were entitled to protection, peaceful enjoyment of their personal property, free speech, freedom of religion, habeas corpus, and such natural rights, but Du Pont refused them any participation in the government ; for only those who "owned the country" should have the right to decide how it was to be administered. To give the ballot to a floating population of industrial workers, unattached to the soil, who had nothing to sell except their labor, was "to brew a revolution, to pave the way for the Pisistrates, the Marius, the Caesars, who represent themselves as more democratic than they really are and than is just and reasonable, in order to become tyrants, to violate all rights, to substitute for law their arbitrary will, to offend morality and to debase humanity." [1]

This was a doctrine which Jefferson could not accept, for it was in direct contradiction to the tenets he had formulated early in his life and held to during all his career. Because he had read Locke, and more probably because he was trained as a lawyer, he opposed the contractual theory of society to this economic organization. He maintained that society was a compact, that all those who had become signatories to the compact were entitled to the same rights, and consequently

[1] Jefferson Papers. Library of Congress. December 12, 1815.

should have the same privilege to share equally in the government, except, and this proviso was important, when they freely agreed to delegate part of their powers to elected magistrates and representatives.

This was the theory, the inalienable principle to be proclaimed in a bill of rights, the necessary preamble to any constitution. In practice, however, various limitations to universal suffrage were to be recognized. One could not even think of granting the ballot to minors, to emancipated slaves or to women. It did not follow either that, all citizens being endowed with the same rights, they were equally ready to exercise the same functions in the government. Men are created equal in rights but differ in intelligence, learning, clear-sightedness and general ability. In other words, there are some natural *aristoi*, and John Adams brought Jefferson to this admission without any difficulty. If this fact be accepted, the next step is to recognize that "that form of government is the best, which provided the most effectually for a pure selection of these natural *aristoi* into offices of the government." It was the good fortune of America that all her constitutions were so worded as "to leave the citizens the free election and separation of the aristoi from the pseudo-aristoi, of the wheat from the chaff. In general, they will elect the really good and wise. In some instances, wealth may corrupt, and birth blind; but not in a sufficient degree to endanger society." [1]

According to this theory, the real function of the people is not to participate directly in all governmental activities, but to select from among themselves the most qualified citizens and the best prepared to administer the country. In a letter to Doctor Walter Jones, who had sent him a paper on democracy, Jefferson made his position even more definite by establishing a very important distinction which gives more than any other

[1] October 28, 1813. Memorial Edition, XIII, 396.

statement his true idea of a progressive democracy — an ideal to be striven for, not a condition already reached:

I would say that the people, being the only safe depository of power, should exercise in person every function which their qualifications enable them to exercise, consistently with the order and security of society; that we now find them equal to the election of those who shall be invested with their executive powers, and to act themselves in the judiciary, as judges in questions of fact; that the range of their powers ought to be enlarged. . . .[1]

In these circumstances, Jefferson's reluctance to encourage both his French and Spanish friends to establish at once a government modeled on the American government in their respective countries, is perfectly intelligible. Of all the nations of the earth, England alone could "borrow wholesale the American system."

They will probably turn their eyes to us, and be disposed to tread in the footsteps, seeing how safely these have led us into port. There is no part of or model to which they seem unequal, unless perhaps the elective presidency, and even that might possibly be rescued from the tumult of the elections, by subdividing the electoral assemblage into very small parts, such as of wards or townships, and making them simultaneous.[2]

As for the other nations, they were no more qualified to exercise the duties of a truly representative government than were the inhabitants of New Orleans at the time of the purchase. The French, in particular, had proved in several instances that they could not be intrusted with the administration of their own affairs.

More than a generation will be requisite — he wrote to Lafayette — under the administration of reasonable laws favoring the progress of knowlege in the general mass of the people, and their habituation to an independent security of person and property, before they will

[1] January 2, 1814. Memorial Edition, XIV, 46.
[2] To John Adams, October 16, 1816. *Ibid.*, XVI, 85.

be capable of estimating the value of freedom, and the necessity of sacred adherence to the principles on which it rests for preservation. Instead of that liberty which takes root and growth in the progress of reason, if recovered by mere accident or force, it becomes, with an unprepared people, a tyranny still, of the many, the few, or one.[1]

From these declarations, to which many other similar passages could be added, a capital difference between the idealism of Jefferson and the idealism of the French philosophers becomes quite obvious. The author of the Declaration of Independence had proclaimed that all men are born free and equal, but he never thought that women, Indians and newly enfranchized slaves should be admitted to the same rights and privileges as the other citizens. In like fashion, although representative government remains the best possible form of government, he found it desirable that some people, who are still children, should not be granted at once the full enjoyment of their natural rights. Thus self-government, which had become a well established fact and a reality in America, should remain for other peoples a reward to be obtained after a long and painful process of education. It could be hoped that some day, after many disastrous experiments and much suffering, the peoples of Europe and South America might deserve the blessings enjoyed by the American people. But nothing was further from the character of Jefferson than to preach the gospel of Americanism to all the nations of the world. Instead of considering as desirable a close imitation of the American Constitution by the newly liberated nations, he maintained that each people should mold their institutions according to their own habits and traditions. Far from being a Jacobin, a wild radical, or a "closet philosopher", this practical politician had come to the conclusion that each people have the government they deserve, and that durable improvements can come only as a result of the improvement of the moral qualities of every

[1] To Lafayette, February 14, 1815. Memorial Edition, XIV, 245.

citizen — from within and not from without. Such a moderate conclusion may surprise those who are accustomed to damn or praise Jefferson on a few sentences or axioms detached from their context; but, after careful scrutiny of the evidence, it seems difficult to accept any other interpretation.

Comparatively perfect as it was, the government of the United States presented certain germs of weakness, corruption and degeneracy. The Sage of Monticello did not fail to call his friends' attention to some of the dangers looming up on the horizon. As he had warned them against inflation, he opposed the formation of societies which might become so strong as "to obstruct the operation of the government and undertake to regulate the foreign, fiscal, and military as well as domestic affairs." This might be taken already as a warning against lobbying. He was fully aware that a time might come when the speeches of the Senators and Representatives "would cease to be read at all" and when the Legislature would not enjoy the full confidence of the people. He deplored the law vacating nearly all the offices of government nearly every four years, for "it will keep in constant excitement all the hungry cormorants for office, render them as well as those in place sycophants to their Senators, engage in eternal intrigue to turn out and put in another, in cabale to swap work, and make of them what all executive directories become, mere sinks of corruption and faction." [1]

Serious and pressing as these dangers were, they could be left to future generations to avoid, but at the very moment he wrote another fear obsessed his mind:

The banks, bankrupt laws, manufactures, Spanish treaty are nothing. These are occurrences which, like waves in a storm, will pass under the ship. But the Missouri question is a breaker on which we lose the Missouri country by revolt, and what more God only knows. From the Battle of Bunker's Hill to the treaty of

[1] To James Madison, November 29, 1820. Memorial Edition, XV, 295.

Paris, we never had so ominous a question . . . I thank God that I shall not live to witness its issue.[1]

No New Englander had done more to promote the cause of abolition than Jefferson; on two occasions he had proposed legislative measures to put an end to the scourge of slavery and he had never ceased to look for a solution that would permit the emancipation of the slaves without endangering the racial integrity of the United States. But this was no longer a question of humanity. What mattered most was not whether slavery would be recognized in Missouri or not. Slavery had become a political question; it had created a geographical division between the States, and the very existence of the Union was at stake. As on so many other occasions, the old statesman had a truly prophetic vision of the future when he wrote to John Adams early in 1820:

If Congress has the power to regulate the conditions of the inhabitants of the States, within the States, it will be but another exercise of that power to declare that all shall be free. Are we then to see again Athenian and Lacedemonian confederacies? To wage another Peloponesian war to settle the ascendency between them? Or is this the tocsin of merely a servile war? That remains to be seen; but not, I hope, by you or me.[2]

The whole question was fraught with such difficulties that Jefferson refused to discuss the abolition of slavery with Lafayette when the Marquis paid him a last visit at Monticello. With his American friends he was less reserved. When, as early as 1811, James Ogilvie asked him to suggest an important and interesting subject for a series of lectures he intended to deliver in the Southern States, Jefferson could think of nothing more momentous than a discourse "on the benefit of the union, and miseries which would follow a separation of the States, to be exemplified in the eternal and wasting wars of Europe,

[1] December 10, 1819. Memorial Edition, XV, 233.
[2] To John Adams, January 22, 1821. *Ibid.*, XV, 309.

in the pillage and profligacy to which these lead, and the abject oppression and degradation to which they reduce its inhabitants." [1]

Jefferson has so long been represented as the champion of State rights, he stood so vigorously against all possible encroachments of the States' sovereignty by the Federal Government, that we have a natural tendency to forget this aspect of his policies and to see in him only the man who inspired the Kentucky resolutions. It must be remembered, however, that he never ceased to preach the necessity of the union to his fellow countrymen, that when President he lived in a constant fear of secession by the New England States, that he stopped all his efforts in favor of abolition lest he should inject into the life of the country a political issue which might disrupt national unity. While he claimed that theoretically the States had a right to secede, he could no more consider actual secession than he would have approved of any man breaking the social compact in order to live the precarious life of the savage.

From these dangers nothing could preserve the United States except what Du Pont de Nemours called once "the cool common sense" of their citizens. It was the only foundation on which to rest all hopes for the future, for American democracy is not a thing which exists on paper, it is not a thing which can be created overnight by law, decree or constitution, it is not to be looked for in any document. "Where is our republicanism to be found," wrote Jefferson to Samuel Kercheval. "Not in our constitution certainly, but merely in the spirit of our people. Owing to this spirit, and to nothing in the form of our constitution all things have gone well." [2]

One of the most reassuring manifestations of this spirit was seen in the willingness of the people to choose the best qualified persons as their representatives, executives and magistrates.

---

[1] August 4, 1811. Memorial Edition, XIII, 68.
[2] July 12, 1816. Ibid., XV, 32.

But if the Republic was to endure, it was necessary to enlighten and cultivate the disposition of the people, and it was no less important to provide a group of men qualified through their natural ability and training, to discuss and conduct the affairs of the community. Thus Jefferson was induced to take up again in his old days one of his pet schemes, the famous bill for the diffusion of knowledge.

As a matter of fact, he had never abandoned it completely, and its very purpose had been explained already in the "Notes on Virginia":

In every government on earth there is some trace of human weakness, some germ of corruption and degeneracy. . . . Each government degenerates when trusted to the rulers of the people alone. The people themselves are therefore its only safe depositories. And to render even them safer, their minds must be improved to a certain degree. This is not all that is necessary, though it be essentially necessary.

During his stay in Europe, Jefferson had become acquainted with great universities, particularly those of Edinburgh and Geneva, and after coming back to America he shifted somewhat the emphasis. It was not so immediately necessary to improve the minds of all the citizens as to form an *élite*, a body of specialists who might become the true leaders of the nation. This seems to have been the object of his plan, to bring over to America the whole faculty of the University of Geneva to establish a national university at Richmond or in the vicinity of Federal City. This scheme was only defeated because of the opposition of Washington who, with great common sense, realized how incongruous it would be to call National University an institution where the teaching would be conducted entirely in a foreign language and by foreigners.

Even after this plan had failed, Jefferson did not give up his ambition to establish somewhere in America and preferably in Virginia, an institution of higher learning. On January 18, 1800, he wrote to Joseph Priestley to ask him to draw up the program of a university "on a plan so broad, so liberal, and modern, as to be worth patronizing with the public support. The first thing is to obtain a good plan."

Priestley sent him, in answer, some "Hints Concerning Public Education" which have never been published and probably did not arouse any enthusiasm in Jefferson. The English philosopher had simply taken the main features of the English system, placing the emphasis on the ancient languages and excluding the modern: "For the knowledge of them as well as skill in fencing, dancing and riding is proper for gentlemen liberally educated, and instruction in them may be procured on reasonable terms without burdening the funds of the seminary with them." He ended with a very sensible piece of advice:

> Three things must be attended to in the education of youth. They must be *taught, fed,* and *governed,* and each of these requires different qualifications. In the English universities all these offices are perfectly distinct. The *tutors* only teach, the *proctors* superintend the discipline, and the *cooks* provide the victuals.[1]

At the same time Jefferson had sent a similar request to Du Pont de Nemours. Curiously enough, the Frenchman manifested little enthusiasm for the proposal of his friend. To establish a university was all very well, but first of all one had to provide solid foundations and to place educational facilities within the reach of the great mass of citizens — the university being only the apex of the pyramid. On this occasion Du Pont reminded Jefferson that he had expressed himself to such an intent some fifteen years earlier in his "Notes on Virginia", which developed the excellent view that colleges and universities are not the most important part of the educational system of the State:

[1] Jefferson Papers. Library of Congress. May 8, 1800.

All knowledge readily and daily usable, all practical sciences, all laborious activities, all the common sense, all the correct ideas, all the morality, all the virtue, all the courage, all the prosperity, all the happiness of a nation and particularly of a Republic must spring from the primary schools or Petites Ecoles.[1]

By July, 1800, Du Pont de Nemours, who had already proposed a similar scheme to the French Government, had completed his manuscript and sent it to Jefferson at the end of August. This was more speed than Jefferson had expected, and Du Pont's plan was far too elaborate and too comprehensive to be of immediate value. "There is no occasion to incommode yourself by pressing it," wrote Jefferson, "as when received it will be some time before we shall probably find a good occasion of bringing forward the subject." [2]

During his presidency, Jefferson had had to lay aside all his plans and postpone any action for the organization of public education in his native State until after his retirement. In the meantime, he read and studied the project of Du Pont de Nemours and corresponded with Pictet of Geneva; he had in his hands several memoirs of Julien on the French schools, and he looked everywhere for precedents and suggestions. His views were finally formulated in a "Plan for Elementary Schools" sent to Joseph C. Cabell from Poplar Forest, on September 9, 1817. The act to be submitted to the Assembly of Virginia was far more comprehensive than the title indicates. It provided for the establishment in each county of a certain number of elementary schools, supported by the county and placed under the supervision of visitors; the counties of the commonwealth were to be distributed into nine collegiate districts, and as many colleges, or rather secondary schools, instituted at the expense of the literary fund, "to be supported

---

[1] Jefferson Papers. Library of Congress. April 21, 1800.
[2] *Ibid.*, July 26, 1800.

from it, and to be placed under the supervision of the Board of Public Instruction."

"In the said colleges," proposed Jefferson, "shall be taught the Greek, Latin, French, Spanish, Italian and German languages, English grammar, geography, ancient and modern, the higher branches in numeral arithmetic, the mensuration of land, the use of the globes, and the ordinary elements of navigation."

A third part of the act provided for

. . . establishing in a central and healthy part of the State an University wherein all the branches of useful sciences may be taught . . . such as history and geography, ancient and modern; natural philosophy, agriculture, chemistry, and the theories of medicine; anatomy, zoölogy, botany, mineralogy and geology; mathematics, pure and mixed, military and naval science; ideology, ethics, the law of nature and of nations; law, municipal, and foreign; the science of civil government and political economy; languages, rhetoric, belleslettres, and the fine arts generally; which branches of science will be so distributed and under so many professorships, not exceeding ten as the Visitors shall think most proper.

Finally, in order "to avail the commonwealth of those talents and virtues which nature has sown as liberally among the poor as among the rich, and which are lost to their country by the want of means of their cultivation", the visitors would select every year a certain number of promising scholars from the ward schools to be sent to the colleges and from the colleges to be sent to the University at the public expense.

This was essentially the Bill for the Diffusion of Knowledge proposed to the Assembly in 1779. Jefferson had incorporated in it such modifications as he may have borrowed from Du Pont de Nemours, but essentially the plan was his own. That Jefferson himself was perfectly aware of it appears in a short mention of the fact that "the general idea was suggested in the 'Notes on Virginia.' Quer. 14." [1]

[1] To Thomas Cooper, January 16, 1814. Memorial Edition, XIV, 60.

It was soon realized that neither the Assembly nor the public were ready for such a comprehensive scheme. Part of the plan had to be sacrificed, if a beginning was to be made at all. Jefferson did not hesitate long; the elementary schools could be organized at any time without much preparation or expense; secondary education was taken care of after a fashion in private schools supported from fees; but nothing existed in the way of an institution of higher learning. Young Virginians had to be sent to the northern seminaries, there "imbibing opinions and principles in discord with those of our own country." The university was the thing, and, in order to provide sufficient funds to start it, Jefferson proposed that subsidies from the literary fund to the primary schools be suspended for one or two years. In his opinion this measure did not imply any disregard of primary education, and Jefferson vehemently protested to Breckenridge that he had "never proposed a sacrifice of the primary to the ultimate grade of instruction"; but, "if we cannot do everything at once, let us do one at a time." [1]

The fight in which Jefferson engaged to obtain recognition for his project, to have Central College or, as it was finally to be called, the University of Virginia, located near Monticello, where he could watch its progress and supervise the construction of its buildings, has been told many times and does not need to be recounted here.[2]

On the board of visitors with Jefferson were placed James Madison, James Monroe, Joseph C. Cabell, James Breckenridge, David Watson and J. H. Cocke. Jefferson was appointed Rector of the University at a meeting held on March 29, 1819, at a time when the university had no buildings, no faculty, no students and very small means. Everything had to be done

---

[1] February 15, 1821. Memorial Edition, XV, 315.
[2] The latest account is the monumental "History of the University of Virginia" by Professor Philip Alexander Bruce, New York, 4 vols., 1920. See also the excellent study of Herbert B. Adams, "Thomas Jefferson and the University of Virginia", United States Bureau of Education. Circular of information No. 1, 1888.

and provided for.   It would have been possible to put up some sort of temporary shelter, a few ramshackle frame houses, but Jefferson wanted the university to endure and he remembered that he was an architect as well as a statesman.   It was not until the spring of 1824 that he could announce that the buildings were ready for occupancy — the formal opening was to be held at the beginning of the following year — but the master builder could be proud of his work.   The university was his in every sense of the word : not only had he succeeded in arousing the interest of the public and the Assembly in his undertaking, but he had drawn the plans himself with the painstaking care and the precision he owed to his training as a surveyor.   He had selected the material, engaged the stone carvers, the brick layers and the carpenters, and supervised every bit of their work. After his death he would need no other monument.

Then, as everything seemed to be ready, a new difficulty arose.   Ever since 1819, the visitors had been looking for a faculty.   Ticknor, with whom Jefferson had gotten acquainted through Mrs. Adams, had refused to leave Cambridge although disgusted with the petty bickerings of his colleagues.   Thomas Cooper had proved inacceptable, and the very mention of his name had aroused such a storm among the clergy that the appointment had to be withdrawn.   After a long and fruitless search for the necessary talents at home, Jefferson and his fellow members on the board of the university decided to procure the professors from abroad.   This time, however, they were not to repeat the mistake of the proposed transplantation of the University of Geneva.   Several prominent Frenchmen suggested by Lafayette were turned down as too ignorant of the ways of American youth and the language of the country.   There remained only one place from which satisfactory instructors could be obtained; this was England.   Their nationality did not raise any serious objection, for, to the resentment of the War of 1812 had succeeded the "era of good feeling", and

Francis Walker Gilmer was commissioned to go to England in order to consult with Dugald Stewart and to recruit a faculty from Great Britain, "the land of our own language, habits and manners." [1]

Eighteen months later, the Rector declared the experiment highly successful, and the example likely to be followed by other institutions of learning.

It cannot fail — wrote Jefferson — to be one of the efficacious means of promoting that cordial good will, which it is so much the interest of both nations to cherish. These teachers can never utter an unfriendly sentiment towards their native country; and those into whom their instruction will be infused, are not of ordinary significance only; they are exactly the persons who are to succeed to the government of our country, and to rule its future enmities, its friendships and fortunes. [2]

Thus after fifty years, Jefferson was able to make real his educational dream of the Revolutionary period, to endow his native State with an institution of higher learning in which the future leaders of the nation would be instructed. They would no longer have to be sent abroad to obtain the required knowledge in some subjects; nor would they have to study in "the Northern seminaries", there to be infected with pernicious doctrines; above all, they would be preserved from any sectarian influence during their formative years; for no particular creed was to be taught at the university, although the majority of the faculty belonged to the Episcopal Church.

The University of Virginia was the last great task to which Jefferson put his hand, an achievement of which he was no less proud than of having written the Declaration of Independence. To bring it to a successful conclusion this septuagenarian displayed an admirable tenacity, a resourcefulness, a practical

[1] To Richard Rush, April 26, 1824. Memorial Edition, XVI, 31.
[2] To the Honorable J. Evelyn Denison, M. P., November 9, 1825. *Ibid.*, XVI, 129.

wisdom, a sense of the immediate possibilities and an idealistic vision, the combination of which typifies the best there is in the national character of the American people. It would take many pages to study in detail Jefferson's educational ideas, as he expressed them in the minutes of the board and in his many letters to John Adams, Thomas Cooper and Joseph Cabell. The most remarkable feature of the new institution was that, for the first time in the history of the country, higher education was made independent of the Church, and to a large extent the foundation of the University of Virginia marks the beginning of the secularization of scientific research in America. Its "father" certainly gave some thought to the possible extension of the educational system that had finally won recognition in his native Virginia, to all the States in the country; but he was too fully aware of the difficulties to follow his old friend Du Pont de Nemours and to propose a Plan for a National Education. At least he "had made a beginning", he "had set an example", and he built even better than he knew. The man who wished to be remembered as the "father of the University of Virginia" was also, in more than one sense, the father of the State universities which play such an important part in the education of the American democracy.

CHAPTER III

THE PHILOSOPHY OF OLD AGE

OLD people are often accused of being too conservative, and even reactionary. They seem out of step with the younger generations, and very few preserve enough resiliency to keep in touch with the ceaseless changes taking place around them. But a few men who, born in the second half of the eighteenth century, lived well up into the nineteenth, were able to escape this apparently unavoidable law of nature. After witnessing political convulsions, commotions and revolutions, they clung tenaciously to the faith of their younger days. They refused to accept the view that the world was going from bad to worse; they looked untiringly for every symptom of improvement and thought they could distinguish everywhere signs foretelling the dawn of a new era. The growing infirmities of their bodies did not leave them any illusion about their inevitable disappearance from the stage and they were not upheld by any strong belief in personal immortality. But however uncertain and hazy may have been their religious tenets, they had a stanch faith in the unlimited capacity of human nature for improvement and development. They believed in the irresistible power of truth, in the ultimate recognition of natural principles and natural laws, in the religion of progress as it had been formulated by the eighteenth-century philosophers. Thus, rather than follow the precept of the ancient poet and unhitch their aging horses, they had anticipated the advice of the American philosopher by hitching their wagon to a star.

Du Pont de Nemours, experimenting with his sons to develop American industries in order to make America economically

independent from Europe; Destutt de Tracy, almost completely blind, dictating his treatise on political economy and
appearing in the streets of Paris during the glorious days of
1830; Lafayette, yearning and hoping for the recognition of his
ideal of liberty during the Empire and the *Restauration* — all of
these were more than survivors of a forgotten age. Even to the
younger generations they represented the living embodiment of
the political faith of the nineteenth century. It is not a mere
coincidence that most of them were friends and admirers of the
Sage of Monticello, whose letters they read "as the letters of the
Apostles were read in the circle of the early Christians."

Jefferson could complain that "the decays of age had enfee-
bled the useful energies of the mind",[1] but he kept, practically
to his last day, his alertness, his encyclopædic curiosity and
an extraordinary capacity for work. A large part of his time
was taken by his correspondence. Turning to his letter list
for 1820 he found that he had received no less than "one thousand two hundred and sixty-seven communications, many of
them requiring answers of elaborate research, and all of them
to be answered with due attention and consideration." [2] I may
be permitted to add that a large part of the letters he received
as well as those he wrote deserve publication and would greatly
contribute to our knowledge of the period.

Among them essays and short treatises on every possible
subject under heaven will be found. With Du Pont de
Nemours, Jefferson discussed not only questions of political
economy, education and government, but the acclimation of the
merino sheep, the manufacturing of woolen goods and nails,
the construction of gunboats and the organization of the militia.
With Madame de Tessé, Lafayette's aged cousin, he resumed the
exchange of botanical views, interrupted by his presidency and
the continental blockade. He undertook to put together the

---

[1] To John Brazier, August 24, 1814. Memorial Edition, XV, 207.
[2] June 27, 1822. *Ibid.*, XV, 387.

scraps of paper on which he had scribbled notes during Washington's and Adams' administrations and compiled his famous
"Anas"; he wrote his "Autobiography", furnished documents
to Girardin for his continuation of Burke's "History of Virginia"; he answered queries on the circumstances under which
he had written the Declaration of Independence, the Kentucky
Resolution, on his attitude towards France when Secretary of
State and President; he criticized quite extensively Marshall's
"History of Washington" and one of his last letters, written on
May 15, 1826, was to inform one of his friends of the facts concerning "Arnold's invasion and surprise of Richmond, in the
winter of 1780–81." [1]

His interest in books was greater than ever; he had scarcely
sold his library to Congress when he undertook to collect
another, going systematically through the publishers' catalogues, writing to booksellers in Richmond, Philadelphia, New
York and even abroad, requesting his European friends to
send him the latest publications and asking young Ticknor to
procure for him, in France or Germany, the best editions of
the Greek and Latin classics.   He drew up the plans for the
University of Virginia and supervised the construction of the
building.   Between times he took upon himself the task of
rewriting entirely the translation of Destutt de Tracy's "Review
of Montesquieu" and directed the printing of his treatise on
"Political Economy."   After writing letters, regulating the
work of the farm, he spent several hours on horseback every
day and during the balance of the afternoon read new and old
books, played with his grandchildren, walked in the garden to
look at his favorite trees, listened to music and, during the
fine weather, received the visitors who flocked to Monticello
by the dozens.   Some were simply idlers coming out of curiosity, many were old friends who stayed for days or weeks; but
all were welcomed with the same affable courtesy and the same

[1] Memorial Edition, XVI, 173.

generous hospitality, according to the best traditions of old Virginia.

They came from all nations, at all times — wrote Doctor Dunglison — and paid longer or shorter visits. I have known a New England judge bring a letter of introduction and stay three weeks. The learned abbé Correa, always a welcome guest, passed some weeks of each year with us during the whole time of his stay in the country. We had persons from abroad, from all the States of the Union, from every part of the State — men, women, and children. . . . People of wealth, fashion, men in office, Protestant clergymen, Catholic priests, members of Congress, foreign ministers, missionaries, Indian agents, tourists, travellers, artists, strangers, friends.[1]

No sound estimate of the extraordinary influence exerted by Jefferson upon the growth of liberalism can be made at the present time. It would require separate studies, careful investigation and the publication of many letters, safely preserved but too little used, which rest in the Jefferson Papers of the Library of Congress, and with the Massachusetts Historical Society. I have already printed Jefferson's correspondence with Volney, Destutt de Tracy, Lafayette and Du Pont de Nemours; many other letters, no less significant, remain practically unknown. He encouraged his European friends, Correa de Serra, Kosciusko, the Greek Coray, to keep up their courage, to hope against hope. To all of them he preached the same gospel of faith in the ultimate and inevitable recognition throughout the world of the principles of American democracy. This was not done for propaganda's sake, for no man would deserve less than Jefferson the dubious qualification of propagandist. The many letters written to his American friends on the same subject clearly show that this was his profound conviction and almost his only *raison d'être*. His was not an over-optimistic temperament; he did not fail to notice all "the specks of hurricane on the horizon of the world." Yet, all considered, and in spite of

[1] Doctor Dunglison's Memorandum, in "Domestic Life", p. 402.

temporary fits of despondency, his conclusion on the future of democracy can be summed up in the words he wrote to John Adams at the end of 1821 :

I will not believe our labors are lost. I shall not die without a hope that light and liberty are on a steady advance. We have seen indeed, once within the record of history, the complete eclipse of the human mind continuing for centuries . . . even should the cloud of barbarism and despotism again obscure the science and liberties of Europe, this country remains to preserve and restore light and liberty to them. In short, the flames kindled on the 4th of July 1776, have spread over too much of the globe to be extinguished by the feeble engines of despotism; on the contrary, they will consume these engines and all who work them.[1]

Jefferson felt such a dislike for unnecessary controversies that he was apt to adopt the tone and the style of his correspondents and apparently to accept their ideas, so that many contradictions can be found in these letters. To a chosen few only he fully revealed his intimate thoughts and without reticence, without fear of being betrayed, communicated his doubts, his hopes and his hatred. The letters he wrote to Short, Priestley, and Thomas Cooper are most remarkable in this respect. But with none of them did he communicate so freely as with his old friend John Adams. The correspondence that passed between them during the last fifteen years of their lives constitutes one of the most striking and illuminating human documents a student of psychology may ever hope to discover. To those who have had the privilege of using the manuscripts to follow month by month the palsied hand of Adams until he had to cease writing himself and dictated his letters to a "female member of his household", it seems unthinkable that the wish expressed by Wirt in 1826, — to see the correspondence between the two great men published in its entirety, — should not have received its fulfillment.

[1] September 12, 1821. Memorial Edition, XV, 334.

They had been estranged for a long time, and no word had passed between them for more than ten years after Adams' sulky departure from Washington on the morning of March 4, 1801. At the beginning of 1811, Doctor Benjamin Rush made bold to deplore "the discontinuance of friendly correspondence between Mr. Adams and Mr. Jefferson." Jefferson answered quite lengthily, giving a long account of his difficulties with Adams, including the letter written by Abigail Adams in 1802, but adding that he would second with pleasure every effort made to bring about a reconciliation. However, he did not entertain much hope that Doctor Rush would succeed, for he knew it was "part of Mr. Adams' character to suspect foul play in those of whom he is jealous, and not easily to relinquish his suspicions." [1]

It was not until the end of the same year that Jefferson took up the subject again, having heard that during a conversation Adams had mentioned his name, adding: "I always loved Jefferson, and still love him." This was enough, and it only remained to create an opportunity to resume the correspondence without too much awkwardness; but "from this fusion of sentiments" Mrs. Adams was "of course to be separated", for Jefferson could not believe that the woman wounded in her motherly pride had forgotten anything. This was no insuperable obstacle, however: "It will only be necessary that I never name her" wrote Jefferson.[2]

Adams took the first step, sending to Jefferson "a piece of homespun lately produced in this quarter", which was nothing but the lectures delivered by J. Q. Adams at Harvard. Jefferson could but acknowledge the peace offering, which he did most gracefully, without mentioning Mrs. Adams.[3] But he was too much of a Southern gentleman to hold a resentment long, even

---

[1] January 16, 1811.   Memorial Edition, XIII, 9.
[2] December 5, 1811.   *Ibid.*, XIII, 114.
[3] January 21, 1812.   *Ibid.*, XIII, 123.

against a woman of such a jealous disposition. Two months later he sent for the first time the homage of his respects to Mrs. Adams, after which he never forgot to mention her. On two occasions he even wrote her charming letters, in the same friendly tone as he had used with her twenty-five years earlier, when he used to do shopping for her in Paris. On hearing of her death on November 13, 1818, he sent to his stricken old friend a touching expression of his sympathy:

Will I say more where words are vain, but that it is of some comfort to us both, that the term is not very distant, at which we are to deposit in the same cerement our sorrows and suffering bodies, and to ascend in essence to an ecstatic meeting with the friends we have loved and lost, and whom we shall still love and never lose again.[1]

Quite naturally, as the circle of his friends grew narrower and one after the other were called by death, Jefferson's thoughts turned to the hereafter. In his youth he had apparently settled the problem once for all; but the solution then found was scarcely more than a temporary expedient. It may behove a young man full of vigor, with a long stretch of years before him, to declare that "the business of life is with matter" and that it serves no purpose to break our heads against a blank wall. There are very few men, if they are thinking at all, who can entirely dismiss from their minds the perplexing and torturing riddle, as the term grows nearer every day. Such an ataraxia may have been obtained by a few sages of old, but it is hardly human, and Jefferson, like Adams, was very human. This is a subject, however, which I cannot approach without some reluctance. Jefferson himself would have highly disapproved of such a discussion. After submitting silently to so many fierce criticisms, after being accused of atheism, materialism, impiety and philosophism by his contemporaries, he hoped that the question would never be broached to him again.

[1] Memorial Edition, XV, 174.

With those who tried to revive it, he had absolutely no patience.

One of our fan-coloring biographers — he wrote once — who paint:small men as very great, inquired of me lately, with real affection too, whether he might consider as authentic, the change in my religion much spoken of in some circles. Now this supposed that they knew what had been my religion before, taking for it the word of their priests, whom I certainly never made the confidants of my creed. My answer was: "Say nothing of my religion. It is known to my God and myself alone. Its evidence before the world is to be sought in my life; if that has been *honest and dutiful* to society, the religion which has regulated it cannot be a bad one." [1]

Unfortunately the controversy is still going on and at least a few points must be indicated here. The simplest and to some extent the most acceptable treatment of the matter was given a few years after his death by the physician who attended him up to the last minutes:

It is due, also, to that illustrious individual to say, that, in all my intercourse with him, I never heard an observation that savored, in the slightest degree, of impiety. His religious belief harmonized more closely with that of the Unitarians than of any other denomination, but it was liberal, and untrammelled by sectarian feelings and prejudices.[2]

But Doctor Dunglison's declaration is somewhat unsatisfactory and misleading, for Jefferson once gave his own definition of Unitarianism. From a letter he wrote to James Smith in 1822 it appears he was not ready to join the Unitarian Church any more than any other:

About Unitarianism, the doctrine of the early ages of Christianity . . . the pure and simple unity of the Creator of the universe, is now all but ascendant in the Eastern States; it is dawning in the West,

---

[1] January 11, 1817. Memorial Edition, XV, 97.
[2] February 21, 1825. "Domestic Life", p. 423.

and advancing towards the South; and I confidently expect that the present generation will see Unitarianism become the general religion of the United States. . . . I write with freedom, because, while I claim a right to believe in one God, if so my reason tells me, I yield as freely to others that of believing in three.[1]

On the other hand, one might easily be misled by some declarations of Jefferson to his more intimate friends. "I am a materialist — I am an Epicurian," he wrote on several instances to John Adams, Thomas Cooper and Short, with whom he felt that he could discuss religious questions more freely than with any others. Rejecting the famous *Cogito ergo sum* of Descartes, he fell back when in doubt on his "habitual anodyne": "I feel therefore I exist." This in his opinion did not imply the sole existence of matter, but simply that he could not "conceive *thought* to be an action of a particular organisation of matter, formed for the purpose by its Creator, as well as that attraction is an action of matter, or magnetism of loadstone." Then he added: "I am supported in my creed of materialism by the Lockes, the Tracys and the Stewarts. At what age of the Christian Church this heresy of immaterialism or masked atheism, crept in, I do not exactly know. But a heresy it certainly is. Jesus taught nothing of it."[2]

In the same sense he could write to Judge Augustus S. Woodward: "Jesus himself, the Founder of our religion, was unquestionably a Materialist as to man. In all His doctrines of the resurrection, he teaches expressly that the body is to rise in substances."[3]

His definition of Epicurism would seem equally remote from the popular acceptation, and certainly Jefferson was never of those who could deserve the old appellation of *Epicuri de grege porcus;* for his Epicurus is the philosopher "whose

[1] To James Smith, December 8, 1822.   Memorial Edition, XV, 410.
[2] To John Adams, August 15, 1820.   *Ibid.*, XV, 269–276.
[3] March 24, 1824.   *Ibid.*, XVI, 17.

doctrines contain everything rational in moral philosophy which Greece and Rome have left us." [1]

All through the year 1813 and on many occasions after that date, Adams tried to draw him out on the question of religion. "For," as he said, "these things are to me, at present, the marbles and nine-pins of old age; I will not say beads and prayer books." But Jefferson could not have declared, as did his old friend: "For more than sixty years I have been attentive to this great subject. Controversies between Calvinists and Arminians, Trinitarians and Unitarians, Deists and Christians, Atheists and both, have attracted my attention, whenever the singular life I have led would admit, to all these questions." [2]

Not so with Jefferson, who felt a real abhorrence for theological discussions and considered them as a sheer waste of time. They belonged to a past age and were to be buried in oblivion lest they create again an atmosphere of fanaticism and intolerance; at best, they could be left to the clergy. But tolerant as he was, there were certain doctrines against which Jefferson revolted even in later life, as he probably did when a student at William and Mary:

I can never join Calvin in addressing *his God*. He was indeed an atheist, which I can never be; or rather his religion was dæmonism. If ever man worshipped a false God, he did. The God described in his five points, is not the God whom you acknowledge and adore, the Creator and benevolent Governor of the world; but a dæmon of malignant spirit.

But right after this virulent denunciation comes a most interesting admission. If Jefferson's God was not the God of Calvin, he was just as remote from the mechanistic materialism of D'Holbach and La Mettrie as he was from Calvinism

---

[1] October 31, 1819. Memorial Edition, XV, 219.
[2] July 13, 1813. *Ibid.*, XIII, 319.

and predestination. Leaving aside all questions of dogmas and revelation he held that :

When we take a view of the universe, in its parts, general or particular, it is impossible for the human mind not to perceive and feel a conviction of design, consummate skill, and indefinite power in every atom of its composition. So irresistible are these evidences of an intelligent and powerful Agent, that of the infinite numbers of men who have existed through all time, they have believed, in the proportion of a million at least to a unit, in the hypothesis of an eternal pre-existence of a Creator, rather than in that of a self existing universe.[1]

From this passage, it would seem that Jefferson founded his belief in the existence of God on the two well-known arguments : the order of the Universe and the general consensus of opinion. If it were so, he would follow close on the steps of the English deists of the school of Pope. But religion to him was something more than the mere "acknowledgement" and "adoration of the benevolent Governor of the world";

It is more than an inner conviction of the existence of the Creator; true religion is morality. If by *religion* we are to understand *sectarian dogmas*, in which no two of them agree, then your exclamation on that hypothesis is just, "that this would be the best possible of all possible worlds, if there were no religion in it." But if the moral precepts, innate in man, and made a part of his physical consititution, as necessary for a social being, if the sublime doctrines of philanthropism and deism taught us by Jesus of Nazareth, in which we all agree, constitute true religion, then, without it, this would be, as you again say, "something not fit to be named even, indeed, a hell."[2]

On this point as on so many others Jefferson is distinctly an eighteenth-century man. One of the pet schemes of the philosophers was to prove that there is no necessary connection between religion and morality. It was an essential article

[1] To John Adams, April 11, 1820. Memorial Edition, XV, 427.
[2] To John Adams, May 5, 1817. *Ibid.*, XV, 109.

of the philosophical creed from Pierre Bayle to Jefferson, and long before them, Montaigne had filled his "Essays" with countless anecdotes and examples tending to prove this point. But Jefferson went one step farther than most of the French philosophers, with the exception of Rousseau. Morality is not founded on a religious basis; religion is morality. This being accepted, it remains to determine the foundation of morality. In a letter written to Thomas Law during the summer of 1814, Jefferson examined the different solutions proposed by theologians and philosophers and clearly indicated his preference.

"It was vain to say that it was truth; for truth is elusive, unattainable, and there is no certain criticism of it." It is not either the "love of God", for an atheist may have morality, and "Diderot, d'Holbach, Condorcet, are known to have been the most virtuous of men." It is not either the *to kalon*, for many men are deprived of any æsthetic sense. Self-interest is more satisfactory, but even the demonstration given by Helvétius is not perfectly convincing. All these explanations are one step short of the ultimate question.

The truth of the matter is, that Nature has implanted in our breasts a love of others, a sense of duty to them, a moral instinct, in short, which prompts us irresistibly to feel and succour their distresses. It is true that these social dispositions are not implanted in every man, because there is no rule without exceptions; but it is false reasoning which converts exceptions into the general rule. Some men are born without the organs of sight, or of hearing, or without hands. Yet it would be wrong to say that man is born without these faculties. When the moral sense is wanting, we endeavor to supply the defect by education; by appeals to reason and calculation, by presenting to the being so unhappily conformed other motives to do good. But nature has constituted utility to man the social test of virtue. The same act may be useful and consequently virtuous in a country which is injurious and vicious in another differently circumstanced. I sincerely then believe, with you, in the general existence of a moral instinct. I think it is the brightest gem with which the human character is studded, and the want of it is more degrading than the most hideous of the bodily deformities.[1]

The test of morality then becomes, not self-interest, as Helvétius had maintained (and Jefferson reproved Destutt de Tracy for having accepted this theory), but general interest and social utility. This is almost the criterium of Kant and one would be tempted to press this parallelism, if there was any reason to believe that the Philosopher of Monticello had ever heard the name of the author of "Practical Reason." On this point, as on so many others, Jefferson differs radically from Rousseau, who admitted also a benevolent governor of the world and the existence of a moral instinct, but who would have strenuously denied that this moral instinct was nothing but the social instinct. Jefferson, on the contrary, is led to recognize the existence of morality, chiefly because, man being a social being, society cannot be organized and subsist if it is not composed of moral beings.

Reading, reflection and time have convinced me that the interests of society require the observation of those moral precepts in which all religions agree, (for all forbid us to murder, steal, plunder or bear false witness,) and that we should not intermeddle with the particular dogmas in which all religions differ, and which are totally unconnected with morality. In all of them we see good men, and as many in one as another. The varieties of structures of action of the human mind as in those in the body, are the work of our Creator, against which it cannot be a religious duty to erect the standard of uniformity. The practice of morality being necessary for the well-being of society, he has taken care to impress its precepts so indelibly on our hearts that they shall not be effaced by the subtleties of our brain.[2]

[1] June 13, 1814. Memorial Edition, XIV, 141.
[2] To James Fishback, September 27, 1809. *Ibid.*, XII, 315.

This was stated more humorously by John Adams after they had treated the subject exhaustively in a series of letters: "Vain man, mind your own business. Do no wrong —; do all the good you can. Eat your canvasback ducks, drink your Burgundy. Sleep your siesta when necessary, and TRUST IN GOD." [1]

This being the case, it remained to determine whether man could not find somewhere a code of morality that would express the precepts impressed in our hearts. In his youth, Jefferson had copied and accepted as a matter of course the statement of Bolingbroke that:

It is not true that Christ revealed an entire body of ethics, proved to be the law of nature from principles of reason and reaching all duties of life. . . . A system thus collected from the writings of the ancient heathen moralists, of Tully, of Seneca, of Epictetus, and others, would be more full, more entire, more coherent, and more clearly deduced from unquestionable principles of knowledge. [2]

In order to realize how far away Jefferson had drawn from his radicalism, it is only necessary to go back to his "Syllabus of an Estimate of the Merit of the Doctrines of Jesus, compared with those of others", written for Benjamin Rush, in 1803, after reading Doctor Priestley's little treatise "Of Socrates and and Jesus compared." [3] There he had declared that

His moral doctrines relating to kindred and friends, were more pure and perfect than those of the most correct of the philosophers, and . . . they went far in inculcating universal philanthropy, not only to kindred and friends, to neighbors and countrymen, but to all mankind, gathering all into one family, under the bonds of love, charity, peace, common wants and common aids. A development of this head will evince the peculiar superiority of the system of Jesus over all others.

---

[1] May 26, 1817. Memorial Edition, XV, 122.
[2] See my edition of "The Literary Bible of Thomas Jefferson." Paris, Baltimore, 1928, p. 58.
[3] April 21, 1803. Memorial Edition, X, 379.

Jefferson had been won over to Christianity by the superior social value of the morals of Jesus. In that sense, he could already say, "I am a Christian, in the only sense in which He wished any one to be, sincerely attached to His doctrines, in preference to all others."

This profession of faith made publicly might have assuaged some of the fierce attacks directed against Jefferson on the ground of his "infidelity", and yet even at that time he emphatically begged Doctor Rush not to make it public, for "it behooves every man who values liberty of conscience for himself . . . to give no example of concession, betraying the common right of independent opinion, by answering questions of faith, which the laws have left between God and himself." To a certain extent, however, his famous "Life and Morals of Jesus", compiled during the last ten years of his life [1] may well be considered an indirect and yet categorical recantation of Bolingbroke's haughty dogmatism. Age, experience, observation had mellowed the Stoic. He was not yet ready to accept as a whole the dogmas of Christianity, but the superiority of the morals of Jesus over the tenets of the "heathen moralists" did not any longer leave any doubt in his mind.

Whether after the death of the body something of man survived, was an entirely different question — one that human reason could not answer satisfactorily. It cannot even be stated with certainty that he would have agreed with John Adams when the latter wrote : "*Il faut trancher le mot.* What is there in life to attach us to it but the hope of a future and a better? It is a cracker, a rocket, a fire-work at best." [2]

He never denied categorically the existence of a future life, but this life was a thing in itself, and after all, it was worth living. Altogether this world was a pretty good place, and

[1] See the introduction of Doctor Cyrus Adler, in the Congressional Edition reproduced in the Memorial Edition, XX.

[2] May 3, 1816. Memorial Edition, XV, 10.

when John Adams asked him whether he would agree to live his seventy-three years over again, he answered energetically: "Yea. — I think with you," he added, "that it is a good world on the whole; that it has been framed on a principle of benevolence, and more pleasure than pain dealt to us. . . . My temperament is sanguine. I steer my bark with Hope in the head, leaving Fear astern. My hopes, indeed, sometimes fail, but not oftener than the foreboding of the gloomy." [1] His old friend was far from attaining such an equanimity and could not help envying the Sage of Monticello sailing his bark "Hope with her gay ensigns displayed at the prow, Fear with her hobgoblins behind the stern. Hope springs eternal and all is that endures. . . ." But Jefferson was bolstered up in his confident attitude by the intimate conviction that he had done good work, that he had contributed his best to the most worthy cause and that he had not labored in vain.

This was not only a good world, but it was already much better than when he had entered it. He had

. . . observed the march of civilization advancing from the sea coast, passing over us like a cloud of light, increasing our knowledge and improving our condition, insomuchas that we are at that time more advanced in civilization here than the seaports were when I was a boy. And where this progress will stop no one can say. Barbarism has, in the meantime, been receding before the steady step of amelioration; and will in time, I trust, disappear from the earth.[2]

Scarcely two weeks before he died — and this is practically his last important utterance — he recalled in a letter to the citizens of the city of Washington who had invited him to attend the celebration held for the fiftieth anniversary of the Declaration of Independence, how proud he was that his fellow citizens, after fifty years, continued to approve the choice made

---

[1] April 6, 1816. Memorial Edition, XIV, 467.
[2] To William Ludlow, September 6, 1824. *Ibid.*, XVI, 75.

when the Declaration was adopted. "May it be to the world,"
he added, "what I believe it will (to some parts sooner, to others
later, but finally to all) the signal of arousing men to burst the
chains under which monkish ignorance and superstition had
persuaded them to bind themselves, and to assume the blessings
and security of self-government." [1]

This faith in the ultimate recognition of the ideals, which he
had defined with such a felicity of expression half a century earlier,
was, even more than any belief in personal immortality, "the
rocket" that John Adams thought so necessary to attach us to
this life.   It was a real religion, the religion of progress, of the
eighteenth century which had its devotees and with Condorcet
its martyr.   Strengthened by the intimate conviction that he
would be judged from his acts and not "from his words", he
saw the approach of Death without any qualms, and he turned
back to his old friends of Greece and Rome, for "the classic
pages fill up the vacuum of *ennui*, and become sweet composers
to that rest of the grave into which we are sooner or later to
descend." [2]   On many occasions he expressed his readiness to
depart : "I enjoy good health," he wrote once to John Adams ;
"I am happy in what is around me, yet I assure you I am ripe
for leaving all, this year, this day, this hour." [3]   It took almost
ten years after these lines were written for the call to come.
Most of his biographers have dealt extensively with the remarkable vigor preserved by Jefferson even to his last day.   For
several years after his retirement he remained a hale and robust
old man.   But he felt none the less the approaching dissolution
and watched anxiously the slow progress of his physical limitations.   His letters do not completely bear out on this point the
statement made by Mrs. Sarah Randolph in her "Domestic
Life of Thomas Jefferson."

[1] June 24, 1826. Memorial Edition, XVI, 181.
[2] To John Brazier, August 24, 1819. *Ibid.*, XV, 207.
[3] August 1, 1816. *Ibid.*, XVI, 56.

At seventy-three he was still remarkably robust and, with the minuteness of a physician, described his case in a letter to his old friend Charles Thomson :

> I retain good health, am rather feeble to walk much, but ride with ease, passing two or three hours a day on horseback. . . . My eyes need the aid of glasses by night, and with small print in the day also; my hearing is not quite so sensible as it used to be; no tooth shaking yet, but shivering and shrinking in body from the cold we now experience; my thermometer having been as low as 12° this morning. My greatest oppression is a correspondence afflictingly laborious, the extent of which I have been long endeavoring to curtail. Could I reduce this epistolary corvée within the limits of my friends and affairs . . . my life would be as happy as the infirmities of age would admit, and I should look on its consummation with the composure of one *"qui summum nec metuit diem nec optat."* [1]

This remarkable preservation of his faculties he attributed largely to his abstemious diet. For years he had eaten little animal food, and that "not as an aliment so much as a condiment for the vegetables", which constituted his principal diet. "I double however the Doctor's glass and a half of wine, and even treble it with a friend, but halve its effects by drinking the weak wines only. The ardent wines I cannot drink, nor do I use ardent spirits in any form." [2]

Yet he had to admit to Mrs. Trist in 1814 that he was only "an old half-strung fiddle",[3] and as he advanced in age the "machine" gave evident signs of wearing out. The recurrence of the suffering caused by his broken wrist, badly set in Paris by the famous Louis,[4] and still worse the very painful "disury" with which he was afflicted [5] gave him many unhappy hours. To die was nothing, for as he wrote then in his old "Common-

---

[1] January 9, 1816. Memorial Edition, XIV, 385.
[2] To Doctor Vine Utley, March 21, 1819. *Ibid.*, XV, 187.
[3] Jefferson Papers. Massachusetts Historical Society, March 5, 1814.
[4] *Ibid.*, To Short, December 17, 1822.
[5] *Ibid.*, To Samuel Smith, October 22, 1825.

place Book", "I do not worry about the hereafter, even if now the doom of death stands at my feet, for we are men and cannot live forever. To all of us death must happen."[1] But "bodily decay" was "gloomy in prospect, for of all human contemplation the most abhorrent is a body without mind. To be a doting old man, to repeat four times over the same story in one hour", if this was life, it was "at most the life of a cabbage."[2] He was spared this affliction he dreaded so much, and when Lafayette visited him in November, 1824, the Marquis found him "much aged without doubt, after a separation of thirty-five years, but bearing marvelously well under his eighty-one years of age, in full possession of all the vigor of his mind and heart."[3] Six months later, when Lafayette took his final leave, Jefferson was weaker and confined to his house, suffering much "with one foot in the grave and the other one uplifted to follow it."

Death was slowly approaching, without any particular disease being noticeable; after running for eighty-three years "the machine" was about to "surcease motion." The end has been told by several contemporaries and friends. No account is more simple and more touching in its simplicity than the relation written by his attending physician, Doctor Dunglison :

Until the 2d. and 3d. of July he spoke freely of his approaching death; made all arrangements with his grandson, Mr. Randolph, in regard to his private affairs; and expressed his anxiety for the prosperity of the University and his confidence in the exertion in its behalf of Mr. Madison and the other visitors. He repeatedly, too, mentioned his obligation to me for my attention to him. During the last week of his existence I remained at Monticello; and one of the last remarks he made was to me. In the course of the day and night of the 2d of July he was affected with stupor, with intervals of wakefulness and consciousness; but on the 3d the stupor became

[1] "Literary Bible", p. 36.   Paris, Baltimore, 1928.
[2] To John Adams — August 1, 1816. Memorial Edition, XV, 56, and June 1, 1822. *Ibid.*, XV, 371.
[3] November 8, 1824, "Mémoires", VI, 183.

almost permanent. About seven o'clock of the evening of that day he awoke and, seeing me staying at his bedside, exclaimed, "Ah, Doctor, are you still there?" in a voice, however, that was husky and indistinct. He then asked, "Is it the Fourth?" to which I replied, "It will soon be." These were the last words I heard him utter.

Until towards the middle of the day — the 4th — he remained in the same state, or nearly so, wholly unconscious to everything that was passing around him. His circulation, however, was gradually becoming more languid; and for some time prior to dissolution the pulse at the wrist was imperceptible. About one o'clock he ceased to exist.[1]

A few days before he had taken his final dispositions and seen all the members of his family. He was not a man to indulge in a painful display of emotions, but he told his dear daughter Martha that "in a certain drawer in an old pocket book she would find something for her." It was a piece of paper on which he had written eight lines "A death bed adieu from Th. J. to M. R." There was no philosophism nor classical reminiscence in it; it was the simple expression of his last hope that on the shore

"*Which crowns all my hopes, or which buries my care*" he would find awaiting him "two seraphs long shrouded in death", his beloved wife and his young daughter Maria.

He was buried by their side in the family plot of Monticello. According to his wishes no invitations were issued and no notice of the hour given. "His body was borne privately from his dwelling by his family and servants, but his neighbors and friends, anxious to pay the last tribute of respect to one they had loved and honored, waited for it in crowds at the grave." A typically American scene, without parade, without speeches and long ceremonies — almost a pioneer burial in a piece of land reclaimed from the wilderness.

[1] "Domestic Life", p. 425.

INDEX

INDEX

Selected Ann Arbor Paperbacks
Works of enduring merit

For a complete list of Ann Arbor Paperback titles write:
THE UNIVERSITY OF MICHIGAN PRESS ANN ARBOR